THE ECONOMIC
TRANSFORMATION OF AMERICA:
1600 TO THE PRESENT

Third Edition

THE ECONOMIC TRANSFORMATION OF AMERICA: 1600 TO THE PRESENT

Third Edition

ROBERT HEILBRONER
New School for Social Research

AARON SINGER

HARCOURT BRACE COLLEGE PUBLISHERS

*Fort Worth   Philadelphia   San Diego   New York   Orlando   Austin   San Antonio
Toronto   Montreal   London   Sydney   Tokyo*

PUBLISHER *Ted Buchholz*

SENIOR ACQUISITIONS EDITOR *Drake Bush*

DEVELOPMENTAL EDITOR *Kristie Kelly*

PROJECT EDITORS *Nicole Boyle, Jeff Beckham*

PRODUCTION MANAGER *Debra A. Jenkin*

ART DIRECTOR *Nick Welch*

Address for Editorial Correspondence: Harcourt Brace College Publishers, 301 Commerce Street, Suite 3700, Fort Worth, TX 76102.

Address for Orders: Harcourt Brace & Company, 6277 Sea Harbor Drive, Orlando, FL 32887. 1-800-782-4479, or 1-800-433-0001 (in Florida).

Credits and permissions acknowledgments are on page 401.

Printed in the United States of America

ISBN 0-15-501092-1

Library of Congress Catalog Card Number 93-78561

3 4 5 6 7 8 9 0 1 2 016 9 8 7 6 5 4 3 2 1

To Shirley and Audrey, again.

CONTENTS

Part I
THE COLONIAL STRUGGLE

New York in the seventeenth century

A London market in the seventeenth century

Chapter 1
ECONOMIC TRANSFORMATION AS A THEME OF HISTORY

We are about to begin the study of American history from an unaccustomed perspective—the perspective of the economic transformation of American life. And we are going to open our examination of this perspective by asking an unaccustomed question: *What is history?*

WHAT IS HISTORY?

This may seem a roundabout and pointless way to broach our subject. Why not proceed directly to the matter at hand? What is to be gained by asking so simple a question? Is history not the record of what has happened, the chronicle of what we know about the past?

The question is not so simple, however. For *which* among many pasts is our history? Is it the past that we learn when we memorize lists of presidents? Is it the past memorialized by the dates of wars? Is it the past reflected in the archives of newspapers? Or is it all these pasts together, some immense volume in which we find presidents, wars, the news, and all else?

The inquiry brings us to a disconcerting recognition. There is no such immense volume. Indeed, none is possible. A history that included all the threads of our past would require us to know everything that had ever happened. That is more than we can know about our own lives, much less the lives of others. History in this all-encompassing sense can never be written.

3

We are left, then, with the need to write history from some perspective, highlighting one theme or another from our "total" history. There are innumerable such possibilities. We can write histories of American politics, art, social life, crime—each with its own cast of characters and plot. Needless to say, the same event may enter into more than one such history, and different histories may feature quite different events. The assassinations of Lincoln and Kennedy, for example, certainly bulk large in the history of politics, but they would figure as well in a history of American crime—although in that context they would be reduced to the insignificant status of mere homicides. The development of jazz figures large in American social history but not in American diplomatic history. *Thus the choice of a theme is a decisive determinant of what we will find in "history."*

These brief reflections help us when we now turn to the theme of this book. For the choice of economic transformation causes us to view events from a perspective different from that of the usual American history. Its cast of characters features business leaders, working men and women, and inventors rather than the usual presidents, generals, or patriots. Its plot ignores the great epic of American democratic development and dwells instead on the less familiar currents of economic expansion and conflict. Technical processes, such as steelmaking, play a role as central as those usually accorded to political processes such as lawmaking. Enormous events like the Civil War appear only in the background; whereas matters that we ordinarily overlook, such as J. P. Morgan's purchase of the Carnegie Steel Company, suddenly loom very large.

Why study the past from such an unusual angle? The answer is that our perspective has an extraordinary power of illumination. Not all themes of history shed equal light on other themes. It is the property of the theme of economic transformation that it touches on so many others. In fact, it is not too much to say that without a comprehension of the American economic transformation, many other histories of American life remain unintelligible. Certainly the great drama of our democratic evolution loses most of its meaning unless we project it against the changeful backdrop of economic events. So, too, the histories of social change, of science or literature, or even fashion—in short, most of the innumerable histories that can be written about America—require for their full understanding a grasp of the profound economic transformation through which America has passed.

THE INTERTWINED STRANDS OF HISTORY

Material Life

And so we arrive at our beginning and can put forth the question we have been waiting for: What do we mean by the economic transformation of America?

In one sense we know immediately what we mean. America in the beginning was a vast, untamed wilderness; today it is a complex industrial civilization. Where there were once virgin forests there are today interstate highways. Where rivers met in solitude there are great cities. Where the voice of the continent was the murmur of nature it is now the chatter of trade and commerce. The economic transformation of America is the narrative of that all-embracing change, a change we are all generally familiar with, however imprecisely we can describe its historic course.

Peasants plowing with wooden plow and sowing by hand

But we need something more sharply focused if we are to study the transformation in a systematic rather than an impressionistic way. Here it is useful to view the great transformation in terms proposed by the great modern French historian Fernand Braudel.[1] Braudel sees in history three intertwined but distinguishable strands.

One of these he calls *material life.* By material life Braudel means the routines of daily work, the everyday round of the tasks by which we sustain ourselves. Thus material life covers the means by which we travel to work, the efforts we perform there, the products we make and use. We would not be far wrong if we thought of material life as the technology at hand and the goods we enjoy. Needless to say, both change dramatically over time: compare the material life of the peasant walking to his task, swinging his scythe, eating his coarse bread, with that of today's worker, driving to his office, using his computer, shopping on the way home.

Part of the economic transformation therefore consists of the evolving technology with which we undertake our worldly tasks. Braudel has a phrase that highlights vividly its importance: material life, he says, sets "the limits of the possible." We cannot understand the overarching narrative of our economic transformation without understanding how those limits have changed.

Economic Life

A second strand of our economic transformation touches on a level that Braudel calls *economic life.* Braudel does not mean the whole range of activities that we think of as "economic," but a level of activity just above the routines and techniques of workaday activity itself. Mainly it encompasses market activity—the jostling of buyers and sellers on the market square, the complex acts of offer and bid, purchase and sale, that make possible the essential social relationship of exchange.

Perhaps we would not ordinarily think of economic life as constituting an aspect of economic experience of equal importance with material life. But we would be wrong. As Braudel points out, it is in the marketplace that the peasant first transcends the narrow world of family and friends and fellow workers to enter into relationships with utter strangers, thereby becoming aware, however dimly, of a world beyond that of his or her immediate experience. In the same way, economic life today continues to bind us into a larger (and still often

Modern four-wheel-power tractor

dimly perceived) world when market forces that we ordinarily ignore suddenly take on hurricane force and raise the price of oil fivefold, or blow away the whole market for the goods we produce or the skills we offer.

Thus another strand of our overall theme is the evolution of our involvement with the market, both as buyers of goods and as suppliers of our energies. A vital part of the economic transformation of America is the enlargement of economic life, from the near self-sufficiency of Pilgrim days, when market influences were reduced to a minimum, to contemporary life when its forces affect our destinies as decisively as the material foundation on which we stand.

Capitalism

Third, Braudel refers to *capitalism* itself. Capitalism is not an easy term to define. It embraces material and economic life, but it is also something more than the concrete processes of production and the realities of consumption, something larger than the skein of market relationships. Capitalism is a historic structure—a framework of forces, an ongoing process of historic change—that arches over both material and economic life, imbuing them with its particular dynamism, its unique influence.

And what is that dynamism, that influence? There is no single, and certainly no simple way of describing how capitalism molds and shapes and impels material and economic change. But we can gain some understanding of the nature of capitalism as the third, and most all-inclusive aspect of our economic transformation, if we pay heed to three elements that it introduces into material and economic life: capital, the market mechanism, and the division of economic and political activity.

1. *Capitalism is oriented to the continual accumulation of material wealth—as capital.*

Capitalism is not unique in its quest for wealth. All social systems above the level of the most primitive cultures accumulate wealth. Indeed, one might say that one of the hallmarks of the first formation of "states"—whether they be kingdoms, empires, or what Karl Marx called "Asiatic despotisms"—is that they seek to amass wealth. Moreover, the wealth amassed by these early imperial states can be dazzlingly great. The Great Wall of China, the immense pyramids of Egypt, the temple complexes of India or of the Inca and Aztec civilizations all testify to the ability of societies with low levels of material life to accumulate vast surpluses from sheer human labor. What is quintessentially different about capitalism is that its wealth takes on a form unlike that of any of these societies—the form of productive *capital.*

Precapitalist societies all used their accumulations of wealth for consumption purposes. The consumption was partly private—the luxuries made available to the ruling strata—and partly public—the great works whose splendors were shared by the populace, even though they were mainly intended to glorify the name of some ruler. Thus many centuries of Asian and European history present us with endless variations on a common theme—a vast, usually impoverished peasantry on the bottom, a ruling personage, with his entourage, on top celebrating his power with lavish consumption and magnificent works to immortalize his name.

Capitalism also has a ruling stratum that enjoys the wealth the system produces, and capitalism also builds mighty public works. But under capitalism the accumulation of society's wealth is put to a use that cannot be found in prior societies. *Wealth is used to build machines and equipment whose sole purpose is to create still more wealth.* The primary purpose of capitalist accumulation is not consumption for the upper classes or public monuments, but the creation of *capital*—wealth-in-general, produced for the sake of producing still more wealth. The nature of this wealth often takes the form of things that would never even be considered as wealth in a precapitalist society—steel ingots, or vats of chemicals, or parts of machines. The form does not matter, as long as the products can be sold and proceeds invested to create still more saleable wealth, more "capital." As a consequence of this search for capital—wealth in any saleable form—capitalism takes on a property not to be found in prior societies. It becomes *expansive*—not so much in geographic extent (although capitalism does indeed move from its original locales into peripheral areas), as in the value and volume of its output. "Taken at face value, the quantity of manufacturing production in the world increased by about 1,730 times [from 1785 to 1971]," writes economic historian W. W. Rostow.[2] This expansive, explosive character of capitalism is the

An urban U.S. business—one seller with many items

source of its extraordinary historic impact, both for good and bad. It is a force that will dominate the economic transformation of America.

2. *Under capitalism, the production and distribution of wealth is entrusted to the market mechanism.*

All societies require some means of assuring the performance of the tasks necessary for their survival, as well as those that create new wealth. Prior to the advent of capitalism, societies depended mainly on the hand of tradition for the first task and on that of command for the second. Thus the basic perpetuation of society was established because son followed father, and daughter followed mother into the traditional routines of planting, reaping, weaving, and maintaining the household; while the Great Wall and pyramids and cathedrals were built because rulers *ordered* them to be built, sometimes paying gangs of workmen to perform their bidding, sometimes literally dragooning armies of laborers to toil on their immense projects.

What was absent in the organization of social effort was the market. Of course, from earliest times, markets played some role in bringing production into being. All through history a trickle of production finds its way from the fields to the village square where it is sold by the

A Guatemalan village market—many sellers with few items

peasant's wife squatting over her tiny stock of fruit or her heap of rye or wheat. And beyond the village square we find more ambitious market ventures—as far back as neolithic times, when there was trade among distant tribes, bronze axe heads being exchanged for we do not know what, perhaps with the use of cowrie shells as money.[3]

But market squares, or even adventurous trading expeditions, are not market *systems*. A market system describes a society in which the village square expands to include the entire city and countryside, and in which relations of purchase and sale extend like many-spoked wheels from a thousand sources of production to ten thousand places of distribution. *A market system comes into being when a society entrusts its own basic replenishment to the forces of the marketplace—* when decisions formerly guided by tradition and command are handed over to the push and pull of market forces, to negotiations between buyers and sellers whose aim is simply to make money, not to abide by age-old routines or to follow anyone's orders.

How can such a system work? How can society rest its very continuance on such a self-regarding, uncoordinated process? That question takes us into the field of economics, beyond the bounds of this book. But the essential elements of the answer are not difficult to give. As we have said, the market system depends on a powerful driving force, the drive to make money. At its most basic level this is the drive to survive by finding work. At its most elevated level it is the drive to succeed in the manner recognized and admired in a commercial society, by running a profitable enterprise. Economists call this essential motive "maximizing"—a technical way of describing a kind of behavior generally familiar to all of us.

The market requires a maximizing drive, but it would not be a *system* without another element, competition. It is the competition among workers vying for work, as well as among capitalists seeking to establish or to steal away shares of the market, that guides the economic energy generated by the maximizing motive. Competition forces both workers and capitalists to direct their energies toward those tasks that society wants done, and to perform their services at prices that society will pay. Both can, of course, ignore the pressures and signals of the marketplace—but at the risk of unemployment or bankruptcy.

The market system is therefore a combination of maximizing drive generated throughout society, and the disciplining pressures exerted by the pressure of other, rivalling, maximizing drives. It is this combination that gives to capitalism its historic dynamism—its restless search for economic opportunities, the constant organization and reorganization of its efforts to match production to demand.

It is important to stress that this combination does not only yield economic triumphs, such as its vast increase in output, it is also the source of another attribute of capitalism—a built-in insecurity, a self-endangering changefulness. The market system can bring disruptions as well as successes. Supply may not match demand. Markets may "disappear." The expansive drive may falter. Tensions between workers and employers may block the accumulation process, or a failure to distribute rewards properly may undermine the creation and growth of the purchasing power required to justify continued business growth.

Thus the market system is as much the cause of instability as it is the source of growth. Capitalism is intrinsically as vulnerable as it is powerful. As we shall see in the economic transformation of America, the process of development is a two-sided affair, failure accompanying success, success emerging from failure.

3. *Capitalism creates a new division between economic and political activity.*

Here we must again look back for a moment to precapitalist societies to understand the change that capitalism brings. Under feudalism, or in the imperial societies of antiquity, there was no clear distinction between "political" and "economic" activity. The serf performing his field tasks, the lord filling his granaries, the tax official attending to the payment of imposts, were at one and the same time ensuring the continuation of the pattern of command and obedience that is the core of political authority, and of the material provisioning that lies at the heart of the economic process. In precapitalist society, political and economic activity were indissolubly one.

In this seamless web the merchant always fitted poorly. The inherent changefulness of market dealings, and the possibility of winning wealth without deferring to imperial pleasure, placed the merchant outside the structure of unified economic and political rule. That is why the fall of the Roman Empire bulks so large in economic history. For the collapse of its central structure created a new fragmentation and compartmentalization of power, as a thousand contesting dukes and lords and barons filled the space once occupied by imperial Rome. In this unprecedented fragmentation of power, mercantile influence could establish itself on a wholly new footing.

This did not happen at once. In the disorganization that followed the collapse of the empire, trade dried up and the merchant nearly disappeared from view. But beginning about the tenth century economic life began to quicken. More important, in the absence of a unified imperial system, the function of the merchant became increasingly indispensable. It was only through trade, not through the direct exercise of imperial power, that goods could now be brought across the face of Europe to isolated castles. It was only through merchants, not tax officials, that feudal lords could raise cash for wars or special luxuries. As the strategic role of the merchant increased, so did his power. By the twelfth and thirteenth centuries, merchants had secured the *independence* of many towns from lordly rule, an assertion of power unimaginable in the empires of the past.

What we then begin to see across the face of the continent is the emergence of two distinct spheres of authority and power. One of them, the political sphere, retains from the imperial past the functions of statecraft—the waging of war, the conclusion of alliances, the promulgation of law, and the responsibility of internal order. The other, the economic sphere, takes into its charge the production and distribution of material goods—no longer under the command of a central imperial power but more and more under the sway of market forces, commanded by merchants competing in search of a profit.

This separation of an economic realm from the political state does not achieve its final clarity until well into the nineteenth century. In the seventeenth century, when our own narrative really begins, there is nothing like the public and private "sectors" of a later age. On the contrary, economic and political life are still intimately entwined, both at the summit of European society where great merchants are directly supported by royal prerogatives, and at the lower levels of the market system where elaborate rules and regulations usually surround the way in which economic life is carried on.

Nonetheless, a cleavage had been introduced. Economic power had been separated from political power in a manner that will become a central feature of capitalism. Indeed we can now see that the division of unitary imperial power into two spheres is an essential element of the capitalist structure—an element that brings with it new conceptions of economic freedom, and new sources of political conflict.

The Dynamic of Capitalism

Our brief survey of capitalism helps us understand and define more sharply the focus of our studies. For it must now be clear that the theme of the economic transformation of America is in fact the theme of the development of American capitalism. To follow the development of capitalism means, of course, that we watch the unfolding of material life as it constantly expands the limits of the possible, and it obviously requires that we observe the expansion of economic life as market transactions knit us ever more tightly together.

But over and beyond these subthemes, America's economic transformation will direct our attention to the contours, the rhythms, the achievements and failures of the larger structure that we call capitalism. It is the explosive drive and tensions of the accumulation process, the successes and failures of the market mechanism, and the changing relationships between the exercise of political and economic power that will become the great threads of our narrative; and we now see that these threads constitute nothing less than the historic evolution of capitalism itself.

The task now is to take up our main theme, but the question is where to begin. Let us imagine that we are examining an album of American life, looking for illustrations of its material, economic, and capitalistic life. We begin in the present with the panorama that we know. We turn back the pages to the 1930s with its photos of the breadlines of the Great Depression; then further back to the imposing figures of the great financiers and entrepreneurs of the turn of the century—the Carnegies and Rockefellers and Morgans. From there we go back still further to the daguerreotypes of the Civil War with glimpses of railroads and iron cannons; still further to the Currier and Ives prints that show New England scenes of horse-drawn sleds and the sugaring of maples; then to the illustrations, drawn from the imagination, of Pilgrim life; until finally we turn the last page and arrive at the beginning.

Where would it be? In Europe, of course. That is where the study of the American economic transformation must start.

Notes
[1] *Civilization & Capitalism, 15th–18th Century* (3 vols., 1979–84), I: 27–29.
[2] *The World Economy* (1979), p. 48.
[3] *Cambridge Economic History of Europe* (1952), 2:4.

English women carding, combing, and spinning with distaff

Chapter 2

OUT OF THE EUROPEAN CRADLE

In many ways Europe at the beginning of the seventeenth century would be familiar to us, especially in England where our study begins. It is the end of Queen Elizabeth's reign. The defeat of the Spanish Armada is not long past. We recognize the costumes of the velveted aristocracy and manners of the ragged peasantry from our introduction to them in the works of the period's greatest, and then living playwright, William Shakespeare. We might even be prepared for an atmosphere of violence and paranoia—it is the time of popish plots and of the burning of heretics at the stake.

MATERIAL LIFE IN EUROPE

But this is not the aspect of history that we are looking for. Our gaze is riveted on a side of Elizabethan times that we normally ignore—its material life. As we might imagine, most of this life is connected with the processes of agriculture, because the vast majority of working men and women live in close contact with the land. They work in the fields, not in workshops. Save for a very few establishments, usually under royal patronage, nothing resembling a place of massed labor under one roof—a factory—could be found, and as for retail stores, there are none. They have not been invented.

Perhaps three-quarters of the 100 million people living in Europe in 1600 worked the land—not as farmers tilling their own fields and selling their output, but as tenants or serfs with various degrees of bondage—unable to leave the land, unable to marry, without the express consent of their lords and masters.

What would strike us forcibly, as we toured the rural areas, would be how small and poor this agricultural population was. In all of England there were only five million people, and much of what would in time become cultivated land or even cities was still fen and bog and forest. London, a city of 250,000 at the beginning of the seventeenth century, was roughly ten times the size of any other English city. Whether in the countryside or in the villages, the prevailing poverty would be impossible to miss. The peasants in England—and England was one of the richest countries in Europe—were small in stature because they did not eat enough. They did not eat enough because agricultural yields were low; in good years a peasant household produced enough food for itself and for another one or two persons. In bad years this slim surplus disappeared and famine stalked the land. Famines were a constant presence in the seventeenth century: in 1697 a quarter to a third of the population of Finland died of hunger; in terms of the proportion of victims, one of the most terrible events in European history.[1]

Famine was a constant threat because production methods were poor. Grain was harvested by the hand sickle, not by the sweeping scythe, the long stubble left for grazing or for the poor to glean; plows, often wood not iron, were pulled by slow, straining oxen rather than by stronger, quicker horses; an efficient system of land rotation and nitrogen-fixing crops had not yet evolved, so that too much land had to lie fallow to regenerate its strength; roads as we think of them were virtually nonexistent. We get some inkling of what this last element of material life meant for the "limits of the possible" when we learn that it took Napoleon as long to invade Italy from France as it had taken Caesar to go the other way—and this was two centuries *after* the period we are examining.

It was not only on the land that the level of material life was cramping. There was very little energy available for the processing of raw materials save for that of human muscle or animal power. Water wheels turned millstones and, especially in Holland, windmills were beginning to harness the energy of the wind, but the technology of production was generally primitive. Iron ores, for example, were still reduced by the heat of wood fire, for a workable coal furnace had not yet been invented. Hence metal implements were scarce, brittle, and none too sharp. Steel was utterly unknown as a household material. In aristocratic mansions steel sword blades were largely imported from the East. In peasant huts, steel implements were unknown. There were no steel axe heads, knives, saws, or nails.

A full account of material life would take us to inspect the way in which Europeans tanned leather and spun wool, wove cloth, made wheels and carts, preserved food, built their huts. But our first impression would only be confirmed if we looked more closely into the countryside or town. Except for the upper classes, life in the seventeenth century was meager and poor, largely because the level of development of material life was low. This is a fact that we must bear in mind when we turn in our next chapter to the initial struggles of the colonists to establish viable settlements. They had to tame a wilderness without steel, cement, or any systematic knowledge of agriculture; without machinery of nearly every kind. Material life in the 1600s was closer by far to its medieval parentage than to its still unsuspected industrial offspring.

ECONOMIC LIFE

Economic life in the 1600s interests us for a different reason than material life. Tools and techniques explain the low level of productivity against which the colonists would soon have to struggle. Economic life speaks to us of something else—of stirrings of change, absent in the modes of planting and harvesting, spinning or weaving, but visible in the manner in which the entire panorama of planting and spinning and weaving was integrated into a functioning social whole. As we already know, it will show us evidence that the market mechanism is becoming a central order-bestowing force within society.

One instance of this change would be particularly noticeable in England where it had developed further than on the continent. It was the sight of merchant-organizers riding out from their establishments in town into the countryside to distribute raw wool or flax thread to spinners and weavers who would work the material up on their own spinning wheels and looms in their cottages. When the merchant made his next trip, he would pay his cottage workers for what they had done and deliver a fresh batch to be worked up in turn. This "putting-out" system was far from satisfactory since it offered no chance for supervising the work or assuring a standard quality of product, but in its extent and organization it presaged the day when workers would be gathered under a common roof to work up raw material on machinery owned not by themselves, but by the merchant-capitalist himself.

More important, the putting-out system represented a basic break with tradition and command in the production of a vital commodity. The putting-out organizer followed no guild rules, for none existed, and heeded no commands, because none were given. His sole guide was the marketplace—the expected demand for cloth of this or that color and fineness, the cost of producing this cloth, and the margin of difference, his profit.

Of equal significance was the fact that the cottage workers were *paid* for their work. This was a sharp break from the feudal, or prefeudal past. In earlier societies labor itself rarely entered the marketplace. The peasant was not paid for his labors when he cultivated the lord's fields or performed his mandatory tasks in mending the roads. Even in the towns, where apprentices labored for their masters, there were no regular payments for their work. For seven years, according to tradition, an apprentice worked for his master in exchange for board and lodging and a pittance, until he could become a master himself. The serf labored for life.

Thus the putting-out system represented a decisive break with the past in that the merchant-organizer paid his cottage workers for their output. Even more striking was the payment procedure for the work force that produced the *fluitschips*—the flat-bottomed, unprepossessing, and very efficient fishing boats of Holland. They got *wages*—payment for a day's or week's labor, not for any product that they produced and then sold to their employer. This was truly a decisive step, for now the act of laboring itself became a commodity and the organizer of a *fluitschip* gang simply paid his men for a certain number of hours of toil. When the work force was paid, the employer had no further obligation to them. Unlike the guild master who owed his apprentices a roof over their heads whatever the fortunes of his workshop, or the lord who could no more dismiss a serf than a serf could quit his land, the wage-paying employer, having paid his wages, was quit of all responsibility. If there was no work to be had the next day, that was his worker's lookout, not his own. They were not "his" men—only their labor was his, and that he had paid for.

All these changes had important implication for the economic life that would be transported to America. Market relations are on the rise, but they are not yet fully developed. Wage labor has appeared, but it is by no means the predominant way of engaging a work force. The putting-out system presages the organization of work in a factory-like manner, but factories are not yet part of the economic landscape. The social classes of the seventeenth century are poised halfway between the old and the new—the lord of the manor is becoming the landlord, interested in his rents, but aristocratic ideas are still very much in the air. Peasants and town laborers are more and more engaged in market relationships, but the institutions of life tenancies and of apprenticeships are far from over. Shares in *fluitschip* ventures are actually sold among successful artisans or rich peasants, but a true market in capital has not yet arrived.

These half-formed institutions and mixed roles tell us that the transition from feudalism into capitalism is still incomplete. But it is precisely from this incomplete capitalism that economic life in colonial America would spring. Like the level of its material life, the character of its economic life would profoundly shape the first century of American economic history. In our next chapter we will watch these influences at work.

The Spice Trade

But we have still to consider one very important aspect of economic life in the seventeenth century in Europe, an aspect more immediately connected with the colonization of America than any we have yet observed. This was the thrust of mercantile activity overseas.

The thrust begins long before the seventeenth century, and we should take a moment to follow its development. We have already noted in passing that medieval Europe depended on its merchants to bring goods that no longer flowed over established imperial channels. Of these goods the most highly prized were spices from the East. Medieval Europeans went without many foods that we today consider commonplace. They had no potatoes, rice, or corn; little butter or cheese; fresh fruits and green vegetables only in season; almost no sugar. Their ordinary diet was bread and gruel, enlivened by onions, lentils, peas, and turnips. In the manor house there was meat, but it was stringy and often near spoiled; tough fowl; occasionally fish. Hence it is not surprising that spices were treasured because they could disguise bad food or give piquancy to sauce. Spices were also used in the preparation of medicinal drugs and in the manufacture of incense for religious ceremonies. Pepper was frequently used as a royal gift, and even as a means of payment.

The spice trade had traditionally flowed into Western Europe by way of the Italian city-states. As early as the eleventh century the Venetians had established a thriving trade with the East via Constantinople. There, in the great entrepôt that linked Europe and Asia, Moslem merchants brought their cargoes of pepper and ginger, cloves and cinammon to exchange them for European wood, iron, wine, and staple foods; and from Venice in turn the precious cargoes of spices moved slowly and expensively to the courts of Europe.*

Thus as vitality returned to the medieval world, it is understandable that monarchs cast their eyes eastward, seeking for a way to break the Italian stranglehold on the spice trade. The most imaginative of these efforts was made by Prince Henry of Portugal (1394–1460). Prince Henry, soon dubbed "Henry the Navigator," created a true research institute for exploration where experts came to work on ship design, maps, and instruments for navigation. Of particular significance in this area was the Portuguese design of the caravel, a small, light, three-masted sailing ship that would soon become the favorite of explorers. In addition to being highly maneuverable, the caravel did not require large crews of oarsmen and was therefore far less expensive to operate. From these efforts Portuguese captains were gradually able to transform the Atlantic Ocean, the "Sea of Darkness" that stood like an impassable barrier between the West and the fabled but hopelessly distant East, into an avenue for adventure—and more important, for profitable commerce. Bartolomeo Dias rounded the Cape of Good Hope early in 1488, and between 1497 and 1498 Vasco da Gama made his epochal voyage to India, bringing back a cargo of spices and jewels worth sixty times the cost of his venture. In the *Wealth of Nations,* published in 1776, Adam Smith would call this journey and Columbus'

---

*Of almost as much interest to Europeans as spices were the precious gems of the East, used for personal ornament and for the enrichment of shrines and religious vestments. In fact, it was the publication in 1477 of Marco Polo's fascinating account of his twenty-four year journey through the whole of China (1271–95) and the riches that he found there that stimulated European interest in the Orient in general. (Polo, it should be noted, was also a Venetian.)

discovery of America "two of the greatest and most important events recorded in the history of mankind."[2]

The actual discovery of America was itself part of this commercial momentum. Around 1484 Christopher Columbus, an experienced Genoese sailor, approached King John II of Portugal with a plan to reach the East by sailing boldly across the Atlantic. According to Columbus' calculations, China was only 4,500 miles west of Spain and Portugal, and Japan a mere 2,400 miles. When King John refused to sponsor his voyage, Columbus turned to the Spanish court and finally persuaded Queen Isabella to finance his expedition. On October 12, 1492, the tiny flotilla sighted land—not Asia, as Columbus confidently believed, but the Americas, specifically the little island of San Salvador in the Bahamas. This was only the first of four voyages Columbus made to the Americas, although never to North America. Like many pioneers, Columbus did not quite know what he had done. To the day

Refining sugar cane in the New World, c. 1590

of his death in 1506, he thought he was exploring the outlying islands of the Indies.

Gradually it became clear that Columbus had stumbled not upon the Indies, but on a tremendous barrier to the Indies—a vast continent that stood in the way of the hoped-for spice route. For decades explorers sought a passage to the Orient through the great North–South American land mass. It was finally achieved by Ferdinand Magellan, a Portuguese mariner sailing under the Spanish flag, after a voyage of horrendous trials, during which Magellan himself was killed. When the *Victoria,* alone of the original five ships, returned home in 1522 only eighteen men survived of the original 237; but the globe was now circumnavigated and its systematic exploration and exploitation began.

THE AGE OF MERCANTILISM

Although many governments spoke openly of their desire to Christianize the indigenous inhabitants, wealth was the driving force behind the European exploration and conquest of the New World. As the great Spanish dramatist Lope de Vega (1562–1635) had the devil say in his play *The New World,* "It is not Christianity that leads them on, but rather gold and greed." The human story of that era is among the darkest in Western history—in the area that we today call Mexico, for example, the population fell from twenty-five million to one million as a consequence of war, brutal practices, and disease. In the area that was to become the United States, about 90 percent of the native population was killed by the time of the first English settlements: a population of ten to twelve million was reduced to approximately 850,000. But the economic consequences of the age of exploration and exploitation feature large in our historical narrative. A torrent of gold poured from the ravaged lands of Central and South America into Spanish hands, and from Spain circulated out into Europe, largely as a result of Spanish expenditures in its futile war against the Dutch. The result of the torrent of gold was an unprecedented inflation, prices rising some three and a half times in Spain and more than doubling in France and England.

In turn, the outcome of that inflation was a tremendous strengthening of merchant power itself. For the aristocracy in most European lands was still dependent on rents and dues from its peasantry which, like all feudal levies, were fixed and immutable. They had, however, been converted from dues in kind—so and so many bushels of wheat or days of labor—to dues in *coin*—so and so many coppers or pence or sous. The conversion from kind to coin was itself testimony to the importance that was now attached to *money* incomes, which the nobility needed to purchase merchants' wares. As inflation swept over Europe in the sixteenth century, the buying power of these fixed incomes was cut in half or worse, while rising prices worked in favor of sellers of goods—especially merchants.

As a result, by the seventeenth century the balance of power was clearly tipping in favor of the mercantile elite. At the very apex of society we now find companies of merchant adventurers who had organized truly gigantic undertakings of global trade. The Dutch East India Company, for instance, sent forty ships a year, on the average, to the

West India Docks, London

East and employed 12,000 people. We gain some appreciation of its importance when we learn that in its two-century history it sent a *million* men to Asia (only a third of whom survived the five-year round trip).[3] And in England a similar East Indies Company, a Turkey Company, and a Levant Company carried on comparable globe-straddling enterprises; and the same again in France and elsewhere.

From the rise of international trade emerged the first form of capitalism. It was not quite the capitalism of a later age, for it differed in two vital respects from what was to follow. *First, it sought its profits from trade rather than from production.* The putting-out ventures that were precursors of a later industrial capitalism were still dwarfed in importance by international trading ventures in spices, metals, and not least important, in human beings, slaves. As an indication of the profits of these ventures, it has been estimated that the treasure brought back by Francis Drake in 1580 on his fabled *Golden Hind* was enough, compounded at interest, to equal the entire pre-World War I wealth of England.

Second, merchant capitalism did not yet depend on competition as a central regulator of the system. On the contrary, monopoly was its organizing principle. The great trading companies of Europe all held royal charters that entitled them to exclusive national trade rights with their designated Eastern ports. Hence merchant capitalism—mercantilism as it is often called—was an openly monopolistic system, very different from the competitive market system that Adam Smith would advocate a century later.

Mercantilist Economics and the Colonies

Mercantilism interests us not only because it is a kind of way station en route to capitalism, but also because it is a way station en route to the explanations of capitalism we call *economics*. The merchants of the great trading companies had to explain to the uncomprehending courtiers of the courts of Queen Elizabeth or Louis XIV how trading activities could be justified in terms of the military calculus that appealed more naturally to the nobility. The answer put forward by merchant pamphleteers was that trade brought gold and silver—*treasure,* it was called—into a nation, thereby enhancing its military power. As Jean Baptiste Colbert, Louis XIV's finance minister, said: "[E]veryone agrees that the might and greatness of a state is measured entirely by the quantity of silver it possesses."[4] Closely related to this belief was another mercantilist perception: that the wealth of the world was more or less fixed and that a nation could therefore grow wealthier, and stronger, only at the expense of another. As Thomas Mun, a director of the East India Company, put it in his famous *England's Treasure by Forraign Trade,* published in 1630: "The ordinary means to encrease our wealth and treasure is by *forraign trade,* wherein wee must ever observe this rule; to sell more to strangers yearly than wee consume of theirs in value."

We can hardly fail to be struck by the naiveté of this early mercantilist economics, for clearly *every* nation cannot sell more than it buys. But the mercantilists applied their policy with special emphasis in their trade relations with distant, rather than neighboring, nations. The great trading companies soon established intimate relations with local sovereigns in their Eastern ports, and from these first connections, by diplomacy, bribery, and ultimately by military conquest, the trading companies became the spearheads of *colonies*—territorial extensions abroad of English, French, Spanish, Dutch, and other national sovereignties.

It was in relation to these colonies that the mercantilist policy of selling more than the mother country purchased in return was applied with a vengeance. The colonies were uniformly regarded as markets into which the mother countries could have the exclusive right to sell their own, mainly manufactured, products, but were regarded as places in which the mother country would only buy the treasures and spices or vital raw materials it needed for its military or economic power. Paramount in the mercantilist economic policy was the stern refusal to permit the colonies to develop industries that might compete with the home country. For example, when the imports of Indian calicoes—cotton fabrics—became so large that they threatened the prosperity of the English textile industry, their importation was forbidden by an Act of Parliament in 1721.

Mercantilism thus put forward an economic policy that placed the colonies in a deliberately subordinate economic position with respect to their overseas sovereign nation. Speaking generally, a colonial nation could only buy from its "home" country; could not freely sell to any other country except its colonial master; and could not sell there any wares that competed with its sovereign's favored industries. All this, we can anticipate, was to have huge consequences for American economic development. For the American colonies, founded from many motives—religious and idealistic, as well as profit-seeking—were soon to be caught up in the economic currents of the mercantilist age. It would be much too much to claim that America's final declaration of independence represented the culmination of its efforts to throw off the restrictions of mercantilist economic policy, but it is not too much to assert that without understanding those restrictions, the American need for independence cannot be fully understood.

Notes

[1] Fernand Braudel, *Civilization & Capitalism, 15th–18th Century* (3 vols., 1979–84), I: 77.

[2] *Wealth of Nations* (1937), p. 590.

[3] Jan De Vries, *The Economy of Europe in an Age of Crisis, 1600–1750* (1976), pp. 131–32.

[4] Quoted in C. W. Cole, *Colbert and a Century of French Mercantilism* (2 vols., 1939), I: 337.

Virginia slaves curing and treating tobacco

Chapter 3

THE COLONIZATION OF AMERICA

We have gotten ahead of our story. It is the end of the sixteenth century and no successful English colony has yet been planted in America. Indeed, by comparison with English efforts in India and elsewhere, the American experience had been very disappointing. Early efforts by Sir Humphrey Gilbert to colonize the bleak shores of Newfoundland had come to naught in 1578 and again in 1583. Gilbert's charter was inherited by his half-brother Walter Raleigh, who sent a reconnaissance fleet to explore the coast south of Chesapeake Bay. When the advance party returned with a glowing account of the fertile soil and friendly Indians, Raleigh decided to colonize in earnest. As encouragement, the Queen knighted him and permitted Raleigh to name the new land in her honor, Virginia (for Elizabeth, the Virgin Queen).

In 1585, Sir Walter fitted out an expedition to settle Roanoke Island, a swampy piece of land, ten miles long and two miles wide, in what is now North Carolina. Instead of planting crops and building homes, the colonists wasted their time searching Virginia's shores unsuccessfully for gold. When the famous buccaneer Sir Francis Drake dropped anchor off Roanoke in June 1586 on his way back from ravaging Spanish settlements in the West Indies, the colonists eagerly accepted his offer of passage back to England. A second effort to found a settlement in Roanoke came to a more tragic end, all its settlers having disappeared without a trace when a relief expedition arrived there in 1591.

FIRST SETTLEMENTS

Things would not change until 1606, when King James I gave a group of merchants permission to plant a colony in Virginia. The expedition is interesting in what it tells us of the colonists' expectations. Among the first party of 101 men and four boys who settled Jamestown (named in honor of their sovereign) in 1607 were thirty-six gentlemen adventurers who had never worked with their hands and had no intention of doing so, and a few artisans, including jewelers (no doubt to appraise the gold and rubies that were still the great temptation of America), but not a single farmer, miner, or fisherman. During its early years the infant colony went through a "starving time," when the settlers almost suffered the fate of Raleigh's "lost colony." The death rate in Jamestown was terrifying: roughly 60 percent in 1607, 45 percent in 1608 and 1609, and more than 50 percent in 1610.

Disease and malnutrition were the two biggest problems to afflict the settlers. While Jamestown was well situated for defense, it had a very unhealthy location, on the edge of a swamp. In addition to being a haven for malaria-bearing mosquitoes, the water on this stretch of the river became contaminated in summer by sea water, so that anyone who drank it encountered salt poisoning. Disease swept through the colony like a brush fire. By the end of the first summer about half the settlers had died. Moreover, because the planting season had ended before they had finished building their houses and fortifications, the colonists were unable to get a crop in the ground. The infant colony survived, but only barely.

Jamestown was not a secure settlement until the arrival of Governor Thomas Dale in 1611. A soldier with a reputation for sternness, Dale imposed rigorous disciplinary laws. But the best answer to Jamestown's economic survival was provided by John Rolfe, who turned the colonists' attention away from dreams of gold to the realities of a different kind of treasure—tobacco. Shortly we will look more carefully into the material and economic life they built on that first successful crop.

The harsh experiences of the pioneers in Virginia exerted a salutary effect on the expectations of subsequent colonists. Among them were the Pilgrims, as Americans have come to call them—the sober group of 101 religious dissenters who risked their lives to found a colony in

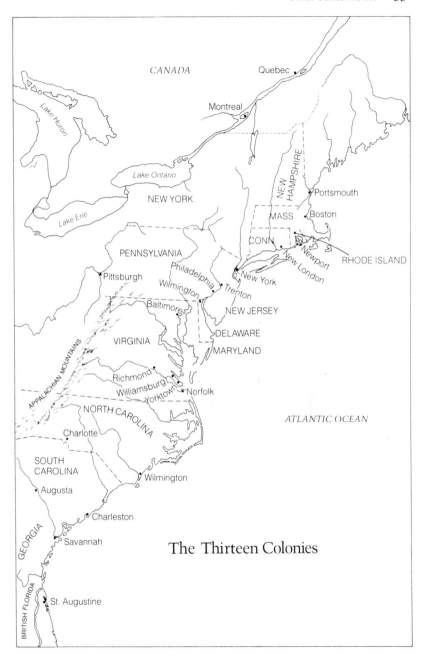

The Thirteen Colonies

First settlements

Virginia where they could practice their "separatist" form of Anglican-ism. The Pilgrims never reached Virginia. On November 9, 1620, they sighted land on Cape Cod Bay, far from their destination. With winter approaching, the party decided not to risk the rough waters, but to settle where they were, and since that was outside Virginian jurisdic-tion, they determined to form a government of their own. In the cabin of their ship they drew up the famous Mayflower Compact, binding the signers into a body politic whose laws—as yet unpromulgated—they promised to obey.

The Pilgrims entertained no visions of golden harvests, but even they were unprepared for the rigors of survival. Within a month they relocated at Plymouth (named after the English city from which they sailed) where they also nearly vanished. William Bradford described the situation in February and March of 1621:

> . . .there died some time two or three of a day in the foresaid time, that of the 100 and odd persons, scarce fifty remained. And of these, in the time of most distress, there was but six or seven sound persons who to their great commendations, be it spoken, spared no pains night or day, but with abundance of toil and hazard of their own health, fetched them wood, made them fire, dressed them meat, made their beds, washed their loathsome clothes, clothed and unclothed them. In a word, did all the homely and necessary offices for them which dainty and queasy stomachs cannot endure to hear named.[1]

Through the efforts of the heroic few and the assistance of a friendly Indian, Squanto, half the colonists survived, the rest dying of malnutri-tion, scurvy, and other related diseases. But the Pilgrims were steeled rather than broken by the ordeal. They had worsted a hostile wilder-ness, created a government, built their churches. The colony grew steadily, from 124 souls in 1624 to almost 300 in 1630, 579 in 1637, then to over 3,000 in 1660.

The Settlement of the North

The cluster of settlements established by the Pilgrims was annexed in 1691 by their neighbors, the Puritans of Massachusetts Bay colony. The Puritans who migrated to New England as early as 1630 were drawn to the New World by the deep desire to establish a religious community based upon the laws of God as found in the Scriptures. To effect this plan it was essential for the Puritans to control the religious and moral life of the community. People could not be allowed to spread out over the land on individual farms. The Puritan settlements therefore took the form of compact villages, with the farming land stretching around the periphery. These communities usually included a central village green, or common, a church, and a school. Each family head received a house lot on the land adjoining the common along with about fifty acres of arable land.

By the end of the 1640s about 15,000 Puritans had crossed the Atlantic, most of them settling near Boston. From this central group various religious splinter movements broke off, establishing settlements in Connecticut, Rhode Island, New Hampshire, and Maine.

The story of the founding of the New England colonies is an important part of the American political and moral chronicle. From our perspective it is interesting because we shall have to see how the colonists in the north managed their economic and material lives in the face of such different conditions—and in the grip of such different ideas—from their southern counterparts.

But we must first complete a rough outline of the colonization of the Atlantic coast. Below New England the Dutch established a trading post at Fort Orange, the site of present-day Albany, as early as 1624. Two years later they founded New Amsterdam, on Manhattan Island at the mouth of the Hudson River. Based on the idea of a semifeudal form of government—anyone who brought fifty settlers was to receive a great estate along the Hudson River and the power to rule it like a lord—the Dutch experiment was doomed to failure. In 1664, the English King Charles II dispatched four warships to remove the Dutch beachhead in the New World. New Amsterdam became New York, and from this territory the colony of New Jersey would subsequently be formed.

South of New York arose the remarkable colony of Pennsylvania, the achievement of William Penn, surely among the most farsighted, courageous, and successful of the first colonists. A royal grant gave Penn the land between New York and Maryland. Although Penn's primary purpose was to conduct a "holy experiment" in Christian living and popular government, he worked prodigiously to assure that he would profit from the venture by making the colony itself profitable. From the beginning Pennsylvania was built along the lines of a hard-working farming community. The Penn family attracted settlers by granting its lands in "fee simple," that is, with no semifeudal restrictions or taxes, but prospered from the sale of its enormous holdings. To obtain a port to export the surplus crops that the industrious farmers in Pennsylvania produced, Penn in 1682 acquired a grant of land to the south on Delaware Bay. This region, known as Delaware, became a separate colony in 1704.

The Settlement of the South

Below Delaware, the tenor of colonization changed. The middle and northern Atlantic settlements had been founded on religious hopes and based on the idea of a kind of free agriculture. The colonies to the south were more aristocratic in their original leanings. Maryland, for example—the ten-million-acre tract of land on Chesapeake Bay—was given by Charles I to a Catholic nobleman named George Calvert. The colony was to be a medieval palatinate and, at the same time, a refuge for Calvert's co-religionists. Calvert and his heirs governed the colony in the grand manner, owned all the land, and granted "manors" to their friends. Settlers to the colony swore an oath of allegiance not to the King of England, but to Lord Baltimore, as the respective heads of the Calvert family were called. There might have been serfs bound to the soil, as in medieval England, but the colonists who came to Maryland insisted on freehold land tenure, and the Calverts had no choice but to yield to their demands in order to attract settlers.

Even more ill-suited to the American scene was the plan of settlement envisioned by the eight noblemen who were awarded the Carolinas—the territory between Virginia and Spanish Florida—by Charles II. The proprietors hoped to populate three-fifths of their property with ordinary settlers while retaining the rest as manorial estates for a hereditary nobility. This impossible scheme rapidly fell apart, and two Carolinas emerged—North Carolina where settlements were isolated and scattered, and material and economic life was cramped, and South Carolina, from the beginning prosperous and cosmopolitan, and based on an active economic life of trade.

To the south of the Carolinas was the colony of Georgia, founded by a group of London philanthropists (led by James Oglethorpe), partly to provide a military base against the Spanish foothold in Florida to the south, partly to open a haven for Englishmen imprisoned for debt. The colony began by giving each of its original 100 settlers fifty acres of land and enough tools and supplies for a year. Land-holdings above 500 acres were prohibited and strict laws forbade drinking and slave-holding, not alone for moral reasons, but to guard against conditions that might lessen the military preparedness of the white colonists. The settlers, alas, did not share the idealism of the founding trustees. The restrictions on rum and slavery were soon removed; and a year before its idealistic charter was to expire in 1752, the discouraged trustees turned the colony itself back to the king.

Thus a wide variety of motives, institutions, and results attended the actual process of colonization. Yet the variety of colonial experience, although of great importance for the subsequent political and cultural development of the thirteen colonial entities, masks certain unifying strands of their history. It is these strands that we need to examine as we now turn aside from this cursory sketch of the adventure of settlement to look more carefully into the less adventurous, but ultimately far more significant theme of the development of American material and economic life.

MATERIAL AND ECONOMIC LIFE IN THE COLONIES

Material Life in the North

Let us begin with a rash generalization. The crucial elements in the first chapter of America's economic transformation consist of the creation of a viable *material* life in the rigorous setting of the North, and in the creation of a viable form of *economic* life in the more favorable geography of the central and southern regions.

Certainly the colonists who landed on the Massachusetts shores knew first-hand the meaning of the limits of the possible imposed by the stony, infertile "hardscrabble" fields of New England. Agriculture as the colonists knew it in the old country was impossible in this inhospitable terrain. Given the short planting season of New England, there was simply not the time to cultivate much land, and the cultivation itself had to be differently practiced than in the well-tilled soft soil of the English country. Thus the typical New England farmer, who might possess 100 acres, was often unable to plow more than an eighth of the area. Plows themselves were in short supply—as late as 1760 only one farm in five owned its own plow—and those on hand were light wooden implements, sheathed with iron (and later steel), incapable of turning the soil very deeply. Even with two or three horses, or with a yoke of four to six oxen, a farmer could hardly plow more than a single acre in a day.

The limits of the possible imposed their barriers, but also stimulated adaptation and innovation. New Englanders learned to cultivate strips of ground a mere hoe's width across and four to five inches deep, to drop in a few grains of corn, and to fertilize the seeds with a dead fish, a technique used by the Indians. Because corn was easy to tend, one farmer was capable of planting six to eight acres, which produced eighty to 120 bushels, enough to feed five to seven persons a year.

Meanwhile tools gradually changed to meet new demands. The necessity of clearing away the forest made the axe an indispensable agricultural implement. The heavy axe of England, with its long bit and light poll (hammerlike head) was shortened and made more compact, until bit and poll were more nearly equal in mass. Later the handle itself became gracefully curved and was often shaped to the height and swing of the user. The result was a dramatic improvement in its efficiency. Trials showed that an American could fell three times as many trees in a given time with his axe than could someone using the European model.

Equally important was the adaptation of the traditional handsickle to the demands of the short growing season that required rapid harvesting. Using a sickle, a farmer could reap and stack no more than half an acre per day. Much of his crop might spoil in the fields while he struggled to cut and bundle it. The challenge resulted in the development of the "cradle," a long-handled scythe with a framework of four or five long wooden "fingers" extending above the cutting blade. As the blade of the scythe cut the grain, the stalks fell onto the cradle, perfectly aligned for gathering into a sheaf. This innovation made it possible for an experienced farmer to reap nearly two acres per day, effectively multiplying his productivity fourfold.

Yet another vital means of improving the limits of the possible was the adaptation of crops. Wheat, rye, and oats, the mainstay of English agriculture, did poorly at first, and the colonists were forced to try an Indian triad—corn, beans, and pumpkins. Corn yielded three or four times as many bushels per acre as the English grains, and the colonists admitted that this Indian "wheat" had to be their "staffe of life."

Nevertheless, the soil of New England provided little encouragement to large-scale conventional farming. Hence the efforts of the set-

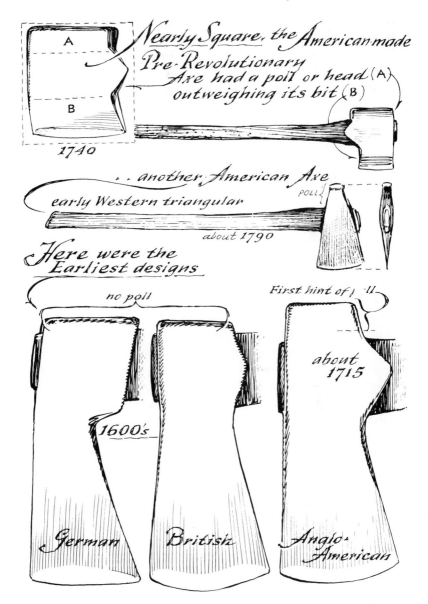

Nearly Square. the American-made
Pre-Revolutionary
Axe had a poll or head (A)
outweighing its bit (B)

A

B

1740

... another American Axe

early Western triangular

POLL

about 1790

Here were the Earliest designs

no poll

First hint of poll

German

British

1600's

about 1715

Anglo-American

Evolution of the American axe head

tlers soon turned in another direction—fishing. First harvesting the inland waters, then venturing out into the bays and ocean, the New Englanders developed the skills of fishing that would soon become the very symbol of their region's occupational specialization. We shall later see how important was this reorientation of material life for the economic trade that New England would develop.

By adaptation, Puritan striving, and ingenuity—the famed Yankee ingenuity that will figure large in the development of American technology—the limits of the possible were thus gradually enlarged. A simple but adequate diet; often windowless but warm houses; rough but substantial clothing changed the level of material existence in New England from a perilous encounter with survival itself to a secure and even ample subsistence, within the space of a single generation.

Economic Life in the South

"Take foure of the best kingdomes in Christendome and put them all together, they may no way compare with this countrie [of Virginia] either for commodities or goodnesse of soil."[2] Thus wrote Thomas Dale upon his arrival in Virginia in 1611. The words bespeak a striking difference between the harsh north and the benign central and southern regions. In these areas, too, the first settlers had had their life-and-death struggles—during the starving time at Jamestown, for example, some of the colonists had been reduced to cannibalism—but once the foolish vision of treasure had been replaced by more realistic ones of commercial crops, nature worked with, rather than against, the colonists. Early on, the middle and southern states found that they could practice a varied agriculture, raising traditional English crops in more or less traditional English ways, borrowing Indian crops where conditions indicated their usefulness, and soon specializing in three staple crops for purposes of trade—tobacco, rice, and indigo, in the South, wheat and barley in the Mid-Atlantic region.

From the middle years of the seventeenth century, then, Virginians, Carolinians, Pennsylvanians, and Georgians turned their efforts to raising crops that would be used not just to provide food or fibre for their growers, but to provide *cash incomes,* by being exported, mainly to an eager market in England.

That is why the life of the marketplace makes its appearance as an important current of economic development earlier in the central and southern regions than in the North. As we would expect, its appear-

Indigo production at a South Carolina plantation

ance generates trading connections that will soon link southern ports with Europe as well as with the rest of the colonies: we will look more deeply into them at the end of the next chapter.

But the emergence of an active economic life brought an even deeper consequence than new trade relations. "I hear . . . that servants would be more advantageous to you than any commodities," wrote a Londoner to a Virginian in 1648.[3] The words tell of the profound difference between North and South. In the North, the task of agriculture was mainly concerned with feeding the immediate family of the farmer, with a little left over to sell to the local merchant; there was scarcely any need for labor beyond that supplied by the household itself or by cooperation among neighbors. But once the aim of agriculture became the production of a commercial crop, an entirely new situation arose. Now the farmer could use as many hands as he could get. A new demand developed—a demand for agricultural labor. Indeed, as early as 1621, the wages of day laborers in Virginia were already three or four times higher than the amounts their counterparts earned in England.

But where was this labor to be found? By 1650 there were perhaps 49,000 white people along the entire English Atlantic coast, an extraordinary increase since the first frail beachheads, but obviously not enough to provide a body of laborers looking for work. Even by 1700, the white colonists numbered only 223,000, but since the number of children was very large, there were probably no more than 100,000 adult male and female workers, most of whom were tending to their own farms or small artisan workshops and were not interested in working for someone else. To entice new colonists, therefore, many colonies offered liberal land terms—for example, fifty acres free of charge for anyone paying his way to Virginia plus another fifty for anyone whom he brought along. But this *headright* system mainly attracted relatively well-to-do immigrants who quickly became farmers themselves, not hired hands.

SYSTEMS OF SERVITUDE

Indentured Servants

How then was a supply of labor created for the promising commercial crops of rice, indigo, and tobacco?

The answer was provided through the development of *indentured servants*. Under this system, those wanting to come to America but unable to pay their passage (which cost about £10, the equivalent of about fifteen months' wages in England), signed an indenture, a legal contract binding them to servitude for a term of years, usually five. Typically the contract was signed with a ship owner or recruiting agent who in turn sold it at a nice profit to a planter or merchant, once the ship arrived in the colonies. In buying the contract, the planter undertook to feed, house, and clothe the worker, and to provide "freedom dues"—a plot of land, tools, or a sum of money—when the contract expired.

About half the migrants arriving in the colonies south of New York prior to 1700 made their crossing in this fashion. Most of them were young, usually male, about equally divided among farmers or artisans, unskilled casual laborers, and domestic servants. Some, of course, were social outcasts or criminals, but the great bulk were simply upwardly mobile, adventurous Englishmen who came to America because it offered opportunity on a scale unimaginable in England.

Nevertheless, the lot of an indentured servant was a difficult one, far worse than in England, where servants had well-established traditional and legal rights. In the New World, because of the pressing need for able-bodied laborers, they were worked as hard as possible and then replaced with new migrants. Put simply, they were treated as exploitable and expendable objects. Typically, they worked six days a week, ten to fourteen hours per day. The backbreaking toil, disease, and general conditions of life in the Chesapeake region exacted an appalling toll: approximately 40 percent of the male servants did not survive long enough to collect their freedom dues.

Female servants, too, had a difficult experience. Although some worked in the fields, most performed domestic service. Typically they were precluded from marrying during their term of indenture, since masters did not want pregnancy to deprive them of workers. Because their marriages were delayed, female servants had fewer children— one to three—than women in England, who generally had at least five.

The indenture contract provided the single greatest contribution to the labor supply in the early years of America's developing economic life. Despite their servile status, the living standard of the servants was probably not much, if at all, below what they were accustomed to in the Old World. The planters gained as an exportable surplus only 25 to 50 percent of what their servant laborers produced, all the rest being needed to feed the workers themselves. Thus even in the commercial South, the constraints of material life exerted their impact on the pace of growth.

Redemptioners

In the eighteenth century a new system of bondage was introduced, the redemption agreement. Unlike the indenture, which was a legally binding contract, the redemption agreement was vague and unwritten. The redemptioner was a partially paid-up passenger. On arrival in the New World he or she was given a few weeks to find someone to pay the balance to the captain. Failure to pay resulted in the sale of his or her service for a period sufficiently long to cover the unpaid sum, often as much as four years. The redemptioner could be sold anywhere in America, for whatever the traffic would bear.

Tens of thousands of Germans, largely from the war-ravaged Rhineland, came to America as redemptioners, many lured by glib misrepresentations of promotion agents who received a commission for every person they gulled aboard a ship. What was not explained to the redemptioners—or to the indentured servants either—were the rigors of the voyage they were to undergo. It took from five weeks to several months to cross the Atlantic, depending on the vagaries of currents and winds. The weak or sick usually died at sea; many of the healthy perished as well. One vessel in 1731 that set sail with 150 passengers arrived with but thirty-four. The *Sea Flower* which left Belfast, Ireland, with 106 passengers in 1741 was at sea for four months and lost forty-six passengers from starvation.

In addition to the hazards of prevailing headwinds and ferocious storms, there was the danger of shipboard disease. Passengers and crew frequently contracted smallpox and other contagious diseases. By the time they made port, many immigrants had been reduced to a state of helpless passivity, unable to make out what had happened to them or why.

And Slaves

One other crossing must not be lost to our sight. This was the crossing of blacks captured or sold into slavery in Africa, packed into spaces that were too low to stand in, too narrow to lie flat, too fetid to breathe freely, brought to America like animal cargoes, and sold on the block—wives separated from husbands, children from mothers. The average size of a slave ship's cargo was about 250 slaves; of this number, about 10–20 percent died en route to the New World.

Slavery was a very small part of the labor supply needed to sustain economic life in mid-seventeenth century America. In 1650, in all of Virginia with its 20,000 inhabitants, scarcely 300 were slaves. But already in other nations the slave population was large—200,000 blacks toiling in Portuguese Brazil, 100,000 in the British West Indies. These islands, the so-called Sugar Islands, would soon become the jewels in Great Britain's New World crown. Sugar was to the West Indies what tobacco was to the Chesapeake colonies—and even more lucrative.

By filling the ever increasing demand for sugar and sugar products, especially molasses and rum, the West Indian planters contributed powerfully to the mother country's wealth and amassed fortunes of their own. As Adam Smith pointed out in his *Wealth of Nations*, "The profits of a plantation in any of our West Indian colonies are generally much greater that those of any other cultivation that is known either in Europe or America."

Slaves were used to plant, cultivate, cut, grind, and boil the cane. About 250,000 Africans were sent to the West Indies between 1640–1670. Of this number about half came to Barbados, the rest going to Jamaica and the Leeward Islands.

America was still relatively free from this most terrible of all the channels of trade and sources of labor, but it would not long remain so. During the century to come slavery would more and more come to provide the great source of agricultural labor that white immigration, free or indentured, could no longer fill, bringing with it decisive changes for every aspect of American history, all rooted in the need to sustain and accelerate the growing currents of commercial life.

CURRENTS OF AMERICAN TRADE

Of course economic life was not confined to the southern colonies, although the search for a labor supply was more acutely felt there than in the North. But the northern colonies, once having established their viability, also began to cast about for products that were marketable in England. As we know, they turned in the direction of fishing—to this very day the "sacred cod" hangs in its place of honor in Boston's State House. On the eve of the American Revolution, fish accounted for more than one-third of New England's exports.

Closely related to fishing but more specialized was whaling. Already during the seventeenth century, whalers captured a few of these great mammals from shore stations along Cape Cod and Nantucket, but it was not until the eighteenth century that whaling took on its extraordinary, ocean-ranging aspects. By 1770 over 250 vessels set sail each season to harpoon the Moby Dicks whose oil was used for illumination and lubrication, for leather and soap, and for high quality candles.

A second market crop was provided by the New England forests themselves. By the seventeenth century England was experiencing a growing shortage of wood for building materials and fuel, and wood imports from Scandanavia and Northern Europe were growing ever larger. England's leaders considered this a dangerous dependency, especially for a nation that depended so heavily on its fleet. Hence the exploitation of the New England forests was encouraged, especially as a source of tall timber for masts. English shipwrights could use a single white pine, 120 feet in height, to fashion a mast that was much stronger than those pieced together from the shorter trees of Europe. It is not surprising that the colonists also began to develop their own shipbuilding industry. By the late 1690s, New England had an enormous fleet of 2,000 shipping and fishing vessels, virtually all of local manufacture; and more and more English ships were also being built in colonial yards. By the eve of the American Revolution a third of the British fleet had been made in New England.

We can see in this direct use of colonial resources for the strengthening of the mother country the clear imprint of mercantilist policies. Equally clear was the use of the colonies as an outlet for English manufactures. As we can imagine, the colonial regions could not possibly develop their own manufactures while they were struggling to find a workable agricultural base; and after they turned to shipbuilding and fishing, there was neither manpower nor the necessary capital equipment to establish a range of textile or metal-working industries. Those

Colonial shipbuilding

would come later, as we will see, but in the seventeenth century the colonies relied exclusively on England for its bolts of better cloth, its shoe buckles and pewterware, its glass windows for the more substantial homes that were beginning to be built. In 1701 the American colonies (including the West Indies) took only about 10 percent of England's exports, but this modest share was almost 100 percent of American-manufactured imports.

Looking at the colonial seaboard as a whole, we can see the development of complex channels of trade. The middle colonies, with their agricultural surpluses, exported wheat, flour, and salted meats to southern Europe and the English West Indies. New England sent dried fish to southern Europe, and a variety of wood, whale oil, and maritime and other products to the Caribbean. In return, the northern colonies bought rum, molasses, and sugar from the English plantations in Barbados and the neighboring isles. Most of the rum was consumed in the colonies; the remainder was shipped largely to Newfoundland. How were these transactions concluded? The question raises an interesting point about the medium of exchange available in America. Although by 1750 most of the colonies had experimented with several forms of paper currency, there was little in America resembling the wide array of monetary notes of England. Business in the colonies was conducted largely by credit in the form of bills of exchange. Essentially, these were promissory notes in which one merchant pledged to pay another an agreed-upon sum on demand. Bills of exchange passed from hand to hand, circulating much as currency does today. (The fabled exchange of rum against African slaves has been shown, on careful research, to have been almost nonexistent—perhaps one percent of colonial trade in the 1760s.)

The Economy of Tobacco

Southerners were much more bound to England. Tobacco, rice, and indigo—their great export crops—went almost exclusively to English ports, including of course to the "English" ports of Boston, Baltimore, and the West Indies.

Tobacco plantations generally lined the banks of the major rivers as far as a hundred miles inland. These broad, deep, and slow-moving rivers were the planters' highways to the world. Every fall English and

Scottish merchants would dock at the wharf of each plantation to pick up barrels of cured tobacco* and to leave off goods ordered by the planter and brought from London. The typical Chesapeake farmer, with only his immediate family as a labor source, planted about three acres in tobacco. Producing roughly 2,400 pounds of saleable tobacco annually, he earned £10 to £20 for his efforts. This represented from 10 to 25 percent of his total income.

Curiously, tobacco was not inherently a plantation crop. The planting, cultivation, and harvesting of tobacco was done entirely by hand. There were no mills or sophisticated engineering systems required for its cultivation, no elaborate storage facilities, no great capital expenditures which required a large output to offset the costs of fixed equipment. What successful tobacco cultivation did require was abundant land. This was because the crops drained the soil of nutrients. Typically, a field produced about three crops before it had to lie fallow for several years to regain its fertility.

Tobacco was marketed almost exclusively under the consignment system. Under this system, the London merchants were primarily intermediaries. They advanced funds for all the necessary charges—transportation, taxes, storage—and repaid themselves, with a handsome profit, when the crop was finally sold. To attract more consignments and hold old accounts, the tobacco merchants sometimes offered growers "advances," that is, they allowed planters to draw funds prior to the sale of the tobacco in Britain, with the understanding that the forthcoming crop served as collateral for the loan.

After 1720, however, aggressive Scottish merchants initiated the practice of buying tobacco directly in the colonies for spot cash or its equivalent. Concentrating mainly on the interior of the Chesapeake region, the Glasgow merchants opened branch stores along the shores of the major rivers, where they bought their tobacco from growers and supplied them with European imports. This practice appealed powerfully to many smaller planters because it eliminated the risks and uncertainties associated with later sales by a consignee in an overseas market. As a result of their entrepreneurship, the Glasgow merchants

---

*A hogshead of tobacco, it should be noted, weighed nearly half a ton. It would have been physically grueling, as well as cost prohibitive, to roll or haul it over miles of rough countryside.

quadrupled their trade in tobacco between the late 1730s and the early 1750s.

Rice and Indigo

Rice was grown largely on plantations located in the swampy lowlands along the Atlantic coast. In contrast to tobacco, slave labor was used extensively in cultivating this commercial food crop. Rice plantations were normally large economic units, and slave populations of thirty to 100 were common. This fact helps explain why South Carolina became the only colony where black slaves outnumbered white inhabitants, by a margin of fifty percent.

Rice cultivation was physically demanding and technically troublesome. The fields were flooded by building dikes and irrigation ditches, and by trapping fresh water that was backed up by the incoming ocean tides. This process demanded meticulous engineering to ensure against seepage of salt water. The large amount of labor and the heavy equipment required in production made rice cultivation relatively labor-intensive and capital-intensive compared with tobacco and other forms of agriculture. Nevertheless, rice was a very profitable crop. In terms of aggregate output, it was the most important crop in the Deep South. Yields were from two to four barrels per acre, and most plantations had two to three acres under cultivation for each field hand. Based on an average price of £2.3 per barrel from 1768 to 1772, each slave who worked knee-deep in the muddy rice fields swarming with malaria-bearing mosquitoes generated revenues annually of from £1.2 up to £27.6, with around £15 probably the average figure. Curiously, this average was virtually identical to the annual per capita income of an ordinary free worker.

South Carolina planters also grew indigo, a plant that yielded a brilliant copper or purple dye highly valued by the English textile industry. Indigo was first grown in America by Eliza Lucas, one of America's first female entrepreneurs. While still in her teens, Lucas was running three large South Carolina plantations owned by her father, a colonial official in the West Indies.

Like rice, indigo production also required great skill, but it nicely complemented rice production because it could be grown on high ground where rice would not grow and its planting and harvesting times did not conflict with those of rice. Indigo was harvested by sickle, the leaves often cut three times a year. Straining the dye residue in large vats was a fairly complicated chemical process that determined in large part the value of the final product. But a skilled slave could usually care for two acres of indigo plants and produce 120 pounds of dye substance worth £20 to £30 for the export market. Probably no other colonial crop produced a greater income per acre, or per worker. Moreover, because indigo production fell at slack times in the rice-growing season, planters who grew both crops were able to create a year-round work routine for their slaves. This efficient and effective use of land and labor made it possible for planters to recover their costs for their slaves in as little as two to three years.

Southerners also found an overseas market for the tall pines that grew in their forests. Like the timber that was exported from New England, these tall, straight logs became masts of ships in the Royal Navy. The resin from these trees was made into tar and pitch that were used to preserve rope and make the hulls of ships watertight.

Intercolonial Commerce

If we were to look at colonial trade as a whole, we would find a very complex pattern. To begin with, most of it travelled by ship. Roads were worse in America than they were in England, and there, we will remember, they were often little better than paths. There was, for all intents and purposes, no inland trade route that linked North and South. Goods had to go by coastal vessel, so that by the end of the seventeenth century, we find a considerable trade plying the American shores, bringing northern whale oil south, Pennsylvanian wheat north, and southern tobacco to New York.

As the eighteenth century opens there is an active mercantile life in America, with a well-organized trade in the various regional specialties. From this trade were forged the first bonds that tied the colonies together. A series of settlements founded for often divergent social and political reasons—compare the feudal visions of the Carolinas with the communal life of the Puritans—was being slowly and without conscious intent formed into an economic entity. It was not, and it never would be, an entity with a single purpose, for the interests and inclinations of North and South (and later of East and West) would be very dissimilar, but it was an entity in that mutual dependencies, articulated through a chain of market connections, created economically "united" colonies before there was a political feeling of unification.

The Colonies in the Mercantilist World

Stepping back still further, we can see the complex trade patterns of the colonies, linking themselves with one another and with the English motherland and its West Indian outposts, in a still larger perspective as part of the prevailing mercantilist structure of trade and thought. We recall that mercantilism put forward a view of foreign trade as an active and aggressive instrument of national economic and military power, seeking to sell more to "strangers" than it bought in return, and using its colonies as strategic sources of supply and as monopolized markets.

From 1651 to 1733 the English Parliament passed a series of acts that gave active expression to these ideas. So far as the colonies were concerned, the acts had three important provisions. First, all trade to England from America (as well as from other colonies) had to be carried in English ships whose crews were also to be at least three-quarters Englishmen. Since the colonies were considered to be a part of England, and the colonists Englishmen, this was actually favorable for colonial development.

Second, all colonial imports, except wine and salt from southern Europe, had to come from England—or at least pass through England, en route to the colonies. This was, of course, a means of preserving the colonial market for the exclusive benefit of British producers and merchants.

Last, the acts "enumerated" certain colonial products that could only be shipped to England—all sugar, tobacco, and indigo, for instance. This was also less favorable for the colonists because it prevented them from disposing of their crops or products where the demand might be highest. The adverse impact fell especially heavily on the southern colonies who felt, quite rightly, that tobacco, indigo, and rice might be much more profitably sold elsewhere than in England, whereas few of the northern exports were on the "enumerated list," which left northern merchants free to trade as they wished.

All things considered, as we shall review later in more detail, the Navigation Acts were no great burden—perhaps even, on balance, of some benefit to the colonies. Were they a benefit for England? For the economic side of things, unquestionably. As early as the 1660s, duties on tobacco from the Chesapeake colonies accounted for 25 percent of England's customs revenues and 5 percent of the mother country's entire revenue. Although England did not regularly sell more than it purchased in America—there were many years in the late seventeenth century when the balance of trade was in the colonists' favor—England was certainly the beneficiary of indirect profits gained from its Navigation Acts. For instance, large volumes of tobacco, indigo, and rice passed through England to Europe, so that its mercantilist policy allowed England to make a middleman's profit that would otherwise have accrued directly as a gain to the colonies. Of the fifteen million pounds of tobacco shipped to England from the colonies in 1670, roughly 50 percent was re-exported; of the 100 million pounds sent in 1770, 85 percent was reexported.

The importation of raw materials and unprocessed foodstuffs from the colonies also stimulated the creation of new enterprises in England. Tobacco processing and sugar refining, for example, both became profitable businesses based on colonial crops. Such new businesses increased employment, expanded the domestic market in England for manufactured products, and transformed imported products into more valuable commodities, which could, in turn, be sold both to Europe and back to the American colonies.

Thus from a strictly economic view, as well as from a perspective that emphasizes the strategic importance of such imports as the tall masts or the raw materials of commerce, mercantilism paid handsome dividends to England. From another view, however, the policy was to introduce complications that would in the end prove its undoing. For the Navigation Acts in particular, and the mercantilist policy that lay behind them, prevented the emerging American economy, slowly coming into being as a self-conscious entity, from pursuing its own interest in an age in which the free pursuit of economic maximization was becoming an ever more attractive political rallying ground.

As part of its mercantilist policy, in 1699 Parliament had forbidden the export of woolens beyond the boundary of any colony, in an attempt to discourage an American industry that threatened to press too hard on English woolen manufacturers. In 1732, in response to loud complaints from the London hatters, another parliamentary act barred the colonial exportation of hats, and in 1750 Parliament prohibited the construction or continuance of any mill or engine for slitting or rolling iron, or any plating forge or furnace for making steel.

Had these acts been strictly enforced they might have dealt a fatal blow to the tiny nuclei of colonial industry. Fortunately, the restrictive legislation appears to have been largely ignored. New iron mills, for example, continued to be set up and even advertised, and American axes acquired such repute that some British firms actually passed off their own products as American.

Nevertheless, the political consequences of mercantilism would ultimately be costly for England, for it was clear that England was not prepared to see the colonists follow the currents of profits wherever they might lead. As we shall see, that thwarting of economic motives would have important effects on American political ambitions. Indeed, it would lead, in less than a century, to the watershed of the American Revolution.

Notes

[1]Samuel Eliot Morison (ed.), *Of Plymouth Plantation* (1952), p. 77.
[2]Alexander Brown, *Genesis of the United States* (1890), 1:494.
[3]Carl Degler, *Out of Our Past* (rev. ed., 1970), p. 2.

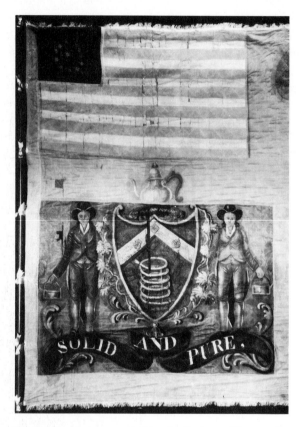

Processional banner carried by the Society of Pewters in
New York City, 1788

Chapter 4

SETTING THE ECONOMIC STAGE

We have been stressing hardships and obstacles, and the earliest years of colonization saw plenty of both. But it would give a mistaken impression of the colonial experience to paint the era only in tones of gray. For once the initial adjustments were made—once a viable form of material life had evolved and the initial economic networks established—colonial America was anything but a land of hardship and penury. On the contrary, it rapidly gave evidence of the most extraordinary vitality the world had ever seen.

There is no more dramatic proof of this than to look at the figures for population, for these figures give incontrovertible testimony to the success of the colonial efforts.

In 1630 there were fewer than 5,000 people in the English settlements, all engaged in a life-and-death struggle for survival. In 1730 the number had grown to 629,000. By 1770, at the eve of the Revolution, it was 2,148,000. Nothing resembling such an explosion of population had ever been witnessed before. Indeed, it was the spectacle of the American colonies, doubling their size every twenty-five years, that was one of the reasons for Thomas Robert Malthus' famous *Essay on the Principle of Population* that warned in 1798 of the horrendous consequences of runaway population increase: pestilence, famine, and war.

POPULATION EXPLOSION

White Immigrants

Where did this staggering increase come from? The first source was, of course, immigration.

New England received an influx of about 20,000 English settlers between 1620 and 1645; it is doubtful if the colonies would have survived without them. So, too, in the Chesapeake Bay region, the flow of white immigrants—many of them coming under various systems of indentured servitude we have described—was a key factor in boosting population in Virginia, Maryland, and North Carolina from barely 900 in 1619 to over 90,000 by 1699. Taking the seaboard as a whole, it has been estimated that between 450,000 and 500,000 white immigrants arrived in America between the turn of the century and 1776.

Unlike the earlier comers, who were mainly English, the wave of immigrants in the eighteenth century was largely Scotch-Irish and German. About 50,000 Scotch-Irish immigrants came directly from Scotland, and about three times that number from Ulster in Northern Ireland. Some of this wave settled in New York and New Jersey, but most went to Pennsylvania.

German immigrants also tended to gravitate toward Pennsylvania, but not all of them stayed there. Some moved west and then south along the eastern slope of the Appalachian Mountains, eventually finding homes in Maryland and Virginia. Others settled in the interior of South Carolina and Georgia.

By the eve of the Revolution, the Scotch-Irish and the Germans each accounted for about 7 percent of the total colonial population. In numbers this was small, but in cultural impact it was not. Here was the first sign of the melting pot that would become a hallmark of American life and a very important part of its economic life as well. Much of the entrepreneurial zeal and drive of American growth was due to the spirit of its non-English immigrants who found in the open social setting of the colonies, and later the states, an opportunity to unleash talents that were bottled up in repressive European countries. Much of the grueling and exploited labor in the colonies, and later in the states, was also performed by newcomers to the melting pot, who brought their muscle power but little else, and who were glad to undertake the hardest and dirtiest work for the lowest pay.

Slave Growth

A second source of population increase is directly related to the melting pot in one way, in that it is the consequence of non-English arrivals, but very different in another way, in that the newcomers were not allowed to enter America on an equal footing with all others. This was, of course, the slave trade at which we have already briefly glanced.

How much of the population growth was provided by slavery? Actually, between 1492 and 1770 more Africans than Europeans arrived in the New World, but just 4.5 percent of them, or 275,000, were imported to America during the eighteenth century. The rest, as we have seen, were sent to the Caribbean and South America. In 1630 slavery did not exist, and a century later there were still "only" 91,000 slaves in all the colonies. Fifty thousand of them were in Virginia and South Carolina, working on the emerging plantation system of rice, indigo, and tobacco. Thereafter the number began to leap: 150,000 slaves in 1740; double that number in 1760; almost half a million when the Revolution erupted.

It is important to recognize that not all of the increase in slave population came about through the slave trade itself. It is one of the more terrible aspects of slavery that the children of enslaved men and women became themselves slaves at birth. Thus, of the increase in the number of black inhabitants in the American colonies between 1700 and 1770, less than a quarter was the consequence of the infamous slave trade.

The rest was the result of the natural increase of the slave population—the excess of births over deaths. A recent study has shown that native-born black women in the colonies typically married before the age of twenty and produced seven to eight children, a much higher rate of increase than in the West Indies. The reason tells us something about the condition of being a slave. In the West Indies, as we have seen, the plantations mainly produced sugar, so that plantation owners had to import foodstuffs for their slave populations. The high cost of food gave little incentive to the owners to provide a nutritious diet—it was cheaper to import new slaves than to incur the costs needed to maintain a slave population in good enough health to give birth to and rear a large number of children. In the colonies, by contrast, foodstuffs in the South, where 90 percent of all slaves lived, were grown on the farms and plantations. The result was a healthier slave population whose natural rate of increase was correspondingly high.

Natural Increase

What we have seen with respect both to white and black populations makes it clear that the main reason for the explosion of colonial population after the seventeenth century was not immigration, free or non-free, but simply a high birth rate, indeed the highest in the world. A combination of a youthful population, economic opportunity, early marriages, and rural life all worked in favor of big families. Patrick Henry, for example, who was born on a Virginia plantation in 1736, was one of nineteen children. Benjamin Franklin, born in Boston in 1706, was the youngest of seventeen. Taking the colonies as a whole, the average number of children per marriage among white settlers was about six or seven, compared with four or five in Europe. Not only were more children born, per couple, but more children survived. The English death rate for infants was probably about 20 percent; in New England it is estimated to have been as low as 10 percent. Moreover, once the hazards of infant death were passed, the chances for longevity were also considerably better in America. The diet, the housing, the healthy life*—and not least, the absence of epidemic-prone cities—all contributed to the American rate of population increase, an amazing 3 percent per year, a rate of growth that has seldom been matched in any other place or time in history.

SOCIAL CLASSES

Agricultural Workers

What sorts of economic tasks did this burgeoning population undertake? The vast majority were, of course, involved with agriculture, whether as farmers raising food for their own households and selling their surpluses in local markets, or as owners of large and small tracts who raised the export crops that we have noted. One of the reasons for the increase in population in the South was the skyrocketing demand for tobacco itself: between 1619 and 1699 tobacco exports

---

*By the late 1700s, the healthier, white, native-born colonial population averaged two to four inches taller than their English counterparts.

from the upper South soared from 387,000 pounds to over thirty million pounds.

Farming, plantation farming with gangs of slaves in the South, and fishing in the North, were not only major activities, but created distinctive social and economic classes. At the bottom of the socioeconomic structure were the slaves themselves, largely concentrated, as we have seen, in the southern regions. At the lower end of the spectrum we would also have to place the indentured servants—not so numerous in the eighteenth century—who also tilled the soil, although a vast gulf separated them from black slavery. We have no exact statistics for the years around 1750, but it is likely that 85 percent of the population lived on the land and engaged in agricultural pursuits. Of this agricultural work force, roughly 20 percent were black slaves, about 2 percent were indentured servants of one sort or another, and the remainder were independent farmers tilling their own lands, sometimes with free hired help. Why were indentured servants so few? There are two answers. First, the number of persons—mainly Englishmen—offering themselves into indentured servitude was fast drying up as the eighteenth century progressed. This reflected better times in England, and the availability of generous settlement terms in colonies like Pennsylvania where cheap land was readily available. Who would offer himself into indenture when he could become an independent farmer himself, no matter on how small a scale?

The second reason for the decline in the importance of indenture is less agreeable. It was the rise of slavery. Planters were beginning to realize that a *permanent* slave costs only two or three times as much as the *temporary* services of an indentured servant. In the 1730s, for instance, the trustees of the colony of Georgia calculated the annual cost of upkeep for a male white servant to be £9 compared with less than £3½ for a slave. An able-bodied slave could be bought for £18 to £30. Thus the demand for indentured servants declined at the same time as the supply. By the middle of the eighteenth century, indentures were vanishing from the American scene, to be replaced with something infinitely worse.

The Planter

At the apex of the agricultural world we find a figure of great economic and political importance. This was the southern planter, the owner of a plantation. The planter typically lived in a large Georgian-style house, surrounded by attendant buildings: smokehouse, kitchen, laundry, and workshops, in a manner that reminds us of the manorial estates of medieval Europe. Although not "noble" by birth, the planter was certainly an aristocrat in wealth and influence. English by descent, Anglican by religion, linked to his fellow planters by ties of kinship and economic interest, the southern planter ruled by the deference paid him by humbler folk. And no wonder: when a tobacco farmer might consider himself well enough off in 1740 with 100 or 200 acres, one Virginia planter, William Byrd II, owned 179,440 acres.

Although extremely rich, even by planters' standards, Byrd typified the southern aristocracy in many ways. He was intensely interested in the practical management of his estate, personally fussing over its orchards and gardens, the operation of its sawmill and gristmill, its ventures into mining—all the while continuing his father's trade with the Indians, his own traffic in slaves, and his service on the Council of State, the supreme court of Virginia.

This active life, mixing business and politics, clearly separated the southern aristocrat from his counterpart in Europe. Unlike the traditional blueblood of Europe who often looked down his nose at trade, the southern blueblood threw himself wholeheartedly into the pursuit of profit. "The men who founded the aristocracy of Virginia," writes Louis B. Wright, a leading historian of the subject, "were working gentlemen busy with the supervision of their estates and occupied with the commerce which resulted from the sale of plantation products and importation of manufactured goods from overseas."[1]

Thus the popular stereotype of the southern planter as someone interested only in the rearing of fine thoroughbreds or in the indolent life of a country gentleman seriously misrepresents his actual role. In the absence of active commercial centers in the regions the planters became, in fact, merchants and bankers as well as growers—often buying the output of their smaller neighbors for sale in overseas ports, while selling in return goods they imported from England. So, too, it was the great planter who naturally became a source for loans and credit to friends and neighbors. According to historian Aubrey C. Land, the wealth of the great Chesapeake Bay planters stemmed as much, and perhaps more, from their entrepreneurial activities as from their plantation operations.[2]

A tidewater plantation

Merchants

Just as planters controlled the economic and political life of the southern colonies, so merchants dominated the affairs of those in the North.
This was the case because the key to prosperity in the North was
trade, just as cash crops were the key farther south. Since merchants
coordinated the flow of trade between farm and town, between town
and overseas ports, and then between ports and foreign nations, they
occupied the strategic points in the network of economic life, and
prospered accordingly.

On the frontier and in remote regions, a merchant was often little
more than a country storekeeper, conducting business out of one
room of his house and perhaps maintaining a farm on the side.
Despite his low place on the mercantile ladder, the country storekeeper provided a number of critical services for the local economy.
He was usually the only source of goods from the outside world, aside
from rare itinerant peddlers; he provided the only cash buyer of farm
surpluses; and he was the only source of credit for small farmers. In
the towns, of course, merchanting was full-time business, where the

proprietor often served as an intermediary between his country counterpart and "big merchants" in the cities.

Even in the cities, however, mercantile business was small-scale in
terms of personnel, even though large sums might be handled. A merchant firm was usually a single proprietorship or a partnership among
relatives, and the owners themselves carried on the business. The pace
of transactions was slow by modern standards: between 1752 and
1767 one of the leading merchants in New York averaged only five
transactions a day.[3]

What sorts of transactions? At their most impressive, they were
arrangements concerning foreign trade—the delivery of goods for
shipment overseas, or payment for a consignment that had arrived and
would be transferred to the merchant's warehouse. A merchant might
very well own a ship, or several ships, or hold a third or a fifth interest
in other ships and their cargoes. Usually the merchant established regular connections with fellow merchants in the important ports of call;
if not, the captain of the ship often acted as the merchant's agent.

Not surprisingly, merchants were among the wealthiest men in the
northern colonies, playing a role in their economic and political affairs
akin to that played by the planter in the South. In Massachusetts, for
example, the merchant class dominated the upper chamber of the legislature after the 1690s, and by the mid-eighteenth century, it provided
half the leadership in the lower assembly as well. Just as an example,
we might note that John Hancock, whose flourishing signature to the
Declaration of Independence gained him a permanent place in American history books, was the richest Bostonian of his time. This because
he was heir to Thomas Hancock, a thriving merchant who had worked
his way up from a bookseller's apprentice to a trader in molasses, an
importer of Dutch tea, an agent for English merchants with interests in
Boston, an investor, and a shipowner. The successful merchant, like
the successful planter, was a center of power in his colony.

The Working Classes of Town and City

Below the merchants were important strata of town and city society,
about which we are less well informed. There was an important group
of artisans, variously known as tradesmen, mechanics, artificers, and
"leather apron" men that included such occupations as silversmiths
and hatters, shoemakers and tailors, shipworkers, masons, and other
skilled trades. Working largely with wood, leather, and metal, and

using their own tools, these artisans made "bespoke" goods—articles that had been "spoken for" (ordered) by individual customers. They were really very small-scale businessmen, the counterparts of the independent garage mechanic today. They were the forerunners of the manufacturing activity whose crucial role we will examine in our next chapter.

Below the artisans were groups of whom we know even less. There were considerable groups of workers in commerce and fishing, some offering their services as "street porters," others regularly employed on a fishing vessel. In Boston or Philadelphia this accounted for a fifth or even a quarter of the cities' populations. Another 5 to 10 percent worked in shipbuilding, working for wages like their Dutch counterparts who built the *fluitschips.* And as always in port cities, there was a floating population of seamen looking for a ship, or scrounging for work between voyages, immigrants who had not yet found their relatives, or simply unattached casual laborers.

At the very bottom there were, of course, the poor—cripples, beggars, a few homeless children. Compared with Europe, America was exemplary in the lack of any large ragged underclass. One reason, as Benjamin Franklin wrote in 1751, was that land was so cheap in America that "a labouring man who understands husbandry can in a short time save enough money to purchase a piece of land whereon he may subsist a family."[4] In general, real wages for colonial laborers were 30 to 100 percent higher than their English counterparts. Every hungry wretch on the docks of Baltimore or New York did not understand husbandry or possess the few pounds needed to buy land, but the steady absorption of newcomers into agricultural life at least prevented the development of the fearful urban poverty that was the scourge of Europe.

RICHES AND POVERTY

Poverty raises the question of how well off Americans were during these years of early economic growth. In the beginning, as we have seen, the colonists fought for survival itself. Was this poverty? The question takes us by surprise. The Pilgrims would certainly have considered their lot very difficult and perilous—but poor? It is hard to use the word unless there is a comparison with others who are not poor. We all know of individuals raised under very sparse and demanding circumstances who did not learn until later that they were "poor." To answer the question of whether Americans were rich or poor, therefore, requires us to look into the *distribution of wealth*.

If we could take a census among the colonial population just before the Revolution, we would discover that the *average* wealth per free colonist—that is, the average amount of land and other property, including money, owned by a free colonist—was about £76. That figure, painstakingly calculated by Alice Hanson Jones on the basis of probated wills, would have compared very favorably with average wealth per capita in England, the richest nation in the world at that time. But very few Americans felt rich or poor in comparison with Europeans. It was the range of wealth *within* their own colonies that counted. What do we know of that?

Until recently, it has been generally believed that colonial America enjoyed an extremely egalitarian distribution of wealth and income. Recent studies have cast doubt on that assumption. It now appears that there was considerable inequality—not merely between North and South, but within each colonial region.

As we might expect, the average wealth in the South was greater than in the North. This was not the consequence of slaveholding alone. The value of livestock, farm tools, household equipment, and land itself was also much higher per person in the plantation regions. There is, however, some statistical bias introduced into the figures because the wealth owned by the very richest planters was so large. These concentrations of wealth pull the *averages* up for the region as a whole, compared with the North where concentration of wealth on this scale did not exist. Nonetheless, with all allowances made, it is not far wrong to suggest that southern Americans were substantially richer, in the typical case, than northerners—owning perhaps twice as much land, equipment, and valuables per household than we might have found in New York, Connecticut, or New Hampshire.

Within the colonies there was also a marked difference among social classes. In New England the wealthiest 10 percent of the population owned 40 percent of the wealth; in the middle colonies 32 percent. Further, if we divide the New Englanders and the middle colonists with the wealthier on one side and the poorer on the other, the rich half in New England would own 89 percent of the wealth, and in the middle colonies 77 percent.

Moreover, new studies make it likely that the unequal distribution of wealth was growing more unequal in colonial times.[5] As frontier settlements became subsistence farms, and as subsistence farms slowly became commercial farms, and as farm communities gradually became more urban in their characteristics, the importance of economic life steadily increased, and with it, the chances for inequality of wealth and income.

Thus, as a counterpart to the concentration of wealth in the hands of the great planters in the South, we find a growing concentration in the hands of merchants in the North. An analysis of Boston tax lists of 1687 and 1771 shows that the top 10 percent of Boston's taxpayers owned 42 percent of the city's wealth in the earlier date, but 57 percent not quite a century later.[6] Looking at the colonies as a whole, on the eve of the American Revolution more than half of the wealth held in the colonies was in the hands of the richest 10 percent of the population.

Baltimore, 1752

THE MOMENTUM OF GROWTH

Early Expansion

It is clear, then, that there were rich and poor in America from the mid-seventeenth century onward. Yet, when all this is said, the fact remains that most Americans enjoyed what was called "middling" wealth, and that the extremes of riches and poverty did not offend the sensibilities of the colonists. This may well have been the case because the pace of change was so rapid and so favorable. Americans living in the eighteenth century could almost literally see the country grow before their eyes. Everything they could count or measure was bigger—population, the value of colonial shipments, the size of urban centers, the volume and value of colonial manufactures.

A few instances may make the pace of growth more tangible. Within the memory of Charles Carroll, a signer of the Declaration of Indepen-

Baltimore, 1827

dence, Baltimore grew from a hamlet of seven houses to a city of 70,000. Philadelphia, a large town of 4,000 people in 1690, became the second largest city in the English-speaking world by 1776, with 35,000 inhabitants. As cities grew, the countryside changed. In 1650 a trip from Boston to New York was an expedition; by 1705 a middle-aged schoolteacher could make the journey in two weeks with only mild trepidations concerning the "savage" Indians through whose territories she had to pass. In another seventy-five years the Indians were a curiosity in the settled parts of New England.

Meanwhile, from the colonial ports poured a rising stream of exports for the table (rice), taste (tobacco), mills (indigo), and navy (the tall masts). Between the beginning of the eighteenth century and the outbreak of the Revolutionary War, the value of colonial shipments to England rose fivefold, from £395,000 to £1.9 million. More striking, a colonial nucleus of manufactured production was also burgeoning, along with agriculture. By 1776 flour mills at the head of Chesapeake Bay reportedly had the finest equipment in the world, distilleries in Philadelphia exported well over 200,000 gallons of rum annually, and most surprising of all, the thirteen colonies possessed more forges and furnaces than all of England and Wales and exceeded them in the output of pig and bar iron. In fact, American iron output totaled one-seventh of world output.

Clearly, an astonishing momentum of economic advance could be discerned in the colonial world almost from its inception. The economic transformation of the nation seems to have begun instantly and effortlessly. No wonder that in retrospect it seems "inevitable."

Was Growth Inevitable?

Why did America grow so rapidly? One reason is that it was never afflicted with some of the handicaps that held back growth in other colonies, such as India or the colonial empire of Spain. The debilitating climate, the poor soils, the overworked land—and above all, the heavy hand of an ancient empire—never weighed on American efforts. On the contrary, the colonists brought with them attitudes of economic and political activism and cultural adaptability that provided an immense advantage over other colonial parts of the world. The colonies were, in fact, a part of England itself that had managed to make the arduous voyage across the seas, and that found in the New

World the chance to develop the expansionist tendencies of a market system that were still hobbled abroad.

Part of that indispensable attitude of striving was no doubt the consequence of what we call the Puritan ethic, a fusion of spiritual and material views that encouraged business and worldly enterprise. Cotton Mather, the famous Puritan minister, stated the case vigorously in 1695:

> Would a Man *Rise* by his Business? I say, then, let him *Rise* to his Business. It was foretold (Prov. 22.29) *Seest thou a man Diligent in his Business? He shall stand before Kings.* . . . Yea, how can you ordinarily enjoy any rest at *Night,* if you have not been well at work in the Day? Let your *Business* ingross the most of your time.[7]

Perhaps the conjunction of the appetite for gain and the approval of industriousness reached its clearest expression in 1757 in Benjamin Franklin's famous *Almanack,* where "Poor Richard" tells his countrymen how to prosper:

> The Sleeping Fox catches no Poultry, and . . . there will be sleeping enough in the grave. . . . Let us then be up and doing. . . . Sloth makes all things difficult, but Industry makes all easy, so Poor Richard says. . . . [So] drive thy business, let not that drive thee; and Early to Bed, and early to rise, makes a man healthy, wealthy and wise.[8]

"Born Free"

Was growth inevitable, then? Certainly climate, land, and ambitious self-selected individuals all combined to make the economy expansive, once growth had begun. Still, imponderables remain. How important, for example, was the spirit of freedom, the absence of a rigid social structure? Canada, with nearly all of the American blessings, did not "take off" on a steep gradient of growth. Hence we cannot assume that we have fully explained why the momentum of growth was attained so early simply by saying that America was never forced to surmount the physical and social and political obstacles of an underdeveloped land. As many historians have remarked, America was "born free." Perhaps that fortunate accident, more than any other single cause, contributed to its economic destiny.

Notes

[1] Quoted in Thomas C. Cochran, *Business in American Life* (1972), p. 17.

[2] "Economic Base and Social Structure: The Northern Chesapeake in the Eighteenth Century," *Journal of Economic History* (December 1965), 646–47.

[3] William S. Sachs and Ari Hoogenboom, *The Enterprising Colonials* (1965), p. 52.

[4] For Franklin's views on land and the colonial population, see his "Observations Concerning the Increase of Mankind," in Leonard Labaree (ed.), *The Papers of Benjamin Franklin* (1961), 4:225–34.

[5] Jackson Turner Main, *The Social Structure of Revolutionary America* (1965).

[6] James Henretta, "Economic Development and Social Structure in Colonial Boston," *William and Mary Quarterly* (January 1965), 93–105.

[7] *Two Brief Discourses* (1695), p. 48.

[8] Leonard Labaree (ed.), *The Papers of Benjamin Franklin* (1963), 7:341–42.

Part II
AN AMERICAN ECONOMY TAKES SHAPE

Lockport on the Erie Canal

Power-loom weaving in the 1840s

Chapter 5

THE DECLARATION OF ECONOMIC INDEPENDENCE

In the eyes of the historian, the colonial system manifested its extraordinary momentum because it was "born free." But that is certainly not the way it appeared in the eyes of the colonists themselves. Originally—and indeed, among the great majority of the population until the very eve of the Revolution—the colonists thought of themselves as *Englishmen,* not as "Americans." Yet from early on they were conscious of not being treated as such by their mother country. They were *colonials,* not quite the political equals and certainly not the economic equals of their English cousins at home.

The theme of the next great chapter of the transformation of the American economy is therefore the gradual formation of the notion among colonists that they were *Americans*—not merely inhabitants of America, but citizens of a still unformed, even undefined new nation. That nation required its political independence, first and foremost for the sake of independence itself, but in no small measure because the colonists recognized that they could not make use of their economic vitality unless they broke the restrictions of their colonial ties.

ECONOMIC FRICTIONS

The history of the political rifts between the colonies and the mother country is of supreme importance in understanding the events that led up to the American Revolution. Yet it is a theme that we will relegate to the background in this book—never denying its importance, but fastening our attention on other threads in the narrative that are more closely woven into our concern with the formation and unfolding of the American economy. Thus we will not begin with vexations of the colonists about the lack of representation in Parliament—a vexation that culminated in the famous cry, "No taxation without representation"—but will examine instead some of the strains that were pulling the colonies away from the mother country because of economic divergences of interest.

The Navigation Acts

The most visible of these strains were the Navigation Acts that we have earlier mentioned. From the privileged position of hindsight, we do not regard these acts as pressing very onerously on the colonists. The additional costs of all the red tape and restrictions imposed by the acts have been estimated to amount to less than 1 percent of the income of the average colonist, a very small "sales tax" in exchange for the not inconsiderable benefits that the acts also conferred.

But the colonists did not take so objective a measure. In the South, planters particularly resented the requirement that all American goods had to be shipped to Europe via England. In the North, entrepreneurial-minded merchants objected equally strenuously to the discouragement, and in some cases, as we have seen, the outright prohibition of domestic manufacturing operations by which the English sought to protect their own home industries. And as we have just mentioned, all the colonists chafed under the taxes that Britain imposed without colonial representation in Parliament, especially after the Seven Years' War (1756–63) when the home country teetered at the edge of bankruptcy. Not least, the annual cost to support British troops in North America during the conflict was between £300,000 and £400,000, an enormous sum for those days.

Once again we must distinguish between hindsight and the view at the time. We can see that the protection offered by England to the colonies—not only military protection, but the assurance of a large English market for their wares—was a considerable quid pro quo; and we also know that taxes in the colonies were much lower than in England. In the home country an average Englishman paid as much as a third of his income to the government—not as income tax, but in the form of various sales and excise taxes laid on the articles he bought. In the colonies the average tax was only about 5 percent. Americans were, in fact, probably the lowest taxed people in the world. It is true that taxes were rapidly rising—after 1750 the tax burden in New York and Boston almost doubled, and in Philadelphia it rose as much as 250 percent.[1] It is often *increases* in taxes, rather than the level of taxes, that bring discontent; and certainly the rise in English imposts, whether or not tax levels were low by comparison with England's, brought discontent to the colonies.

To make matters worse, after 1763 the British government, hard-pressed for revenues, began to enforce the Navigation Acts strictly rather than carelessly and loosely as it had done before. The smuggling trade, winked at by British customs officials, was suddenly declared a practice that had to be stopped, and the outcry from merchants and customers alike revealed how important that trade had been.

POLITICAL SELF-DETERMINATION

The Articles of Confederation

Perhaps because their economic complaints were noisier than the facts justified, the colonists put their case largely in political rather than economic terms. Many of their protestations to the Crown make reference to arbitrary actions of the English government that injured the economic interests of the colonists, but the ultimate justification of the cause was political self-determination, not economic independence. As economic historians John J. McCusker and Russell R. Menard have written: "The conflict centered on the issue of power over the long haul, on the shape of things to come, on who would determine the future of the British Empire in the Americas."[2]

In this struggle for political freedom, Thomas Jefferson's Declaration of Independence was the first great victory, for Jefferson's words literally echoed around the world; and the last victory was the extraordinary campaign that Washington fought five years later when his makeshift army of plowmen and artisans outmaneuvered and outfought the British army itself, until Cornwallis surrendered at Yorktown, Virginia, in 1781.

As is so often the case in history, victory brought as many problems as it solved. For the colonists the supreme challenge was to create a unified government from thirteen enormously diversified colonial entities, none of which felt any deep allegiance to a nonexistent American nation, and all of which had learned from their experience with the

British to distrust authority imposed from above. The results were the Articles of Confederation, ratified in 1781, which created an entity entitled "The United States of America," but which refused to give this entity any power to enforce its resolutions, or to tax its member states or their citizens, or to regulate commerce between the states. These restrictions on the power of the government reveal how suspicious Americans were of any power imposed on them from above or outside. The Articles, it must be remembered, were written in the shadow of the Revolutionary War. Having just suffered at the hands of a distant British government, Americans were wary of allowing much authority to their own central government.

The Articles of Confederation were a recipe for disaster in the face of a situation that rapidly required strong, concerted action by the newly independent colony-states. With the end of the war, Americans were soon exposed to the competition of lower priced and better made British goods against which they could not protect themselves, since the new government did not have the power to impose a tariff. Hence, at the same time that Great Britain increased its penetration of the American market, it restricted American entry into English markets. As a result, the value of American exports to Great Britain and the British West Indies fell from a yearly average of $7.5 million between 1771–73 to an annual average of $5.8 million between 1785–87. The newly constituted congress also had difficulty negotiating favorable commercial treaties with other nations because of a general belief in Europe that the states would not comply with agreements, even if they were reached. When John Adams arrived in England as America's first minister to the Court of St. James's, he was asked whether he represented one nation or thirteen. Sensing this weakness in the American government, the British refused to withdraw their troops from the western frontier; the Spanish government closed the mouth of the Mississippi River at New Orleans to all American commerce; and the Barbary pirates freely looted American shipping in the Mediterranean.

No less serious was the inability of the new government to tax the states. In 1785 the Congress billed the states $3 million, the money to be used to reduce the war debt and pay the government's few employees. By 1787 it had received less than 4 percent of the amount requested. To pay its wartime bills the Congress was forced to print a large amount of paper money, and after the war this practice continued. By way of example, in 1778 it took seven dollars in Continental bills to buy goods that cost one dollar in gold and silver. This ratio increased to 100 to 1 in 1780, and finally to 146 to 1 in 1781, when the currency depreciated to such an extent that "not worth a continental" became a stock phrase to describe anything worthless. The result was severe inflation and general loss of confidence in the paper money of the thirteen states. To regain control, some states cut their issuance of paper money and raised taxes to pay for their own expenses. The demand for goods thereupon declined, and a severe recession began.

Despite these difficulties, the Confederation Congress did effect some important achievements: it brought the War for American Independence to a successful conclusion and then signed a peace treaty with Great Britain; it opened up a permanent channel of communication among the states; and, most important of all, it was able to take control of the vast territory between the Appalachian Mountains and the Mississippi River and to provide for orderly settlement and government there. In a series of laws, climaxed by the Northwest Ordinance of 1787, Congress established the basic set of rules under which new land could be organized into territories and then into states.

The Making of the Constitution

However, peace also made it clear that the Articles of Confederation were painfully inadequate for the needs of the new nation. Thus paradoxically, the absence of any strong central authority proved as vexatious as had the autocratic rule of the British government. Clearly what was needed was a new institutional framework that could preserve the liberty won in the Revolution while at the same time ensuring a greater degree of unity and effective authority among the states.

The first tentative steps were taken in January 1786, when the Virginia legislature suggested that delegates from the states meet at Annapolis, Maryland, to discuss trade, taxes, and related matters. Only five states sent representatives. Despite this obvious failure, Alexander Hamilton of New York persuaded the group to issue a call for another meeting, with the more ambitious plan of revising the entire Articles of Confederation. Hamilton's suggestion was approved, and in May 1781, delegates from all the states except Rhode Island converged on Philadelphia.

The purpose of what was to become the Constitutional Convention was to create a union of individual states with a strong and representative central government. As such, its primary concern was political—to

forge a unity of purpose for member states jealous of their prerogatives, and to meet the desire for a democratic form of government with
appropriate safeguards against "mob rule." From our perspective,
however, the interesting question is the degree to which the Constitution served the economic needs of the states. The lessons of the recent
past were clear. The new government had to have powers formerly
denied to it—powers to levy and collect taxes, to regulate currency, to
impose tariffs, and to regulate commerce among the states. Behind
these apparent needs was a still deeper necessity, clearly recognized
by the men of property and ambition who constituted the delegates.
This was the necessity to recognize the rights of private property and
to prevent the federal government from arbitrarily invading those
rights. The Founding Fathers, as the Constitution makers have come to
be called, completed their work on September 12, 1787. On September 17, thirty-nine delegates signed the new Constitution of the United
States. Their work complete, the delegates adjourned to await
ratification by the states.

The work of the Founding Fathers was to be put to the test by special ratifying conventions, which were to be elected by the citizens of
each state. The Constitution was to go into effect when nine states had
approved it. Hence the new charter became legally effective when
New Hampshire approved it on June 21, 1788.

In 1913, historian Charles A. Beard suggested in a famous book, *An
Economic Interpretation of the Constitution of the United States,* that
the Constitution itself could only be understood if one put the economic interests of the delegates in the forefront, where they assumed
at least equal, perhaps prior, place to the political considerations of a
separation of powers and of building a workable republican form of
government.

There is clearly something to be learned from Beard's position, but
most historians today see the Constitution as primarily a political, not
an economic document. Its establishment of a form of government
respecting private property was, of course, essential for the development of American capitalism, but this was nothing more than the
widely held view of the most enlightened thinkers of the time, certainly including Franklin and Jefferson.

Here it is useful to recall that Adam Smith's great book, *The Wealth
of Nations,* was published in 1776, the very year of the Revolution and

was well known to many of the delegates. Smith never used (or knew) the word "capitalism." He called the economic framework described in his book a "society of perfect liberty" because of its emphasis on freedom of economic contract; and he recommended it, not because such a society would work for the benefit of the rich alone, but for the enhancement of the wealth of the entire nation. That is surely the economic philosophy that inspired, and that is embodied in, the Constitution that finally emerged from the convention.

DOUBTS, MISGIVINGS, AND FALSE STARTS

The Manufacturing Sector

The forging of a workable constitution was the necessary step for the achievement of true political independence, but there remained an equally necessary step before economic independence could be won. That was to break the dependency on England with respect to manufactured goods, a step that could only be taken by establishing a viable *manufacturing sector* in the newly united states. Manufacturing—the word means making by *hand,* but the practice means making by *machine*—was to be the decisive step in the evolution of material life in America. Here we must examine the origins of what would become the basis of American capitalist development.

As the eighteenth century opens, we would hardly think in terms of a manufacturing "sector." Even in 1800, after manufacturing had received the impetus of the Revolutionary War, it is doubtful if one person in thirteen worked in either trade or manufacturing (although we must bear in mind that many farmers were also artisans who produced much of their own "manufactures," such as woven cloth, simple tools, candles, soap, and the like).

Such "industry" as existed was largely centered in the cities and towns where owner-craftsmen, often with an apprentice or two, carried on a variety of trades for the local community. A survey in Philadelphia in 1787, for example, shows us some sixty kinds of manufacture—potash, woodworking, carriages, leather crafts, grain-milling, woolens, nails, clocks. What strikes us in surveying this incipient industry, however, is the tiny scale of its endeavor—papermaking in which each ream was an accomplishment; bootmaking by the individual pair; woodturning to order; the forging of axes and scythes and plowshares for the individual customer; the production of crockery in lots of a few dozen. Even when we turn to the most important industries we are still struck by the minuscule scale of production. The iron foundries of the colonies may have outproduced those of England, but they nonetheless turned out only 30,000 tons of iron a year—about twelve pounds per capita, or no more than the least-developed country today. Nails, for instance, were so scarce that pioneers burned their cabins to the ground to recover them before moving on. Similarly, the flour industry, for all the excellence of its equipment, exported only 250 tons in a good year, and the entire output of the shoemakers of New England was only 80,000 pairs, or one pair per forty (white) population.

For all its small size, the advent of the war quickly revealed the strategic role of manufacturing. For the Revolution soon came to depend on America's small manufacturing capacity. The colonial iron industry assumed a critical importance—Washington located his winter camp at Valley Forge (note the significance of the name) to guard its essential metal-working shops. The tiny textile and leather industry was suddenly indispensable for providing the army with its issue of four shirts, two pairs of overalls, two pairs of shoes, breeches, coat, and cap.

Despite subsidies from the Continental Congress, the tiny industrial core was clearly unable to expand fast enough to support the war effort. Woolens were scarce and the army shivered for lack of adequate clothing. More telling, in the vital matter of arms, the scale of manufacture and delivery remained pitifully small. The largest Treasury payment of which we have record was $1,200, or roughly the price of a hundred muskets, and the average delivery was probably a dozen or two. Had it not been for the receipt of 80,000 muskets from France, the Revolutionary army would have been reduced to fighting with pitchforks.

Thus it was the war that first revealed the need for a strong manufacturing sector. But with the return of peace, the considerations of national self-sufficiency were relegated to second place behind those of immediate profit. With the conclusion of hostilities, old trade connections with England were gradually resumed. A backlog of orders existed for all the goods denied by the war—linens and silks and fancy materials, "good" tableware, household bric-a-brac of various sorts—and dealers in these wares turned naturally to the makers they knew in London rather than to untried possibilities of production in New Haven or Boston.

The Lure of Trade

Further, as the war ended, the expansive thrust of American business again turned to the alluring prospects of trade and agriculture. Near the end of the war, John Ledyard, a young New Englander, returned from China where he had sold pelts, bought for a song on the Pacific coast of America, for $100. Soon thereafter the China trade became a source of lucrative profit and steady commerce; in 1801, fifteen American ships put in at Canton with 18,000 skins valued at over $500,000. In the face of such profits, the lure of manufacturing was small. "The brilliant prospects held out by commerce," reminisced an observer in 1818, "caused our citizens to neglect the mechanical and manufacturing branches of industry; fallacious views, founded on temporary circumstances, carried us from those pursuits which must ultimately constitute the resources, wealth and power of the nation."[3]

It was not surprising that the wartime enthusiasm for manufactures waned. John Adams, Washington, Franklin, all partisans of manufacturing during the war, now regarded prospects as unpromising, while abroad the general opinion prevailed that American manufactures would not take firm root. Thomas Cooper, an English economist who wrote a book of advice for émigrés, opined that the prospects for American woolens, linens, cotton goods, and pottery were dim, although he took a more hopeful view of glass, gunpowder, paper, and iron. Lord Sheffield, surveying the outlook for English exports in 1783, wrote, "British manufactures will for ages ascend the great rivers of [the American] continent. . . . It will be a long time before the Americans can manufacture for themselves. Their progress will be stopped by the high price of labor, and the more pleasing and profitable employment of agriculture. . . . If manufacturers [by which he meant workers in manufacturing] should emigrate from Europe to America, nine-tenths of them will become farmers; for they will not work at manufacturing when they can earn a greater profit at farming."[4]

Technical Problems

If these were not enough discouragements for manufacturing, there was yet another—the difficulty of creating an efficient industry in a nation that was technologically behind England and severely short of capital-building facilities. Take, for example, the case of textiles, a prime candidate for manufacture in every nation that is commencing the development of its economy. As we have already seen, the colonial wool-manufacturers were early denied access to the British market. But this economic barrier was not as difficult to surmount as a *technical* problem. England was the home of a cluster of epochal inventions that had matured around the time of the Revolutionary War: Arkwright's and Hargreaves' spinning jennies, Crompton's mule, Cartwright's power loom.

The British government had no intention of sharing these breakthroughs with colonials or anyone else. It quickly prohibited the export of textile-making machinery and drawings and even forbade the emigration of skilled textile workmen—a policy continued until

The Slater mill at Pawtucket, Rhode Island

1845. Thus for nearly a decade before the Revolution, American textile enthusiasts struggled to found an industry by smuggling in models and drawings of English mill machinery. The effort was of little avail. Some models were intercepted in transit and destroyed; others arrived only to prove inoperable or of antiquated design. Thus it is not surprising that most of the early textile ventures were unsuccessful; typically, a factory established in Beverly, Massachusetts, was operating at a deficit after four years, despite exemption from taxation and subsidies from the legislature.

When the textile industry finally became established, it was largely the result of the efforts of Samuel Slater, a former employee of English textile pioneer Richard Arkwright, the inventor of the jenny and a cotton manufacturer on a vast scale. Slater landed in New York in 1789 and quickly established contact with Moses Brown, a Rhode Island textile pioneer who had tried in vain to establish an efficient cotton mill. Slater persuaded Brown to allow him to build a machine with seventy-two spindles with the aid of the local blacksmith. In 1791 the machine was "done." Actually, it refused at first to work, but after some desperate last-minute repairs the machinery, tended by nine children, turned out its first yarn. The yarn from the mills went to hand weavers who wove the yarns into cloth in their farm homes—that is the thread was "put out," just as the British merchant capitalists of the seventeenth century had distributed raw wool or flax thread to the cottage weavers. Slater's accomplishment was proudly announced in Alexander Hamilton's *Report on Manufactures,* of which we shall learn more shortly. By 1801 the mill was a solid success, with a work force of over 100 children and adult overseers.

The Jeffersonian View

Despite Slater's success, it was clear that the path to manufacturing profit was uphill. Twenty-seven mills were spawned within a few years by the Slater-Brown venture. Most of them failed within a short period. A *Society for Establishing Useful Manufactures,* founded in New Jersey with ambitious plans to produce hats, cloth, and other goods, foundered within five years, although it was promoted by no less skillful an organizer than Hamilton himself. The irrefutable fact confronting American businessmen was that powerful adverse market forces subjected all manufacturing ventures to the gravest perils. And

Jeffersonian visions

finally, one last current of opposition had also to be faced. This was the widely held view that manufacturing was inherently corrupting and debasing—a view that claimed the introduction of the factory system into the United States would bring with it the horrors of the factory towns in England and Wales.

Of all the protagonists of this view, the most articulate was Thomas Jefferson. Although he personally delighted in inventions and extolled household crafts, Jefferson set himself squarely against the enlargement of manufacture beyond the modest role it played in sustaining an independent and self-sufficient *household,* and did not translate this idea into the scale of an independent and self-sufficient *economy.** At

---

*Upon his brief "retirement" from public office in 1794, Jefferson returned to Monticello to become not only a farmer but a nailmaker. Jefferson personally supervised the construction of the nailery, making certain that the most efficient machinery available was used. Later he built a grist mill at his Shadwell plantation on the Rivanna River and a textile manufactory for his household at Monticello.

bottom his objection rested on two conceptions of the manufacturing process. One sprang from a classical estimation of farming and a correspondingly dark picture of nonagricultural toil: "Those who labor on the earth," he wrote in his *Notes on Virginia* (1785, Query XIX), "are the chosen people of God, if ever He had a chosen people. . . . Generally speaking, the proportion which the aggregate of other classes of citizens bears in any state to that of its husbandmen, is the proportion of its unsound to its healthy parts, and is a good enough barometer to measure its corruption."

Jefferson's second objection was that manufactures were not really a national necessity but a luxury. In America, he felt, the immensity of the land allowed nearly everyone the possibility of becoming a husbandman, and should any manufactures be required they could be obtained by trading agricultural surpluses for the products of the grimy manufactory.

Jeffersonian fears

One final, philosophical point must be made about Jefferson's deeply rooted predilection toward agriculture. As America's pre-eminent spokesman of republicanism, Jefferson believed that the essence of liberty was independence, which—according to Jefferson and others—required the ownership of productive capital. A man dependent upon others for a livelihood could never be truly free. Nor could a subservient class form the basis of a republican polity; it would be constantly threatened by corrupt manipulations of power.

Jefferson feared the development of manufacturing and industrial capitalism precisely because wage labor was a form of dependency that seemed to contradict the republican principles of liberty upon which the country was founded. To quote Jefferson, "Dependence begets subservience and venality, suffocates the germ of virtue and prepares fit tools for the designs of ambition."[5]

THE TURN TOWARD INDUSTRY

Thus, however predisposed toward economic growth, it was not at all clear that America was equally well predisposed toward *industrial* growth. Indeed, the obstacles we have noted strongly imply the opposite. The powerful guidance of natural economic forces, the absence of the needed technology, and the inclinations of native sentiment in favor of agriculture all tended to direct American economic effort away from industry.

What changed the course of American economic growth? In retrospect we can discern sources of a gradual shift in economic direction. The first was simply that by hard trial and numerous errors the young economy discovered a few nooks and crannies of manufacturing in which it could meet and better English competition. One such nook was a low grade of cotton goods, well suited to American needs. Another was the flour-milling industry, already well established by Revolutionary times and sheltered by transportation costs from effective competition from abroad. A third was the small-arms industry, favored and patronized by the government; yet another was the domestic iron industry, also protected by the high costs of transportation against English competition. In these industries the first roots of an industrial economy were firmly planted.

Equally important was the slow growth of an articulate philosophy that could be used to rebut the Jeffersonian view. In the 1780s a small but determined group of manufacturing protagonists began to present the manufacturers' view: Was there, as the pro-agriculture side claimed, a shortage of labor that would impede the establishment of an expansive industry? The remedy for that was simple: women and children would work in the mills. As one mill owner put it:

> Teach little hands to ply mechanic toil
> Cause failing age o'er easy tasks to smile;
>
> So shall the young find employ
> And hearts, late nigh to perish, leap for joy.[6]

Was the work of manufacturing degrading, as the agriculturalists claimed? On the contrary, asserted the proponents of manufacturing, it could be made the occasion of moral improvement by the incorporation of courses of religious instruction. Samuel Slater did in fact found a Sunday school for his child employees, and we shall see in our next chapter that the early mills tried at first to combine profitable employment with workers' uplift.

Finally, was there a shortage of necessary capital? That too could be remedied by assistance from the state—by extending bounties and grants to pioneer businessmen and by strengthening the general credit and currency of the nation.

Hamilton's Reports

All through the Revolutionary period these sentiments gathered strength. It was not until after the new government was established, however, that they found an effective and articulate spokesman on the national level in Alexander Hamilton.

As Secretary of the Treasury, Hamilton's burning ambition was to build a strong, prosperous, diversified economy in which political independence would find its roots. Ten days after his appointment, Congress directed Hamilton to prepare a report on the national credit. The United States owed more than $11 million to foreigners and over $40 million to its own citizens. Most of the debt was in the form of certificates, like the United States savings bonds which are sold today. In the first of his three famous reports to Congress, the *Report on Public Credit* (January 1790), Hamilton suggested that this debt be *funded at par,* which meant calling in all outstanding securities and issuing new bonds at the same face value in their place, and establishing an untouchable "sinking fund"—that is, a treasury reserve built from the revenues of certain fixed taxes—to assure payment of principal and interest. Hamilton also proposed that the government assume all state debts (about $20 million) on similar terms.

Hamilton's *Report on Public Credit* was the cornerstone of his economic edifice. Such a bold measure, he believed, would restore the nation's creditworthiness both at home and abroad, and, at the same time, win the allegiance of the business elite to the new government, thereby laying the groundwork for a climate of confidence needed to advance the shaky cause of manufacturing.

Although most congressmen agreed that it would be wise to fund the debt at par, they objected to Hamilton's desire to benefit already powerful interests. Some of the old securities had been issued to soldiers of the Continental Army as pay for their services. Others had been given to farmers and merchants who had been forced to accept them in lieu of cash. Still others had been purchased by patriotic citizens to advance the war effort. But by 1789 most of the certificates were held by speculators who had bought them at much less than their face value. Hamilton insisted that payments be made to whomever held the certificates. But congressmen like James Madison of Virginia believed the speculators should be paid only half their face value. The original holders should get the other half, he argued.

Madison also opposed Hamilton's plan to assume the state debts. Many of the southern states had already paid a large proportion of the debt. The largest debts were owed by Massachusetts and South Carolina. Why should Virginia be taxed to pay off the debts of the other states? Madison asked. Secretary of State Jefferson seconded Madison's argument. The disagreement over funding and assumption was settled by a classic political bargain. Madison and Jefferson swung a few southern votes to Hamilton, and he in turn convinced some of his followers to support the southern plan for locating the permanent capital of the United States on the Potomac River.

Hamilton next urged Congress to pass a bank bill establishing a national bank (December 1790). There were only three commercial banks in the entire country in 1790. A bank would provide a safe place to deposit the money the government collected in taxes, Hamilton explained. It would also serve as a source of credit and loans for industrial and commercial enterprise.

Congress passed the bank bill in 1791, but Washington hesitated to sign it. He could not find anything in the Constitution giving Congress the power to charter a bank. He therefore asked Hamilton and Jefferson if they thought the bank was constitutional. Hamilton advanced a "loose" interpretation of the Constitution, arguing that Congress had "implied" powers that permitted it to legislate in areas not specifically prohibited by the Constitution. Jefferson, on the other hand, rejected the constitutionality of the bank and insisted that Congress could only exercise power specifically authorized by the Constitution. Neither argument wholly satisfied Washington. Nevertheless, he signed the bank bill on February 25, 1791. The new institution soon helped to alleviate the problem of credit for would-be manufacturers.

In December 1791, Hamilton submitted his *Report on Manufactures,* the capstone to the economic edifice he proposed to build. The *Report* forcefully enunciated all the arguments we have already reviewed and pressed the case that a manufacturing sector was essential to the security and prosperity of the nation. What interests us here, however, is not merely Hamilton's vision of an economy in which manufactures existed side by side with agriculture. More striking are his proposals that *government itself should take an active hand in bringing this new partnership about.* Hamilton's *Report* urged tariffs to exclude foreign goods competitive with those made at home; controls to prevent the export of raw materials that might be needed by American manufacturers; bounties and subsidies for enterprising manufacturers; rewards for American inventions and embargoes to prevent American industrial secrets from leaking abroad; a national board to promote arts, agriculture, and manufacture. A strong believer in private enterprise, Hamilton was nonetheless the first proponent of a form of national "planning," in which the government sought to channel the energies of enterprise in directions that presumably served the national interest better than the unguided pull of the marketplace.

The Napoleonic Wars

Hamilton's broad-gauged program received a cold reception in Congress; it was too far ahead of its time. Even though Congress had actually passed its first tariff bill on July 4, 1789, levying a 5 percent tax on all imports, opposition came from farmers and merchants who feared that protective duties would prompt retaliatory measures by other countries against American agricultural exports. The proposed aids to manufacturing were ignored, and the country continued its easy dependence on Europe's manufactures, bought with the proceeds of its agricultural exports.

That situation came to a jolting halt with the Napoleonic Wars.* Napoleon sought to close the Continent to British manufactures; Britain sought to weaken Napoleon by cutting off his sources of raw materials. As a result, both nations systematically searched and seized all vessels, including those of neutrals. In growing exasperation, President Jefferson sought to bring counterpressure by closing off American trade from both sides. The Embargo Act of 1807 prohibited all vessels in the United States from leaving for foreign ports and required special bonds for those engaged in coastal trade.

The results were extremely painful for many. American exports fell from $108 million in 1807 to $22 million in 1808, with devastating effects on anyone engaged in exporting. Imports also took a nose-dive. Why should foreign shipowners carry goods to America if they had to return to their home ports empty handed? Once bustling harbors became a forest of idle masts; counting rooms and exporters' offices were deserted. Thousands of sailors and laborers were thrown out of work. So damaging to the economy was the Embargo Act that many New England sailors sought employment in the British merchant marine. The economy ground to a halt.

---

*Napoleon's decision to end his efforts to revive French imperialism in the New World after his soldiers failed to crush a slave rebellion in Santo Domingo (Haiti) in 1802, and to renew warfare against Great Britain on the European continent, did produce an important, positive result for the United States: the Louisiana Purchase. Finding himself in need of funds for his European adventures, Napoleon offered the United States 828,000 square miles of lush but practically uninhabited country for $15 million. The United States took possession of New Orleans in December 1803.

Some two weeks after selling Louisiana to the United States, Napoleon picked a quarrel with England over the tiny island of Malta in the eastern Mediterranean. The titanic death struggle did not end until 1815, when Napoleon was safely exiled on the lonely island of St. Helena in the South Atlantic.

A New Sector Is Born

Yet if the embargo ruined the export trade, it brought sudden profits to anyone who could make the articles that were no longer available from abroad. As a result, whereas only fifteen cotton mills had been built prior to 1808, eighty-seven mills were erected in 1809, and the textile industry continued its expansion, albeit at a slower pace, until 1812.

No less important than the stimulus given to industry, and the consequent diversion of capital and talent from shipping into manufacture, was a gradual change in national views about the proper place of manufacturing. The ultimate conversion was that of Jefferson himself. In a letter written to Benjamin Austin in 1816 Jefferson admitted that he had originally been opposed to the spread of manufactures. But that had been before the economic hardships of war. "We have experienced," he wrote, "what we did not then believe . . . that to be independent for the comforts of life we must fabricate them ourselves. We must now place the manufacturer by the side of the agriculturalist."[7]

Jefferson's conversion came *after,* not during, the war. Its late date was symptomatic of a persisting national reluctance to admit the necessity of founding a strong manufacturing sector. For with the conclusion of the Napoleonic Wars, as previously with the end of the Revolutionary War, English manufactures again came flooding into the country, bringing bankruptcy to those new industries that could not meet English competition or had not found a niche of their own. When trade resumed in 1815, British textile manufacturers "dumped" a total of seventy-one million yards on the American market—that is, sold it at prices below what was being charged in England. This took place at a time when the total annual United States production was about ninety million yards.

Thus the actual implementation of Hamilton's *Report on Manufactures,* with its belated Jeffersonian endorsement, would not come for some time. An outright protectionist tariff was not passed until 1828, and then it was labeled the "Tariff of Abominations" by the southern interests who remained adamantly opposed to the Hamiltonian vision. Indeed, the setting of an industrial course would not be fully made until the terrible gauntlet of the Civil War had been run and the contest between the industrializing North and the agricultural South had been bloodily resolved once and for all.

But the process of change was only recognized and endorsed, not begun, by these later events. Economic growth, so strongly evident from the earliest days of the colonies, had to be diverted away from agriculture and trade toward manufacturing by a lengthy experience during which the nation gradually came to understand the need for, and the requirements of, a strong manufacturing capacity. The early lessons, blows, and growing convictions from which the nation made up its mind have been the main subject of this chapter. Now we must look into some of the supporting changes in economic and social institutions that were necessary to give effect to the change of heart.

Notes

[1] Gary Nash, *The Urban Crucible* (1979), pp. 223–63.

[2] *The Economy of British America, 1607–1789* (1985), p. 357.

[3] Quoted in Douglass C. North, *The Economic Growth of the United States, 1790–1860* (1961), pp. 47–48.

[4] *Observations on the Commerce of the United States*, pp. 101, 105.

[5] *Notes on Virginia* (ed.), T. P. Abernathy (1964), p. 157.

[6] Quoted in Samuel Rezneck, "Rise and Early Development of Industrial Consciousness in the United States," *Journal of Economic and Business History* (August 1932), 373

[7] P. L. Ford (ed.), *The Writings of Thomas Jefferson* (1899), 10:10.

Building the railroad westward

Chapter 6

PREPARATIONS FOR THE
AGE OF MANUFACTURE

An observer in 1815 would have been pardoned if he had failed to understand the country's new ambitions for manufacture. The nation was still overwhelmingly rural in aspect and agricultural in occupation. Even in its most densely populated areas of the Northeast, barely 10 percent of the population lived in "urban" concentrations of 2,500 or more, while in the South the ratio was only half that. Moreover, even in the cities, "industry" was an unusual calling. In 1820, for example, New York City, well on its way to becoming the most productive manufacturing city in the nation, had only thirty-five companies that employed ten or more workers. The great bulk of the city workers were employed in mercantile businesses, in seafaring, or in the handicraft and service trades that catered to city life. The number found in mills or manufactories was negligible—throughout the entire nation probably only 15,000 people, perhaps 1 percent of the gainfully employed, were engaged in iron or textiles, the two most promising candidates for industrial growth, and less than 4 percent in manufacturing of all kinds.

Lacks and Requirements

There were, moreover, serious problems that hindered the growth of the tiny nuclei of industry—the flour mills, sawmills, papermills, woolen "factories," and artisan establishments that dotted the countryside. One of them was the marked isolation of the average American establishment. A comparison with England is useful here. In England, thanks to the smallness of the nation and to its peculiarly indented coast, a network of transportation bound the parts of the country into a more or less unified market. With no town more than seventy miles from the sea and with at least 20,000 miles of turnpike-highway (much of it admittedly execrable), England was knit together into an economic whole.

By contrast, America was fragmented into unconnected economic parts. In 1776, it took twenty-nine days for news of the Declaration of Independence to travel from Philadelphia to Charleston, the same amount of time it would have taken to sail from Philadelphia to Paris. When the British cut off coastal traffic during the War of 1812, transportation costs on a barrel of flour from New York to Boston shot from seventy-five cents to five dollars. In those days it took two yoke of oxen three days to make a thirty-five-mile round trip, so that it cost more to drag a ton of iron ten miles through the Pennsylvania hills than to bring it across the ocean, and the inland freight on corn was so high it was unmarketable outside a radius of a few miles from its origin.

A lack of adequate transportation was not the only handicap facing American industrial aspirations. Equally serious was the absence of a supply of labor to man its hoped-for mills. Here too England had a decided edge. The long, slow growth of English population, combined with the steady expulsion of poor "cotters" from the land, brought a steady stream of men, women, and children into the English mill towns. In America, population was booming, but the easy availability of land offered farm employment—and better, farm ownership—to the growing population.

Finally, America was technologically backward. Already by the early nineteenth century, as we shall see, the country had produced more than its share of individual technical brilliance, but it lacked the sheer scale of capital to enable it to build the machinery it needed. Significantly, when Robert Fulton designed the engine that was to propel the *Clermont* up the Hudson in 1807, he had to write to James Watt and Matthew Boulton's factory in England to make the contraption, because there was no place in America that could produce so complicated a piece of machinery.

Thus the foundation, the infrastructure, the material basis, of an industrial economy had to be laid down. The country had to be unified physically as well as politically. A labor force had to be freed from the land and made available to the mills. To set into motion the new forms of material life, new patterns of economic life were needed. Until those tasks were complete—and that would not be until the very eve of the Civil War—an all-important aspect of the economic transformation of the country would be incomplete, and a full-scale entrance into the manufacturing age could not commence.

THE WEB OF TRANSPORTATION

The first need was transportation. Already in 1808, Albert Gallatin, Jefferson's national-minded Secretary of the Treasury, had proposed a broad and far-reaching system of "internal improvements" by which the nation would be tied together from north to south and east to west by a net of federally sponsored turnpikes and canals. Unfortunately, the plan perished in a flood of bickering, not so much over the principle of federal aid (although there was doubt as to the constitutionality of Gallatin's proposals) as from intense sectional jealousies and the fear that one state might get ahead of another. Of Gallatin's ambitious network, only one road was actually built—the great westward-leading pike from Cumberland, Maryland, on the Potomac River through the lower western corner of Pennsylvania to the site of present-day Wheeling, West Virginia, on the Ohio River. Construction on the National Road, as it was called, began in 1811 and was completed in 1818. Later it was extended as far as Vandalia, Illinois. Built at a cost of $7 million ($10,000 to $13,000 per mile), the road was a remarkable engineering achievement. It was constructed on a solid stone foundation with a gravel topping. Over it rolled an endless caravan of Conestoga wagons carrying population westward. Its sturdy stone bridges still carry traffic today.

In the absence of a national plan to create arteries of commerce, there grew up a kind of capillary system under private or state sponsorship. By 1800 there were already seventy-two profit-seeking turnpike companies in the Northeast, and ten years later the number had multiplied into the thousands: in New York alone there were 400 toll roads, though most of them were barely passable. Since the cost of construction rather than speed of travel or convenience was the main factor, the pikes were built as straight as possible, marching resolutely over hill and dale rather than seeking a more level, but longer, route through the valleys. The first turnpikes were built over very short stretches: five, ten, or twenty miles. We can judge their quality by an Ohio law of 1804 prohibiting the leaving of stumps over a foot high in *state* roads, and from the appellation "mudboats" given to the sledges that pulled cotton in the South during the rainy season.

Nevertheless the pikes were the first effective answer to the transportation challenge. They provided not only a slow circulation of commerce and travel but an economic boom of considerable dimensions. In New England alone, by 1840 over $6.5 million of private funds had been invested in turnpikes, much of it in small companies with capitals of less than $100,000; in Pennsylvania another $6 million, two-thirds private, one-third public, had also been spent. Indeed, not many years after the Revolution, a sum as great as the total domestic debt at the close of the Revolution had been invested in roads, thus providing a valuable economic as well as a physical stimulus.

The Erie Canal

Not surprisingly, many of the turnpikes failed. Of the 230 turnpikes constructed in New England, for example, only five or six were profitable. They were built with high expectations, little or no planning, and poor execution; by 1835 more than half of the turnpike ventures in the country had been either partially or wholly abandoned. Moreover, their demise was hastened by the coming of a new and much more efficient means of transportation, the canal.

Canals were not of course a new invention. In 1761 the Duke of Bridgewater built a famous canal in England to carry coal barges—a canal that actually crossed over streams on elevated waterways (an etching of the time shows a boat being towed by horses, crossing over another sailing by the wind), and Gallatin had proposed ambitious canal-digging along with his plans for national roads. The problem was that whereas turnpikes cost $5,000 to $10,000 a mile, canals cost $25,000 to $80,000 a mile, and they took not a year or two to build but eight or ten. With the nation's sparseness of population and the long distances between cities, canals thus seemed impossibly costly for the United States. By 1816 barely more than 100 miles of canals had been dug, most of them only two to three miles in length.

The event that moved canal construction off dead center was the tremendous adventure of the Erie Canal, in the words of one historian "the most decisive single event in the history of American transportation."[1] The idea of such a canal, linking the Great Lakes and the Atlantic, had appealed to a few imaginative persons since the early 1800s, and in 1809 a delegation actually went to visit Jefferson to interest him in the scheme: Jefferson observed that it was a fine project and might be realizable in a hundred years.*

That the canal was built was largely owing to the fortunate endorsement of the Erie project by Dewitt Clinton, who was then casting about for an effective program for his campaign as Governor of New York. Voyaging with a few companions, Clinton surveyed the route and returned bursting with confidence that the immense undertaking could be done with funds and labor available within New York State alone.

By 1817 the legislature had been convinced as well, and on July 4th of the next year the work digging "Clinton's Big Ditch" was actually commenced. Within a year 3,000 workers, largely immigrants, were digging; by the end of 1819 a middle section of some seventy-five miles was opened to traffic. By 1825 the canal was completed, an overnight wonder of the world.

And it *was* a wonder of the world. In parts it ran along embankments high enough for the barge-travelers to look down on the tops of trees; at one point it went through seven miles of rock, sometimes to a depth of twenty-five feet; it sailed for miles through flat country crossed by light and airy bridges that stitched together the bisected land and forced the passengers to duck or go below deck. At a speed of four miles an hour and for a fare of four cents a mile, with "excellent provisions and comfortable lodgings on board," the barges brought their travelers on a romantic 363-mile journey and, more important, conveyed their cargoes on an incredibly economical basis.

For the canal worked a veritable revolution in the economic relationships in the area. Before the opening of Erie, the cost of bringing grain from the western regions of the state to New York City was three times the value of wheat, six times that of corn, ten times that of oats. Now, overnight, this stifling weight of transportation costs disappeared, as freight rates fell by 90 percent. In 1817 freight moved from

---

*It was typical of Jefferson that, after the canal was opened, he was quick to admit his mistaken judgment and mused on the motivations that made such a bold venture possible.

Buffalo to New York via wagon at just under twenty cents a ton-mile; in the mid-1850s it was moving at less than a cent a ton-mile. Tolls in the first full year of operation reached nearly $500,000 and soon paid off the entire cost of construction.

As a result, the volume of goods entering into commerce soared. Tonnage on the canal amounted to 58,000 tons by 1836; by 1860 it had reached 1.8 million tons. Moreover, as early as 1840 it was apparent that the canal was imparting a visible stimulus to the development of manufacturing, now that lowered freight rates greatly reduced the cost of raw materials and vastly extended the possibilities of marketing the output.

The Canal Boom

The success of the Erie Canal touched off an era of canal-building even more important for the economic integration of the country than the turnpikes. Within a year after Erie there were a hundred major projects for canals; by 1840 the combined length of completed canals exceeded the distance across the continent. Penetrating as far to the west as the far side of Indiana, with some fingers going even farther—the Illinois and Michigan Canal linked Chicago with the Illinois River and thus with the Mississippi—the canals provided a skein of broad water highways that did indeed unite East and West and (to a lesser extent) North and South.

The magnitude of the financial effort also far exceeded that demanded by the turnpikes. The decades of the 1820s and 1830s saw the huge sum of $125 million spent on canals. Unlike the financing of the turnpikes, most of this spending was state-financed, often with private participation.* Reviewing the role played by government in these pre-Civil War years, Robert A. Lively has described what he called "the American System":

> . . . the elected public official replaced the individual enterpriser as the key figure in the release of capitalist energy; the public treasury, rather than private saving, became the main source of venture capital; and community purpose outweighed personal ambition in the selection of

---

*A significant portion of the private funds invested in canals came from overseas. Between 1834 and 1844, for instance, 60 percent of the $72 million invested in canals came from foreigners.

large goals for local economies. "Mixed" enterprise was the customary organization for important innovations, and government everywhere undertook the role put on it by the people, that of planner, promoter, investor and regulator.[2]

This is not to say that the government was a generally successful investor, either in the era of canal-building or later when it helped underwrite the railroads. In the canal era, financial failures outweighed financial successes by far; more than one state courted bankruptcy by overambitious building.

Yet even with the unsuccessful ventures came benefits. The vigorous spending served to stimulate economic activity at large. And when canals were themselves financial losers, they nonetheless brought business opportunities and profits to the enterprises they served. In similar fashion, our present-day road system would not be adjudged an economic failure simply because toll revenues failed to cover its costs: we measure the benefits of the road to the larger economy. So it was with the pikes and the canals. By 1859 the ton-mileage on the canals (already adversely affected by the railroads) totaled 1.6 *billion*. The canals had opened up the interior so that Ohio and Indiana grain could be sold in Europe and European or New England wares could be sold in Ohio. Moreover the canals (and to a lesser degree, the turnpikes) made possible an astonishing redistribution of population. Between 1790 and 1840, before any rail line breached the Appalachians, the percentage of the national population on the far side of that barrier increased from next to nothing to an astonishing 40 percent. This westward expansion of the population was greatly helped by the liberal land policy pursued by the federal government. Unoccupied lands were sold at very low prices—from $1.25 to $2.00 per acre—and purchasers were given several years to complete their payments. Not only was land cheaper and more abundant than in the East, but it was also more fertile, yielding about twice as much per acre. But without the means of getting there, the cheap lands would have remained unoccupied.

Steamboats

Still, travel by canal was slow and cumbersome. Goods were carried through canals on barges towed by horses or mules. The animals plodded patiently along towpaths on the banks of the canal. A mule could pull through water a load fifty times or more heavier than it could over any road; but the animal could only travel at a snail's, or rather, a human's pace—about three miles an hour. What was needed was a new source of power, one that would replace the energy of beast and human beings. Once again British technology supplied the answer. In 1769 a Scotsman named James Watt had patented a practical steam engine—a source of power vastly greater than men or mules could provide.

The first American to apply the power of steam to water transportation was John Fitch, a silversmith and clockmaker. In 1787 Fitch launched a twelve-paddle steamboat, the *Perseverance,* on the Delaware River. Yet it would be another twenty years before these smoke-belching monsters would begin to change transport and travel. In 1807 Robert Fulton's *Clermont** dazzled the nation by making the trip up the Hudson River from New York to Albany, about 150 miles, in sixty-two hours. Next, Fulton explored the possibilities of sailing steamboats up and down the Mississippi. Shipping freight by flatboat or keelboat was essentially one-way, time-consuming, and costly. Typically, farmers floated their produce downstream to New Orleans where the flatboat was broken up and sold for lumber. The power of steam would enable boats to breast the current and would transform the Mississippi into a huge two-way traffic route.

In 1811, Nicholas Roosevelt, an associate of Fulton's, built the *New Orleans* on the Monongahela River in Pittsburgh. In the winter of 1811–12 the ship made the 1,950 mile trip from Pittsburgh to New Orleans in only two weeks. Previously the trip had taken four to six weeks. An even more dramatic breakthrough occurred in 1815, when the *Enterprise* was piloted up the Mississippi from New Orleans to Pittsburgh against the current. The trip took about a month. Before that time a trip upstream by sail or keelboat from New Orleans to Pittsburgh took more than four months. Soon dozens of steamboats (built with so shallow a draft it was said they could sail in a heavy dew) were plying the western rivers. In 1817 there were only seventeen; by 1840, over 500.

---

*To guard against any mishaps caused by the primitive steam engine, Fulton had large square sails attached to the ship's masts.

Steamboats made possible much more upriver traffic and reduced shipping costs both up- and downstream. By 1860 upstream rates on the Ohio and Mississippi rivers were about 6 percent of what they had been in 1815; downstream about one-quarter of 1815. The drop in rates made it more profitable for northwestern farmers to sell their produce in New Orleans. Because farmers had an incentive to expand production for the market, another result of the burgeoning traffic on the western rivers was an increase in the settlement of the Midwest.

The Railroad Age

Thus when the railroads came, they appeared not as the main agents of the necessary transportation infrastructure, but as its capstone. The Baltimore and Ohio, the first operating steam railway in America, did not commence operations over its thirteen miles of track until 1828. In the next two years, while canal building was booming, only seventy-three miles of track were laid down. The general opinion was that rail-roads would not amount to much.

The doubts were understandable. Rails were generally made of flat strips of iron fastened to wood with spikes. Frequently the spikes would loosen and the rail would curl up around the wheels of the engine or even pierce the floor of the cars. Some lines laid their rails directly on stone and suffered their equipment literally to be pounded to pieces. Sparks from the engines set fields afire; engines jumped their tracks; railroads were said to run at unhealthy (as well as unsafe) speeds.

But by the 1840s it was clear that doubts had been ill-founded. During the ten years following 1830, while 3,326 miles of canals were dug, 3,328 miles of track were laid, and a rapidly improving technology had already put to rest many of the fears of the past. In the next ten years almost 9,000 miles of track were laid down; in the 1850s, 22,000 more would be put into place. During the 1840s alone over $200 million was spent on railroad building—a sum larger than the entire invest-ment of the previous four decades in turnpikes, canals, and steam-boats. As Louis Hunter has pointed out, the construction costs of a sin-gle mile of well-built railroad were enough to pay for a fully equipped steamboat of average size.[3] Even a small railroad, perhaps thirty to forty miles long, required about $1 million in capital, in comparison to a giant textile mill which required only $500,000 to $750,000. It is not

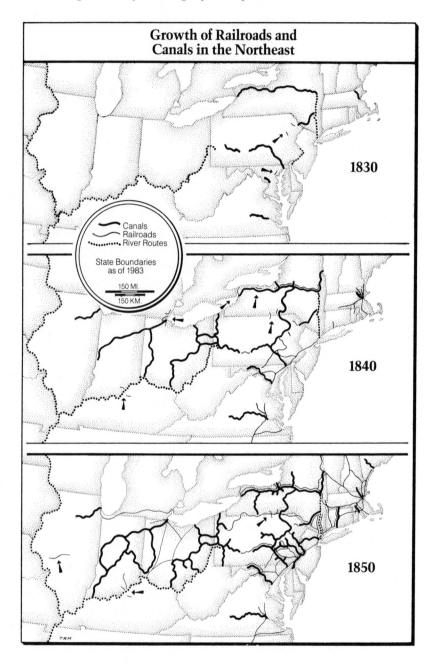

Growth of Railroads and Canals in the Northeast

Canals
Railroads
River Routes

State Boundaries as of 1983

150 MI.
150 KM.

1830

1840

1850

surprising, then, that by the eve of the Civil War railroads had become the first billion-dollar industry in America.

The Effect of the Industry

The impact of railroadization, as these figures show, was profound and pervasive, although our inquiry into the canals and steamboats makes it plain that railroads were merely an advance in the transportation revolution and did not in themselves initiate the nation's industrial or agricultural growth.

Yet, in some ways the railroads imparted a different stimulus to the nation's economic transformation. Like the canals and steamboats, the rails cheapened rates and quickened the pace of activity, but unlike the canals, they never froze over. Hence economic activity became less tied to the seasons. Much more than the canals and riverboats, the railroads served as stimuli for the development of such crucial industries as iron and later steel, locomotive manufacture, and metalworking in general. Indeed, railroads consumed more than 40 percent of the output of iron and steel–rolling mills in this period. Again unlike the canals and steamers, they mobilized the industrial imagination of the country: Frederika Bremer, a Swedish novelist visiting the nation before the Civil War, noted that boys in school amused themselves by drawing locomotives (or steamboats)—always in motion, always smoking. She concluded that "interest in locomotive machinery had a profound connection with life in [this] country."[4]

Not least, the development of the railroads was even more effective than the canals in stimulating the flow of capital into the economy. A good portion of this, about three-quarters, came from private sources—just the reverse of the financing of the canals. As early as 1838 the Eastern Railroad of Massachusetts had 2,331 stockholders, and the original Pennsylvania Railroad was financed almost entirely by house-to-house sales of stock. In the West, farmers often mortgaged their properties to help finance a short line through their region, and many manufacturers underwrote all or part of the spurs or short lines to their places of business.

Some of these investments turned out very badly. The first great depredations of finance made their appearance in these years as the president of the New York and New Haven Railway sold 20,000 shares of unauthorized stock, the proceeds of which went entirely into his own pocket. And the president of the Vermont Central dispersed 10,000 shares of illegal stock so skillfully that the legislature had to increase the authorized capital of the firm to save the unidentifiable victims from being fleeced.

Despite these harbingers of much larger depredations to come, the railroads never lacked for investors eager to put their money to work through rails and engines and cars. In particular, European investors rushed to buy American railway bonds and shares. By 1853 more than one-quarter of all American railroad bonds were foreign-owned. As a machine for siphoning European wealth into American capital equipment, the railroads were as effective as they were in completing the network of transportation indispensable for the industrial development of the nation.*

The Marshall Court

Supporting the forces that were reshaping the American landscape and altering the character of American life in these years was the Supreme Court. In ruling on questions of constitutional law, the Court indirectly contributed to economic development.

---

*Like all large-scale technological change, the advent of the railroads brought gain to some, loss to others. In *Life on the Mississippi,* Mark Twain vividly described the impact of the railroad on the previously flourishing steamboat trade:

These railroads have made havoc with the steamboat commerce. The clerk of our boat was a steamboat clerk before these roads were built. In that day the influx of population was so great, and the freight business so heavy, that the boats were not able to keep up with the demands made upon their carrying capacity; consequently the captains were very independent and airy—pretty "biggity". . . . The clerk nutshelled the contrast between the former time and the present one, thus:

"Boat used to land—captain on hurricane-roof—mighty stiff and straight—iron ramrod for a spine—kid gloves, plug tile [hat], hair parted behind—man on shore takes off hat and says:

"'Got twenty-eight tons of wheat, cap'n—be great favor if you can take them!

"Captain says:

"'I'll take two of them'—and doesn't even condescend to look at him.

"But nowadays the captain takes off his old slouch [hat], and smiles all the way around to the back of his ears, and gets off a bow which hasn't any ramrod to interfere with, and says:

"'Glad to see you Smith, glad to see you—you're looking well—haven't seen you looking so well for years—what you got for us?

"'Nuth'n,' says Smith and keeps his hat on, and just turns his back and goes to talking with someone else."

Between 1801 and 1835, the Court was dominated by the powerful and persuasive personality of Chief Justice John Marshall. A staunch advocate of national supremacy, Marshall's opinions frequently pronounced the same nationalism, broad interpretation of the Constitution, and regard for property rights that were expressed in the views and programs of Alexander Hamilton.

Probably the Marshall Court's most direct and effective contribution toward the promotion of a national economy was its curtailment of state power. In *Fletcher v. Peck* (1810), the Court, for the first time, declared a state law void because it conflicted with the U.S. Constitution. Marshall reinforced this principle in *Dartmouth College v. Woodward* (1819), granting corporations federal protection from state modifications of their charters. But his most comprehensive expression of national supremacy was in the case of *McCulloch v. Maryland* (1819), in which the high court struck down a Maryland law taxing the federally chartered Second Bank of the United States. Maryland had adopted the tax in an effort to destroy the bank's Baltimore branch. The lines were clearly drawn: at issue was state versus federal power. Speaking for a unanimous court, Marshall asserted the supremacy of the federal government. Thereafter he went on to consider whether Congress could issue a bank charter. His response was a ringing endorsement of Hamilton's doctrine of implied powers and, by extension, a validation of the promotion of national economic development.

FORGING A LABOR FORCE

Self-Employed America

It is an illuminating commentary on early nineteenth-century America that whereas nearly everyone worked—on a farm a child was useful for small chores as soon as he or she was ready to carry things—by 1800 only 10 percent of the labor force were "employees." *Self-*employed farmers, *self-*employed "mechanics" or artisans, small *independent* tradesmen made up the bulk of the white working force. What was lacking was the personage we associate with the very essence of the industrial process—the factory worker, selling his or her labor power to the factory owner.

There were several reasons for this absence. One, to which we have already referred, was the easy availability of land. A second, with which we are familiar, was the organization of manufacture on a putting-out basis, in which a merchant capitalist distributed yarn to be woven, or straw to be plaited, or leather to be sewn, to workers in their homes, returning later to pick up the finished work. A third reason, with which we are also acquainted, was the general distaste, even horror, in which "mill work" or factory work was held. As one author put it:

> Cotton mills! In England the very words are synonymous with misery, disease, destitution, squalor, profligacy and crime! The buildings themselves are huge edifices which loom like gigantic shadows in a smoky dense atmosphere. Around them are wretched houses and places of the most infamous resort; and blasphemies and curses are the common language of those who frequent them.[5]

A consequence of this ubiquitous self-employment was that the organizers of the first mills and large plants had difficulty in rounding up a work force. One of Samuel Slater's original child employees, risen to become a textile-mill owner himself, wrote to the Secretary of the Treasury in 1833 that "our greatest difficulty at present is a want of females, women and children; and from the great number of factories now building, [I] have my fears we shall not be able to operate all our machinery another year."[6]

The complaint summed up a real difficulty. Men preferred not to work in the mill when they could find work on the farm. Women and children were the preferred employees, but they could be attached to a mill only if the mill owner managed to house the family nearby. That was manageable when the required labor force was only a few dozen hands. It became unmanageable when the technology made it possible to design mills that could employ hundreds, even thousands. To staff the bigger mills, a new system was needed. A form of economic life suited to the new technology was as necessary as the new technology itself. Let us see how this adaptation was brought about.

Lowell's Cotton Mill

That adaptation was the creation of an American businessman of considerable talents, Francis Cabot Lowell, son of a comfortable Boston family, and a successful merchant himself. In 1810 he took his family abroad for their health and while in England he toured the cotton mills at Manchester and Birmingham. Deeply impressed by what he saw, Lowell tried to memorize the layout of the mills and the construction of the machines. He hoped to be able to reproduce them in New England.

Lowell's opportunity to test his memory came sooner than he expected. When he returned to America the War of 1812 was under way. Foreign trade had come to a virtual standstill. With European goods unavailable, almost anyone who could reproduce articles that were usually imported could make fabulous profits. Sensing this opportunity, Lowell and his brother-in-law, Patrick Tracy Jackson, purchased a water-power site on the Charles River in Waltham, obtained a charter of incorporation from the Massachusetts legislature for their newly created Boston Manufacturing Company, and sought investors for the enterprise within their circle of friends and relatives among Boston's merchants. Lowell then hired a brilliant mechanic named Paul Moody to help him construct a power loom. By the end of 1813 the factory and machinery were ready to operate. The plant both spun cotton and thread and wove it into cloth by machine, thus making it the first "integrated" cotton textile factory in the United States. The Boston Manufacturing Company was a success from the start. After seven years of operation, the stockholders received more that a 100 percent return on their investment.

The Lowell System

What interests us here, however, is the manner in which Lowell provided himself with the necessary labor force to put his new plant into motion. Determined not to have a mill village of poor, dependent families, he set out to revolutionize the labor supply by attracting intelligent young farm girls of good character to his mills. He did so by building dormitories and rooming houses, staffing them with housemistresses of unimpeachable respectability, and then scouring the countryside for young girls who would accept two or three years' employment as a means of gathering a small dowry or bettering themselves. Every effort was made to disassociate the mills from their English reputation of looseness and moral depravity and to create a spirit of earnestness, moral uplift, and financial self-improvement.

The Lowell system succeeded so well that within a short time the Boston Associates—as Lowell and his wealthy business partners were called—began thinking about expanding their operations. Unfortunately, Lowell lived only until 1817, long enough to bask in the glory of his successful experiment in labor-management relations but before practical plans for the industrial town that would bear his name had begun. That factory complex—located on the Merrimack River, northwest of Boston—was completed in 1823. The company's six factory buildings were grouped around a spacious square bordering the river and landscaped with trees, shrubs, and flowers. The dormitories, with intervening strips of lawn, were constructed in rows of double houses, at least thirty girls to a unit. Each bedroom was shared by six to eight young women, two to a bed.

Everyone who visited Lowell was dazzled. The town quickly emerged as the idealized countertype to satanic Manchester. By the 1830s Lowell had become something of a preindustrial Mecca for sociologically minded sightseers. Michel Chevalier, a French engineer, noted that Lowell was "new and fresh like an opera scene." An English visitor found himself searching in vain for the "tall chimneys and the thick volumes of black smoke" that personified British manufacturing towns.

Even more impressive to visitors were the young women workers, called operatives. Europeans were especially surprised by the fact that these young women, who worked twelve hours a day, six days a week, still found time to read, to attend lectures, and even to publish their own magazine. No less a critic of the British factory system than Charles Dickens—who visited Lowell in 1842—wrote that "from all the crowd I saw in the different factories that day, I cannot recall or separate one young face that gave me a painful expression; not one young girl whom, assuming it to be a matter of necessity that she should gain her daily bread by the labour of her hands, I would have removed from those works if I had the power."[7]

Life and Labor in the Mills

Lowell offered its operatives real economic and social advantages. Wages at Lowell—about $2 to $4 a week, from which $1.25 was deducted for room and board—were higher than could be earned in any other occupation open to women at that time. The community attracted women from all over New England. This gave the operatives an opportunity to broaden their horizons; and the close working and living conditions helped the operatives develop a sense of community.

But Lowell was considerably less benign beneath the surface than it appeared. The young women were not entirely happy with conditions in the mills and the boardinghouses. They were accustomed to long hours and hard work on the farm, but the demands of factory labor were different. On the farm, the rising and setting of the sun, the seasons, and the cycle of crops regulated the patterns of life and work. Now, instead of being guided by nature, work was calibrated by a time clock, a whistle, a bell. Industrialization standardized irregular labor rhythms and made time the measurement of work. The factory bell woke the operatives at 4:00 in the morning. Work began at 5:00. There was a breakfast break at 7:30 and at noon a half hour for lunch. At 7:30 each evening the factory bell dismissed the work force. At 10:00 it rang for the last time, signaling lights out.

Work in the Lowell factories was under the watchful eye of a superintendent, his office strategically placed between the dormitories and the mills. Each work room had a foreman, who was responsible for the work and the proper conduct of the operatives. Supervision was thus constant. It was a life without privacy.

Inside, the factories were not as celestial as they seemed when viewed from the outside. They were badly lit and stuffy, for foremen often nailed windows shut because it was necessary to keep the air damp in order to prevent the thread from breaking.

The Deterioration of the System

How shall we balance the advantages and disadvantages of the Lowell system? On the one hand there was the excitement of leaving the family farm, and the opportunity to accumulate some money, meet new people, experience a different way of life. On the other hand there was the relentless factory routine, the close supervision, the long hours of work. In the early days, the advantages probably outweighed the disadvantages for many. As time passed, the reverse became true.

For Lowell was growing as the factories prospered. Between 1825 and 1840 it changed from a village of 2,500 to a city of 21,000. Unfortunately, the building of housing did not keep pace with the population. "One week ago I entered a house in a central location," declared a town resident in the Lowell *Courier* in 1840, "and found it occupied by one store and twenty-five different families embracing 120 persons.

. . . " Two years later the Reverend Henry Wood, minister-at-large at Lowell, found several cases of six to ten people inhabiting one room, sometimes one bed.

Women made up by far the larger portion of this population increase, and by 1850 women and girls comprised two-thirds of the labor force in the textile industry. Mill owners sent out a wagon called a "slaver" to tour the farm roads of New England for prospective operatives. The "commander" of the wagon received a dollar a head for any girl he could "bring to the market."

Like most workers, the Lowell operatives did not readily embrace the transition from an agrarian-based economy—or, for that matter, a localized craft economy—to an expanding capitalism. In particular, they and their fellow workers rejected the increasing control over the work process. Americans still preferred to labor at their own pace, performing work or services by the task or job, rather than laboring in lockstep.

Unfortunately, efforts to improve working and living conditions at Lowell failed. Strikes—or, as they were called, turnouts—were crushed in 1834 and again in 1836. Partly this was because Lowell was a company town. In addition to owning the homes the workers lived in, the manufacturers controlled the newspapers, played an important role in electing town officials, and controlled every aspect of town life. This was an aspect of Lowell that Dickens did not see.

Industrial Immigration Begins

Meanwhile the mill owners were discovering another, more docile source of labor. At the very time that the supply of young girls was nearing exhaustion, a growing pool of Irish and English (and some German and Canadian) workers began streaming into Boston, desperate for work, willing to take anything. The names on the factory lists in Chicopee, Massachusetts, changed from Lucinda Pease and Wealthy Snow to Bridget Murphy and Patrick Moriarty. In Fall River in 1826 only twenty-six out of 612 operatives were foreign, but by 1846 the majority of the plant was Irish. "By 1850," writes one historian who has studied this period in depth, "the white gowned girls who marched to welcome Presidents, who talked so intelligently to foreign visitors, who write poetry and stories filled with classical allusions, were no longer to be found in the factory mills."[8]

Elsewhere in the country, employers had long since turned to immigrant labor as a means of supplementing the labor force available to them. As early as 1828 the Chesapeake and Ohio Canal Company sent agents abroad to recruit Irish workers from the famine-ridden counties of Cork, Kerry, Galway, and Clare at rates well below prevailing American levels. The immigrant accepted work on the canals under hideous conditions that broke 5 percent of the labor force each year from fever and disease. Many of them stumbled into factory towns where they formed the first permanent urban proletariat in America. It would not be long before urban reformers would be describing with shock the conditions in the cellars and garrets and hovels that housed the urban poor.

Even more disquieting were the conditions of life and labor in the early mining towns. Unlike textile villages, which were located near farms and seacoasts, the early mining towns were far removed from the centers of "civilization," and became islands unto themselves. In the earliest days of mining, before railroads and corporations became involved in this industry, mining communities were similar to feudal villages, with one difference. The similarity was that the iron master's home was the manor and the workers his serfs. The difference was that the iron masters owed their industrial serfs none of the reciprocal obligations that were part of the feudal system.

When the mining industry began to grow, mine operators began employing recruiting agents. In the 1830s and 1840s thousands of Irish miners flocked to the Pennsylvania coal fields. There they established their own coal "patches," where they tried to preserve their cultural identity.

Life in a mining town did not differ substantially from that in a textile village. Miners worked the same long hours, lived in jerry-built houses, brought their children into the hazardous tunnels to supplement the family income, shopped at what they labeled the company's "pluck-me" store, and were often at the mercy of their bosses. The catalogue of sufferings in these communities was endless.

Yet it is a telling commentary on the comparative standards of Europe and America that immigration—"that great referendum on American conditions," as historian E. C. Kirkland has dubbed it[9]—rapidly swelled to vast proportions. Between 1820 and 1840 immigration rose from roughly 10,000 to 90,000 a year; by 1850 it had jumped to over 300,000; by 1854, to nearly 500,000. Nearly half the increase in the nonslave working force between 1830 and 1850 was supplied by foreign labor.

The swelling tide of immigrants was not merely a continuation of the initial immigration that had founded the colonies. Those earlier arrivals had been on the whole literate, often skilled, fired up to get ahead. The new wave, by and large, was illiterate, unskilled, easily exploited. We catch a glimpse of the prevailing managerial spirit in this excerpt from the report of a mill agent visiting Fall River in 1855:

> I inquired of the agent of a principal factory whether it was the custom of the manufacturers to do anything for the physical, intellectual, and moral welfare of their work people. 'We never do,' he said. 'As for myself, I regard people just as I regard my machinery. So long as they can do my work for what I choose to pay them, I keep them, getting out of them all I can. What they do or how they fare outside my wall I don't know, nor do I consider it my business to know. They must look out for themselves as I do for myself. When my machines get old and useless, I reject them and get new, and these people are part of my machinery.'[10]

We will look again at the role played by the immigrant worker, but here it is useful to reflect on the broader problem that the issue raises. Not only Karl Marx but the conservative German sociologist Max Weber has held that capitalism could not function without a property-less proletariat—a mass of workers who had no choice but to sell their labor on the market, accepting whatever terms and conditions the "market" offered. Certainly the industrial system in America could not find its needed workers as long as land was cheap and easily available. In the Lowell system, and then in the army of immigration, we find efforts to *create* a work force willing to perform hard work for low wages. To put it differently, the principle of a market relationship—first buffered by the Lowell system, then harshly impersonal in the purchase and sale of immigrant labor—was gradually replacing the older and more traditional master-servant or employer-apprentice relationship of the precapitalist world. The same transformation that was altering the material aspect of everyday life was bringing into being an organization of work that would irreversibly change the original aspect of America as a nation of predominantly independent working men and women. In short, Jefferson's worst fears were being realized. His vision of an America of farmers and artisan producers who owned the means of production and depended on no man for a living was becoming more and more imperceptible.

TECHNOLOGY AND GROWTH

The network of transportation undergirded the growing American economy; the new labor force gave it its necessary factory hands; but for the emerging economy to "take off," there was required yet another factor—the creation of an industrial "know-how," a general expertise, a native technology.

Yankee Ingenuity

At the outset of the nineteenth century, and certainly in the eighteenth and seventeenth centuries, America lagged far behind Great Britain in most technology. There were good reasons for this. By 1850, for every two Englishmen who worked the land, three worked in some kind of industry, broadly defined. By way of contrast, in America in 1850 not even 15 percent of the labor force was in manufacturing. Thus England had a far greater weight and a variety of industry, a finer specialization of labor, and a more massive concentration of business talents in the area in which America was now beginning to seek its fortune.

Yet from the beginning, some advantages were to be found on the American side. One of them was a widely admired American propensity to innovate and experiment. A parliamentary committee, touring America in 1854, reported that every workman seemed to be continually devising mechanical aids to his work. In the same vein, James Nasmyth, the famed British inventor of many machine tools, told a parliamentary committee that English workmen and manufacturers were hampered by a "certain degree of timidity resulting from traditional notions and attachment to old systems, even among the most talented persons."[11] Typically, inventions spread more rapidly in America for the same reason: in 1859, fifteen years after the sewing machine had been invented, America had fifteen times as many sewing machines as England.

Whence this "Yankee ingenuity"? In part it was the product of farmer–mechanics, trained in country mills and blacksmithing shops,

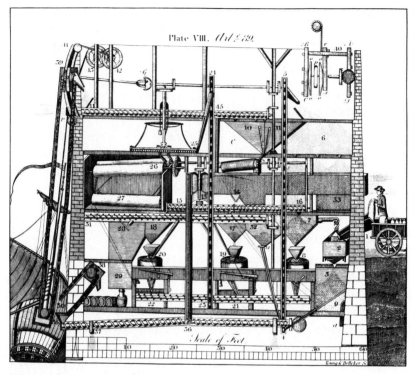

Diagram for a mechanical flour mill built in Delaware in 1785. The mill is considered to be the first automatic factory and the prototype of the continuous production line.

who apparently achieved an extraordinary self-reliance and versatility. From an early date, many tools, such as the hatchet, were altered by these craftsmen so that American axes and hammers early acquired a reputation abroad. In a society freed from the heavy hand of traditional class barriers and guild rules and regulations, such inventiveness found a natural outlet.

Add to this an economic incentive to invention posed by the high price of American labor. If there is a discernible pattern in American innovation, it seems to have been the adaptation of processes originally used in Europe in ways that would allow for a greater economy of labor. Thus Oliver Evans, an extraordinarily fertile mind, devised an automatic mill in 1783 that processed grain into flour through a series of conveyors and gravity feeds, virtually without the need for human effort. And of course the famous invention of the cotton gin by Eli Whitney in 1793—an overnight stroke of genius—was said by Whitney himself to make the necessary labor of cleaning cotton "fifty times less."

Interchangeable Parts

The great triumph of Yankee ingenuity, however, unquestionably lay in its early emphasis on a technique that would become more and more associated with "American" manufacturing techniques. This was the technique of mass production. But mass production is not a means of manufacture that can be adopted directly from handicraft. There is needed a crucial intervening step—the development of a technology of *interchangeable parts* in which the components of a finished article are so much alike that one can be substituted for another, at random, to make the final article.

The American style of this radically innovative system becomes more apparent when we learn that the technology itself was first developed in France and Britain. In 1785, as American minister to France, Thomas Jefferson was shown an interchangeable set of flint-lock parts, but despite his efforts Congress refused to bring the inventor to this country. In England another interchangeable system, developed to manufacture pulley blocks, was also curiously neglected by Britishers, so that the idea never spread to other products.

A happy but not altogether fortuitous conjunction of circumstances led to the eventual application of interchangeable parts in America. At the close of the century Eli Whitney was already famous for his invention of the cotton gin, but he was also in considerable financial straits, having been unable to patent the gin. He determined to remedy his fortunes by undertaking a daring scheme. "I should like," he wrote to Oliver Wollcott, Secretary of the Treasury, "to undertake to manufacture ten or fifteen thousand stand of arms."

Since Whitney had never manufactured so much as a single gun, and in view of the fact that the entire output of the federal arsenal at Springfield, Massachusetts, was only 245 muskets over two years, his proposal was indeed audacious. But Whitney had a plan. As he wrote to Wollcott:

> My general plan does not consist of one great complicated machine, wherever one small part being out of order or not answering to the

purpose expected, the whole must stop and be considered useless. If the mode in which I propose to make one part of the musket should prove by experiment not to answer, it will in no way affect my mode of making any other part. *One of my primary objects is to form the tools so the tools themselves shall fashion the work and give to every part its just proportion—which, once accomplished, will give expedition, uniformity, and exactness to the whole.*

. . . *the tools which I contemplate are similar to an engraving on a copper plate from which may be taken a great number of impressions, perceptibly alike.*[12]

The American System

We know little of the actual tools that Whitney designed to make possible his system of interchangeable parts. We get some inkling of the difficulty of the task, however, when we learn that in the Lowell textile machine shops blacksmiths still cut each nut to fit its own bolt and that mechanics considered a tolerance of 1/32 inch to be the best that could be hoped for. In England, where the firm of Watt and Boulton turned out superb steam engines, it was considered a triumph when a cylinder head was made accurate within the thickness of an "old shilling."

Thus we are not surprised to learn that Whitney's contract was long delayed in being carried out. For twenty-eight months he labored to create his grinders and borers and lathes, and then in 1801 he brought ten (not 10,000) muskets to show President Adams and Vice President Jefferson. Before their eyes he took the guns apart, separated the pieces into piles, and offered to assemble ten new muskets from parts selected at random. His audience was dumbfounded. Yet they did not begin to appreciate the extent of the revolution that was latent in those scattered bolts and stocks and barrels.*

The "American system," as it was soon called, was not instantaneously successful. It would not be so until a general technology of machine-tool production made the task of creating multiples a simple rather than a demanding one: as late as 1824 it was considered a feat when the Harpers Ferry arsenal produced muskets with interchangeable bayonets. In 1815 the new technique was applied to the manufacture of wooden clocks, and Eli and Seth Thomas began to assemble

---

*Another gun-maker, Simeon North, shared honors with Whitney for his vision of interchangeable parts but was never so successful in applying the idea.

500 wooden clocks at a single time. Thereafter Chauncey Jerome applied the idea to brass clocks; then in 1846 it was used in the making of sewing machines; in 1847, for farm machinery; in 1848, for watch parts; in 1853, for the famous Colt revolver.*

However slow in spreading (the technique was used in only about twenty industries in 1860), the use of interchangeable parts was still

An early factory in Ohio and its manufactures

*The mention of the Colt revolver provides an opportunity to comment briefly on another employer's efforts to create a model workplace that would, like Lowell's original plan, combine paternalism and profits. In the community established by Samuel Colt in Hartford, Connecticut, in the 1850s, all workers labored a maximum of ten hours per day, were given a full hour for lunch, and were provided with clean washrooms and a fully equipped social center. When Colt recruited German immigrants to staff his new willow-furniture factory, he even tried to reproduce the hamlet of his workers' native country.

almost exclusively an American process. When Colt set up a plant in London for the manufacture of small arms (perhaps the first multinational company!), he had to take his own equipment and personnel with him, for the American system was still largely unknown to English manufacturers. Indeed, James Nasmyth, who inspected the Colt factory, reported that it made him feel quite humble.

It was not, of course, just the "system" that provided the needed technological impetus to the nation. The first half of the nineteenth century also saw a flowering of American inventiveness applied to areas where American needs were different from those of the Continent. In agriculture, for example, American efforts to cope with high ratios of acreage to labor led to early experiments with farm machinery. A man working with an old-fashioned cradle could harvest only two acres a day. By 1837 with the very imperfect Hussey reaper, he could bring in ten to fifteen, and the McCormick reapers made in 1849 were warranted to cut at least two acres an *hour.*

The Readying of the Economy

It is impossible to itemize all the technical improvements that now came with increasing rapidity—in water wheels, steam engines, blast furnaces, methods of canning, slaughtering, hat-making, building. Let us merely note that between 1840 and 1860 the number of patents increased by 1,000 percent.

Rather, what asks for emphasis is that the period of industrial preparation comes to fruition somewhere around the middle years of the nineteenth century. A transportation network had by then been solidly laid into place. A labor supply, willing to perform the monotonous tasks of machine tending, had been discovered. A technology capable of producing an industrial apparatus was well advanced. A new basis for material life was emerging from the quickened means of transportation and the increasingly complex, interconnected, power-driven means of production. Matching this was the expansion of economic life, evidenced not only in the ever more ramified networks of trade that bound the states to one another, but also in the rise of market relations between worker and employer.

All this set the stage for an immense change in the trajectory of the overarching system of capitalism itself. We have scarcely talked of capitalism yet, for the system as we know it today was only beginning to form in the decades to which we have paid attention. But in this age of preparation we can already see the outlines of an impending change of vast dimensions, a change that would not burst with full force until after the Civil War, but one that was already capable of working deep changes within the structure of the nation.

Notes

[1]Carter Goodrich, *Government Promotion of American Canals and Railroads,* 1800–1890 (1960), pp. 52–55.

[2]"The American System," *The Business History Review* (March 1955), 81.

[3]*Steamboats on the Western Rivers* (1949), pp. 308, 110–112.

[4]Quoted in Leo Marx, *The Machine in the Garden* (1964), p. 205.

[5]Quoted in Marvin Fisher, *Workshops in the Wilderness* (1967), p. 87.

[6]*McLane Report,* 1833, 1:1046.

[7]*American Notes* (1842), p. 28.

[8]Norman J. Ware, *The Industrial Worker* (1924), p. 153.

[9]*Industry Comes of Age* (1961), p. 6.

[10]Ware, *The Industrial Worker,* pp. 76–77.

[11]Quoted in John E. Sawyer, "The Social Basis of the American System of Manufacturing," *Journal of Economic History* (1954), 377.

[12]Jeanette Mirsky and Allan Nevins, *The World of Eli Whitney* (1952), pp. 200–201.

Steam engine, mid-nineteenth century

Chapter 7

THE STRUCTURAL TRANSFORMATION

By every standard, the country was vastly richer in 1860 than it had been in 1800. Population had increased from five million to thirty-one million and was growing at a rate of about 35 percent per decade, doubling every twenty-three years. Yet the source of this growth was changing. Before the 1840s most of the population increase resulted from the unparalleled fertility of the American people. By the 1840s it was the swelling stream of immigration that sustained the previous rate of natural growth, but the birth rate was declining, so that by the 1850s the proportion of foreign-born in the populations of port cities such as New York and Boston actually climbed to over 50 percent, although in the nation as a whole it was still under 15 percent.

Meanwhile the cities themselves were rapidly expanding. In 1800 there was no city over 70,000; now there were already two cities with more than 500,000 people. In Washington's time 95 percent of the population lived in rural settings; in Lincoln's time the figure had fallen to 80 percent—one-fifth of the nation was already "urban." And whereas only 350,000 people worked in factories or mills or hand trades in 1820 (the earliest date for which we have statistics), by the time of the Civil War there were two million men and women laboring in tasks that were neither agricultural nor "service" but industrial.

ECONOMIC GROWTH AND CHANGE

The Rate of Growth

Was this extraordinary change the direct product of that process we call "economic growth"? The question is not altogether easy to answer, for economic growth itself is not an easy concept to describe or measure. It would be one thing if economic growth consisted only in the augmentation of a *given* set of commodities—more and more corn, bricks, miles of turnpikes. But that is not the way in which growth occurs. Growth is an economic process of change as well as simple expansion. It is a process in which corn gives way to wheat, bricks to cement or steel, turnpikes to canals to rails—and then back to roads.

How can we measure growth under these conditions of change? The answer is that economic statisticians compute the dollar value of total output—*gross national product* (GNP) is the official designation. For the early years of the nation, this is a difficult task, given the paucity of statistical information and the fact that much output in those early years did not come onto the market for sale and therefore did not have an official price. From the estimated figures, economists then calculate the rate of increase of the total volume of output of the economy in dollars, making due allowance for changes in prices or (if they wish to discover how much output increased per person) for changes in population.

The calculation of actual growth rates is a technical matter into which we need not enter here. Suffice it to sum up the best estimates as showing a per capita growth rate of about 1.3 percent a year over the period from 1790 to 1860.[1] A rate of 1.3 percent may not seem very impressive, but it is more than sufficient to double per capita incomes over the period in question.

The Sources of Growth

For our purposes it is less important to calculate the rate of growth than to reflect on the sources of growth. We have watched the development of America from an untilled, untapped continent to a thriving society of farms and businesses. But we have not yet systematically inquired into the nature of the growth process itself. How can we now explain the process that has been at the center of our attention for so many pages?

The first source of the expansion in the value of total output must be self-evident. It is the sheer increase in the amounts of labor and capital that enter the production process. In 1860 our total labor force was about eleven million, over five times the 1800 labor force of 1.9 million. During the period 1810–1860 the total value of manufactures increased roughly tenfold, from $200 million to just under $2 billion, while capital invested in manufactures actually grew twentyfold, from about $50 million to $1 billion.* By 1860 the United States was second only to Great Britain in manufacturing.

Together, the increases in the man-hours of labor and "machine-hours" of capital explain much of the growth in GNP. But the increase in the quantity of inputs is not sufficient to explain the entire rise in the volume of outputs. Economists also emphasize the rise in *productivity* that augmented the contribution of both labor and capital. An average worker in 1860 was capable of turning out over 50 percent more than a worker in 1800.[2] This in turn was the consequence of two main improvements. First, the labor force was shifting out of agriculture into manufacturing, where its productivity per worker was higher. According to recent estimates, factory workers were about twice as productive as farm workers. Second, labor was working with larger quantities and far better "qualities" of machines and tools of all kinds.

It is the second source that we should stress, for economic growth is much more attributable to improvements in the quality of inputs than to their increased quantities. Technology plays a central role here—the cotton gin, as we have seen, gave a tremendous impetus to the momentum of growth by multiplying the productivity of labor perhaps fiftyfold. So too the development of the "American system" of interchangeable parts greatly enhanced labor productivity.

From Quantity to Quality in Material Life

In discussing the role of technology in growth, we reemphasize a point of great importance. It is that the economic transformation to which we give the name of "growth" is not just a change in volume of goods but in kinds of goods. The GNP of 1860 was not merely larger in the sense that it contained many more tons of wheat than the GNP

---

*These figures are expressed in constant dollars of 1860 purchasing power—that is, they are corrected for inflation or deflation.

of 1800; it also contained new products that made the output of the later date *different* from, as well as more valuable than, that of the earlier. The texture of material life was changing as dramatically as its sheer quantitative abundance.

One immediately visible sign of the new times was the effect on the national imagination of the railroad. To quote from one social historian of the period, "Stories about railroad projects, railroad accidents, railroad speed [filled] the press; the fascinating subject [was] taken up in songs, political speeches, and magazine articles, both factual and fictional."[3] The cliché of the age, as one critic has observed, was "the annihilation of time and space," the telegraph here sharing honors with the railroad. It was, however, by no means an empty cliché. Chicago, once three weeks' distance from New York by canal, was now but three days removed. The railroad became a part of the life experience of millions of Americans, from the poorest immigrant families who traveled in boxcars across the nation to the social elites who traveled to spas and resorts in "saloon cars."

Less dramatic than the railroads but not less important was the introduction into daily life of objects that depended on machine production. There were the safety pin; large, cheap panes of window glass; the omnipresent cotton textiles; the new carpeting from the power looms of New England. In good but not lavish homes of the 1860s there were cast-iron stoves, spring mattresses, roller shades at the windows, flush toilets, wallpaper, gaslights, "patent" furniture, silver-plated tableware, a daguerreotype on the wall. Perhaps the most important change, in terms of the quality of life, was the invention of chloroform, the first effective anesthetic.

All these things were either unknown to or extremely expensive for Americans in the 1830s and 1840s, and unimagined by most Americans of 1800. Chester Wright has commented shrewdly on the importance of small articles in the wills of that earlier time: "The care with which a silver spoon, a silk dress, a bed, a chest of drawers, or a head of livestock is bequeathed shows a society where scarcity made little things important." But this concern for small articles of household wealth is lacking sixty years later.[4]

The Distribution of Wealth

In terms of comfort and convenience, the material life of the moderately well-off classes was appreciably above the level at the beginning of the nineteenth century, although in cities such as Pittsburgh another side of industrial abundance was already visible in a layer of soot and grime that lay over everything within miles of the iron foundries.

We should recognize, however, that the enjoyment of industrial abundance was mainly confined to the middle and upper reaches of the population and did not extend to the general run of the working class. Mostly this was because economic inequality increased markedly over this period. Around the time of the American Revolution, the top 10 percent of the wealthholders in New England controlled 47 percent of the total wealth. On the eve of the Civil War, the top 10 percent of wealthholders controlled over 70 percent of the total wealth. The great majority of this elite group had benefited from inherited wealth and from certain social and educational advantages; in effect, the rich got richer. Looking at the nation as a whole, by 1860 the top 5 percent of free adult males owned 53 percent of the wealth; the bottom half owned only 1 percent.

As in colonial days, the distribution of wealth varied significantly by region. Southern slaveholders retained their hold on first place, owning five times as much wealth as the average northerner, and more than ten times as much wealth as the average nonslaveholding southern farmer.

The Lower Classes

For the working class the negative side of industrialization—the soot, the crowding—was all too evident, while the products of the new industry were beyond the reach of most. In the 1850s in Newburyport, Massachusetts, for example, the pay of a common laborer was insufficient to enable him to support his family without outside assistance,[5] and the situation was far worse in the larger cities into which the immigrants poured. In the crowded tenements of Boston and New York, conditions sometimes approached the depths of the English slums that Americans had once thought would never appear on their side of the Atlantic. At the same time that a local guidebook identified New York City's Fifth Avenue as "the most magnificent street on the continent," perhaps even "the finest in the world," the New York *Tribune* reported that in 1850 some 18,456 people were inhabiting 8,141 cellars; one out of every twenty New Yorkers lived in one of these "Dens of Death."

Between 1810 and 1859 the crude death rate for the city rose from one death per 46.5 persons to one in twenty-nine. Dr. Henry Clark, visiting Half-Moon Place in Boston, in 1849, discovered:

> One cellar . . . occupied nightly as a sleeping apartment for thirty-nine persons. In another, the tide had risen so high that it was necessary to approach the bedside of a patient by means of a plank which was laid from one stool to another; while the dead body of an infant was actually sailing about the room in its coffin.[6]

The worsening slums make it clear that the meaning of economic growth was not a general improvement enjoyed equally by all. From a more general perspective we can also see that the transformations of material life, though highly visible on the surface, had not yet penetrated into the whole structure of society. The persistence of log cabins and sod houses in the West testifies that the incursion of manufactures was a phenomenon mainly confined to the centers of population. Life expectancy at birth in 1855, if we judge by the statistics of Massachusetts hospitals, was still less than forty years, only four years more than in 1790. Municipal sanitation systems, fire-fighting forces, and public libraries were still rarities. The total number of school days in the lifetime education of an average citizen was less than 500. Little as this seems, the American figures for school enrollments were the highest in the world. Moreover, by 1860 the literacy rate at age twenty had attained modern levels, exceeding 90 percent.

The Effect on Life

Can we then sum up this irregular change with its differential impacts? We can venture three generalizations: The first is that *the transformation of material life also changed the character of economic life, displacing many tasks formerly done at home into the market arena.* In the upper classes the home had never been an important locus of productive activity, except perhaps insofar as servants performed various tasks. But in the great majority of families milling, bolting, brewing, distilling, spinning, weaving, even simple metalwork were all done at home—even up to the Civil War every well-conducted farm had its salt tub, its smokehouse, its trying kettle, ash-leach, and candlemold.

Gradually the new "machinofacture" made these tasks unnecessary. Clothes were no longer made at home, nor were beer or soap or flour or tools. The tasks of lighting and heating the home were simplified by the invention of the safety match, the cast-iron stove, and the gaslight. The preparation of food had begun to change from a domestic chore to a factory task with the development of a canning industry.

A second general change was *the homogenization of material culture*—a leveling of material standards in many areas. The availability of cheap watches, railway travel, vulcanized mackintoshes, and machine-sewn shoes narrowed the gap between the middle and the upper classes. There was still a vast difference between middle and upper, and a gulf between lower and upper; but the introduction of machine-made products set into motion a "democracy of things" that we can trace through the ensuing years down to our own time.

Third, there was an effect that was intangible, yet perhaps the most powerful of all. It was *the introduction of a new state of common expectation, a new state of mind about the material environment itself.* One can do no better than cite the words of the venerable historian of American manufacture, Victor Clark:

> Manufacturing is the phase of production that has modified most our national character and the constitution of society. The prolific output of machinery has made us prodigal in respect to things of which we were formerly thrifty, and has substituted a thirst for change in place of an earlier love for fixed order and familiar ways. The material environment, like the intellectual environment, of our forefathers was permanent. They lived in the same houses, used the same furniture, employed the same implements, wore the same clothes, and viewed the same scene from youth to old age. Their minds reflected the conservative habit of their surroundings. . . . In its fuller sense variety was the privilege of the few. That this condition has changed, whether for better or worse, is due mainly to the growth of manufactures, whose very end is to diversify our material surroundings.[7]

Perhaps we can add a word to Clark's eloquent description. It is that the imagination as well as the techniques of the American economy were slowly steering the system into the swift-running currents of industrialism. The older merchant-oriented capitalism of the past was making way, without even being aware of it, to a new production-oriented capitalism. This brings us ahead of our story, but it is well to identify the direction of change before it finally surfaces after the Civil War.

The machine process in rope-spinning

THE COMING OF THE WAR

The culminating and dominating event of our period was not, of course, the invention or introduction of machinery. At least on the surface it was not even an economic event. The terrible war toward which the country moved with a quickening pace and inevitability towered over the economic events of the times, and for all the economic motives and frictions so intimately entwined in the hostility of the North and South, no one then believed, and few today would hold, that the war was purely the result of an irreconcilable difference between a plantation economy and a factory economy. In the end the moral and political issue of slavery hung like a great noxious cloud between the sides, awaiting only a chance spark to flare into an immense conflagration.

Nevertheless, behind the immediate drama of political tensions and moral division, economic factors played an immensely important role. One factor was the fateful combination of cotton and slavery, which together turned the southern economy in a direction that would ultimately bring it into head-on conflict with the North. Let us therefore follow our economic narrative by paying heed to this aspect of the story.

King Cotton

Before the invention of the cotton gin, cotton was a profitable export only for sea-island planters along the coast of Georgia and South Carolina, who grew the high-quality, long-staple variety, in which the seed could be easily separated from the fibers by squeezing it between a pair of simple rollers. The short-staple cotton—or, as it was sometimes called, upland cotton—that grew easily in the interior was unmarketable because its sticky seeds lay tangled in the fibers.

The first cotton gin

As we have already noted in passing, Eli Whitney's cotton gin, an invention of inspired simplicity, broke this bottleneck and created a tremendous cotton boom in the South. Output rose a hundredfold between 1790 and 1820—from 3,000 bales to 335,000—and then quadrupled to 1,438,000 bales by 1840. On the eve of the Civil War, total output had risen to almost 4 million bales. More important, the 1860 crop was sold abroad for $191 million, or 57 percent of the total value of all American exports.

Even those states that grew little or no cotton benefited by the boom. In 1850, approximately 95 percent of Dixie's cotton crop was grown in the lower South. States of the upper South, such as Virginia, Missouri, Kentucky, and North Carolina, with economies based on hemp and tobacco, profited by selling their excess slaves to the planters who flocked westward into Alabama, Mississippi, Louisiana, and beyond. The rest of the nation also gained. The transportation, insurance, and marketing of cotton fell largely into the hands of northern merchants, who profited accordingly. Cotton cultivation also made the rapid growth of the northern textile industry possible. With the money received from the cotton trade, the South purchased all kinds of manufactured goods from the Northeast and foodstuffs from the West. As economic historian Douglass C. North has remarked, cotton was the "major expansive force" in the economy between 1800 and 1850. The American economy "was geared to the expansion of the southern cotton economy."[8]

Cotton and Slavery

Cotton obviously paid; and cotton was, unhappily, a slave crop. Of the four million slaves in the South in 1860, about three-quarters worked in agriculture, and of those two-thirds worked in cotton. The remainder of the agricultural slave force worked on tobacco, rice, indigo, and sugar; the nonagricultural slave force was used for domestic service, and to a minor extent in industry, construction, mining, lumbering, and transportation.

Essentially, then, the cotton crop rested on slavery. This did not mean, however, that most southerners were slaveholders. The South was principally a region of small farms, not great pillared mansions and vast plantations, and on the small farms slaves were rare. Of 568,000 agricultural units in the South in 1850, less than one in five could be classified as a "plantation." On the remaining four-fifths of the farms, the owner was an independent farmer who raised numerous crops, mainly for self-support rather than for the market. Of some 1.6 million white families in the region, only 384,000 owned the 4,000,000 slaves, and of those who did own slaves, 88 percent held fewer than twenty (and were therefore not classified as "planters"). Indeed, half the slaveowning farmers possessed fewer than five slaves.

Slavery was thus concentrated on the great plantation estates where gangs of fifty to 100 slaves were used. There were about 10,000 such big planters, dominated by 3,000 very wealthy planters who owned more than 100 slaves, and capped by fourteen "plutocrats" who had over 1,000 slaves.

Curiously, most of the great planters were self-made men rather than descendants of the colonial gentry that we studied earlier. Many, in fact, were relative newcomers to agriculture, having channeled their profits from banking, land speculation, commerce, and slave trading into plantation ownership.

Slave Life

Most slaves did not live on small agricultural units. More than half of them lived on plantation units of more than twenty slaves, and one-fourth labored on units of more than fifty. A field hand's routine varied little from day to day, year to year. The day's work lasted from dawn to dusk, or as the saying went, from "can see, 'til can't," with short breaks for the breakfast and lunch rations. Everyone worked: older children served as water carriers or began to learn the lighter tasks of field work; slaves too old to labor in the fields cared for the small children and tended the stables, gardens, and kitchens. Sundays were free, as were several days at Christmas, when there were parties and small presents for everyone.

The slave's food was simple. The basic ration was cornmeal, pork fat, molasses, and occasionally coffee. Fortunately most slaves were allowed to tend small vegetable gardens of their own, to fish in the streams, and to trap small animals in the forest. Their clothing, too, was plain, coarse, and inexpensive—overalls, cotton and woolen shirts, work shoes, and a hat for protection against rain and the summer heat. Slave cabins were small, drafty, and scantily furnished. Logs chinked with mud formed the walls, dirt was the only floor, and a stone chimney vented the fireplace that provided heat and light. According to economic historians Roger L. Ransom and Richard Sutch, slaves on cotton plantations received in the form of food, clothing, and shelter only 22 percent of the earnings produced by these plantations. Still, the standard of living was above subsistence: it made economic sense for the planters to maintain their human "capital."

Most slave masters were neither excessively cruel nor exceptionally permissive. Nevertheless, slavery could not have been sustained without the power to punish. Except for the intentional murder of a slave, the master's power to administer punishment was virtually unlimited, and planters could delegate this authority to white overseers who were hired to supervise the field hands. Thus the stern hand of control, compulsion, and immediate punishment lay heavily over the slaves at all times. Probably the greatest fear among slaves was that their families would be broken up by sale; about a fifth to a third of slave families *were* broken up in this way.

But this did not preclude the slaves from giving their labor reluctantly and irregularly, or from resolutely testing the limits of the system under which they were forced to live. Slaves exercised a variety of means to circumscribe and frustrate white authority. Some used subtle forms of subversion, such as destroying crops, breaking tools, faking illnesses, and inflicting injuries on themselves. Others resorted to arson. Still others joined slave conspiracies that pledged themselves to an all-out race war against the whites. The bloodiest slave uprising was the Nat Turner Insurrection in Southampton County, Virginia, in 1831, in which fifty-seven white people were murdered before Turner and his followers were captured. Fear of slave rebellions, it should be added, was intense and omnipresent among white southerners. When captured, rebellious slaves were always killed.

To bring dignity and hope to their daily lives, the slaves created a rich cultural world of their own. Within their quarters, self-esteem and an independent perspective were communally nurtured by strong family ties, inspired and emotional religiosity, and a folk culture pulsating with African patterns of song, dance, and storytelling. These, too, were efforts to resist the pervasive dehumanization of slavery.

Slavery Defended and Opposed

The growing number of slave conspiracies during the 1820s and 1830s also caused white southerners to change their attitude toward their "peculiar institution." Before that time, southerners tended to apologize for slavery, as though it were an ugly heirloom willed to them by some malevolent relative. Blame for this "necessary evil" was placed not on themselves but on Dutch, British, and Yankee slave traders who had brought the blacks to America in the first place. But with insurrectionist threats rocking the South, terror-stricken whites began loading their guns, forming vigilance committees, and moving away from their ever-ready "necessary evil" rationalization to an unconditional defense of slavery as a "positive good." They found citations in the Bible that were interpreted to sanction slavery and command slaves to obey their masters. Southerners pointed to the glory of ancient Greece and Rome—both slave societies; they called attention to the paternalistic side of slavery, arguing that, unlike northern workers who had to toil in the factories and face the vagaries of "wage slavery," slaves were cared for from the cradle to the grave; and they quoted pseudoscientific evidence that analyzed the innate inferiority of blacks.

Another cause of this more aggressive posture was the rising abolitionist movement in the North. Demands for black emancipation could, of course, be traced back to the colonial era. But in the 1820s and thereafter, abolitionists swelled antislavery sentiment from a trickle to a respectable stream of opinion. This was partly because of the humanitarian impulse that coursed through the nation during these years. Abolitionists believed in the ideal of freedom. Slavery was a visible blemish on the republican complexion of the nation. It was sinful, they argued, to stand by idly while a disease like slavery poisoned the body politic. Americans could atone for their sins only by immediate repentance: the instantaneous and uncompensated emancipation of all slaves. Abolitionists punctuated their arguments by quoting the Declaration of Independence and by advancing religious views stressing that all human beings are equal in the eyes of God.

These were powerful arguments, but they failed to convert most Americans, even northerners. Mostly this was because northerners were as hopelessly antiblack as southerners themselves. Only New York and the five New England states allowed Negroes to vote. Most whites in states like Ohio, Illinois, and Indiana were virulent racists and made it strikingly clear that they did not want any blacks, free or slave, living in their midst. Slavery withered away in the North only because it was not economically viable. Because the growing season in the North was relatively short, idle slaves would have to be supported during the cold winter months. Northern crops, such as wheat and corn, also did not demand as much attention as, say, tobacco, which required (and still does) careful tending from the first planting to the packing of the cured leaves almost a year later.

Southerners, for their part, considered the abolitionists to be violent incendiaries out to provoke slaves to rebellion. Northerners also saw the abolitionists as dangerous radicals because there seemed to be no legal way to do away with slavery in the United States. Under the Constitution each state could decide whether or not to allow slavery to exist within its borders. Aside from a few quixotic abolitionists, no one believed that southerners would see the light and release their slaves voluntarily. Slavery could, of course, be abolished by amending the Constitution. But an amendment would require the approbation of three-quarters of the states. In 1850 half of the thirty states in the Union permitted slavery. No antislavery amendment could possibly be ratified. To campaign for abolition under these circumstances seemed like advocating revolution and civil war.

Economic Conflict

Alas, that war did come, as the nation stumbled from one disaster to another. The problem was not so much the threat posed to the North by the presence of a slave economy in the South—at worst, this resulted in the exasperating refusal of southern congressmen to vote for measures wanted by northern businessmen, such as a northern route for a transcontinental railway or a protective tariff.

In point of fact, aside from slavery, the tariff was the single most divisive sectional issue in pre–Civil War America. Northern manufacturers were the most irrepressible tariff advocates. Protective tariffs, they argued, would shield America's infant industries against foreign competition. By 1828 the entire northeastern section of the nation chorused this protectionist argument. But the export-conscious South rejected it, as we have seen in its reaction to the so-called Tariff of Abominations of 1828. High duties, southern congressmen insisted, would raise the cost of everything their constituents consumed—especially the price of manufactures they could not make at home. Their argument seemed plausible. If the British were to be expected to buy southern cotton, for example, the South had to be willing to accept manufactured goods in exchange. This exchange worked well when tariffs were low. Protective tariffs, however, would produce a vicious cycle. Both parties would be forced to raise their prices to earn profits.

The southern argument caused the West to divide on the issue. The Southwest, where cotton was the major crop, favored low duties; the Northwest and much of Kentucky, which had a special interest in hemp production (used for baling cotton), favored protective tariffs.

So bitterly opposed to a protective tariff was the South that when Congress passed a new tariff in 1832 (slightly lowering the duties of 1828), South Carolina held a convention in Charleston and declared both the tariffs of 1828 and 1832 null and void: South Carolina would not allow the tariff to be collected within its borders.

Although President Andrew Jackson was not much interested in tariffs, he knew that the idea of nullification was incompatible with the very concept of union. He therefore applied all the power of the presidency and all the force of his personality to check the "nullies," as he called them. Tension mounted, but was finally abated when Congress passed a compromise tariff in 1833, which called for the gradual reduction of tariff duties.

The economic threat was far more frightening when viewed from the southern side. For not only was the North openly opposing the crucial institution of slavery on which the plantation system depended, but for all the contrary efforts of southern congressmen it was evident that the industrial interests in the nation were clearly rising to dominance over the agricultural.

To put it bluntly, the North was rich and growing richer, and the South by comparison was poor and growing poorer. Two statistics will serve to round out the picture. First, in 1860 Massachusetts alone produced more manufactured goods than all the future Confederate states *combined,* while New York and Philadelphia *each* produced more than twice the goods manufactured by all future Confederate states.* Second, New York had nearly as much banking capital in 1860 as all fifteen slave states combined. In 1860, not counting its slaves, the South possessed almost a quarter of the nation's population, but only a tenth of its capital. Worse was the seemingly unbreakable hold of

---

*According to the 1860 Census, the North had approximately 1.3 million industrial workers, the South only 110,000.

War becomes mechanized

agriculture, especially cotton, over the southern economy. Central to this fatal involvement was the plantation aristocracy. Unlike its commerce-minded forebears, the great planters had increasingly distanced themselves from business. They complained endlessly about their dependence on Yankee middlemen and resisted rather than welcomed capitalist attitudes in their daily affairs.

Perhaps this reflected the fact that their investment in slaves—about $4 billion—represented half the value of all the assets in the cotton region of the South. Slavery is not a capitalist institution, and it is not surprising that as the South found itself ever more dependent on slavery, at least in its cotton economy, it also found itself more and more hostile to a capitalist way of life. Thus although the southern economy was growing in wealth, it was not growing qualitatively. It remained a "colonial" economy, impervious to the modernizing ethos of the North.

So the two regions were from early times embarked on courses that were bound to bring them into conflict. In the South an economy had been built on a cheap, localized, oppressed labor force; in the North the economy had been adapted to an expensive, mobile, and active working force. In the South the ruling elites spurned the pursuit of money that was more and more the openly espoused social goal of the North. In the South, an absence of manufacturing made the region welcome the influx of cheap goods from Europe; in the North the presence of manufacturing caused the region to seek to exclude foreign wares. All these conflicts were integral to the growing tension, although they cannot be said finally to have precipitated that tension into outright war.

AFTER THE WAR

There has been a continuing debate among historians over the precise effect of the war on growth. No one doubts, however, that the end of the war witnessed a sharp change. Between 1860 and 1865 overall industrial production advanced only 7 percent. *Between 1865 and 1870 it rose by nearly 47 percent.* Per capita growth of GNP, long steady at 1.3 percent, now rose by about one-third.

It was as if the four years of the war, when the advance of manufacturing was slow, were a period during which the momentum of growth was actually being dammed up, waiting for release. For certainly progress was extraordinary once the war was over. Cotton-textile production doubled from 1865 to 1866, then climbed another 50 percent by 1869. Pig-iron output jumped from under a million tons in 1865 to two million tons in 1869, then to almost three million in 1873. New railroad trackage climbed from 819 miles in 1865 to 1,404 miles in 1866, 2,541 miles in 1867, over 4,000 miles in 1869, over 6,500 in 1871.

Did the Civil War cause this tremendous industrial spurt? The question is not easy to answer. The trend toward industrialism was already in motion, as we have seen, and part of the spurt was, therefore, nothing but the release of demands and plans that had been postponed by the war. Then, too, we must not forget that the war also brought enormous destruction in its wake. As Thomas Cochran pointed out,[9] one major effect of the war was to set back southern production so badly that even by 1880 the values of southern farms and livestock were still one-fourth below those of 1860. Hence, the accelerated growth rate after the war may have reflected in part the rebuilding of the war-torn southern economy and represented what economic historian Stanley L. Engerman has called "a 'catching-up' process induced by the decline in per capita commodity output during the Civil War decade."[10]

Moreover no discussion of the economic impact of the Civil War would be complete without mention of the horrendous cost of the lost energies and talents of 620,000 Americans killed in the conflict. It was not just a war; it was a carnage. Estimates of the total cost of the conflict run as high as $20 billion—five times the total expenditures of the federal government from its inception to 1865.

CHANGES AND STIMULI

No one could declare, in the face of these figures, that the war was an unambiguous cause for the postwar boom. As we have seen, the boom itself was gestating, slowly gathering force before the conflict erupted. Nonetheless, the war itself, with all its disruptive results, also brought changes and stimuli that played a positive and even a powerful role in the expansion that followed. Let us look at some of them.

Technology

First, the war provided encouragement to a few major industries. One instance was the clothing industry. The Northern army was wearing out 1.5 million uniforms and three million pairs of shoes a year. This required a substantial expansion in the woolen and leather processing industries. A ready-to-wear clothing industry was already established before the war, but wartime demand accelerated the need for standardization of men's clothing and for the mechanization of production. The number of sewing machines doubled between 1860 and 1865; and from the standard sizes for army uniforms emerged the standard sizes of the men's clothing industry.

Another high-powered technical advance was the invention of the universal milling machine. First developed in 1862 to drill holes in gun parts, it was soon generalized into a machine capable of cutting all sorts of metal shapes. Within ten years of its development, the Brown and Sharp Company was selling the machine to makers of hardware, tools, cutlery, locks, instruments, locomotives—in short to a whole spectrum of industrial companies.

Yet another specific impetus was given to the iron industry, impelled by the needs of war to improve its metal-handling abilities. At the outset of the conflict American mills had been unable to fill orders for $1\frac{1}{2}$-inch steel plates because they had no way of trimming them. By the end of the war they were rolling and forging and cutting five-inch plates.

Finance

A second direct effect of the war was its impact on finance. Many of the fortunes that would power postwar expansion had their origins in the war itself.

Some of those fortunes were earned by dubious tactics or by outright fraud. A congressional committee investigating contracts for army provisions discovered that tents were made of such cheap stuff that soldiers testified they could better keep dry "out of them than under." Purveyors of knapsacks passed off as "linen" the shoddiest of cloth; suppliers of foodstuffs sold as "coffee" a mixture of roasted peas, licorice, and just enough coffee to give it a faint taste and aroma of the real thing. Blankets were often little better than rags. Freight rates charged to the government were higher than those charged to private commerce.

In other words, the war was the source of much "ill-gotten gains." But those same gains, in the period that followed, would be the source of investments that would account for much of the rush of growth and for the widening and deepening apparatus of industrial production.

Moreover, the rise of war-based fortunes accorded with the growing admiration of businessmen and business ways. Henry Adams, returning from Europe in 1868 after a ten-year stay, found himself in a world utterly strange to his prewar values. A new money-oriented, expansion-minded, hard-headed class had moved into prominence, elbowing aside the leaders of the prewar era to whom business was still a subsidiary and not a commanding social value. "One could divine pretty nearly where the force lay," commented Adams, "since the last years [have] given to the great mechanical energies—coal, iron, steam—a distinct superiority over the old . . . agriculture, handwork, and learning. . . ."[11]

From Slavery to Sharecropping

Apart from settling for all time the issue of disunion that had haunted the nation through much of its history, the most important result of the Civil War was the destruction of slavery. What did emancipation mean for the four million ex-slaves? Freedom meant first of all the right to decide what to do with one's own time. For most freedmen the first need was to test their liberty, to make some kind of symbolic move, to convince themselves that they really were free. Some decided to leave their plantations and roam the countryside. To quote one ex-slave: "Right off colored folks started on the move. They seemed to want to get closer to freedom, so they'd know what it was—like it was a place or a city."[12] Others decided to put down their tools and relax. According to one recent estimate, the reduction in labor-force participation and hours worked caused the per capita work effort of the black population to decline by about one-third between 1860 and 1870. Whites of course blamed the decline on the Negroes' desultory work habits.

Another use that blacks made of freedom was to seek education. In 1860 only about 10 percent of the slaves could read and write. To escape from the bondage of ignorance, blacks enthusiastically availed themselves of all educational opportunities provided by the Freedmen's Bureau (an army-run agency that had been created to care for refugees) and the many missionary societies that were established in the South. By 1877 southern schools enrolled 600,000 blacks.

But the one vital support that northerners did not provide to the freedmen was land. This meant that the blacks would once again be economically dependent on the whites. But because most white southerners were hard-pressed for cash at the end of the war, a new system of labor had to be developed. This was called sharecropping. Under sharecropping, the landowner provided the laborers with small plots of land, tools, seed, and work animals. The sharecroppers provided the skill and muscle needed to grow the crop. When the harvest was gathered, the sharecroppers typically turned over between one-half and two-thirds of this crop to their landlords. Although sharecropping afforded blacks a semblance of freedom, it would be a long time before many black farmers owned the land they cultivated. As late as 1900 three-quarters of all black farmers in the South were still share-croppers or tenant farmers, the victims of past injuries and contemporary oppressions. To this day we are suffering from the economic as well as the social wounds of slavery.

New Legislation

One last result of the war was a far-reaching change in the attitude of government toward manufacturing. The change was noticeable in many ways. As we have already mentioned, for a decade before the war southern congressmen had blocked the approval of a transcontinental railway that would strengthen the hands of the nonslave states or territories. By 1862 that decisive step had been taken, and in 1869 the Central Pacific, building eastward from San Franscisco, joined the Union Pacific heading west across Nebraska and Colorado. A golden spike joined the lines at Promontory Point, Utah, on May 10, 1869. Thereafter a traveller could ride, dine, and sleep his way in a Pullman Palace Car from the Hudson River to the Golden Gate in about ten days.

Less dramatic, but perhaps more important, was a change in tariffs. With the South no longer in the Union, Congress was able to pass a strongly protectionist measure in 1861. The tariff was subsequently revised upward until average duties stood at 47 percent after the war compared with 18.8 percent at its beginning.

Not less important was the passage of a National Banking Act (1864) that greatly strengthened the banking system and eliminated the wild-cat banks that had seriously undermined commercial progress. Before the passage of this act, the United States had been without a central bank for over a quarter of a century. The charter of the First Bank of the United States had expired in 1811. The Second Bank of the United States was not created until 1816, but it was "destroyed" twenty years later by President Andrew Jackson, who believed that the institution was a monopoly, a protector of special interests, and a threat to America's republican virtues. It mattered little to Jackson that the Supreme Court, as we have seen, had already affirmed the constitutionality of the Second Bank of the United States in the case of *McCulloch v. Maryland*. Jackson believed that the president had as much right as the Court to interpret the Constitution.* After his re-election in 1832, Jackson ordered his secretary of the treasury, Roger B. Taney,** to place current government income from taxes and land sales into state banks and to pay government expenses from existing deposits in the Bank of the United States. Hence the national bank lost its best depositor. The charter of the Second Bank was allowed to expire in 1836.

Homesteading and Other Acts

Yet another crucial act was the disposal of vast quantities of the public domain. The Homestead Act of 1862 opened the public lands to individual ownership and development; the principle was soon to be applied to the railways and other interests as well. In the eight years after the passage of the Homestead Act five times as much land was granted to the railroads as over the preceding twelve years—a total of 131 million acres, or 10 percent of the area of the states through which the lines passed, was handed over to the railroad-builders. Perhaps the lines could not have been built without this largesse, but largesse it assuredly was.

Nor does this recital exhaust the acts of the government favorable to business. Timber and mineral interests benefited from the Timber Culture Act in 1873, the Desert Land Act in 1877, and the Timber and

---

*To Jackson and his followers, the Bank was a "monster." By the mid-1820s the Bank had, in fact, become one of the most powerful institutions in the nation. Its president, Nicholas Biddle, once boasted that he exercised more power than the president of the United States. Despite his arrogance, Biddle was a man of considerable talent. Under his careful direction the Bank and its twenty-nine branches performed essential services for the government and public at large. It stored government revenues, helped arrange for the transfer of federal funds from one part of the country to another, bought and sold government bonds, helped obtain favorable terms of payment of the national debt, advanced loans to the business community, and exerted a restraining influence on the lending policies of state banks by forcing them to back their notes with adequate specie reserves.

**Taney, curiously, would also be the person to succeed John Marshall as Chief Justice of the Supreme Court, serving from 1836–1864. As chief justice, his decisions encouraged free enterprise and individual economic opportunity. At the core of Taney's judicial philosophy was the Jacksonian principle that the public interest must always take precedence over vested interests. "The object and end of all government," he wrote in the famous *Charles River Bridge v. Warren Bridge* case (1837), "is to promote the happiness and prosperity of the community by which it is established. . . ." By engraving free, fair, and open competition as the economic hallmarks of the Court, the judiciary further buttressed economic development.

Stone Act of 1878—all of which made land available on very favorable terms. Meanwhile, to ease the labor problems of both coasts, the Immigration Act of 1864 legalized the entry of cheap labor from Europe and China under contracts that have been called as harsh as those that brought indentured servants to America in the seventeenth and eighteenth centuries. And the capstone measure was the passage of the Fourteenth Amendment in 1868, which assured that "No State shall . . . deprive any person of life, liberty, or *property* without due process of law. . . ." A measure framed in the name of human rights was soon to become a bulwark in the defense of property rights.

This is not to imply that every act of the victorious North was unequivocally in favor of business, or that business interests themselves were always of one mind. What stands out, however, is the contrast between pre– and post–Civil War government. As Barrington Moore has pointed out, one must compare the program that we have just outlined with that of the South in 1860—"federal enforcement of slavery, no high protective tariffs, no subsidies or expensive tax-creating internal improvements, no national banking or currency system"— to realize the extent to which the victory of the North represented a victory for industrial capitalism.[13]

The "New South"

What of the South's economic plans after the war? Although southern businessmen had long cast a wistful eye toward their northern counterparts, it was not until after the removal of federal troops in 1877 that they made a sustained effort to transform their region's economy. Their object was to solicit northern capital with which to rebuild a South cast in the image of the North. The old order would be replaced with a business civilization of factories, cities, and commerce, with a new scale of values and new aims.

The leading booster for this "New South" movement was Henry Grady, publisher of the Atlanta *Constitution*. To draw northern capital southward, Grady wrote editorials on behalf of sectional harmony and spoke out in support of laissez-faire capitalism and freedom of restraints on business. His most effective speech on behalf of southern modernism, "The New South," was delivered before the New England Society of New York City on December 21, 1886. "The Old South rested everything on slavery and agriculture," he said, "unconscious that these could neither give nor maintain healthy growth." The New South, on the other hand, would be characterized by "a hundred farms for every plantation, fifty homes for every palace—and a diversified industry that meets the complex need of this complex age."

Grady's dreams were slow to materialize. A full generation after Appomattox, the South actually had a smaller percentage of the nation's factories and a slightly smaller percentage of the nation's capital than it had on the eve of the war. Partly this resulted from the massive devastation wrought by the war. Partly it was because the character and economic realities of the Old South were slow to change and hard to cast off. As late as 1900, only about 9.5 percent of the population of the South Atlantic states below Maryland was urban. The South was the most rural and agrarian section in the settled regions of the nation. The manufactures that did take root in the region were low-wage industries such as cotton and tobacco manufacturing. Another barrier was the inability of southern farmers to acquire either land or credit. Aside from causing widespread hardship, this condition hindered farmers from developing a "capitalistic spirit."

End of a Chapter

Like all "turning points" in history, the change from the prewar to the postwar economy was irregular, and it grows increasingly indistinct as we examine it closely. We have already pointed out that manufacturing had its roots deep in the past; we should emphasize as well that the age of agriculture did not come to a sudden stop with the war. Indeed, the period from 1860 to 1890 saw a doubling of cultivated land in the West, and to this very day farming continues to be one of the most productive economic sectors in the nation.

Nevertheless, there is an unmistakable contrast between the nature of the economic transformation of the country before and after the war. We have watched the transformation of an undeveloped wilderness into a major economic power. Next, the world would watch the transformation of a major economic power into an industrial civilization.

Notes

[1] Paul David, "The Growth of Real Product in the United States Before 1840," *Journal of Economic History* (June 1967), 195.
[2] David, "Growth of Real Product," 169.

[3]Leo Marx, *The Machine in the Garden* (1964), p. 191.

[4]Chester Wright, *Economic History of the United States* (1941), pp. 1022, 1025–32.

[5]See Stephan Thernstrom, *Poverty and Progress* (1964), p. 32.

[6]Norman J. Ware, *The Industrial Worker* (1964), p. 13.

[7]*History of Manufactures* (1929), p. 578.

[8]*The Economic Growth of the United States, 1790–1860* (1961), pp. 67–68.

[9]"Did the Civil War Retard Industrialization?" in Ralph Andreano (ed.), *The Economic Impact of the Civil War* (1967).

[10]"The Effects of Slavery upon the Southern Economy," *Explorations in Entrepreneurial History* (Winter 1967), 71–97.

[11]*The Education of Henry Adams* (Modern Library edition, 1931), p. 238.

[12]Quoted in Eric Foner, *Reconstruction* (1988), p. 80.

[13]Barrington Moore, *Social Origins of Dictatorship and Democracy* (1966), p. 151.

Part III
INDUSTRIALIZATION TAKES COMMAND

Tornado Windmill Company factory, Elba, New York, c. 1876

The Cincinnati Chamber of Commerce, 1902

Chapter 8

THE AGE OF THE BUSINESSMAN

THE BUSINESS THRUST

We are about to examine a "chapter" in our history of economic growth that will change the character of life far more dramatically and decisively than anything Americans had witnessed up to that point. In a dazzling period of sixty years following the Civil War, the face of the country will literally be made over. Railroads will cross and recross the continent; enormous cities will arise out of prairie wilderness; gigantic mechanical monsters will devour mountains in search of ore; astonishing inventions will enable individuals to talk to one another over wires; carriages will carry people about their business without horses. Between 1790 and 1860 the U.S. Patent Office granted a total of 31,000 patents; over the period 1860 to 1930 it awarded 1.5 million.

In the background of these alterations a tremendous structure of steel will come to undergird the economy, and a torrent of power will come to drive it: the 16,000 tons of steel produced in 1865 will multiply to fifty-six million tons; the sixteen million horsepower of energy used in the nation after the Civil War will become 1.6 billion horsepower by 1929. Perhaps we can sum up the change by saying that the omnipresence of machines will become more and more noticeable in the period from 1865 to 1929, when still another "chapter" of economic history will begin. We call this era of intensified machine building and machine use the *industrialization of America,* and in the chapters to come we shall examine the process as it took place. But here we must take a moment to think back on our frame of reference, to help us place the entire drama in clear perspective.

Three Effects of Industrialization

Industrialization changes America in three ways. First, it alters—indeed, it truly revolutionizes—material life. The daily routines of work, the objects of everyday use, are more profoundly affected by the advent of industrial technology than by any previous change in the economic history of mankind.

Second, industrialization changes economic life. The reach and penetration of the market expand. The manner in which men and women are mobilized for the economic tasks will shift from a relationship of indenture and apprenticeship to those of wage work in factories.

Third, the rhythm and pace of capitalist expansion will also undergo a vast change. Growth will move more rapidly. Instability will become more pronounced as production takes place more and more in factories, not on farms. The texture of institutional life will take on a new aspect as huge business enterprises arise, as buccaneers become bureaucrats, and as the government itself is presented with new tasks and challenges.

All these changes await us in the pages to come. We mention them here to trace out in advance the central thread of the narrative whose complicated path we are now about to examine.

The Market Mechanism

There is no better way to begin than to ask: Who planned the industrialization of America? Who determined where the railroads would go? Where the cities would grow and the iron mines be developed? Who planned the changeover from horse-drawn to horseless carriages, or the knitting together of the nation by telephone wires?

The answer is that no one planned it. In contrast with the late Soviet Union, where every steel mill, every technological change, every major new city was first determined by a group of planners and then built according to the blueprints of a central authority, no single individual or group of individuals designed the industrial transformation of America. Instead, the enormous process was largely left to the working-out of the market mechanism.

That mechanism basically consists of two elements, each equally important. The first is the organization of the bulk of the nation's production as profit-seeking enterprise, free to carry on whatever activities are permitted by law. The drive for profit thus becomes the central driving force of the market system.

This search to make profits pushes business enterprises in two directions. It serves as a force for the expansion of business, because a large business almost always makes more money than a small one. And it also serves to put businessmen on the alert for new opportunities for profit-making. In this way the drive for profit propels business into the development of new products, as well as into the expansion of facilities to provide more of existing products.

Therefore we can see that the drive for profits serves as a generalized imperative for action. That imperative is lodged, however, not in the directives and blueprints of a central command agency, but in the acquisitive drives of thousands of business executives or capitalists.*

But the drive for profits is only one part of the market mechanism. If it were the only operating factor, the market would be better characterized as a profiteering system than a profit system. Each enterprise, out to maximize its income, would be able to charge all that the traffic would bear. Monopoly would be the natural result of such a system, with business enterprises charging extremely high prices, and reaping extremely high returns, on every article sold either to households or to other businesses.**

Thus a control system is a necessary part of the market mechanism. It is not a system of inspectors or rigidly enforced directives, such as we found in the Soviet Union or still find in centrally planned systems. It is the institution of competition that provides control—the institution of businesses vying one against another to obtain the favor of their customers. Competition thereby turns potential profiteering and

---

*It is worthwhile learning a bit of terminology here. A capitalist is someone who owns capital and risks it in a business enterprise. An executive, or an entrepreneur (the word much used by economists), is a business decision-maker. One can be a capitalist without being an entrepreneur, as when a capitalist lends his money to or buys stock in an enterprise run by someone else. (We will learn more about stocks in the following chapter.) One can also be an entrepreneur without being a capitalist—for example, a manager of a business who is paid a high salary or a bonus but who does not himself own a substantial portion of the enterprise.

**Just as a cautionary note, it should be added that monopolies cannot charge *any* price that they like if they wish to maximize their profits. If a monopoly railroad charged a million dollars per ticket, it would not sell many tickets. What a monopoly can do is to establish the price that gives it the highest profit obtainable. A competitive firm has to charge a price that "meets competition," and its profits are accordingly lower.

monopoly into a struggle in which profits are constantly under pressure from enterprises eager to steal away the business of any firm that fails to trim costs or that prices its goods with a higher profit margin than is necessary for business survival.

Businesses

To learn more about the theory of the market mechanism we study economics, for a large part of that subject is concerned with elucidating the way in which the profit drive on the one hand, and the constraint of competition on the other, bring about the process of material replenishment and growth. But here we want to see the market mechanism in action and the overarching dynamics of capitalism. We want to follow the actual careers of nineteenth-century businessmen who were struggling to make money by expanding their businesses or by pioneering in new fields. We want as well to watch the competitive control system at work, for here lies one of the great sources of change in the period we are studying.

So let us begin by taking a survey of the business system as it existed in the first decade or two after the Civil War. There were about 500,000 business firms in America in 1870, not counting the nation's farms. Most of them were very small, employing one or two persons besides the owner-proprietor. A great many were small retail stores. But we are interested in a particular sector of the business world—the sector of manufacturing, for this is where the industrial growth of the nation will mainly take place.

From the census of 1870 we know something about that sector. Of the nation's total labor force of almost thirteen million, nearly 2.5 million worked in manufacturing. The ten biggest industries were flour-milling, cotton goods, lumber, boots and shoes, men's clothing, iron, leather, woolen goods, liquor, and machinery—in that order. However, the biggest employer, lumber, gave work to only 160,000 employees—far fewer than we would find in most giant companies today.

Businessmen-Inventors

Who ran these small businesses that were to play such an important role in our economic growth? They were a varied lot. A few were inventors, such as Thomas Alva Edison, who not only established the nation's first industrial research center—his so-called invention factory—at Menlo Park, New Jersey, in 1876, but who was actively engaged in creating companies to market his many inventions. As one observer noted, Edison was "the first great scientific inventor who clearly conceived of inventions as subordinate to commerce." Edison would have taken this remark as a compliment. Discussing his role as a scientist, Edison said:

> I do not regard myself as a pure scientist, as so many persons have insisted that I am. I do not search for the laws of nature, and have made no great discoveries of such laws. I do not study science as Newton and Faraday and Henry studied it, simply for the purpose of learning truth. I am only a professional inventor. My studies and experiments have been conducted entirely with the object of inventing that which will have commercial utility.[1]

Other businessmen had the prescience to put together other people's innovations to create new industries: Gustavus Swift, for example, who left Massachusetts in the mid-1870s to become a butcher in Chicago, combined the ice-cooled railway car with the ice-cooled warehouse to create the first national meat-packing company in 1885.

Still others were simply men with a talent for organization, finance, and management. James Buchanan Duke made his fortune by welding technology and merchandising. When the company in which he was a partner turned to cigarette manufacturing in 1881, Duke reduced the firm's operating costs by installing the new Bonsack cigarette-rolling machine, a one-ton contraption that fed paper and tobacco in continuous rolls, pasted and cut the tubes, and made 100,000 cigarettes in a single day. By comparison, the fastest worker could roll only 3,000 daily. The resulting output threatened to glut the market. But by 1884, through the use of advertising and the creation of a crushproof sliding cardboard box, Duke had created a national demand for his product. In 1890 he combined the four major cigarette producers in the nation to form the American Tobacco Company.

And Ordinary Businessmen

But most of the nation's businessmen were not inventors, or merchandising pioneers. They were a much more conventional lot, no more remarkable (and no less) than the businessmen who run small factories or stores or wholesale establishments in the United States today. We tend to think of the entrepreneurs whose combined efforts brought so dramatic a change to the economic landscape as Horatio Alger success stories—men who rose from humble beginnings to achieve fame and fortune.* In fact, the business leadership largely came from substantial and conservative backgrounds.

A study by Francis W. Gregory and Irene D. Neu on the social origins of 303 business leaders in textiles, railroads, and steel during the 1870s finds that the overwhelming majority were born in the United States; that of those native-born executives only 3 percent had foreign-born fathers, the rest dating their American ancestry back to colonial times; that some 90 percent were raised in either a middle- or upper-class milieu; that roughly a third were college graduates; and that one-half did not go to work before age nineteen, and that less than one-quarter went to work before age sixteen. Summing up their investigation, Gregory and Neu conclude:

> Was the typical industrial leader of the 1870's, then, a 'new man,' an escapee from the slums of Europe or from the paternal farm? Did he arise from his own efforts from a boyhood of poverty? Was he as innocent of education and of formal training as has often been alleged? He seems to have been none of these things. American by birth, of a New England father, English in national origin, Congregational, Presbyterian, or Episcopalian in religion, urban in early environment, he was rather born and bred in an atmosphere in which business and a relatively high social standing were intimately associated with his family life. Only at about eighteen did he take his first regular job, prepared to rise from it, moreover, not by a rigorous apprenticeship begun when he was virtually a child, but by an academic education well above the average.[2]

THE ROBBER BARONS

Thus the average business enterpriser does not seem like a very promising figure to be the agent for the industrial transformation of

---

*Horatio Alger business romances were about poor, hard-working boys who made good. They were not essentially rags-to-riches stories, but morality fables. Few people read these once-popular tales any more. If they did, they would soon discover an underlying pattern. Alger's heroes did not gain respectability and virtue because they displayed sterling qualities of business acumen, loyalty, etc. Invariably recognition came to them because they had the chance one day to stop a runaway carriage in which sat a terrified golden-ringleted girl who turned out to be—you'll never guess—the boss's daughter. After that, things changed dramatically for plucky Dick, Tom, or Harry.

the nation. But what makes the businessman so dramatic a personage in the post–Civil War era is not the average entrepreneur. Rather, it is a handful of business leaders who arose in virtually every line of business to dominate and drive and dazzle their fellow businessmen. By virtue of their personalities, their ambitions, their talents, or their tactics, these business leaders bestrode the economic landscape like Gullivers in the land of Lilliput, endowing the age with many of their personal characteristics. Because their characteristics included some of the predatory habits of feudal lords who exacted tolls and ransoms from those who strayed within their domains, these dramatic figures have been called by their critics the "robber barons," and the period of industrialization in which they played so powerful a role has been dubbed the Age of the Robber Barons. An examination of the career of perhaps the most notorious of them, Jay Gould, will give us some insight into the group as a whole.

Jay Gould

Jay Gould was the "Mephistopheles of Wall Street." He was perhaps the most money-minded man in a money-minded age. One historian writes: "No human instinct of justice or patriotism caused him to deceive himself, or to waver in any perceptible degree from the steadfast pursuit of strategic power and liquid assets."[3]

Gould moved from one wrongdoing to another with striking virtuosity. His career began in 1856, when he became a partner in a tanning factory in Pennsylvania. It was not long before he began investing a large percentage of the *company's* profits in his *personal* banking and real estate ventures. After those embezzlements were discovered, Gould formed a new partnership—but continued his embezzlements. This time one of his partners committed suicide; the other tried unsuccessfully to remove Gould from the tannery. It was not until 1861 that Gould was ousted, but by that time he had already extracted most of the firm's assets.

It was during this period that Gould first turned his attention to the railroad industry. In 1867, Daniel Drew put Gould and Jim Fisk on the board of directors of the Erie Railway. It was quite a trio. Fisk was a man of rapacious appetites and extraordinary unscrupulousness, of whom it was said that he regarded business "as a kind of joke."[4] Drew was famous for having introduced the idea of "watered stock"—

driving thirsty cattle to the market and then bloating them with water just before they were weighed in for sale.*

Cornelius Vanderbilt

Beginning in 1868 the triumvirate of Drew, Gould, and Fisk engaged "Commodore" Cornelius Vanderbilt, a New York shipping magnate who began investing in railroads during the Civil War, in an Olympian struggle for control of the Erie. The threesome began by issuing some $8 million in "watered" stock—corporate securities as bloated as water-filled cattle—despite a judicial restraining order. Thereafter they dispensed $1 million in bribes to obtain passage of a New York law to authorize the stock issue. These manipulations were too much even for Drew and Vanderbilt. Drew recalled the $8 million stock issue, and he and Vanderbilt turned the Erie over to Gould and Fisk, who thereupon issued $23 million in watered stock.

Even in an age of unbridled acquisitiveness, Gould's tactics earned him an unenviable reputation. Yet we should recognize that his chicanery and unscrupulousness represented an exaggeration of, but not a departure from, the behavior of many of his fellow business titans. Bribery, for example, was not uncommon—even Thomas Edison promised certain New Jersey representatives a thousand dollars apiece if legislation favorable to his interests was passed. Stock-watering and disregard for the law were widespread. After obtaining control of the New York Central Railway, Cornelius Vanderbilt arbitrarily increased its capitalization by $23 million, virtually every dollar of which represented inside profits for himself and his associates. When told this was illegal, he supposedly replied: "Law! What do I care about the Law? Hain't I got the power?"[5]

Fraud and deception were thus all too common practices of the day—the federal government, for example, was billed at three times actual cost by the first transcontinental railway construction company,

---

*Drew was also known for the bandanna trick. Feigning confusion and dismay on the floor of the stock exchange, he would mop his forehead with a red bandanna, causing a slip of paper to fall from his pocket. Another speculator would retrieve the note on which were written Drew's instructions to his brokers to buy or sell stocks. Thinking that Drew's plans were now discovered, his adversary would place his stock orders to take advantage of Drew's plans. But of course the whole thing was a ruse that enabled Drew himself to outwit his opponents because he knew what *their* operations would be.

Jay Gould (1836–1892)

whose expenses Congress had agreed to underwrite; and afterward, when the depredations of the company were in danger of being dragged into the open, the company's books were brazenly burned.

Baron or Builder?

Yet like many of the robber barons, Vanderbilt was also an empire-builder. The enterprise that set the motif for America's post–Civil War expansion was the railroad industry. The iron horse symbolized the boundless energy and forward motion of the nation. When the war broke out there were only 30,000 miles of railroad track in the country. Most roads were short, averaging no more than 100 miles, built to connect two or three local market centers; and there were few direct lines between major cities. Passengers travelling from New York to Chicago, for example, had to be transferred from one line to another seventeen times. The trip took two full days.

The main task of the postwar generation of builders was to consolidate these independent lines into unified networks. Vanderbilt was a pioneer in this development. By 1869 he had obtained control of the New York Central Railroad, which ran between Buffalo and Albany, and two other lines that connected the Central with New York City. In 1870 he picked up the Lake Shore and Michigan Southern railroads, thereby extending his system from New York City to Chicago by way of Cleveland and Toledo, Ohio. Passengers could thereafter travel between the two great terminals in less than a day without leaving their seats. When he died in 1877, Vanderbilt left a railroad network of some 4,500 miles. In the nation as a whole, by 1900 there were 200,000 miles, more than in all the countries of Europe combined.

THE CELEBRATION OF WEALTH

We will have a chance to look more deeply into the business behavior of the age and its relation to economic growth, for the era of industrial expansion could hardly have flourished if Gould's or Fisk's tactics were ubiquitous. Nonetheless, the styles and aims of the robber barons have an important bearing on the tenor of the times. For they typify a country that had become enamored of wealth. Business became the great avenue of success, and anything that delayed one's entrance into the world of business, including education, was frowned on. It was often remarked with approval that Cornelius Vanderbilt, who left $100 million at his death, had read but one book in his life, and that one at an advanced age. (It was *Pilgrim's Progress;* we can doubt that he learned very much from it.)

Not only was the accumulation of wealth regarded as the most fitting and admirable of all careers, but its ostentatious expenditure was generally admired. Social commentators of the period delighted in describing parties where cigarettes made of dollar bills were smoked for the pleasure of inhaling wealth; where extravaganzas of decoration were employed, including the conversion of one New York hotel into a fake coal mine; where newly made millionaires vied with each other for social distinction, one giving a party where monkeys were seated

A horseback dinner

between the guests, another a dinner party on horseback, yet another a party where each lady found a gold necklace tucked in her napkin as a favor.*

Moreover, the love of money and success permeated all ranks of society, not just the top. Historian Henry Steele Commager comments, "The self made man, not the heir, was the hero. . . ."[6] Small wonder, then, that panegyrics and encomiums celebrated the "captains of industry," and that a general philosophy of "rugged individualism" reached down through all the ranks of American society. Even among the working classes, Charles A. Beard remarks, "all save the most wretched had aspirations. There was a baton in every toolkit."[7]

*In several books published at the end of the nineteenth century, economist Thorstein Veblen observed that the very wealthy literally lived to spend money for the sake of proving they had money. Veblen called this pompous extravagance "conspicuous consumption," and the penchant to flaunt it, "conspicuous waste." See, especially, Veblen's *The Theory of the Leisure Class* (1899).

Social Darwinism

The worship of success thus provided an important source of the drive for profit that set into motion the industrialization process. We should note as well that the quest for wealth was supported by an important intellectual current of the day—a current we call Social Darwinism because it translated the biological theories of Charles Darwin into a social theory that blessed the business struggle as an indispensable means to "progress."

Darwin's theory of evolution did not make pronouncements about "progress." It was essentially a generalization about the struggle for survival in which some species survived and some perished. But in the hands of the English sociologist Herbert Spencer, Darwin's theory became interpreted as a process that chose the "better," as well as the tougher or stronger, among competing individuals or species. Thus the competitive struggle of business was viewed as a contest in which the survivors were the "fittest"—not merely as businessmen, but as champions of civilization itself. Hence businessmen transformed their sense of material superiority into a sense of moral and intellectual superiority. As John D. Rockefeller once stated, "I believe it is my duty to make money and still more money and to use the money I make for the good of my fellow man according to the dictates of my conscience."

Little wonder that such a theory won the approval of successful businessmen and that Darwinian phrases and ideas threaded their way easily into the fabric of business speeches and writings. Andrew Carnegie, for example, lionized Spencer and wrote to him as "Master." In a famous article published in the *North American Review* of 1889, Carnegie wrote:

> While the law [of competition] may be sometimes hard for the individual, it is best for the race, because it insures the survival of the fittest in every department. We accept and welcome, therefore, as conditions to which we must accommodate ourselves, great inequality of environment, the concentration of business . . . in the hands of a few, and the law of competition between these, as being not only beneficial, but essential for the future of the race.[8]

A few years later John D. Rockefeller, Jr., defined Spencerian "competition" to a Sunday school class:

The growth of large business is merely a survival of the fittest. . . . The American Beauty Rose can be produced only by sacrificing the early buds which grow up around it. This is not an evil tendency in business. It is merely the working out of a law of nature and a law of God.[9]

Hence Social Darwinism became a means of excusing as well as explaining the competitive process from which some emerged with power and some were ground into poverty. As one millionaire member of the United States Senate said of himself: "I do not know very much about books; I have not read very much; but I have travelled a good deal and observed men and things and I have made up my mind after all my experiences that the members of the Senate are the survivors of the fittest."[10] We understand his sentiment better when we learn that in 1900 the Senate contained twenty-five millionaires among its ninety members.

Thus Social Darwinism joined with the general adulation of wealth to create an atmosphere in which aggressive business expansion was given the unstinting and uncritical approval of virtually all sections of society. Even the churches were strong supporters of the business ethic, equating worldly success and spiritual superiority in a manner that would have made Cotton Mather blush. An estimated thirteen million people heard the Reverend Russell Conwell deliver his "Acres of Diamonds" sermon: riches were to be had almost for the asking by a little hard work, he claimed, and riches were "holy" because money could be used for good purposes. Conwell certainly had *his* acre of diamonds: his publications earned him over $8 million.* We shall see in later chapters how these prevailing attitudes played an important role in determining the character of the industrialization process.

FROM BARON TO BUREAUCRAT

We have looked into the careers of the robber barons to get some feelings for the roistering atmosphere of the post–Civil War period. Yet it must be apparent that industrialization would never have found its realization under a business elite composed only of Goulds and Fisks. Therefore we must acquaint ourselves with another type of business

---

*Most of Conwell's wealth was channeled into social and educational causes, including the founding of Temple University.

tycoon, typified by a man very different from Jay Gould in his view of the aims of the business enterprise. Gould is a caricature of the worst of the robber baron age; Andrew Carnegie represents the best of it.

Andrew Carnegie

Born in the attic of a cottage in Dunfermline, Scotland—a center of the Scottish weaving industry—in 1835, Carnegie was the son of a hand-loom weaver who had been thrown out of work by the coming of the Industrial Revolution. When Carnegie was thirteen the family emigrated to Allegheny, Pennsylvania. There he worked as a bobbin boy in the textile mills at $1.20 a week; then as a machine wiper deep in a

Andrew Carnegie (1835–1919)

factory cellar at $3 a week—to the end of his days the merest whiff of machine oil could make him deathly ill.

In America Carnegie found the thing that was so noticeably absent in Scotland—opportunity. When the telegraph came to nearby Pittsburgh in 1849, he got a job as a messenger boy. Like the hero in a Horatio Alger story, he came to the office early and left it late in order to watch the operators at work; then at night he studied Morse code until he became a skilled telegrapher himself. In fact he was soon one of the very few operators in the country who could take messages direct from the buzzes of the machine rather than from its printed dots and dashes: people used to drop into the telegraph office to watch him take a message "hot from the wire."

Also as in every Horatio Alger story, luck and patronage played an important role. One citizen who saw Carnegie at work was Thomas Scott, then the local superintendent of the Pennsylvania Railroad, later to become a great railway baron in his own right. In 1853 Scott took Carnegie on as his assistant, and after the young man had gained his trust offered him a chance to buy a $600 interest, ten shares, in a company called Adams Express. Carnegie did not have $60, much less $600, but Scott lent the funds to this young man of "great expectations." Adams Express prospered mightily and soon paid its first dividend. It was a turning point for Carnegie. As he later wrote: "I shall remember that check as long as I live. It gave me the first penny of revenue from capital—something I had not worked for with the sweat of my brow. 'Eureka!' I cried. Here's the goose that lays the golden eggs."[11]

In 1859 Scott promoted Carnegie to superintendent of the western division of the Pennsylvania Railroad at a salary of $1,500 a year. And when Scott became Assistant Secretary of War in 1861, he appointed Carnegie superintendent of military transportation and director of the Union's telegraph communications.

Meanwhile, another goose came his way. Riding the railroad in 1860, Carnegie was approached by a stranger carrying a green bag. The stranger introduced himself as T. T. Woodruff and inquired if Carnegie was connected with the railway. Woodruff then opened his bag and showed Carnegie a small model. It was, in miniature, the first sleeping car. Carnegie arranged for Woodruff to meet Scott, and soon a company was formed in which Carnegie was given a one-eighth interest for his services. Within two years the Woodruff Palace Car Company was paying Carnegie dividends of over $5,000 a year.

Investments now became the center of Carnegie's interest and the means to his initial fortune. The Palace Car Company was followed by an interest in the Keystone Bridge Company, the first successful manufacturer of iron railroad bridges, which were needed to sustain the weight of ever heavier locomotives. Next came a share in the Pittsburgh Locomotive Works; thereafter a share in a local iron foundry that would become the nucleus of Carnegie's steel empire.

By 1868 Carnegie was already rich. Yet, unlike the great majority of his fellow budding captains of industry, he was troubled by his wealth. In a suite in the opulent St. Nicholas Hotel in New York he wrote a memorandum to himself:

> Thirty-three and an income of 50,000$ per annum. . . . Beyond this never earn—make no effort to increase fortune, but spend the surplus each year for benevelent *[sic]* purposes. Cast business forever aside except for others. . . .
>
> Man must have an idol—the amassing of wealth is one of the worst species of idolitry *[sic]*. . . . To continue much longer overwhelmed by business cares and with most of my thoughts wholly upon the way to make more money must degrade me beyond hope of permanent recovery.
>
> I will resign business at Thirty-five. . . .[12]

Odd thoughts for a robber baron! And of course Carnegie did not "resign business." On the contrary, his real business career was soon to begin; everything previous had been a harbinger of what was to come. While vacationing in England he had a chance to see the astonishing new way of making steel invented by Henry Bessemer (we will find out more about that method in our next chapter). Although he had known about this method of making steel for some time, it was not until then that Carnegie became convinced that the day of cheap steel had arrived. Perhaps something about the spectacular volcanic eruption of Bessemer's "converter" appealed to his fiery temperament. Carnegie rushed home and built the largest Bessemer plant in America. It is interesting that the year of his return was 1873, and that the United States was in the throes of the most severe business depression it had ever experienced. But Carnegie was convinced that the future was bright. In addition, because of the depression, he was able to build a large up-to-date mill for $1.25 million, about 25 percent less than the cost in normal times. By 1875 the plant was in production and he was on his way to becoming the most renowned industrial businessman in the world.

The Rise of the Business Manager

Carnegie's career is a corrective to that of Jay Gould in that it gives us a sense of the men and motivations that lay behind the market mechanism. But before we are finished with our study of businessmen, we must pay heed to one extremely significant development of the sixty-year period in which we are interested. This is the gradual emergence of a new "style" of businessman—no longer a robber baron, or even a captain of industry, but a corporate manager, indeed a business bureaucrat.

Sociologist Reinhard Bendix describes him this way:

> Entrepreneurs start firms of their own at some point in their careers; bureaucrats do not. At the climax of their careers entrepreneurs are substantial owners of a firm, while bureaucrats are typically salaried executives. Entrepreneurs sometimes spend parts of their careers as salaried employees, bureaucrats do so invariably and for a major portion of their careers.[13]

Bureaucrats are peculiarly creatures of organizations, and it was inevitable that a business bureaucracy should develop as the size of industry grew. A Lowell cotton mill or a Pittsburgh rolling mill was an operation that could still be housed in a single large shed or in a small complex of buildings, where the owner or his mill foreman could take in the entire works in an hour's tour of inspection. But once a certain size of endeavor was reached, the possibility for direct supervision disappeared and an effective *organization* became essential. By the 1850s Henry Varnum Poor, editor of the *Railway Journal* (and later the founder of the first manuals of statistical information for investors), was tracing the misfortunes of the railroads to the fact that the owners of the roads could not manage them, and that the managers did not own them. What was lacking, in other words, was a managerial element—a group of executives subordinate to the ultimate decisional authority of the owners in matters of grand strategy, but possessing the authority to run complex organizations according to their own expertise.

The First Table of Organization

As we might expect, we find the first efforts to create systems of administration in the largest industry of the times, the railroads. The pioneer of industrial organization was Daniel A. McCallum, a talented engineer and inventor who was asked in 1854 to become general superintendent of the Erie Railroad. (It is ironical that the railroad that would one day belong to the greatest industrial pirate, Jay Gould, was also to be the locus of a profound managerial reorientation.) McCallum's task was to establish a system to assure better accountability of both managers and men. He responded to the challenge eagerly. As he pointed out in his report a year later:

> A Superintendent, if a road is fifty miles in length, can give its business his personal attention and may be constantly on the line engaged in the direction of its details; each person is personally known to him, and all questions in relation to its business are at once presented and acted upon; and any system, however imperfect, may under such circumstances prove comparatively successful.
>
> In the government of a road five hundred miles in length, a very different state exists. Any system that might be applicable to the business and extent of a short road would be found entirely inadequate to the wants of a long one; and I am fully convinced that in the want of a system perfect in its details, properly adjusted and vigilantly enforced, lies the true secret of [the road's] failure; and that this disparity of cost per mile in operating long and short roads, is not produced by any difference in length but is in proportion to the perfection of the system adopted.[14]

To achieve his desired system, McCallum drew up what is probably the first table of organization for an American company—a tree with the roots representing the president and the board of directors, and five branches showing respectively the main operating divisions— engine repairs, cars, bridges, telegraph, printing—plus the service division. On the branches, leaves represented the various local agents, train crews, foremen, and so on. Furthermore, within the smaller units of the system, such as the machine shops, the same hierarchical system prevailed, with duties prescribed for each grade, and the grade of each individual indicated on the uniform he wore.

Orders were to go from roots to leaves, but as economic historian Alfred Chandler points out, "McCallum realized that the most essential communication in his organization was from subordinate to superior rather than vice versa."[15] Thus a continuous flow of upward-rising reports constantly informed the managers as to the day-by-day, and sometimes hour-by-hour, location of rolling stock, or the occurrence of tie-ups or accidents, and provided them with a detailed, regular scrutiny of the costs of operating the system, not alone as a unit, but in each of its numerous constituent parts.

Henry Varnum Poor considered McCallum's work so remarkable that he had the organizational tree lithographed and offered it for sale at one dollar a copy; the tree was reported on in Parliament and was even popularized in the *Atlantic Monthly*. Thus its influence on the development of internal business organization was widespread.*

Organization Enters Business

Other large enterprises soon followed suit by "rationalizing" their own internal structures of command. In *The Inside History of the Carnegie Steel Company,* James Howard Bridge describes the metamorphosis there. Of the early days of the company, he writes:

> While the workings of every furnace and every machine were carefully watched and tabulated, the operations of the greatest machine of all, its brain, were spasmodic, unmethodical, and for the most part unnoted. The Board of Managers met by chance, there being no fixed time for meetings. Consultations and deliberations were conducted in a haphazard way, and often no minutes of them were taken. If an important change was to be made, perhaps a meeting would be called; or it might happen that the managers most interested in it would have an informal meeting at the works, when the matter would be decided. The old books of the various companies often show a gap of several months without an entry.
>
> With the accession of Mr. [Henry Clay] Frick to the headship of the concern, this was promptly changed. A rule was made that the Board of Managers should meet every Tuesday at lunch, and that a full report of their subsequent deliberations should be kept. Similarly, every Saturday at noon, the different superintendents and their assistants, some foremen, purchasing and sales agents and their principal assistants, to the number of thirty or more, met about a larger table, and after lunching together, talked over all matters of common interest.[16]

---

*Curiously, the actual illustration itself has disappeared. The once famous ubiquitous lithograph is today only a memory: no known exemplar exists.

We find the same organizational scaffolding arising elsewhere. In Standard Oil, for example, an elaborate system of committees superintended the various aspects of the company's affairs. Each day at lunch at 26 Broadway their work was coordinated and supervised by the management committee that provided the central guidance for the whole concern. Similarly in the very large merchandising and manufacturing operations of Swift or Armour, of Duke, of Preston (who created a merchandising operation for refrigerated bananas similar to that of Swift's for meat), in the promotion of McCormick's reaper and Singer's sewing machine, the functional requirements for growth and success were first and foremost the creation of effective and smoothly running organizations.

Bureaucrats versus Barons

What relationship did these committee men have to the robber barons, whose presence still dominated the years during which the committees were proliferating? At first they tended to assume subsidiary roles in which their rise to power depended on the patronage of the central figure. Thus Carnegie steadily promoted men like Charles Schwab and W. E. Corey, and J. P. Morgan assisted the rise of Charles Mellen to become "Railroad Lord of New England." Mellen candidly admitted that he wore the Morgan collar, saying after Morgan's death, "I did what I was told."[17] Others, such as H. H. Rogers of Standard Oil, served their terms as organization men and then left to become independent capitalists on their own. Still others rose to high rank and salary, while never quite emerging as leaders in their own right.

But the change induced by the need to administer the larger scope of enterprise did not end with the production of internal bureaucracies. Soon we find that the bureaucracy itself was producing the leading business figures—the route to power had changed from the assumption of capitalist risk to the exercise of organizational expertise. A study of over 1,000 biographies of prominent businessmen shows that only 5 percent of the business leaders born before 1800 rose to success by way of the bureaucratic route; 16 percent of those born between 1801 and 1830; 21 percent of those born in the 1831–1860 period; 29 percent of the group born from 1861–1890, and 48 percent of those born between 1891 and 1920.[18] A study by William Miller of 185 business leaders in the decade 1901–1910 confirms this finding (see table on following page).[19]

AMERICAN BUSINESS LEADERS BY TYPE OF CAREER		
Type of Career	**Number**	**Percent**
Professional (lawyers)	23	12
Independent Entrepreneur	25	14
Family	51	27
Bureaucratic	86	47

Thus by the end of the period we are interested in, *nearly half of the great industrial leaders were products of the organizational structure of industrial enterprise.* The managerial-minded men desired by Henry Varnum Poor had moved from a subsidiary to a primary function, no longer merely assisting the personal aggrandizement of the great barons but now taking into their own hands the direction of the great corporations within which they had climbed to the very top.

Their advent brought with it a change in the character of business leadership. The piratical tactics, the zest for competitive combat, the personal generalship so characteristic of the robber barons were not the style of men who had patiently worked their way up the organizational ladder. The new captains of industry were not practiced in the arts of risk but in the arts of negotiation—80 percent of the bureaucratic business leaders studied by Miller had never in their entire careers headed a company or assumed any significant risk of financial responsibility for their business enterprises. Significantly, they were also less successful financially. Of the 303 leading entrepreneurs studied by Gregory and Neu, only fifty-four were considered millionaires. Hence, despite the lingering presence of a few baronial types, the dominant businessmen of the twentieth century would be men who built organizations, not monuments. Theodore Vail, who guided AT&T; Gerard Swope, who made (but did not start) General Electric; Alfred Sloan, who rebuilt General Motors—all were representatives of an entrepreneurial type very different from the dominant figures of the previous generation.

This is by no means to say that they were less successful as businessmen. Indeed, the very point of the shift in the locus of power was that it reflected a changing attribute of the business system itself. Bureaucratization did not mean the slowing down of industrial growth, but rather its adaptation to an environment in which the buccaneer's mode of operation was no longer the mode best suited to the survival of the system.

What is striking is that the profoundly significant rise of business bureaucracy was rooted in the very period when the robber baron seemed to occupy the center of the stage. Thus, at a time when every American knew the names of the greatest enterprisers of the time, the age was already foreshadowed when no one would know any names except those of the great enterprises themselves.

Notes

[1] Harold C. Livesay, *American Made* (1979), p. 148.

[2] Francis W. Gregory and Irene D. Neu, "The American Industrial Elite in the 1870's: Their Social Origins," in William Miller (ed.), *Men in Business* (1962), pp. 193–211.

[3] Matthew Josephson, *The Robber Barons* (1934), pp. 192–3.

[4] Quoted in Edward C. Kirkland, *Dream and Thought in the Business Community* (1956), p. 40.

[5] Quoted in John Tipple, "The Robber Baron in the Gilded Age," in H. Wayne Morgan (ed.), *The Gilded Age* (1963), p. 36.

[6] *The American Mind* (1950), p. 13.

[7] Charles and Mary Beard, *The Rise of American Civilization* (1933), 2:395.

[8] *North American Review* (February 1889), 141ff.

[9] Quoted in W. J. Ghent, *Our Benevolent Feudalism* (1902), p. 29.

[10] Quoted in Matthew Josephson, *The Politicos* (1938), p. 445.

[11] *Autobiography* (1920), p. 80.

[12] Quoted in Joseph Frazier Wall, *Andrew Carnegie* (1970), pp. 224–25.

[13] *Work and Authority* (1956), p. 229.

[14] Quoted in Alfred Chandler, "Henry Varnum Poor," in Miller (ed.), *Men in Business,* p. 260.

[15] *Men in Business,* p. 262.

[16] (1903), pp. 275–76.

[17] Quoted in William Miller, "The American Business Elite in Business Bureaucracies," in *Men in Business,* p. 290.

[18] Reinhard Bendix, *Work and Authority,* p. 229.

[19] "The American Business Elite," in *Men in Business,* p. 290.

Drake's Well, first U.S. oil well, near Titusville, Pa., 1862

Chapter 9
The Technology of Industrialization

The Rise of Steel

We have become familiar with the men who guided the process of industrialization—barons, captains of industry, and, later, bureaucrats. But we have not yet explored the process itself. We are interested, of course, in the gradual introduction of machines and capital goods throughout American life. But we need to examine the technology of industrialization as closely as we examined the reality of the market mechanism if we are to gain a clear sense of what was happening in the eventful years of our study.

Technical Problems

A good place to begin is with steel, for the age of industrialization can almost be summed up as the age of steel. The reason is that machinery requires steel. You can make machines of wood, as in medieval times, but wood has limited strength. You can make them out of iron, as in the early Industrial Revolution, but iron snaps and bends. Hence from earliest times men have sought to improve iron by heating it, combining it with other materials, or cooking it at high temperatures to make what we call steel—a metal of tremendous strength, resiliency, and versatility.

But the cost of converting iron into steel was tremendous. Steel swords were treasures in medieval Europe, rarities to be handed down from father to son. Moreover, not only was the product extremely expensive, but it could not be made in large quantities. At the time of the American Revolution steel was made in crucibles not much larger than a vase. At the great Crystal Palace Exposition of 1851 a 2½-ton ingot of steel (made by combining the outputs of many crucibles) was a sensation.

The steel bottleneck was broken by an extraordinarily versatile English inventor, Henry Bessemer. Bessemer was an inspired tinkerer who had already made his fortune by inventing a way of using brass to make "gold" paint. Thereafter he became interested in increasing the range and accuracy of artillery by designing a projectile that would spin. The projectile, however, required a rifled gun barrel that would far exceed the strength of wrought iron. Since steel barrels were much too expensive, Bessemer set to work to make his projectile practical by inventing cheap steel.

Bessemer devised a solution of amazing simplicity—once it was discovered.* Instead of refining pig iron into steel by heating its surface, he blew air right through the molten metal. The heat generated by the oxidizing iron kept the iron liquid, and the enormous temperatures rapidly burned out the carbon that made untreated iron brittle. Through the Bessemer process three to five tons of iron could be converted into steel in ten or twenty minutes, compared with the laborious process of heating and stirring and reheating, which used to take a day or more. Meanwhile, as the air shot through the container, a veritable volcano of sparks and fire erupted. Then when the miniature hell subsided, pure steel could be poured out.

That was the process that captured Carnegie's imagination. But it was only the beginning of the new steel technology. When Carnegie built his first plant, its converters held five tons of molten iron. Within twenty-five years they held twenty tons—converters as large as small houses were cradled by immense gantry cranes that raised and lowered and tilted them as easily as sandbox toys. Equally important, machines also performed the operations before and after the conversion into steel. Mechanization began at the mines, where the ore was scraped up by shovels capable of loading a freight car in a few swings. The cars themselves rolled directly into the mills, where a giant dumper picked them bodily off the tracks and cascaded their products into vast bins. Electric cars then hauled the ore to the tops of furnaces ten stories high. Emerging from the converters in a Niagara of

---

*In fact, the process was independently discovered by William Kelly, an American ironmaster. Kelly made the great mistake of keeping it secret.

molten metal, the white-hot steel was sent through a succession of rollers that squeezed the glowing metal thinner and thinner and faster and faster until finished rails shot from the last pair of rollers at speeds of forty to sixty miles an hour.

The Birth of an Industry

The Bessemer process did more than revolutionize the making of steel. As costs fell, steel became the basic building material of a host of other industries. In 1873, steel was selling at over $100 a ton. Although railroad executives badly wanted to replace their iron rails with steel—the iron rails were splintering under the weight of the big new engines—they could not afford to do so at that price. But the Bessemer process reduced the cost of steel dramatically. When Carnegie's new plant (thoughtfully named the Edgar Thomson works in honor of a top official of the Pennsylvania Railroad) began production in 1875, it cut the cost of rails to fifty dollars per ton. Two years later the cost had fallen to forty dollars. By 1885 it was reduced to twenty dollars; by the late 1890s, to twelve dollars. Selling his rails at eighteen dollars a ton, Carnegie made a very large profit and still offered the railroads an unprecedented bargain.

The new low-cost steel did more than open a vast market for steel rails ten or fifteen times stronger than iron rails and lasting twenty times as long. Carnegie soon saw the versatile possibilities of steel and converted another mill from steel to structural shapes. Again he was right. By the mid-1870s steel began to edge iron out as the material used for railroad bridges: in 1879, for instance, the builders of New York's famous Brooklyn Bridge decided to construct the entire middle section of steel. Within a few more years another market opened. The Masonic Temple in Chicago, which was to rise a dizzying twenty stories into the sky, gave rise to an order for 4,000 tons of girder, all to be made of steel.

After steel beams came steel nails, steel wire, steel tubes. Total steel output, which amounted to barely 157,000 tons the year before the Thomson works opened, grew to twenty-six million tons by 1910. Carnegie's plants did not produce all of this steel; Carnegie had formidable competitors, and in our next chapter we will be looking into the problem that this competition caused. But the Carnegie complex of mills, valued at $700,000 when the Thomson works were opened,

The Bessemer process

doubled in value in five years, doubled again in three more years, rose to an official valuation of $300 million by the turn of the century. Indeed, by 1901 Carnegie was producing more steel than was produced in all of Great Britain.

Technology and Growth

How did the business grow? In large part, as we have seen, it grew because the master key of technology opened vast new market demands for a commodity that had previously been too expensive for extensive use. First the 100,000 miles of railroad trackage, as of 1881, was converted to steel; then the 100,000 miles of new trackage laid down in the next decade was built of steel; thereafter the entire national network had to be relaid in a heavier grade of steel rail as locomotives continued to grow in weight. In 1907 the Tennessee Coal, Iron and Railway Company placed an order for 150,000 tons of rail, which was only 3 or 4 percent of the nation's steel output.

The demand for structural steel provided another vast new market. When the Thomson plant opened there was very little demand for steel beams, but within twenty-five years over 2.5 million tons of steel went into girders and plates for bridges and buildings. Steel nails alone took 300,000 tons of output by 1889; steel wire soon approached 1 million tons a year as telephone poles festooned railroad tracks and as barbed wire enclosed hundreds of thousands of farms.

In this process of expansion, the Bessemer method paved the way. Without it we would not have had the steel rails, wires, nails, girders, plates, bolts, needles, screws, and springs that gave us the skyscraper and the steamship, the scalpel and the jackhammer, the train and the sewing machine, the tin can (actually made of steel) and the "tin lizzie" (motor car). Yet it must be clear that steel alone could not have changed the face of America. Industrialization also required power— the electric dynamo, the internal combustion engine, gasoline. It required communication—the telegraph and the telephone, the type-writer and the high-speed press. It required enormous supplies of materials to be wrested from the earth and used as inputs into the production process—sulfur, tin, lead, zinc. It required complex processes that were invisible to the eyes of consumers but indispensable to the production of the goods they bought—of making chemicals, for example, without which rubber tires or photographic film or dyed cloth could not be made.

Industrialization was the sum total of all these technological advances, most of them first invented by some gifted individual like Bessemer and then launched into economic importance under the business generalship of a man like Carnegie. Without the generalship the technology would have lain dormant or would have been diffused only very slowly into the bloodstream of the nation. Carnegie threw into it the force of his dynamic, driving personality. Carnegie once remarked that a fitting epitaph for him would be: "Here lies a man who knew how to get other men to work for him."[1] He pitted one manager against another, paying big bonuses for higher output, shaming laggards with telegrams: "Puppy dog Number Two has beaten puppy dog Number One on fuel."[2] Carnegie recognized no substitute for success; and success meant expansion, expansion—and then more expansion.

THE ECONOMICS OF SIZE

The new technology and the aggressive tactics of the age provided a powerful mixture for economic growth. But they were also a dangerous mixture for economic stability. For the technology and the tactics combined to alter the organizational structure of industry quite as profoundly as it altered its physical configuration.

The table below indicates that change:

IRON AND STEEL FIRMS: 1870 AND 1900		
	1870	**1900**
No. of firms	808	669
No. of employees	78,000	272,000
Output (tons)	3,200,000	29,500,000
Capital invested	$121,000,000	$590,000,000

SOURCE: U.S. Department of Commerce, *Census of Manufactures, 1900, Part IV.*

The Increase in Size

The effect of technology is not immediately apparent in these figures, but it quickly becomes apparent when we relate the number of firms to the figures for employees or output or capital. Then it becomes clear that the thirty-year span is marked by a *dramatic increase in the size of the average enterprise.*

In 1870 the average iron and steel firm employed fewer than 100 men; in 1900, over 400. During the same period, average output per firm jumped from under 4,000 tons per year to nearly 45,000 tons, and the capital invested in an average company rose from $150,000 to almost $1 million. Moreover, these figures understate the "look" of what was going on, because the statistics include numerous small but unimportant firms. We get a clearer picture of the change when we learn that it cost about $156,000 to build a new rolling mill in Pittsburgh at the time of the Civil War whereas a new rolling mill in 1890 cost $20 million.

It was not only in iron and steel that the size of the typical industrial establishment grew. A glass furnace in the 1860s was deemed an adequate size if it had the capacity of six tons. By 1900, an efficient glass furnace had to produce 1,000 tons. Between 1865 and 1885, the typical railroad grew in length from 100 to 1,000 miles. The cost of an oil refinery in the 1850s, when a "refinery" was little more than a shed with distilling equipment, came to less than $500. By 1865, when Rockefeller bought his first refinery, he paid $72,500—a sizable fortune for those days. (By the end of the year that one refinery grossed over $1.2 million!) By 1900 a refinery cost over $1 million.

Thus in nearly every industry we witness a vast increase in size. Already in 1888 a middle-sized railway with headquarters in Boston employed three times as many people and enjoyed six times as much revenue as the state that had created it. By 1891 the Pennsylvania Railroad employed over 110,000 workers. The largest U.S. government employer, the post office, then had only 95,000 on its payroll. In manufacturing, an "enterprise" came to mean not a single modest building but a multiacre complex of structures; machinery grew in size from assemblies that fitted comfortably into a room to constructions that required immense sheds; the work force swelled from troops or companies to regiments and divisions that thronged the streets as they entered or left the factory gate. From one industry to the next, this increase in size varied according to the technology of the product or process, but when we look at the country as a whole, and especially at its industrial core, we cannot mistake the phenomenon of business growth.

The Pattern of Growth

Moreover, the growth of business followed certain common patterns. Much as we have seen in steel, businesses in many fields diversified their products, multiplied their sites, expanded their size of plant. In this way the one-man, one-plant enterprise grew into the bureaucratic organization that we have already studied. And the pattern of growth did not merely involve diversification or geographical extension. Companies grew vertically as well as horizontally, buying up sources of supply or reaching forward to the final sale of their products. The arch-example of successful vertical integration was the oil industry.* Standard Oil began in 1870 as a refining company. Shortly thereafter it expanded "backward" into the actual drilling for oil, and it was also extended "forward" as a direct seller of products such as kerosene to the consumer.

Not every enterprise pushed its vertical integration that far. But in many industries we see an effort to grow in "depth" as well as in "extent." Carnegie's great steel plants, for example, were only the disgorging end of a still larger organization that extended far behind the making of steel to a variety of industrial undertakings that fed into the final steel complex. Behind the Thomson and Homestead and Keystone plants were the famous Lucy and Carrie furnaces for making pig

---

*Of the many *new* industries that emerged after the Civil War, none was more important than oil refining. Although people had been watching crude oil, or petroleum, ooze from the earth for hundreds of years, they did not know how to reach it. The man who proved that petroleum could be drilled for like water was E. L. Drake, a retired railroad conductor. In 1859 Drake began what observers called "Drake's Folly" in Titusville, Pennsylvania. When he had drilled down seventy feet he struck oil. Drake's well yielded twenty barrels of crude oil a day. News of Drake's success brought other drillers to the region. By the early 1860s "wildcatters," as oil prospectors were called, were drilling for "black gold" all over western Pennsylvania. A decade later, the oil fields covered 2,000 square miles of Pennsylvania, West Virginia, and Ohio, and production had soared to forty million barrels. Interestingly, the cost of drilling a well was very modest, about $5,000 throughout most of the post–Civil War period.

iron; and behind them was the enormous Henry Clay Frick Coke Company with its 40,000 acres of coal land, its 2,688 railway cars, and its 13,252 coking ovens; and behind this in turn were 244 miles of railways (organized into three main companies) to ship materials to and from the coking ovens; and then at a still more distant remove were a shipping company and a dock company with a fleet of Great Lakes ore-carrying steamers; and then, at the very point of origin of the steelmaking process, was the Oliver Mining Company with its great mines in Michigan and Wisconsin.

Pittsburgh steel mills, c. 1880–1890

What was the point of this vertical organization? Partly it was an effort on the part of business managers to assure a steady flow of necessary raw materials, or to head off the possibility of being "held up" by some strategically placed railroad or mine company. In part it was also a natural avenue of expansion for companies that were seeking profitable areas for investment but feared to extend themselves further in their own markets. And in part the vertical organization of business expressed the "logic" of a technology that was increasingly knitting the production activities of industrial society into one vast, interconnected process.

The Visible Hand

Surveying these motives and maneuvers, historian Alfred Chandler described the entire process in a vivid phrase. It was, he said, "the visible hand of management [replacing] the invisible hand of market forces . . ."[3] What Chandler meant was that the forces of technology were bringing out ever larger and more rapid flows of production, thereby forcing business units to seek ever wider and deeper forms of organization. They did so because horizontal expansion and vertical integration offered corporate managers the opportunity to *administer* the productive process from start to finish, rather than having to deal with the surprises and possible disruptions of the market as that process moved toward completion.

Thus the vertical integration of Carnegie Steel not only assured the steady physical transformation of ore into finished steel, but also removed the necessity of buying and selling, with all its attendant uncertainties, at each linkage along the way. Without the organization that Carnegie (and other entrepreneurs) built, the raw material would have had to be purchased, and then the shipping services that transported it, and then the equipment that processed it, and so on until the final product was made. *Once vertical integration was achieved, no market forces intruded within the long chain of operations from start to finish.* In this way the visible hand of management replaced the invisible hand of the market.

Changing Structures

Recently, Chandler has described in detail the economic pressures that gave rise to the visible hand, not only among firms in the United States but in Germany and England as well.[4] The first of these was the huge savings in cost—"economies of scale"—yielded by massive machinery and equipment. As the rolling mills and blast furnaces increased in size, the river of output swelled out of all proportion. By the late 1890s a dozen men on the floor of a Pittsburgh rolling mill were able to turn out three thousand tons of steel a day, as much as a mill employing several hundred men forty years earlier. The result, as we have seen, was a dramatic drop in the cost of producing steel.

A second impetus to the rise of managerial organization were economies of "scope"—that is, an ability to widen the range of outputs as the sheer size of enterprises grew. In Germany, for example, dye factories first gained cost-cutting economies of scale similar to those of U.S. steel mills, and then used their vast facilities to broaden their markets with new varieties of dyes. By 1913 the Bayer company alone was producing over 2,000 different chemical products. Last, but by no means least, was the replacement of one-man leadership by elaborate managerial teams. The gigantic enterprises were too ramified in their inner workings, and too complex in their connections with the larger economy to be efficiently, or even effectively, run by a single person or a small group of partners. Enterprises were now the size of small armies, and required, as do armies, not only a single general but generals, each with his staff, and not only clear directives but manuals of rules and regulations. Little by little the era of the boss gave way to that of the business bureaucrat.

Did all this mean that the importance of the market mechanism was thereby lessened within capitalism? Unquestionably it meant that the internal organization of business was becoming more and more organized—planned, if you will—by the very actions of businessmen themselves. But still the market retained its powerful influence in the system. For eventually the rivers of output, now part of an engineered flow, met the sea where other rivers of similar outputs also debouched, and there great battles of competition took place—battles that could not be avoided by vertical envelopment. Later in this chapter, and even more intensively in our next chapter, we will see what were the consequences of this battle of competing commodities.

The Leap Overseas

First, however, we must pay heed to a hitherto unnoticed aspect of business expansion. This was the extension of the expansive thrust of business overseas.

Such expansion typically began with exports. As a firm grew larger, its market expanded from locality to region, from region to the nation. But why stop at the frontiers of a nation? Would not Canadians and Mexicans, English and Germans also consume the goods a firm could produce if it could manage to sell them cheaply enough to cover transportation costs and meet competition abroad? That was clearly the trend by the late 1800s. Between 1870 and 1900, total United States exports tripled from $450 million to $1.5 billion, and, even more significant, the percentage of those exports that consisted of manufactures (rather than agricultural or raw materials) jumped from 15 percent to 32 percent.

Thereafter only one avenue of expansion remained to be explored. This was actual production overseas—that is, the establishment of branches abroad, not to sell goods but to produce them. Thus by 1897 American companies had invested some $635 million abroad—in oil wells, railway ventures, mines, plantations, and—most interesting of all—in manufacturing. By that date $94 million was already invested in foreign factories, such as the giant Singer Sewing Machine factory at Kilbowie, Scotland, as large as the company's largest domestic plant. Because Singer was selling half its output overseas, foreign production, rather than exports, made economic sense. It came to make the same sort of sense to a wide variety of industries, some of which expanded overseas "horizontally" (like Singer), some of which expanded "vertically" (like Standard Oil, seeking oil wells).

Thus from an early date business exerted an expansive thrust that brought the American economy into involvement with economies throughout the world. Moreover this internationalist, "imperialist" impulse was strongly encouraged and supported by American government policy. The Caribbean became an American lake. American troops policed the region to guarantee U.S. security and prosperity. From 1900 to 1917 U.S. Marines were landed in Cuba, Panama, Mexico, Haiti, Nicaragua, and the Dominican Republic. American officials took control of the customs houses to ensure that tariff revenues were properly collected and spent; they renegotiated foreign debts with U.S. banks; and they even ran elections. In 1900 the United States dispatched 2,500 American soldiers to join an international European "rescue" expedition aimed at suppressing the Boxer Rebellion—a Chinese uprising against foreign economic influence in Chinese affairs.

Within a few years American foreign policy would openly be called "Dollar Diplomacy." President William Howard Taft was not reluctant to admit—indeed, to advertise—the close association of American military might and the promotion of American commercial interests. In his annual message of December 3, 1912, Taft spoke of the new diplomacy as "an effort frankly directed to the increase of American trade upon the axiomatic principle that the Government of the United States shall extend all proper support to every legitimate and beneficial American enterprise abroad."

In this book we shall not trace the complex story of the expansion of American economic influence abroad. But at least we can see that the roots of the modern multinational corporations can be discovered almost 100 years ago—and that the pressures for international growth were only the final expression of an expansive process of capitalism whose domestic aspects we are now familiar with.

The Struggle for Market Shares

Now we must return to our central theme—the economic transformation of the country. For we have hitherto only attended the causes of the change in size that marked the post–Civil War years. We have yet to investigate the consequences of that change.

The most important immediate effect was a devastating new form of competition. Competition, we recall, was the disciplinary process of the market system. But this disciplinary effect held true only in a milieu of small firms, none of which could take over the entire market. With the coming of the new technology the nature of this disciplining process altered completely. A firm with great economies of scale—the economist's term for the advantages in cost per unit of output resulting from large-scale production—often had the ability to take away the entire business of a competitor. Competition thus awarded to the more efficient firm* the power not merely to "discipline" the prices of a laggard or overly avaricious firm, but literally to wipe out such a firm.

---

*Economies of scale, it should be noted, are available only to those firms that can afford the equipment needed to achieve them. Between 1850 and 1900 the average amount of capital invested in a manufacturing firm more than doubled, rising from $700,000 to $1.9 million.

Fixed Costs

Moreover, technology changed competition in another way. Typically, the expensive new machines and equipment added to the "fixed costs" of business—a steel mill that put in Bessemer converters, for example, had to pay interest on the money it borrowed to pay for them and had to bear the cost of the depreciation of the new investment. These large fixed costs also served as a powerful stimulus for aggressive business behavior.

Suppose, for example, that a steel plant put in a Bessemer process and thereby incurred new interest and depreciation costs of $1 million per year. Those costs had to be paid whether the plant was running or not. Therefore there was a tremendous temptation, whenever business was dull, to cut prices in order to bring in *some* revenues, even if they were not enough to make a profit. Carnegie put the matter in a nutshell when he said that it cost less to keep the machines running, even when there was no market in sight, than to shut down the factories.

Cutthroat Competition

Thus the growing investment in new technology exerted a powerful inducement to price-cutting as a means of stealing a march on competitors. Price-cutting was all right—until the going got rough and the bigger firms, with more wealth, began to cut prices *below* costs, accepting a loss in order to keep revenues coming in. As Carnegie wrote in 1902, "Political economy says that . . . goods will not be produced at less than cost. This was true when Adam Smith wrote, but it is not quite true today."[5]

Not just in steel, but in virtually all industries with heavy fixed costs—railroads, oil, coal, copper—"cutthroat" price wars repeatedly broke out as producers desperately struggled to find markets for their products when business was slack. By the 1880s fixed costs averaged *two-thirds* of a railroad's total annual cost. "A starving man will usually get bread if it is to be had," said James J. Hill, president of the Great Northern Railway, "and a starving railway will not maintain rates."[6]

As we would expect, this cutthroat competition soon forced smaller firms, with less wealth, against the wall. We can see this tendency if we examine the statistics of the iron and steel industry once again. Notice that there were *fewer* firms in operation in 1900 than in 1870, even though the industry's output had increased enormously. Obviously some firms had grown at the expense of others.

It was not just in iron and steel that dog-eat-dog competition winnowed the ranks of the firms. In 1900, for example, the number of textile mills in the country was one-third fewer than in the 1880s, although textile production was up threefold. In similar fashion, the number of manufacturers of agricultural implements had fallen by 60 percent despite a rapid increase in the use of farm machinery.

We can sum up the change in a sentence: *Competition became a process in which firms struggled for shares of the market.* The result was a desperate contest whose consequences would have profound effects on the workings of the entire economy. We shall trace those consequences in our next chapter. But first, while we are still focused on the role of technology in the economic transformation, we must stop to consider another change, without which the thrust of economic growth would have been expressed in very different fashion. This is the *social technology of organization,* and specifically the development of the organizational form we call the corporation.

THE TECHNOLOGY OF ORGANIZATION

Corporations and Proprietorships

The corporation can be traced very far back into history. The early colonial settlers had corporations for the performance of certain activities, such as charity work and other activities that were associated with the public welfare. These corporations were entities organized by the state or colony—that is, organizations that received a corporate "charter" from the local government permitting them to carry on their business.

But certainly the corporation was very much the exception rather than the rule until well into the nineteenth century. Corporations required the approval of legislatures and therefore entailed a degree of government intervention into economic life that appeared both unnecessary and burdensome to enterprisers in the eighteenth and early nineteenth centuries. The typical enterprise was a proprietorship or a partnership—forms of organization in which the principals of a business "owned" it very much as they owned their private assets, such as their house or other personal effects.

There were obvious conveniences to such a simple mode of establishing a business, but there were also difficulties and problems. For if a proprietorship or a partnership failed, its creditors could sue the owners personally, forcing them to pay any debts of the business from their personal assets. Proprietorships thus exposed their owners to considerable financial risk in case of business failure. Moreover, they were ill-suited to businesses that were expected to last beyond the life of the proprietor, because the enterprise had to be legally reorganized every time its owner or partners died.

Corporate Advantages

The corporation avoided those difficulties. Because it was an entity created by the state, it existed in its own right as a "person" created by law. As such a legal person, the corporation could do anything that a private person could—own, buy, or sell property, carry on business affairs, sue or be sued. But it had two extraordinary features:

1. *The "person" of the corporation did not die when any official or shareowner of the corporation died.*

It went on forever—or at least until the state that issued its charter revoked it.

2. *The corporate person was responsible only for "its" own obligations.*

If a corporation went bankrupt, it met as much of its debts as it could from its own assets, but neither its officials nor its shareowners could ordinarily be asked to pay any remaining debts from their personal wealth.

Corporate Ownership

Clearly the corporation had substantial advantages over proprietorships and partnerships. But who owned it? How did it run?

A corporation today as in the past is owned by individuals who buy "shares" in it. Suppose that a corporation is granted a charter to carry on a business, say in retail trade. The charter also specifies how many shares of stock this business enterprise is allowed to issue. For example, a corporation may be formed with the right to issue 1 million shares. If these shares are sold to individuals at a price of ten dollars each, the original shareholders (also called stockholders) will have put

$10 million into the corporation. In return they will receive stock certificates indicating how many shares each person has bought.

These stock certificates are somewhat like a partnership agreement, although there are very important differences. If someone buys 1,000 shares in our imaginary corporation, he or she will own .1 percent of the corporation. He will have the right to receive .1 percent of all income that it pays out as "dividends" on its stock. He will also be entitled to cast 1,000 votes at the meetings of shareholders that all corporations must hold. In this way a shareholder is very much like a junior partner who was given a one-tenth of one percent interest in a business.

But there are critical differences. As we have already said, a stockholder is not personally liable for any debts that the corporation cannot pay from the money it has taken in from its stockholders or from its earnings. If the company goes bankrupt, the shareholder will lose his investment of $10,000 (1,000 shares at ten dollars), but no one can sue him for any further money. *His liability is thereby limited to the amount he has invested.*

Moreover, unlike a partner, who usually finds it very difficult to sell his shares, a stockholder may sell his shares to anyone he likes, at any price he can get. If our imaginary corporation prospers, he may be able to get twenty dollars for each share. He is perfectly free to sell as many of his shares as he wishes at that price. Moreover, marketplaces for stocks and bonds have developed along with the corporation to facilitate sales of stock. The most important of these markets, the New York Stock Exchange, was organized in 1817. By 1900 over 100 million shares a year were being traded on its floor. *Thus with the corporation came the advantage of a much greater "liquidity" of personal wealth.*

Finally, shares of stock entitle the stockholder to the dividends that the directors of the corporation may decide to pay out for each share. But as a stockholder he is not entitled to any fixed amount of profit. If the corporation prospers, the directors may vote to pay a large dividend. But they are under no obligation to do so—they may wish to use the earnings of the corporation for other purposes, such as the purchase of new equipment or land. If the corporation suffers losses, ordinarily the directors will vote to pay no dividend, or only a small one, to be paid from past earnings. *Thus as an owner of ordinary*

The New York Stock Exchange

*"common" stock, the stockholder must take the risk of having his divi-
dends rise or fall.**

---

*Corporations are allowed to issue bonds, as well as common stock. A bond is different
from a share of stock in two important ways. First, a bond has a *stated value* printed on
its face, whereas a share of stock does not. A $1,000 bond is a certificate of debt issued
by the corporation. It makes the bondholder not a sharer in the profits of the company
but a creditor of the corporation—someone to whom the corporation is in debt for
$1,000.

Second, a bond also states on its face the *amount of income* it will pay to its bondholders. A $1,000 bond may declare that it will pay eighty dollars a year as interest.
Unlike dividends, this interest payment will not rise if the corporation makes money,

Ownership and Control

One last matter is also of significance in discussing the organization of the corporation. The new mode of structuring enterprise brought a development of great moment for the captains of industry and their successors, the business managers and the bureaucrats. It enabled a small group of men to direct the affairs of an enterprise *even if they did not personally own it.*

As we have seen, stockholders are the actual owners of a corporation. But it is obviously impossible for large numbers of stockholders to meet regularly and run a company. Many large corporations have over a million stockholders. Where could they meet? How could they possibly decide what the company should do? Even in the 1870s, how could shareowners of a large railway company have gathered to run their enterprise?

Therefore all corporations are run by boards of directors elected by the stockholders. At regular intervals, all stockholders are asked to elect or reelect members of the board, each stockholder casting as many votes as the number of shares he or she owns. In turn the board of directors appoints the main officials of the corporation—for example, its president and vice-presidents. In turn the main officials hire the rest of the employees.

As a result, a corporation is something like a private government. It has an electorate—its shareholders. It has an elected governing body—its board of directors. It has an executive—its officials. Needless to say, there are very important differences between a government and a corporation, but it is not too misleading to think of corporations as a means of governing the complicated affairs of a business enterprise.

Moreover, as the number of shareowners grows, power tends to drift into the hands of the board of directors and the officials whom it

---

nor will it fall if it does not. Thus there is no element of profit-sharing in bonds, as there is in stocks. However, there is compensation for this. The risk of owning a bond is much less than that of owning a stock. A bond is a legal obligation of the corporation, which *must* pay interest, and which must buy back the bond itself when a fixed term of years has expired and the bond becomes "due." (If it fails to do so, the bond-holder can sue the corporation.) A stock has no such obligations attached to it, and a share of stock never comes "due." No stockholder can sue a corporation if it fails to pay a dividend. Last, bondholders' claims come ahead of stockholders' if a corporation goes out of business or becomes bankrupt.

appoints. Consequently, it becomes extremely difficult to round up enough votes to elect a slate of directors different from the directors in office. Who, after all, has the money and the time to write to a thousand—much less a million—shareowners, recommending a special candidate? Thus boards of directors tend to become self-perpetuating, each year mailing to the company's stockholders a mail ballot (called a proxy) on which are printed the names of their own candidates—usually themselves. Except in unusual circumstances, the shareowners obediently vote the slate that the directors have designated.* It is easier for a shareholder who "wants out" to sell his company shares than to get a new management in place of the old. (This is not to say that the directors are indifferent to stockholders' opinions, for they are not. All directors are concerned about their company's image, especially if they plan to offer more stocks and bonds for sale at a future date.)

Thus power comes to settle in the hands of a board of directors whose members may own only a tiny fraction of the total outstanding stock of the company. We do not have statistics for the early years of corporate activity, but in 1929 the board of directors of the United States Steel Corporation held in all only 1.4 percent of the company's stock. In contrast, in 1900 Andrew Carnegie had personally owned over half of Carnegie Steel, Ltd. Needless to say, the passing of effective control from the hands of a few wealthy capitalists into the hands of a small group of self-chosen directors further enhanced the change from the captain of industry to the industrial manager.

The Corporation and Economic Growth

The development of the modern corporation did not take place overnight. In Pittsburgh in 1860 there were seventeen foundries, twenty-one rolling mills, seventy-six glass "factories," and forty-seven other manufacturing establishments to be seen, but not a single one of them was incorporated. As late as 1878 in Massachusetts there were only

---

*Once in a while shareholders may receive letters urging them to vote their stock in a certain way. Usually this is when a corporation is the target of a "takeover" attempt—an effort by another corporation to buy enough of its shares to control the company, or even to merge it in its own company. Takeovers are dramatic battles, but they did not stir up the corporate world in its early days because, as we shall subsequently see, corporations were not yet legally authorized to buy stock in other corporations.

520 businesses organized as corporations out of 11,000 manufacturing enterprises, but those 520 corporations already produced one-third of all the state's manufacturing output. By the turn of the century, 70 percent of the industrial labor force worked for corporations and two-thirds of the nation's industrial output was the product of incorporated enterprise. As we will see in our next chapter, the legal powers and flexibility of the corporation changed considerably as various state legislatures altered the requirements for corporate charters. But we can already understand how this enormously important development in social technology assisted in the growth of the economy.

To the robber barons and the captains of industry the corporation offered immediate advantages. The corporation limited their personal financial risk and increased their liquidity—that is, their ability to raise cash by selling their stock. Therefore their ability to move into and out of businesses was vastly increased. The possibility of steering the policy of a large enterprise without necessarily owning a majority of its shares was still another gain for them.

More important in terms of economic growth was the possibility for successful businesses to tap a source of capital that would have been impossible to reach without the limited liability and high liquidity of stocks and bonds. In the early days of enterprise, businessmen had to look to their own resources, or to those of capitalists at home or abroad, to raise the money needed for their operations. Once the market for stocks and bonds was organized, a whole new layer of capital became available among small merchants or moderately well-to-do citizens who were eager to share in the rising fortunes of the great railways and major companies, or who simply wanted a chance to "play the market" in the hope of getting rich quick. Indeed, many of the early railroads were financed by sales of stock to small stockholders.

Fortunately for the captains of industry there was an enormous pool of capital that was available to underwrite industrial expansion in these years. During the last half of the nineteenth century, as a consequence of their increasing real incomes, Americans began to set aside a larger share of their revenues as savings. Before the Civil War, households and businesses channeled about a seventh of their receipts into savings and investment—that is, into the building of new capital. By the 1870s that share had more than tripled.

To put this money to work, a host of new financial institutions emerged—savings banks, commercial banks, life insurance companies, investment houses—to serve as intermediaries between the investors and the corporations. By 1880 well over two million depositors had placed roughly $819 million in savings banks. Two decades later depositors exceeded six million and funds fell just short of $2.5 billion. Because of the role they played in capital formation, financial intermediaries soon became essential for economic expansion. Like the businesses they served, they were themselves incorporated enterprises.

A last, but important, source of capital was foreign investment. Between 1870 and 1900 foreign investment in the United States rose from $1.4 billion to $3.6 billion. Most of this foreign money, writes economic historian Stuart Bruchey, "went into municipal and other local bonds, and into railroads and public utilities, although a few manufacturing firms were also among the recipients."[7]

The Corporation and Capitalism

The corporation was therefore an indispensable adjunct to the machine technology. It was a social invention every bit as powerful as the technical inventions it controlled. To put the rise of the corporation into Fernand Braudel's organizing framework, we can say that the corporation represented a development of economic life that was the cause of vast changes both in material life and in the dynamics of capitalism.

Without the possibilities of management and discipline brought by the corporation—a discipline that extended from managerial heights down to the factory floor—the dazzling advances in speed and volume of output never could have been achieved. Without the vast market for capital that the corporation brought into being and then tapped, the extraordinary increase in physical capital never could have been financed. And without the organizational focus of creative energies that the corporation made possible, the accumulation of capital on so vast a scale never could have taken place. Thus the corporation changed the pace and the dynamics of capitalism as dramatically as it changed the pace and dynamics of business life, for capitalism is, in fact, the larger shape of historical change that emerges from the business process itself.

Notes

[1]David Brody, *Steelworkers in America: The Nonunion Era* (1960), p. 48.

[2]Quoted in J. H. Bridge, *The Inside History of the Carnegie Steel Company* (1903), p. 113.

[3]*The Visible Hand* (1977), p. 121.

[4]*Scale and Scope: The Dynamics of Industrial Capitalism* (1990).

[5]*The Empire of Business* (1902), p. 154.

[6]Quoted in Thomas Cochran and William Miller, *The Age of Enterprise* (1942), p. 141.

[7]*Growth of the Modern American Economy* (1975), p. 87.

Standard Oil gas station, New Jersey, 1927

Chapter 10

FROM TRUST TO
ANTITRUST

Thus far we have examined particular elements of the industrialization process—the evolution of the businessman who was its main human agency, and the development of the technologies that were its most powerful material agencies. Now we must put these elements together, watching what happened as the aggressive drive of the business search for profit combined with the new industrial techniques and the new forms of social organization.

THE SPIRIT OF THE AGE

A good way to begin is to put ourselves into the business frame of mind of the late nineteenth century. We tend to think of those years as a time of easy money-making, when everyone prospered and businesses grew effortlessly from small firms into large enterprises.

But that is not at all how things looked to the businessmen of the time. The "Gilded Age"* was a period of extreme business uncertainty. Periods of prosperity were interrupted by long and frequent stretches of business depression. Indeed, of the twenty-five years between 1873 and 1897, fourteen were viewed by contemporaries as times of recession and depression.

---

*The phrase comes from the title of a book written by Mark Twain with Charles Dudley Warner. Published in 1873, it captured many aspects of the age—its coarse materialism, its speculative fever, and above all, its corruption. To Twain the 1870s were a base age, covered over with an ornate veneer, but lacking substance and quality. Ever since its publication, Twain's title has become a catchword for post–Civil War America.

Panic and Pain

The businessmen of that time were not mistaken: those *were* difficult years. In the terrible debacle that began in 1873 the general price level dropped by a quarter; the rate of business failures doubled; more than half the nation's steel furnaces and rolling mills were idle; the New York Stock Exchange was even shut down for ten days. "Business since 1873," said the *Commercial and Financial Chronicle* at the beginning of 1879—*six years* after the onset of the recession—"has been like a retreating army on the march."[1] Worse still was the depression of 1893, which has been adjudged the most severe in American history, save only for the Great Depression of the 1930s. On December 30, 1893, *Bradstreet's* wrote: "The business year 1893 promises to go into history with heavier net losses in financial, commercial, and industrial circles throughout the United States than in the more severe panic periods in the past eighty years." Indeed, reflecting on his years in the oil business John D. Rockefeller later wrote:

> [I wondered] how we came through them. You know how often I had not an unbroken night's sleep, worrying about how it was all coming out. All the fortune I have made has not served to compensate for the anxiety of the period. Work by day and worry by night, week in and week out, month after month.[2]

Hence business enterprisers did not enter on their search for profit and expansion confident that all would end well. As a guiding mechanism the market was a harsh pacesetter, urging business into hell-for-leather expansion when the outlook seemed bright, exacting terrible penalties when the outlook changed. The expansion of output and the accumulation of wealth took place, not in an atmosphere of security, but in one of "panic and pain," as historian Edward Kirkland has described it.

The Business Cycle

In a word, economic growth did not proceed along a smooth upward path but took the form of booms and busts. Economists call this irregular wavelike motion the *business cycle:* and they attribute it to the very phenomenon we have seen—a rush of business expansion in one period, normally lasting four to five years, followed by a period of doldrums typically lasting another three, four, or five years.*

These business cycles were not a totally new experience in economic life, for we can trace waves of faster and slower growth back to the years before the Civil War. But the industrialization process brought much sharper swings in prosperity and recession. "In the three decades after the Civil War," write Thomas Cochran and William Miller, "as confident entrepreneurs raced to take advantage of every ephemeral rise of prices, of every advance in tariff schedules, of every new market opened by the railroads and puffed up by immigration, they recklessly expanded and mechanized their plants, each seeking the greatest share of the new melon. The more successful they were in capturing such shares and the more efficient they were in promptly satisfying the new market, however, the greater was the number of buildings and machinery left idle when the new market approached the saturation point and the rate of expansion declined."[3]

But the business cycle was more than just the cause for "panic and pain." It was also a prime factor in that concentration of business in fewer hands that we noted in our last chapter. During the years of panic and depression, many smaller, weak firms went under, and bigger, rich firms survived; so that when the cycle was over and the forward movement resumed, the new (and usually larger) volume of production was lodged in a smaller number of firms than before. And then, quite independent of the cycle, the bigger and more aggressive firms pursued expansive strategies of the kind we have seen, forcing competitors to the wall and further accelerating the "concentration" of industry.

Competition and Combination

Thus the struggle for markets brought fear in its wake. "Competition is industrial war," wrote a large manufacturer of envelopes in 1901. ". . . [U]nrestricted competition, carried to its logical conclusion, means

---

*Actually, there is more than one cycle in the pattern of growth. Statisticians identify at least three different cycles: a short one, of one to three years' duration, commonly associated with swings in inventories; a very long cycle of about twenty years, probably the result of swings in housing construction and household formation; and the "regular" seven-to-ten-year cycle we mention above.

death to some of the combatants and injury for all. Even the victor does not soon recover from the wounds received in combat."[4]

The Pittsburgh *Commercial,* a newspaper concerned with the oil industry, bemoaned "a ruinous competition between refineries, by which all parties have lost money."[5] Even the Social Darwinists, who extolled the virtues of the competitive struggle, felt the strain was too much: "The struggle for existence and survival of the fittest is a pretty theory," said George W. Perkins of the Chicago, Burlington and Quincy Railroad, "but it is also a law of nature that even the fittest must live as they go along."

An obvious response to the anxiety and threat of cutthroat competition was for the firms in a given industry to get together and to agree not to undercut one another—to "live and let live." From pre-1865 days—indeed, back to colonial times—this had been a constant aim of businesses in many fields, who formed "pools"—informal agreements on prices—to avoid their suicidal race for markets.

In 1876 the Cleveland *Gazette* described how a pooling arrangement worked on a local steamboat route:

> The object of the pool line (so called because each boat is required to put up a certain amount of its receipts—about 45 percent—each trip into the hands of the treasurer, when it becomes the property of the line) . . . is to maintain a regular rate on freights at Cincinnati and all points on the river, to, and including, Cairo.
>
> . . . In case of opposition, the pool boat on "berth" will take freight at figures so low that the opposition will lose money, and the regular boat's rate is made up to the established rate out of the pool's fund. . . . After 60 days a division of the pool money is made, retaining 20 percent of the whole amount to maintain organization. The assessment of the pool is very heavy . . . so that it does not take long to get enough money on hand to make all boats "stick," for, if they do not live up to their agreement, they forfeit all the money they have paid into the pool.

By the 1880s there was a cordage pool, a whiskey pool, a coal pool, a salt pool, and endless rail and other pools. For the growing scale of individual firms provided a strong new impulse to avoid the mutual bloodletting of cutthroat competition. As fixed costs grew, the incentive to take in business at any price was often irresistible.

Yet, none of the pools worked. As soon as business worsened, the need to assure revenues led one firm after another to reduce its prices.

At a meeting of railway managers called to agree on a schedule of freight rates, the president of one railroad slipped out during a brief recess to wire the new rates to his company so that it could be the first to undercut them. "I suppose they will cheat," sighed one railroad executive, "but we can stand a great deal of cheating better than competition."[6]

Trusts and Mergers

The basic reasons that pools could not prevent all-out competition was that they were illegal. A long tradition in English and American law forbade *contracts* in "restraint of trade." Therefore no company could sue another for breaking its "gentleman's agreement."

The failure of the pools did not, however, bring to an end the search for a means of enforcing price discipline. It merely turned that search in a new direction—a direction happily provided by the growing predominance of the new corporate means of organizing business. For the corporation was soon discovered to offer a highly effective way of avoiding the internecine economic wars that upset the business community.

The first businessman to benefit from the new method was John D. Rockefeller. Rockefeller was born in Richford, New York, in 1839. After making a modest fortune in the grain and meat business in Cleveland, he decided to go into the oil business. Rockefeller was an extraordinary businessman. Those who worked with him could not help but admire his decisiveness, his sureness of touch, and his infinite resourcefulness. Rockefeller knew how to fasten upon and make the most of the opportunities that were presented to him. When his inner clock told him that the time was ripe, he was capable of acting with a speed, an authority, and, if it was needed, a ruthlessness that never failed to impress his subordinates.

Rockefeller was a deadly competitor. He forced railroads to give him rebates on his huge oil shipments. He sold below cost in particular communities to steal business from local refiners. Then he gave the refiners a choice: sell out to Standard Oil or face destruction. He also paid bribes to informers to gain information about his competitors' activities.

Because he detested waste, Rockefeller kept close track of every aspect of Standard Oil's complicated affairs. His plants were so

John D. Rockefeller (1839–1937)

efficient that he could undersell competitors and still make enormous profits.* Rockefeller's principal objective was to combine all the refineries in the country into one supercompany. Then the industry could develop in a safe, orderly manner. The architect of Rockefeller's supercompany was Samuel C. T. Dodd, the chief counsel of Standard Oil. Dodd saw that the corporation, with its control vested in a small number of directors, provided a legal means of achieving what could not be done under the common law. His brainchild was the trust—a legal arrangement under which stockholders in a corporation gave their stock to a central board of directors "in trust." The board members were authorized to vote the stock as they wished, while the dividends on the stocks continued to be paid to the shareholders, who had surrendered their stock for trust certificates.

In 1882 Dodd established a trust for Standard Oil that permitted its board of directors to control the overall policies of forty corporations from Standard's headquarters in New York City. Soon the trust idea spread to other industries: there was a sugar trust, a cottonseed oil trust, and a dozen more. By the late 1880s, trusts were a well-nigh ubiquitous feature of industry, much talked about in the press. One commentator said that an average citizen was born to the profit of the milk trust and died to the profit of the coffin trust.

The voting trust was, however, only a stepping stone to a still more effective means of avoiding competition. This was the corporate merger, a very simple device by which one corporation bought up the stock of another, thereby winning control of its price and other policies. Why was such an obvious means not used before? The principal reason was that corporations were not at first allowed by their charters to own stock in other companies. Then in 1889 New Jersey amended its incorporation laws to make mergers possible, and businessmen quickly took advantage of the new law.

Morgan and U.S. Steel

One such businessman was John Pierpont Morgan, the dominant (and domineering) figure of finance at the turn of the century. Morgan lorded over the financial world with a passion for order and a fierce hatred for the financial havoc that competition brought. He also had a

---

*In 1892 Rockefeller's fortune was reported as amounting to $815,647,796.89.[7]

shrewd eye for the profits that could be made by merging warring corporations into one giant firm and then selling the stock of the new giant for more than the combined values of the corporations that comprised it. "I like a little competition," he was quoted as saying, "but I like combination better."[8] Between 1892 and 1902 Morgan was instrumental in merging competitive firms to create such new giant corporations as General Electric, American Telephone and Telegraph, and International Harvester. But the capstone of his career was the formation of the United States Steel Corporation, the first billion-dollar company in American history.

One evening in 1900 Morgan was invited to a dinner of leading industrialists, where Charles Schwab, the dynamic young operating president of Carnegie Steel, sketched out his vision of a unified steel

J. P. Morgan (1837–1913)

industry. We have already mentioned that Carnegie had competitors. Other capitalists had also formed Bessemer-based operations that fought Carnegie in every aspect of his operations. There was the American Can Company, American Steel and Wire, Federal Steel, National Steel, National Tube, American Bridge—a whole regiment of steel-producers. Schwab painted the picture of an industry rid of this competitive duplication of factories and mills, guided by a single great corporation charged with the orderly development of American industrial power. Needless to say, such a vast steel corporation would also be immensely profitable.

Morgan's imagination was kindled. He took Schwab aside and plied him with questions about his absent master. On what terms would Carnegie sell his interests? What companies would be inside the new supercorporation; what ones could safely be left outside? In turn Schwab conferred with Carnegie, and the veteran steel-maker, tired of business, agreed on a price for selling out to Morgan: $492 million, of which $250 million would go to Carnegie, the rest to his partners. Morgan looked at the scrap of paper on which the number was scrawled and brusquely said: "I accept."

Morgan then set about acquiring the other firms he needed for his supercorporation. One of them was American Steel and Wire, controlled by John Gates, a swashbuckling robber baron whose latest scandal had been to risk a million dollars on the turn of a single card. (He lost.) Gates was reluctant to sell. At last Morgan stormed into his office, pounded on the table, and, fixing Gates and his associates with his fierce eyes, said, "Gentlemen, I am going to leave this building in ten minutes. If by that time you have not accepted our offer, the matter will be closed. We will build our own wire plant." Gates capitulated.

The firm assembled by Morgan consisted of Carnegie Steel and its eight largest competitors. It had a capacity of two-thirds of the nation's steel castings and ingots. It embraced every aspect of steel-making from ore beds to finishing plants. It had 156 major factories. It was the largest industrial company the world had ever seen, and the wealthiest. For Morgan sold the shares of the new United States Steel Corporation for $1.4 billion. Of this enormous sum, perhaps $700 million was "water." The shares were bought at their inflated price only because Morgan's prestige convinced investors that their value was real.

THE MERGER MOVEMENT

What Morgan brought to pass in steel was also rapidly coming about—often at Morgan's doing—in many other industries. For beginning in 1898, the merger device was producing a tremendous wave of amalgamation.

The effect of the merger wave was to change the structure of American industry almost overnight. In 1865 most industries were competitive, with no single company dominating any field. By 1904 one or two giant firms—usually put together by merger—controlled at least half the output in seventy-eight different industries. In the locomotive field nineteen firms had shared the market in 1860. Two merger-created firms ruled the roost in 1900. In the biscuit and cracker market— formerly a scatter of tiny companies—one giant merged firm, the National Biscuit Company, controlled the great preponderance of the industry's market. In oil, the Standard Oil Company, under the shrewd and aggressive leadership of John D. Rockefeller, grew from insignificant beginnings in the 1860s to a supercorporation that owned well over 80 percent of the nation's refining capacity by the turn of the century.

Another way of looking at the transformation is to note the change in sheer size. In 1865 it is doubtful if there was a single firm in the

THE MERGER WAVE		
Year	Number of Firms Bought	Capitalization of Firms Bought (in $ millions)
1895	43	40.8
1896	26	24.7
1897	69	119.7
1898	303	650.6
1899	1208	2262.7
1900	340	442.2
1901	423	2052.0
1902	379	910.8
1903	142	297.6
1904	79	110.5

United States worth $10 million. In 1896, except for the railroads, there were not a dozen $10-million companies. In 1904, after the merger wave, there were 300 such firms which together owned $20 billion—over 40 percent of all the industrial wealth of the nation. In 1913, two banking groups, one controlled by Morgan and the other by Rockefeller, held thirty-four directorships in twelve corporations with an aggregate capital of more than $22 billion. As two of America's leading economists wrote in 1912, "If the carboniferous age had returned and the earth had repeopled itself with dinosaurs, the change in animal life would scarcely have seemed greater than that which has been made in the business world by these monster corporations."[9]

The Results of Combination

Did the trusts achieve their end? Yes and no. Investigating the course of steel prices from 1880 to 1901, one scholar has discovered that the monthly average price per ton for standard Bessemer rails ranged from $16.50 to $85. For the next fifteen years, following the merger that produced the United States Steel Corporation, they sold for $28 a ton without deviation, save for occasional rush orders. During this period steel prices still fluctuated considerably, and once or twice the price of pig iron rose *above* the price at which rails sold. But rails, which were the main focus of cutthroat competition, held firm. The perils of competition had been effectively eliminated.

In oil, farm machinery, lead, biscuits—in short, in most heavily concentrated industries—one large corporation now emerged by tacit consent as the price-maker, the remaining firms following closely or exactly in its tracks.

We should note, however, that price leadership did not necessarily ensure price stability, despite the extraordinary results in steel rails. Indeed, according to a study prepared by the National Industrial Conference Board in 1929, the trusts as a whole did not diminish the scope of price swings over the business cycle. But we must remember that the purpose of the consolidation movement was not to counteract the business cycle (which was then regarded as beyond the intervention of man), nor was it even to raise prices "unduly." Above all, *the aim of consolidation was to remove the threat of the unrestricted price competition that proved so dangerous for a world of large-scale enterprise.*

Viewed in this light, the combination movement was a considerable success, for it did mute price competition. Yet, surprisingly, the merger movement never succeeded in wholly stamping out competition by other means. In fact, one of the most interesting findings about the trusts is that the shares of the market commanded by the great corporate giants steadily declined, as smaller and more aggressive firms stole business away from the large conservative monoliths, or as new firms were formed to enter the industry. In the following table we see the steady erosion of the market share of the biggest firms over time:

SHARE OF MARKET OF LEADING MERGERS		
	At Time of Merger	**Later Date**
U.S. Steel (1901)	62%	40% (1920)
Standard Oil (1882)	90+	64 (1911)
Int'l. Harvester (1902)	85	64 (1918)
Anaconda Copper (1895)	39	12 (1920)
Am. Can Co. (1901)	90	50 (1913)

Thus the trusts were a mixed success. They did mitigate the severity of the price competition that had demoralized business for so long. They did not, however, secure monopoly positions, or even commanding shares of the markets, for the biggest firms. And perhaps most important of all, by their very efforts to achieve economic success, the trusts brought upon themselves the political animus of the nation. Let us next follow that development.

THE ANTITRUST MOVEMENT

Popular Opposition to the Trusts

Grass-roots opposition to the trust movement was a sentiment of long standing. What historian Arthur Dudden has called a "simmering ferment of anti-monopolistic ideas" was discernible through most of the late nineteenth century: "The corners and pools of the eighteen sixties and seventies," he wrote, "the oil trust of the seventies together with its imitators of the eighties, and the multitudinous mergers and consolidations throughout, were assailed by their detractors not only as particular evils but as overall manifestations of foreboding portent."[10]

These antitrust feelings were at first of little importance. Then, as the railway pools began to squeeze the small businessman and the farmer, voices began to rise in protest. A resolution passed in 1873 by the Illinois State Farmers Association read:

> Resolved, that the railways of the world, except in those countries where they have been held under the strict regulation and supervision of the government, have proved themselves arbitrary, extortionate, and as opposed to free institutions and free commerce between states as were the feudal barons of the middle ages.[11]

Labor organizations, such as the Knights of Labor and the American Federation of Labor, also feared the rise of mighty concentrations of business power: "The great corporations, the trusts, with their capital, their machinery, special privileges and other advantages, are overwhelming the individual, reducing him to the condition of a mere tool, to be used in their great undertakings for their individual profit, and of no more consequence than a dumb piece of machinery," wrote John Hayes of the Knights.

And by no means least influential, a group of journalists began to call attention to the practices of the robber barons. Probably the most important critic of monopoly in these years was Henry George, a San Francisco journalist. His *Progress and Poverty,* published in 1879, was not merely a tract for the times but a major text in American social criticism. The central question to which George addressed himself was one that Americans are still wrestling with: why is economic progress accompanied by poverty? George blamed poverty on the fact that private individuals could own advantageously situated land. Because this land was strategically located, landlords could charge exorbitant rents for their property, even if they had not done anything to improve it. This was immoral, George argued. Land was valuable only because people lived on it and used it. An acre in an empty desert was worthless. Expressed differently, society was the true creator of wealth. The rent that landlords charged for unimproved land should be taken by the government and used for public purposes. This single, massive tax on land, George believed, would destroy monopolies, distribute wealth more equitably, and eliminate poverty.

In *Wealth Against Commonwealth,* published in 1894, Henry Demarest Lloyd excoriated big business in general and the Standard Oil Company in particular. Lloyd's book, detailing the transgressions of the great oil company, was the first of a series of what would later be called "muckraking" exposés that would do much to mobilize outrage against the tactics of business aggrandizement and the general indifference, not to say contempt, evidenced by business for the public.*

As a consequence of all these protests, public sentiment began to change. Significantly, whereas the Anti-Monopoly Party polled but 173,000 votes in the election of 1884, four years later even the Republican Party declared itself against "all combinations of capital organized in trusts," and Democratic President Grover Cleveland asserted that the people were being "trampled to death" beneath the iron heels of the trusts. Clearly a new political theme was being sounded; as Henry Demarest Lloyd wrote, "If the tendency to combination is irresistible, the control of it is imperative." By 1890 twenty-one states had attempted to curb monopoly with antitrust statutes of varying kinds.

The Regulation of Enterprise

The question was: What to do? By the early 1890s one remedy had been tried and was found wanting. Many states had gone to court to sue the trusts on the grounds that they were "restraining" trade—Louisiana sued the cottonseed trust, Nebraska the whiskey trust, New York the sugar trust, Ohio the almighty oil trust. Yet, although the states generally won their court cases, the trusts were not so easily

---

*Muckrakers were investigative journalists who dramatized the need for reform by casting a searching light on dark corners of American life. These writers dug into public records and interviewed anyone with knowledge about whatever subject they were investigating. They were given their name by Theodore Roosevelt, who compared them to the man with the muckrake in John Bunyan's *Pilgrim's Progress,* whose attention was so fixed on "the filth of the floor" that he could not notice the "celestial crown" that was offered him in exchange. Despite the implication, "muckraker" became a term of honor.

vanquished. As we have seen, they abandoned the "trusteeship" idea, only to achieve the same dominating effect through mergers and other corporate devices, or simply by moving their headquarters from a state in which they were being attacked to another, more obliging one.

It was the failure to achieve control over the trust at the state level that brought pressure on Congress to intervene at the federal level. The first target was the railroads, now accused by merchants all over the country of charging exorbitant rates. One newspaper in Sacramento, California, for example, published a schedule of freight rates between that city and a number of points in Nevada, showing that far lower rates had been charged by wagon-teams before the railroad was built! In addition, there was growing outrage at such practices as charging more for some short hauls than for long hauls, or for the nefarious granting of secret rebates or kickbacks to favored shippers.

The Interstate Commerce Commission

In a mood of indignation Congress passed the Interstate Commerce Act of 1887, establishing the first federal *regulatory agency,* the Interstate Commerce Commission. As its title makes clear, the commission was limited to the regulation of railroad rates in interstate commerce, for the Constitution had specifically provided Congress with the authority only to regulate commerce between the states. The act declared that railroad rates must be "reasonable and just," that railroads had to publish their rate schedules, and that most of their shadier practices, such as granting rebates, were unlawful.

The ICC had immense obstacles to overcome. To begin with, the law itself was obscure: What was a "reasonable and just" freight charge? In its *First Annual Report,* the Committee stated:

> Of the duties devolved upon the Commission by the act to regulate commerce, none is more perplexing than that of passing upon complaints made of rates as being unreasonable. The question of the reasonableness of rate involves so many considerations and is affected by so many circumstances and conditions which may at first blush seem foreign, that it is quite impossible to deal with on purely mathematical principles, or on any principles whatever, without a consciousness that no conclusion which may be reached can by demonstration be shown to be absolutely correct.[12]

Yet another difficulty the commission had to contend with was the flood of requests for action that it received. Over a thousand cases were presented to its tiny staff in its first few months of existence. And not least, the ICC had no way of enforcing its decisions except to sue in the federal courts.

Taking advantage of the confusion, the railroads paid little attention to the commission, often continuing to charge their high rates even after the commission had directed them not to. Four or five years later, when the erring railroad was finally brought to court, the roads generally gained from judicial interpretations of the law that gave the benefit of every doubt to the railroads and that regarded the new federal authority with grave suspicions. Of sixteen cases brought to the Supreme Court between 1887 and 1905, fifteen were decided in favor of the railroads. One railroad executive announced that "there is not a road in the country that can be accused of living up to the rules of the Interstate Commerce Law."[13]

In time the situation changed. The powers of the ICC were gradually expanded and its staff enlarged. By the beginning of the twentieth century the commission was effectively regulating the rates on virtually all rail transportation, and no railroad dared flout its rulings.* Ironically, by the midpoint of the twentieth century, the ICC had become the *protector* of the railroads, establishing freight schedules for trucking that prevented this new, aggressive form of freight-handling from undermining the dwindling profits of "their" industry. This conversion of an agency charged with the suppression of abuses into an agency concerned with the protection of its client industry has since been many times repeated, as the ICC model was extended into other fields—banking, food inspection, communications, drugs, airlines.

The Sherman Act

Regulation, however initially ineffective, was not the only sign of a gradual swing of public sentiment against the big corporations. Equally important was the growing movement that we call

---

*This was largely due to the passage of the Hepburn Act (1906), which, among other powers, gave the ICC the authority to inspect the books of railroad companies and reduce unreasonable rates on the complaint of a shipper, subject to the review of federal courts.

"antitrust"—a movement designed to break up the big companies and to restore competition rather than to restrain it.

Like the simmering discontent against the trusts because of their abuse of power, there had long existed an undercurrent of mingled fear and dislike directed against them sheerly because they represented a threat to the ideal of democratic equality. A strain of "populist," anti-wealth, anti-big-business ideas had always tinctured American thought, even in the years of all-out celebration of wealth. Gradually that strain received popular support as the trusts waxed fat and the books of the muckrakers began to make a deep popular impression. By 1890 the political feeling had swelled to such an extent that a bill directed against the trusts—the Sherman Antitrust Act—passed Congress without a murmur of dissent: 52 to 1 in the Senate, unanimously in the House.

The Sherman Act declared that "every contract, combination in form of trust or otherwise, or conspiracy in restraint of trade among the several States . . . is hereby declared to be illegal," and "that every person who shall monopolize or attempt to monopolize or combine or conspire with any other person to monopolize any part of trade or commerce among the several States . . . shall be deemed guilty of a misdemeanor." This surely seemed a radical departure for a nation that had always extolled its business leaders and admired their exploits. How did such a bill pass through a highly conservative Congress whose Senate was called—with good reason, as we have seen—"The Millionaires Club"?

Looking backward we can see a number of explanations. The mood of the country was strongly "antitrust," and the bill satisfied the need of Congress to go to the electorate and declare that it had passed a bill to punish the trusts. Then, too, the bill did not really break new ground in its economic philosophy but merely moved the long-standing disapproval of monopoly from the exclusive concern of the states to the mixed concern of the states and the federal government. Another reason was the genuine desire of Congress to "do something" about the trusts, although no one was able to say exactly what should be done: the bill in its general condemnation of monopoly seemed as good an answer as any. And then there was the knowledge that the actual impact of the law would depend on the interpretation of the judiciary, which in turn could be depended on for a conservative reading of the law.

Business Ignores Antitrust

Certainly Congress was correct in not expecting the law to make a great change. Most business leaders simply ignored it. Testifying before the Stanley Committee investigating the United States Steel Corporation, Carnegie was nonchalant about the Sherman Act: "Do you really expect men engaged in an active struggle to make a living at manufacturing to be posted about laws and their decisions, and what is applied here, there, and everywhere?" Pressed further, as to whether his lawyers might not have advised him about the law, he answered: "Nobody ever mentioned the Sherman Act to me, that I remember."[14] Carnegie's indifference must have been widespread, for, as we have seen, the merger movement gained its greatest impetus in the decade *following* the passage of the Sherman Act. Thus if the act was supposed to halt the growth of trusts, it clearly failed.

The failure was traceable in large part to the extremely conservative interpretation that the Supreme Court put on the law, as expected. In the first important case in 1895, *U.S.* v. *E.C. Knight Co.,* involving the American Sugar Company's control over 98 percent of the nation's refining capacity, the judges decreed 8 to 1 that the company's mergers concerned *manufacture* and therefore did not fall within the scope of interstate *commerce.* How the trust could have disposed of all that sugar without selling it in many different states the high court did not say. In the face of such decisions, we can understand why a humorist of the times wrote, "What looks like a stone wall to a layman is a triumphal arch to the corporation lawyer."

Following the Court's conservative interpretation, the Sherman Act lay dormant, having virtually no effect in breaking up the trusts or slowing down the process of business amalgamation. Then, in 1902, the act was rejuvenated. In that year President Theodore Roosevelt ordered his Attorney General to prosecute the Northern Securities Company under the Sherman Antitrust Act. The Northern Securities Company was a corporation formed by J. P. Morgan to control the Northern Pacific, the Great Northern, and the Chicago, Burlington and Quincy railroads, giving it a monopoly of western transportation. The Court dissolved the Northern Securities Company in 1904, earning for Roosevelt the sobriquet "trust-buster." Roosevelt also initiated a suit against the Standard Oil Company, which was adjudicated under Taft in 1911. Although the Court dissolved the Standard Oil Trust, the Standard

Oil Company of New Jersey promptly reorganized as a holding company (a corporation that owned stock in other corporations) to re-establish direct control over some seventy companies that had been severed from it by the antitrust decision.*

The Effect of Antitrust

Thus, just as in the case of regulation, it is difficult to claim that the immediate aims of the antitrust movement were achieved. Even today, after the Sherman law has been strengthened by other legislation, many economists doubt whether the dynamics of industrial concentration have been much affected by efforts to curb the tendency toward monopoly. Yet, as is also the case with regulation, perhaps it is possible to see the problem from a perspective that does not focus directly on the success or failure of the legislation.

For in retrospect what seems most significant about the Sherman Act or the ICC and its subsequent regulatory agencies is the expression of a new concern on the part of the national government. We have seen how the expansion of business size was intimately related to the whole process of industrialization. During the early years of that process, the change in the texture and scale of business life was a matter of indifference to the national government. Indeed, the government watched with admiration as the captains of industry built a mighty

---

*Roosevelt, it should be noted, never opposed giant corporations because of their sheer size. Indeed, he believed that big corporations were more efficient than smaller ones, and that competition among behemoths in the same field would be dangerous and wasteful. Such companies, he believed, should be allowed to combine and cooperate, but they should not be allowed to use their size or power to tyrannize small producers and the consuming public. To neutralize the power of the great corporations he supported measures to extend the control of the federal government over the national economy, such as the creation of a Bureau of Corporations (1903) to investigate business practices. Only a forceful government could subject big business to a measure of control, he argued—but he continued to apply subjective standards to differentiate "bad" trusts that should be subject to control from "good" ones that should not.

On the other hand, what Roosevelt did oppose was the arrogance of big-monied men. This personal resentment became particularly clear during the anthracite coal strike of 1902, when 140,000 miners demanded a pay raise, a shorter workday, and recognition of their union, the United Mine Workers. When the coal operators imperiously refused to negotiate, Roosevelt settled the strike by threatening to use federal troops to operate the mines. The miners won a modest raise and a shorter work day, but the owners did not have to recognize the union. According to Roosevelt, everyone had received a "square deal."

President Theodore Roosevelt exterminating the
"bad" trusts and restraining the "good" trusts

industrial economy; and both state and federal legislatures were generous with help to hasten that process along.

Slowly, however, another view began to manifest itself—a view
quite different from the uncritical approval of business expansion and
private enrichment so characteristic of attitudes at the beginning of the
period of industrialization. In 1890, ex-President Rutherford B. Hayes,
certainly no radical, wrote in his diary about the "wrong and evils of
the money-piling tendency of our country." Theodore Roosevelt,
though deeply concerned about the "socialistic" tendencies of reformers like Henry Demarest Lloyd, nevertheless shared their disdain for
what he called the "malefactors of great wealth": "I am unable to make
myself take the attitude of respect toward the very wealthy men which
such an enormous number of people evidently feel," he wrote. As we
have seen, it was under Roosevelt's presidency that the first efforts
were made to enforce antitrust legislation against the "bad" trusts.

Woodrow Wilson was even more outspoken in his crusade against the trusts. Unlike Roosevelt, Wilson did not believe in government regulation of big business. Rather, he wanted to use the antitrust laws to break up monopolies. This would restore competition, make business more efficient, and release anew the individualism that had made America a rich and powerful nation. "If monopoly persists," he wrote, "monopoly will always sit at the helm of government. I do not expect monopoly to restrain itself. If there are men in this country big enough to own the government of the United States, they are going to own it."[15] Under Wilson the Federal Trade Commission and the Clayton Antitrust Act (both passed in 1914) greatly strengthened the hand of government vis-à-vis the corporation.*

A Final View

How can we sum up this complicated chapter of economic history? It would be wrong to view the tendency to giant size or to monopoly as an indication of evil intentions on the part of business. The captains of industry, seeking to aggrandize their firms by price competition or by merger, were only following the profit incentive that is the legitimate

---

*The Federal Trade Commission was empowered to conduct investigations of huge business corporations. The Clayton Act outlawed interlocking directorates—that is, it made it illegal for directors of one corporation to be directors of other corporations in the same field—and provided that the directors of a company that violated the antitrust laws could be held personally accountable for their actions. In addition, the law stated that labor unions were *not* to be considered "combinations in restraint of trade." This was, of course, a great victory for labor, into which we will look further in our next chapter.

Two other pieces of legislation signed into law under Wilson are worthy of mention. One of these was the Underwood Tariff Act of 1913, which, in addition to lowering the protective tariff, provided for a graduated income tax. This was possible because the Sixteenth Amendment, authorizing federal income taxes, had just been ratified.

Second was the Federal Reserve Act (1913). At the time of its passage the Federal Reserve Act was intended mainly to assure stability and orderliness to the nation's banking system which was then subject only to the regulation of the states. Gradually, however, the Federal Reserve System became a mechanism for regulating the amount of credit (loans) that its member banks could authorize. By the time of the Great Depression in the 1930s, the Federal Reserve System had become recognized as the "monetary authority" of the nation, the central agency responsible for regulating the amount of spending power, mainly in the form of bank deposits, available to the country.

objective of market behavior. Although their tactics were outlandish by present-day standards, their motives were beyond reproach. Rather, we must see the emergence of giant corporations and of trusts and mergers as the natural, even the logical, outcome of this motivation coupled with the new technologies of mass production and corporate organization that we have previously examined.

In a word, mergers (and before them, trusts and pools) sought to accomplish "horizontally" what the integration movement had accomplished "vertically," namely to remove the disturbing influences of the marketplace from the production and distribution of commodities. Mergers, like vertical integrations, were efforts to replace the invisible hand of market forces with the visible hand of managerial administration.

The businessman was not to blame for this turn of events: he was only the agent of economic forces and developments beyond his control. But the businessman was never the only, though he may have been the dominant, figure in the social system. As the reach and power of business organizations increased, other elements within the body politic began to search for effective countermeasures to be applied against the emerging business monoliths. There was only one agency capable of applying those countermeasures—the government. Thus, from many quarters pressure mounted to use the government as a deliberate force to contain or guide or even inhibit business growth.

As we have seen, the application of government power was halting, was at best only partially effective, and was even used, in the regulatory system, to bolster the fortunes of portions of the business world.* This outcome is hardly surprising. The regulation or curtailment of business does not easily accord with the basic beliefs in "free" and "private" enterprise that underlie the capitalist market system. More-

---

*A school of "revisionist" historians, challenging the conventional interpretations of political and economic history, contends that much of the regulatory or antitrust sentiment came from big business itself, eager to establish rules of behavior that would eliminate the smaller concerns nibbling at their markets. Gabriel Kolko has presented the most effective case for this view in *The Triumph of Conservatism* (1963) and *Railroads and Regulation* (1965). His general contention that "big business led the struggle for the federal regulation of the economy" is still under debate. But there is no doubt that some business leaders did cooperate with the government in seeking a means to achieve through legislation what business could not do by itself—namely, to lessen the pressure exercised against major firms by the price and standards-cutting behavior of smaller companies.

over, efforts to interfere with the natural expansive tendencies of business threaten to dampen the expansive forces of the economy itself. A society that depends on the workings of a business system cannot easily interfere with the dynamics of that system.

Yet it would be wrong to conclude this chapter on a note that stresses the unsolved aspects of controlling big business, although that problem is still very much with us. Rather, we should come away with two conclusions:

The first is that the process of economic growth, though lodged mainly within business enterprises, has gradually required the intervention of government—in part to protect the market mechanism from destroying itself, in part to assert the claims of the larger society over the blind workings of that mechanism. The unresolved question is not whether government should intervene, but where, and how far.

The second is that economic growth, which we have hitherto considered mainly as a force for economic expansion, is also a force for profound structural change. With this change come problems for which no immediate or easy social solution may be at hand. More and more, as we proceed with our theme, this disturbing aspect of economic growth will come to our attention.

Notes

[1] Quoted in Norman S. B. Gras and Henrietta Larson, *Casebook in American Business History* (1939), p. 718.

[2] Quoted in Edward C. Kirkland, *Dream and Thought in the Business Community* (1956), p. 9.

[3] *The Age of Enterprise* (1942), p. 139.

[4] Quoted in Gabriel Kolko, *The Triumph of Conservatism* (1963), p. 13.

[5] Quoted in Allan Nevins, *A Study in Power* (1953) 1:96.

[6] Quoted in Thomas Cochran, *Railroad Leaders* (1953), p. 163.

[7] Nevins, *A Study in Power,* p. 613.

[8] Quoted in John Tipple, "The Robber Baron in the Gilded Age," in H. Wayne Morgan (ed.), *The Gilded Age* (1963), p. 26.

[9] J. B. and J. M. Clark, *The Control of Trusts,* pp. 14–15.

[10] Arthur Dudden, "Men Against Monopoly," *Journal of the History of Ideas* (October 1957), 587–88.

[11] Quoted in Jonathan Periam, *The Groundswell* (1874), p. 286.

[12] Interstate Commerce Commission, *First Annual Report* (1887), p. 36.

[13] Quoted in John A. Garraty, *The New Commonwealth* (1968), pp. 119–20.

[14] Quoted in E. C. Kirkland, *Industry Comes of Age* (1961), p. 323.

[15] Quoted in Richard Hofstadter, *The Age of Reform* (1955), p. 231.

Pre-1920 Ford Motor Co. assembly line

Chapter 11
WORKERS AND WORK

The end of our last chapter provides a good beginning for this one. Until now, we have examined economic growth as if it were a process that mainly affected business. This is because business enterprise, as we have seen, was the agency through which the process of growth was expressed and by which the forces of growth were mobilized. Economic growth in a capitalist market system is set into motion by business expansion, and it makes sense, therefore, to focus initially on the individuals, the techniques, and the problems associated with that business effort.

Yet, as our first pages indicated, we mean more by "economic growth" than just the expansion of output that was its most striking result from a business point of view. Growth was also a process that changed American society at every level, bringing new ways of life, new stresses and strains, new difficulties as well as new advantages and improvements. In our next chapter we will look again into some of the social aspects of the process of industrial transformation. But first we must examine an attribute of the changing society that is closely associated with the development of business, though submerged beneath it. This is the effect that economic expansion—specifically, industrialization—exerted on the working men and women whose energies were harnessed within the business system.

THE CONDITIONS OF WORK

Homestead

Let us start by taking a tour of a great new steel mill that Andrew Carnegie built on the banks of the Monongahela River in 1879. When the site was chosen, Homestead, Pennsylvania, was a hamlet of 600 people. By 1892 the population had swelled to 11,000. Almost every able-bodied man and youth worked in the sixty-acre assemblage of sheds—there were 3,800 employees, including the mayor of the town who worked as an assistant roller earning $65 a month. This was a good wage, considerably above the forty dollars per month average earnings of manufacturing workers. And prices were far lower than they are today: One could keep body and soul together on those wages, especially if more than one member of the family worked or if the family had a small vegetable garden or kept a cow.

We do not know what Homestead looked like before the mill was built; in all likelihood it was another sleepy Pennsylvania town, with a few stores, and a generally rural air. By 1892 that rural aspect had vanished. The Monongahela was so polluted with wastes from the mill that it was said no self-respecting microbe would live there (perhaps just as well, since many a typhoid microbe lived in the Ohio River near Pittsburgh). Cinders and dust covered the area—even the trees were gray with soot, except after a heavy rain. Hamlin Garland, a novelist, found the vista depressing:

> The streets of the town were horrible; the buildings poor; the sidewalks were swaying, sunken and full of holes. . . . Everywhere the yellow mud of the street lay kneaded into a sticky mass, through which groups of pale lean men slouched in faded garments, grimy with soot and grease of the mills.[1]

Life was certainly hard in Homestead, and in dozens of industrial towns like it. The men worked every day of the year except Christmas and July 4th, twelve hours each day except for a swing shift every other week when they worked twenty-four hours straight. There were no lunch periods, no shower rooms, only primitive sanitary facilities. When the day was over the men sloshed off the dirt in the same troughs in which they washed their tools and trudged home for an exhausted sleep—perhaps stopping for a drink at one of the many saloons on Eighth Avenue.

Inside the mills a fearful scene greeted Garland's eye. In the furnace room he saw "pits gaping like the mouth of hell and ovens emitting a terrible degree of heat, with grimy men filling and lining them. One man jumps down, works desperately for a few minutes, and is then

Work in a steel mill

pulled up, exhausted. Another immediately takes his place. . . . "[2]
Garland spoke to the men about the heat. They told him he was lucky
he was there in the winter.

A modern historian of the Carnegie mill describes some of the less
arduous jobs as follows:

> Pressure work in the rolling, blooming, and plate mills (as contrasted to
> hot jobs) was cooler but equally nerve-racking, due to the incessant
> vibration of the machinery and the maddening screech of cold saws rip-
> ping through steel. In time the men became hard of hearing. The din
> within the huge sheds forced them to yell to each other all day long.
> They and their clothes were covered with miniscule [*sic*], shiny grains of

steel. They complained about respiratory ailments and drank liquor after work, as one man said, to 'take the dust out of my throat.'[3]

Work was dangerous as well as hard. We do not have precise statistics of industrial safety for those years, but we know that in a single year 195 men were killed in Pittsburgh's iron and steel mills: twenty-two from hot metal explosions, five from asphyxiation, ten from rolling accidents, twenty-four falling from heights or into the pits. Men worked only inches away from white-hot metal; terrible burns were frequent. In the hot departments the steel floors hissed when water was poured on them. In 1893 Homestead alone had sixty-five accidents, seven of them fatal, two necessitating amputations. Not a cent of recompense was paid for most injuries or even for death—not because Carnegie was a mean-spirited employer—on the contrary, "Andy" was admired and even loved by his men—but because the idea of workmen's compensation had not taken hold in American industry.

The United States as a whole had an appalling industrial accident rate, one of the highest in the Western world. Between 1880 and 1900, some 35,000 workers were killed annually and another 536,000 were injured. Coal mining was the most hazardous occupation. According to some estimates, three miners were killed every two days in the anthracite fields. Some died of accidents (roof collapses, faulty explosives, runaway coal buggies); others of gas poisoning or lung disorders.

It is a chilling picture. Of course we must be careful not to assume that work everywhere in America was as arduous, dangerous, and exhausting. Only a small fraction of the total labor force was exposed to the full rigors of the industrial work process. Total employment in all the iron and steel mills of the nation amounted to less than 1 percent of the jobs in the country. Yet, for reasons that will become clear as we go along, the experience of the industrial force was as decisive for our future as was the experience of trustification, which affected far fewer than 1 percent of all the business firms in America.

Immigrant Labor

But we are not quite finished with our tour. As we go about the plant we notice another thing: how "foreign-looking" so many of the workers are. We are right—about a third of all workers in 1870 in manufacturing industries were foreign-born, perhaps more than a third in "dirty" industries such as steel. By 1907, over four-fifths of the laborers in the Carnegie plants of Allegheny County were eastern Europeans.*

We have already seen how significant was the contribution of immigrant labor before the Civil War. Now, with the full-scale advent of industrialization, the role of immigration in providing a labor force became even more indispensable for the expanding business system. After the Civil War, the costs and stresses of ocean voyages were reduced. The cost of a steerage ticket ranged from ten dollars to twenty dollars, while steamers took only one week to cross the ocean. Driven by hunger and lured by visions of a promised land, beginning in the third quarter of the century, immigrants arrived in enormous numbers: 138,000 in 1878, 789,000 in 1882; in all, over 6 million between 1877 and 1890; fourteen million from 1860 to 1900! The immigrants brought extraordinary vitality and sometimes business acumen. But the greater part of them were pressed into the service of the industrial sector where they helped sustain the momentum of expan-

---

*Before the 1880s most immigrants had come from western and northern Europe, especially from England, Ireland, Germany, and the Scandinavian countries. In the 1880s the immigrant stream began to flow from a different source—southern and eastern Europe. Among the new ethnic stocks were Hungarians, Greeks, Italians, Russians, and Jews from Poland and Russia. In 1851 one lone Russian immigrant had entered the United States; in 1890, 35,600 stepped ashore. Between 1881 and 1891, 135,000 Russian Jews left for America. In 1880 New York held 12,000 foreign-born Italians. By 1900, 145,000 lived in the city. Although many of these newcomers succumbed to waves of nostalgia for their old homelands, only about 24 percent of the immigrants who arrived between 1870 and 1900 returned to the Old World. In fact, they struggled to save their money in order to bring other family members over. By 1900, about one-half of all steerage passengers arrived on steamship tickets prepaid by such sacrifices.

To adjust to city life, immigrants from each country or district tended to cluster together in the same neighborhoods. In 1890, Jacob Riis, a New York reporter, wrote that a map of the city showing where different nationalities lived would have "more stripes than the skin of a zebra, and more colors than any rainbow." These ethnic communities took on the character of a small city. They offered people right off the boat in the strange new world of America a chance to hold on to a few fragments of the world they had left. There the immigrants could find people who spoke their language, houses of worship and clubs based on old-country models, and foods they were accustomed to. The ethnic neighborhood also served as a haven against the outside world. It protected the newcomers while they prepared themselves for the hardships they would have to overcome.

sion, first by providing sheer labor power, second by holding down wages and thereby enabling businessmen to reap larger profits which were plowed back into still more expansion.

Mainly between the ages of fifteen and forty, poor and unskilled, the immigrants were drawn like iron filings to a magnet toward the growing industrial centers of work. By 1880 immigrants made up 80 percent of the populations of New York, Cleveland, Detroit, Milwaukee, and Chicago. There they took on jobs at pay that native-born American working men and women would not accept. "Immigrants work for almost nothing and seem to be able to live on wind—something which I cannot do," said one American worker. Another objected that immigration brought wages "below the bread line."[4] A reporter, Margaret Byington, inquiring into weekly wages at Homestead in 1907, found that native white Americans averaged twenty-two dollars; English-speaking Europeans (mainly Irish and Scots), sixteen dollars; "Slavs" (Slovaks, Croats, Magyars, Russians, Italians), a miserable twelve dollars.

It was not just in steel that the immigrant played a major role in providing the muscle power and the docility that enabled crushing work to be performed at cheap rates. Upton Sinclair, describing the Chicago stockyards in his famous novel *The Jungle,* published in 1906, wrote about "Hunkies" and "Polacks" who performed their work in a sea of blood and miasma of fetid stench. In the West 9,000 Chinese toiled on the plains and in the mountains, building the Central Pacific transcontinental line. In the cities of the East, sweat-shop industries, such as clothing, were "manned"—we need quotation marks because so many workers were women—by immigrant Jews, largely from Poland and Russia.

Labor's Attitude Changes

Immigrants fitted into the picture in yet another way. Because they were often from peasant backgrounds, unused to the ways of city life, and because they had much less independence than native workers— if they lost a job there was often no family to turn to—immigrants were much less likely to join the labor unions of the time. Not only did employers find it easier to persuade them not to unionize, but American workingmen were reluctant to admit "foreigners" into their union lodges.

Unions were, of course, regarded with suspicion and antipathy by almost all employers. Not only were they regarded as a direct threat to profits, but their very existence was seen as a challenge to the ideal of benign parental authority that employers believed to be the proper relation of the owner to "his" working people. Moreover, these feelings were shared by many workers, some of whom had been trained to look up to and respect their "betters," others of whom believed fervently in the American dream of rising from humble origins to wealth and power, and who saw in union membership the surrender of this ideal.

But the gradual change in the environment of work and the breaking down of the older personal relations between the "boss" and his workers began to make these sentiments outmoded. In 1860 the average factory had fewer than ten employees. By 1900 the McCormick reaper plant had 4,000 employees, the Baldwin locomotive works 8,000. Looking at the nation as a whole in 1900, about 1,100 companies had payrolls of more than 500 workers and 443 had more than 1,000 wage earners. The factories of such big companies had to be run like armies. Like the railroads, they required a chain of command in which the scope and limits of each individual's authority and responsibility was clearly defined, and a body of elaborate rules which defined the roles and functions of everyone holding a position in the organization.

Many of the new rules that accompanied the growth of industrialism were degrading. In a Rochester, New York, carriage factory, each worker was known by his number. If he wanted a drink of water he had to get his foreman's permission. To make sure that he did so, the water faucets were locked up. In a Massachusetts tannery, guards patrolled the shop and reported any worker who talked during the day. Because of such draconian rules, workers began to complain that they were being treated like prisoners in a penitentiary. Instead of being responsible to a boss who knew their needs and with whom they were in daily contact, workingmen were now accountable to an impersonal foreman who usually did the hiring and firing. ". . . I never do my talking to the hands," said a New England mill owner, "I do all my talking to the overseers."[5] This new state of affairs was summarized in 1883 by a brass worker:

Well, I remember that fourteen years ago the workmen and the foremen and the boss were all as one happy family; it was just as easy and as free to speak to the boss as anyone else, but now the boss is superior, and the men all go to the foremen; but we would not think of looking the foremen in the face now any more than we would the boss.[6]

Unionization

Unionization was thus labor's response to the problems of technology and large-scale organization, just as trustification was the response of business. Actually, unions of workingmen were very old—we can trace them back to colonial times. But they were mainly unions of craftsmen—skilled workers who joined together to form local mutual-benefit associations and to bargain with employers over wages and working conditions. Indeed, as late as 1860 only 0.1 percent of the labor force was organized.

The idea of a nationwide labor union was slower in coming. In 1866 the so-called National Labor Union was formed in Baltimore. It was an amorphous body, composed of sovereign constituent units and embracing at its height somewhere between 200,000 and 400,000 members. Its financial strength, however, lagged far behind its numerical strength. In 1870, the union's best fiscal year, its expenses were nearly double its receipts. The primary objective of the National Labor Union was to abolish the wage system and to inaugurate worker-owned cooperatives. "By cooperation," said William Sylvis, the union's first president, "we will become a nation of employers—the employers of our own labor. The wealth of the land will pass into the hands of those who produce it."[7] The National Labor Union was short-lived—little wonder, with such ambitious plans and such weak finances.

The Knights of Labor and the AFL

Of longer duration were the Knights of Labor, founded in Philadelphia in 1869. Originally a secret organization with an elaborate ritual, the Knights tried to organize—with the exception of liquor dealers, gamblers, bankers, and lawyers—into one "great brotherhood." Under the leadership of Uriah Stephens, a garment-cutter who had once studied for the ministry, the Knights were an idealistic organization, more interested in the "rights of man" than in the dollar-and-cents concerns of the wage-earner.

By 1879 the Knights claimed some 9,000 members. In that same year the Knights were taken over by Terence V. Powderly, a Pennsylvania machinist and one-time mayor of Scranton, Pennsylvania. While Powderly was in office the Knights abandoned secrecy and opened their ranks to women, blacks, immigrants, and unskilled workers—a radical step in a period when most craft unions would admit none of them. In addition, the Knights came out in favor of the eight-hour workday at a time when ten hours was the norm. Curiously, Powderly matched his radical view of membership requirements with an extremely conservative view of his union's role. His principal objective was to organize society on a cooperative rather than a capitalistic basis. Because he believed so fervently in cooperation, Powderly refused to sanction strikes, engage in collective bargaining, or recognize any discernible difference between labor and management. Paradoxically, it was not until the Knights won several important strikes in the 1880s, despite Powderly's disapproval of them, that it became a significant organization. By 1886 some 700,000 workers belonged to the union. But this was far more than the central leadership could control. Hence its subsequent fall was as meteoric as its rise. The rank and file called strikes that failed. Workers became discouraged and dropped out of the union. Then the Knights were blamed, quite unfairly, for a bombing incident in Haymarket Square in Chicago in 1886. In the national hysteria that followed, the union dissolved.

With the collapse of the Knights, the craft unions took hold. To strengthen themselves, these unions of skilled workers founded the American Federation of Labor (AFL) in 1886. The AFL was led by Samuel Gompers, a cigar maker. Much more practical-minded than Powderly, Gompers concentrated his energies on "bread and butter" issues—higher wages, shorter hours, better working conditions— rather than on vague plans for social change. Samuel Gompers was once asked what was the philosophy of the AFL; he answered succinctly: "More." The way to obtain more, Gompers and other leaders of the AFL insisted, was to bargain collectively with employers and to be ready to strike to enforce union demands.

THE WORKER'S STANDARD OF LIVING

Did the union actually win "more" for its members? In a few pages we shall trace its efforts to do so at Homestead. But we can readily see that as a force for raising wages on a national scale unions could not have been very important. Despite the growing class consciousness among workers, trade unions were still in their embryonic stage, and much too small to be of any significance. In 1870 membership in trade unions was approximately 300,000, and, although the labor force more than doubled by 1890, trade unions could boast of only 370,000 members at that time. In his important work *Wages and Earnings in the United States: 1860–1900,* Clarence D. Long states that "it is highly questionable whether, up to at least 1880, most firms in manufacturing were either touched directly by unions, or obliged in setting wage rates to take the threat of unionization very strongly into account."

Had unions alone been responsible for wage levels there would have been no noticeable improvement in worker's incomes during this period. But unions were not alone responsible. The pace of growth, under the stimulus of industrialization, provided a steady increase in the demand for labor—enough to bring about a very considerable rise in wages. If we compare industrial wages in 1880 with those of thirty years before, allowing for price declines during the period, we find that real wages rose by 40 percent. As an overall generalization, it is probably true that the standard of living of the American worker was higher than that of any country in the world at that time.

Hidden Hardships

But this general truth conceals as much as it reveals. For one thing, the upward trend in purchasing power ignores the "panic and pain" with which working men and women also had to deal during the depression phases of the business cycle. The business collapse of 1873, for instance, took a terrible toll. "Probably never in the history of this country has there been a time," reported the Pennsylvania Bureau of Labor Statistics at the end of 1873, "when so many of the working classes, skilled and unskilled, have been moving from place to place seeking employment. . . . "[8] In its annual report of 1874, for example, the American Iron and Steel Institute said that as of November 1874 "at least a million" workers across the nation were unemployed. The actual figure was probably double that, or more.

Meanwhile, workingmen who were lucky enough to maintain their jobs were forced to accept wage cuts and longer hours of work during periods of depression. Between 1873 and 1879 the McCormick Harvester Company in Chicago cut salaries on five separate occasions; in 1875 the Whitin Machine Works in Massachusetts instituted the first pay cut in its history. Unskilled laborers who were averaging about $1.81 a day in 1873 were getting $1.29 in 1879. Artisans in the New York City building trades who were making from $2.50 to $3.00 for an eight-hour day in 1872 were receiving $1.50 to $2.00 for a *ten-hour day* in 1875.

We could repeat these statistics of unemployment and wage cuts for the depressions of 1882–1885 and 1893–1897. But the point is clear. The rough waves of the business cycle affected labor just as painfully as they affected business. The overall climb in labor's earnings masked a great deal of hardship and uncertainty. When a man enjoys an increase in pay for, say, nine years, but is unemployed for the tenth, it is hard to say that his standard of living has risen.

Moreover, even at their best, the wages paid industrial workers were barely enough to sustain a family. The Homestead laborers, as we have said, earned a modest living wage. Elsewhere in the nation, wages were often not up to subsistence for the family. In Massachusetts, for example, studies show that living costs for a worker's family exceeded the earnings of the head of the family by almost a third. The difference had to be earned by other household members, taking part-time work.* In the coal mines, Robert Layton of the Knights of Labor said that "absolute necessity compels the father in many instances to take the child into the mine with him to assist in winning bread for the family."[9] In the South, particularly, children were sent to work at tender ages under the duress of need: in the nation as a whole in 1880 approximately 6 percent of the children between the ages of ten and fifteen were employed in some kind of industrial work.

---

*One of the most important and sophisticated inquiries into the financial and social condition of the workingman and his family was conducted by the Illinois Bureau of Labor Statistics in 1884. This study covered over 2,000 families living throughout the state. The families interviewed represented sixteen different nationalities and 163 occupations. In this respect alone, the Illinois report dwarfed all previous investigations. Breaking down their findings, the Bureau noted that almost one fourth of the households in Illinois failed to make a living and that an equal percentage had to rely on more than one member of the family for supplementary income. Examining the nation as a whole, another contemporary study indicated that there was an increasing inequality in the distribution of wealth in these years. In 1890, for example, the wealthiest 1 percent of families owned 51 percent of the nation's real and personal property; the 44 percent of families at the bottom of the economic ladder owned only 12 percent of all the property. See Charles B. Spahr, *An Essay on the Present Distribution of Wealth in the United States* (1896).

Women at Work

An increasing fraction of the country's women were also working for wages. In 1870 only about 15 percent of all women aged sixteen or over were at work, and a much smaller percentage of white women. By 1929 over a quarter of the nation's women were working.

Of course women were at work in the 1830s and 1840s. But in those days it was held that there were only seven occupations open to women—teaching, needlework, working as domestics, keeping boarders, setting type, and working in bookbinding and cotton factories. By the census of 1890, of the 369 listed occupations, at least some women were engaged in all but nine. Mainly, as we might expect, women entered fields with which they had some familiarity. The factories they entered were extensions of the work they did at home: clothes-making, textile and millinery work, and food-processing.

Women enter the labor force

Industrialization thus provided new avenues of opportunity for women, for many of the jobs they entered were directly created by the new technology of industry. Between 1870 and 1900 the number of women working in offices increased 2700 percent, from 19,000 to 503,000. (Many of these women served as "typewriters.") By 1920 they made up more than half of the clerical workers in the nation. Moreover, it was no longer unusual for women to think in terms of entering business. The heroine of Sinclair Lewis' novel, *Main Street,* published in 1920, has no hesitation about discussing her business aspirations upon graduating from college. And in Booth Tarkington's *Alice Adams,* published in 1921, a middle-class daughter goes into clerical work because of the failure of the family business.

The entrance of women into the labor market had an effect on men as well. As women proved they were capable of doing many kinds of work, they began to displace men. Salesmen gave way to salesladies, as the number of saleswomen jumped from 7,462 in 1880 to 142,265 by 1900. This figure doubled by 1920, due to the expansion of department and franchise stores. Male telephone operators disappeared and telephone girls became a national stereotype of female employment. In 1870 only 350 women worked in telegraphy (the telephone was not invented until 1876), but by 1907, of roughly 80,000 telegraph operators in the country, only 3500 were male. Yet another area that opened up for women in these years was government employment. Women first entered government service during the Civil War, working for the Treasury Department. By 1900 about one-third of all federal employees were women.

With few exceptions, women earned much less than men for the same work. At the turn of the century men in manufacturing industries averaged about 75 percent more than women. Black women earned only about half the wages of white women. At James Buchanan Duke's factory in Durham, North Carolina, for example, the black women who prepared the tobacco leaves for the machines in the factory's segregated leaf department earned half the wages that white women earned on the so-called cigarette side, even though their work was more difficult and less pleasant. (To keep themselves from inhaling the dust and fumes, they worked with handkerchiefs tied over their noses.) Black men, too, it should be added, received less than half the pay of white men. The day of economic equality was—and still is—in the future. Indeed it was not until 1920 that women gained political equality with the passage of the Nineteenth Amendment to the Constitution.

The Overall Change

Our glance at the changing market for labor makes it clear that it is not easy to generalize about the well-being of the working family. Perhaps it is not even wise to do so. As the nation moved off the farm and into the city, as family size gradually diminished, as new patterns of consumption created new demands for income, as the hours worked per week slowly fell, the meaning of a given dollar income changed. We are probably correct in envisaging a considerable general improvement in the economic situation of most working-class families during our sixty-year period, but we are wise to remember that that impression ignores the periods of severe hardship and the plight of backwater areas or trades. Not least, it overlooks the growing strains and strife of industrial work.

The Strike at Homestead

We will get a glimpse of that strife if we return to the Carnegie mill at Homestead, Pennsylvania, where the AFL had a strong local union of 800 men. Those men were part of the Amalgamated Association of Iron and Steel Workers. With 24,000 dues-paying members and 300 sub-lodges, located mainly in western Pennsylvania, this was one of the largest unions within the AFL, which by then had a quarter of a million members. We focus on 1892 because that was the year of the terrible Homestead struggle. Meeting with the management in a year of adverse business conditions, the Amalgamated was faced with a demand for a *reduction* of wages of about 18 percent. Negotiations were in vain; in desperation the union struck. In retaliation, Henry Clay Frick, Carnegie's partner (with full support from Carnegie, who was enjoying life in his castle in Scotland), closed the plant and announced that he would hire a new labor force. Frick secretly hired the Pinkerton Detective Agency, an organization whose activities included labor espionage and strike-breaking, to send an armed force of 300 men to seize the Homestead plant from the striking workmen who were picketing it.

What happened thereafter was a miniature war. The Pinkertons approached the works by barge along the Monongahela under cover of night, but the landing went astray. To their dismay, the Pinkertons found themselves surrounded, rounded up, and marched as a body of captives toward the main gate. All might have ended without further incident, but along the march someone's anger snapped and the crowd of workmen fell upon the Pinkertons, savagely beating them. When the melee was over, seven Pinkertons and nine workmen were dead.

The victory of the workmen proved short-lived, however. The governor of the state sent in the National Guard; arrests followed; and within a few months the strike was hopelessly lost. Henry Clay Frick had the vindictive pleasure of watching his men file back into the plants on his terms. Of 3,800 strikers, only 1,300 went back on the payrolls—none of them Amalgamated men. The few gains the Amalgamated had won were washed away. The twelve-hour day was imposed on almost all workers. Grievance committees were abolished. Extra pay for Sunday ceased. Labor espionage became an established practice. Wages were reduced not by 18 percent but by approximately 50 percent.

Labor versus Capital

Homestead interests us because it tells us something about the attitudes against which workers had to struggle, as well as about the physical conditions they faced. Frick's hostility toward unions was by no means unusual in that period. Historian John A. Garraty has assembled a collection of views typical of the times:

> *John H. Devereux, railroad general manager:* I would proceed to discharge every man . . . who continued to foment, and cause a disturbance. . . . It would be a sad thing for some of the old white-haired Engineers to be thrown out of work, but I told the Committee I should strike with an unsparing hand.

> *N. F. Thompson, secretary, Southern Industrial Convention:* Labor organizations are today the greatest menace to this Government that exists . . . [A] law should be passed that would make it justifiable homicide for any killing that occurred in defense of any lawful occupation.

> *A Massachusetts textile manufacturer:* As far as [collective bargaining] is concerned, we will not agree to that. Our money built these mills, and we propose to secure whatever benefits may be derived from the business.[10]

Not all manufacturers were so adamantly opposed to unions. Despite his support of Frick's policy at Homestead, Carnegie had written with sympathy about the plight of the workers and had gone so far as to endorse the eight-hour day—as a long-term goal. But even Carnegie could not bring himself to see that the new conditions of industrial labor made his words often seem unrealistic: "The lot of the skilled workman," he had written, "is far better than that of the heir to an hereditary title, who is likely to lead an unhappy, wicked life."[11] We read the words and smile. But then, Carnegie's sentiment aside, what about the *unskilled* workman? What about the immigrants falling into the pits? What about the vast numbers of Homestead employees who were losing their skills because of industrialization itself? There was a side to the industrial expansion of America that Carnegie did not clearly see. Let us take a look at it.

THE WORSENING OF WORK

If we survey the era of industrialization with regard to its impact on labor, it is not the change in the living standards of workers that impresses us. It is the change in the nature of the work itself. For one element that Carnegie either did not see or did not understand was the significance of a process to which he himself was surely a major contributor. This was the increasing division of labor, far and away the most significant effect that industrial growth exerted on the life of the worker.

The Industrial Division of Labor

We are all familiar with the idea of the division of labor. But now we must distinguish between a division that allows workers to specialize in a single craft and one that breaks down that craft into specialized tasks that are performed by several people. In the 1770s, Adam Smith noticed that this second kind of division of labor was taking place in England and wrote about it in a passage that has been famous ever since:

> To take an example . . . from a very trifling manufacture . . . , the trade of the pin-maker. [A] workman not educated to this business . . . , nor acquainted with the use of the machinery employed in it . . . could scarce, perhaps, with his utmost energy make one pin a day, and could

certainly not make twenty. But in the way in which the business is now carried on . . . one man draws out a wire, another straights it, a third cuts it, a fourth points it, a fifth grinds it at the top for receiving the head, to make a head requires two or three distinct operations; to put it on is a peculiar business; to whiten the pins is another; it is even a trade by itself to put them into paper. [T]he important business of making a pin is, in this manner, divided into about eighteen distinct operations. . . .[12]

Why should labor be divided into these "distinct" operations, instead of having each person make pins from start to finish? Smith provided an answer: "I have seen a small manufactory of this kind where only ten men were employed. . . . When they exerted themselves [they could make among them about twelve pounds of pins in a day. There are in a pound upwards of four thousand pins of a middling size. These ten persons, therefore, could make among them upwards of forty-eight thousand pins in a day. . . . But if they had all wrought separately and independently . . . , they certainly could not have each of them made twenty, perhaps not one pin in a day."

The fragmentation of labor, in other words, enormously increases the productive power of human energy—a crucial fact for the phenomenon of growth itself. We will come back to it shortly. But here we want to note two other aspects of the industrial division of labor. First, as Adam Smith makes clear, it requires machinery if it is to be effective (and there would be no point in seeking a division of labor if it were not). Thus the ability to set up a small "manufactory" of ten men, grinding out pins, requires that machinery exist to enable each workman to accomplish his specialized job much more rapidly than he could do it unassisted.

Second, the industrial division of labor requires organization. The flow of work must be studied; the object, the task itself, must be scrutinized as if it were strange and unfamiliar. The product called a "pin" has to be examined very carefully. What does it consist of? How many different activities need one person undertake to make a pin? Can these activities be established as independent tasks, accelerated with machinery, and linked with the activities of other persons working on other aspects of that peculiar object, a pin?

Homestead was a pin factory on a giant scale. For what the Bessemer converter and rolling mill, the giant presses and the railroad cars filled with ore represented was a realization of the principle of the division of labor to a far greater extent than was attainable in Adam Smith's day. Here not ten men, but 3,800 men, were coordinated into a single work team. Not all of them did different tasks, of course; but the plant as a whole divided the complex task of making steel into the much simpler tasks of loading furnaces, cleaning out ovens, guiding machinery, picking up and moving ingots, shoveling fuel. If you had stopped a workman at Homestead and asked him what he did, he would have had to answer that he ran a hoist, or handled billets, or stacked bars, or scrubbed floors. None of them could have answered "I make steel," because no one person did make steel.

The division of labor, as Adam Smith's pin factory reveals, is much older than the era of rapid industrialization. Frederick Olmstead, the architect who designed New York's Central Park, visited Cincinnati in 1850 and described how rows of men transformed a carcass, traveling before them on an overhead conveyor, from hog to pork in a matter of minutes: "No iron cogs could work with a more regular motion," he wrote of their steady chop, chop, chop.[13]

What industrialization did was to give an enormous impetus to the process by which labor could be subdivided and given the strength, speed, and steadiness of machines to augment its human exercise. But industrialization also brought a renewed effort to organize the flow of work in a new manner. Not only machines but method were the secret of the Carnegie plants, and of successful industrial operations everywhere.

Taylorism

One of the most far-reaching suggestions for the reorganization of work was the product of a strange man named Frederick Winslow Taylor. The scion of a well-to-do Philadelphia family, Taylor gave up the study of law at Harvard and decided to work his way up from the bottom in a steel plant. Beginning as an apprentice in 1874, he used his intelligence, diligence, and sheer drive to rise to the position of "gang boss" of the lathe department in the Midvale Steel Works.

By temperament Taylor had been a curious personality since boyhood, given to splitting the world into its smallest parts. He counted his steps when he walked to learn the most efficient stride, calculated the angles of his shots at croquet, and chafed at anything that displayed less than the efficiency of a finely planned machine. The most irritating thing to Taylor was the extreme "inefficiency" with which most men worked. As gang boss he told his men that he intended to get much more work out of them—and he did, by alternately bullying and persuading them to work quicker, more accurately, harder.

But Taylor was not content merely to be a driver of men. He began to see that much more work could be performed if men would break their accustomed habits and perform their tasks in a "scientifically" planned way. Early in his career, he studied a seemingly simple task— the loading of ninety-two–pound "pigs" of iron into freight cars. Picking up his ninety-two–pound pig, walking up an inclined plank to the top of a freight car, and dropping his load into the car, an average worker loaded some $12\frac{1}{2}$ tons of iron a day. Taylor watched each motion, each step; and then he taught his first subject exactly what to do. As he explained it later to a congressional committee in 1912:

> Schmidt started to work, and all day long, and at regular intervals, he was told by the men who stood over him with a watch, 'Now pick up a pig and walk. Now sit down and rest. Now walk—now rest.' etc. He worked when he was told to work and he rested when he was told to rest, and at half past five in the afternoon has . . . $47\frac{1}{2}$ tons loaded on the car.[14]

Taylor's method was to search for the tool or the technique that would be exactly suited to a given purpose. "When we went to the Bethlehem Steel Works," he told the committee, "and observed the shovelers . . . , we found that each of the good shovelers . . . , owned his own shovel. There was a larger tonnage of ore shoveled in that works than of any other material, and rice coal came next in tonnage. We would see a first-class shoveler go from shoveling rice coal with a load of $3\frac{1}{2}$ pounds to the shovel, to handling ore from the Massaba Range, with thirty-eight pounds to the shovel. Now, is $3\frac{1}{2}$ pounds the proper shovel load or is thirty-eight pounds the proper shovel load? They cannot both be right. Under scientific management the answer to this question is not anyone's opinion: It is a question for accurate, careful, scientific investigation."

The "Homogenization" of Labor

Although Taylorism was much talked about in industrial circles, few plants seem to have instituted the system as a whole. What became known as Taylorism more often than not consisted of tighter managerial control of various sorts. Perhaps the most important of these was the gradual elimination of the practice of having gang bosses or foremen hire and fire their own labor crews on a kind of subcontracting basis. More and more, management took the hiring of labor into its own hands. The foreman now became a representative of management rather than a petty boss on his own.

In effect, the new system spelled the end of an era in which the organization of industrial labor still reflected its craft origins, and the establishment of a new era in which labor skills were "homogenized," to use the expression of labor economists David Gordon, Michael Reich, and Richard C. Edwards.[15] Homogenization meant that the making of commodities was more and more entrusted to the direction of management engineers, and less and less to the hand-me-down skills of craftsmen and artisans. In turn, the gradual elimination of skilled labor and its replacement by semiskilled labor—labor that could be trained for its tasks in a matter of a week or two—gave rise to a new, disciplined organization of the work process under the eye of foremen backed by time-and-motion engineers, a system that Gordon and his associates call "the drive system."

The Assembly Line

Machines and method came together most dramatically not in steel but in automobiles, in the famous "assembly line" technique developed by Henry Ford during the first decade of this century. Allan Nevins, the biographer of Ford and his company, has described the process as it existed in 1914:

> Four great principles [were] applied throughout: the use of the latest machinery of original design; the placing of men and machines in operation sequence; the employment of work slides and moving assembly lines; and the installation of overhead carriers to bring up materials. The period for assembling a motor, which only the previous fall had been about 600 minutes of one man's time, had been lowered to 226 minutes. The period for assembling a chassis had been reduced from twelve hours twenty-eight minutes . . . to one hour and thirty-three minutes. . . .
>
> . . . [Y]ou see men whose function is to join parts together and insert a bolt; others who put nuts on bolts; others who tighten the bolts and insert cotter pins; one who uses a hand lever . . . press to impose the

inside ball-bearing cone upon the stub-axle; another who applies a more complicated machine to bring steering arms and stub axles into combination.[16]

Without machines and method, the mass-produced, cheap car would have been impossible, just as without machines and method the production of cheap steel would never have been achieved. But here we want to summarize the effects of Taylorism on the worker who was exposed to it.

Two consequences stand out. First, *the pace of work was deliberately speeded up*. In 1890, Samuel Gompers was quizzed by a special Commission on Capital and Labor:

Samuel Gompers (1850–1924)

Q. Would you say that the new machinery, bringing in more rapid processes of production, has lightened the toil of the operatives?

A. No. . . . As a matter of fact, the velocity with which machinery is now run calls forth the expenditure of nearly all the physical and mental force which the wage-earner can give to industry. . . .

I can say . . . that in every mechanical trade, when European workmen come over to this country and stand beside their American fellow workingmen, it simply dazes them—the velocity of motion, the deftness, the quickness, the constant strain.[17]

Second, *the character of work was changed.* In place of the variety of tasks demanded of a farmer, a fisherman, a potter, a carpenter, or even an old-fashioned "mechanic," work was now more and more patterned after the impersonal repetition of machinery itself. A Massachusetts Bureau of Labor Statistics publication stated in 1872: "Skill, once the strong defense of the artisan, is now trembling . . . before the advance of machinery. In fact it is about conquered." Many years later, an operative in an automobile factory was to tell a visiting researcher:

I work on a small conveyor which goes around in a circle. We call it a "merry-go-round." I make up zigzag springs for front seats. Every couple of feet on the conveyor there is a form for the pieces that make up the seat springs. As that form goes by me, I clip several pieces together, using a clip gun. I then put the pieces back on the form, and it goes around to where other men clip more pieces together. By the time the form has gone around the whole line, the pieces are ready to be set in a frame, where they are made into a complete spring seat. That's further down the main seat cushion line. The only operation I do is work the clip gun. It takes just a couple of seconds to shoot six or eight clips into the spring, and I do it as I walk a few steps. Then I start right over again.[18]

PRODUCTIVITY

Taylorism and the homogenization of labor raises a question of great importance. For in the dehumanization of factory work, we sense the seeds of an immense latent conflict. The struggle between those who "owned" the jobs and those who performed them—between capital and labor—had long provided a major theme for history, a theme that Karl Marx had elevated to the main process of historical change when he wrote in the *Communist Manifesto* that "the history of all hitherto existing society is the history of class struggles."

The Missing Class Struggle

In Europe there was indeed a brooding revolutionary spirit. Though it was mainly muted, it broke into violent expression in 1848, again in Paris in 1870, in Russia in 1917, and in Germany after the First World War. In America, however, a revolutionary temper had never been an integral part of the labor movement. Some labor leaders did, of course, weave Marxian references into their speeches to summon up class consciousness, but these ideas never took hold among American working men and women. As late as 1872, the Marxist First International had only about 5,000 members and virtually no trade union support. As we have seen, labor unions—especially the successful ones— were concerned with defending and trying to better the lot of the worker under the existing scheme of things rather than striking out against the whole framework of capitalist society.* Perhaps this pragmatic, nonrevolutionary turn of mind reflected the pervasive air of American democracy, so markedly different from the European feeling of inherent class differences. Perhaps it was the consequence of the extraordinary openness of the vast American continent with its beckoning, if often delusive, opportunities for the "common" man. Perhaps it was simply the result of the economic improvement that proceeded so much more rapidly in America than abroad.

Whatever the reasons, the idea of a self-conscious, revolutionary working class never made much headway in nineteenth-century America. But with the advent of the de-skilling of labor, the stage seemed set for a decisive change in sentiments. The progressive reduction of the working person within the factory to a mere robot, a pair of hands whose very movements were no longer determined by their possessor,

---

*Let us raise in a footnote a question of deep importance. Lenin believed that trade unions and socialism were incompatible. Unions, he wrote, would produce class consciousness, but not revolutionary resolve—indeed, by obtaining material benefits for their memberships, unions would serve to undermine revolutionary sentiment. In the bitter opposition by the Communist Party of Poland to the Polish union Solidarity, this Leninist belief had been tragically acted out in the early 1980s. How it will finally end, now that the Soviet Union and the Communist Party are no more, we cannot tell.

seemed likely to sharpen the sense of class solidarity among working people and to rouse a feeling of class antagonism against the system that had so diminished their status.

Yet it did not. Why not? The history of the American labor movement is complex, and the reasons for its divergence from the more revolutionary European example are many. But one central part of the answer interests us, because it is intimately connected with the very process of industrialization that degraded the labor process.

This antirevolutionary effect of industrialization lay in the immense impulse that industrialization gave to *labor productivity*. Behind this surge in productivity were many factors with which we are now familiar. There had been an enormous accumulation of capital in the form of machines, buildings, railroads, and highways. There had been dazzling advances in technology. Although we have not heretofore called attention to it, human effort was itself becoming more adept and skillful as the consequence of education. In 1870 only 57 percent of the population between the ages of five and seventeen was in school; by 1929 the percentage had grown to eighty. And not least there had also been the "militarization" of labor—its reduction to the robotized, armylike functions that Taylorism so avidly promoted. Together, all these causes accounted for the stunning increase in productivity that tripled the tonnage of steel produced per man in the thirty years between 1870 and 1900 and that would triple it again in the years between 1900 and 1929.

To be sure, the total output of the nation did not grow at anything like the explosive rates of its most advanced industrial salients, but overall output increased mightily in the period from 1865 to 1929. In round numbers a person living in 1929 produced about four times as much as his father or grandfather living in 1865.

The Effects of Productivity

This increase in productivity meant, of course, that the amount of goods and services available per capita in the nation was steadily growing. And in turn this meant that the standard of living of most working people—with all the exceptions and irregularities that we have pointed out—was gradually increasing. Thus one reason why the harsh process of labor discipline did not give rise to a revolutionary labor movement was that it was tempered by a feeling of slowly improving conditions.

But this was not the only, and perhaps not the most important, reason. For despite the growth in income, had the industrialization process subjected ever more people to the rigors of factory life, the course of American (and, indeed, European) labor history might have taken a different course. But that is not the way industrialization worked. We would think, for example, that the rise of industrial technology meant that vastly larger numbers of men and women worked in factories and manufacturing establishments in 1929 than in 1865. In fact, the actual numbers did increase sharply, from 2.3 million to 10.9 million. But if we look at the *percentage* of the labor force in manufacturing we find an unexpected result. In 1865 about 18 percent of all workers were employed in "manufacturing and hand trades," to use the classification of official government statistics. In 1929 this percentage had indeed grown—but only to 22.5 percent, hardly a dramatic change.

This gives us a new insight into the economic transformation of the country. The rise of a highly mechanized industrial sector, marked by tremendous productive powers, did not mean that a rapidly growing portion of the American working force was subjected to the harsh discipline of the assembly line. On the contrary, it made it possible for more and more labor to be switched from onerous tasks whose output was enormously leveraged by industrialization into other, less physically demanding tasks.

The Reallocation of Labor

This release of labor did not mainly occur within the industrial sector where, after the 1890s, the proportion of the work force remained approximately constant. The main impact of the industrialization process was in another area—agriculture. In 1870 one worker out of every two was employed in agriculture. If there had not been a steady growth of the use of machines on the farm—such as the reaper, the combine, the tractor—Americans would have had to use half of the work force in 1929 just to feed the nation. That would have made it impossible to man the factories, the offices, the stores, the public services that they enjoyed in 1929. It also meant that the United States would have remained a nation of farm workers.

In fact, however, industrialization made labor much more productive in agriculture. From 1870 to 1929 the value of farm tools and equipment increased from $271 million to over $3 billion. Better machinery lowered the number of man-hours required to tend an acre of wheat from twenty to less than twelve. Thus, even though the actual output of all crops tripled from 1865 to 1929, the proportion of the labor force on the farm dropped from one worker out of every two to one worker out of every five. Instead of only half the labor energies of the nation being available for nonagricultural work, four-fifths were available. Today, less than 3 percent of our labor force works on the farm.*

The Rise of the Service Sector

Still more significant, from our point of view, the industrialization process allowed large numbers of the working force to be employed in the growing array of white-collar "service" jobs. In 1865, only 12 percent of the work force was employed in education, professional and personal services, trade, and government. In 1929, these white-collar tasks absorbed almost double that proportion of the labor force. By the middle of the twentieth century, over two-thirds of the working population had moved into service occupations.

Many of these service tasks were as routine as those on the assembly line, but they were typically located in offices and stores and not in factories or farms, they were performed by men and women in street clothes and not in overalls, and they carried with them the feeling that one belonged to a middle-class not a working-class way of life.

Thus economic growth defused the revolutionary potential inherent in factory life by using the productivity of the machine to support the rise of nonfactory occupations. Technology made America a "middle-class" nation. This process was not, of course, the outcome of anyone's decision. Like much of the economic history we have traced, it followed from the blind workings of the market mechanism. But the changing shape, as well as the changing content, of the labor requirements of industrial America helps us understand something more of the dynamics of the economic transformation itself—a process that

---

*We ought to note, however, that many tasks, once considered to be agricultural—such as canning or preserving food—are now done in factories, where it counts as "industrial" production. How much labor is actually connected with food production would be difficult to compute, but it is surely much more than 3 percent of the labor force.

brings change, often difficult to measure in terms of better and worse, along with mere expansion. The radical alteration of the labor process, both within the factory and in the society at large, is perhaps the most dramatic instance of this, but it is not the only one. In our next chapter we will see similar effects of growth and industrialization, for better and worse, in other areas of our national life.

Notes

[1] "Homestead and Its Perilous Trades," *McClure's Magazine* (June 1894), 3:3, 5.

[2] Quoted in R. G. McCloskey, *American Conservatism in the Age of Enterprise* (1951), p. 145.

[3] Leon Wolff, *Lockout* (1965), p. 37.

[4] Quoted in John A. Garraty, *The New Commonwealth* (1968), p. 142.

[5] United States Senate, Committee on Education and Labor, *Report on the Relations Between Labor and Capital* (1885), 3:38.

[6] U. S. Senate, *Report on the Relations Between Labor and Capital*, 1:473.

[7] Quoted in Samuel P. Hays, *The Response to Industrialism* (1957), p. 33.

[8] *Second Annual Report,* 1873–74, p. 433.

[9] U. S. Senate, *Report on the Relations Between Labor and Capital,* 1:19.

[10] *The New Commonwealth,* pp. 144–45.

[11] Quoted in McCloskey, *American Conservatism in the Age of Enterprise,* p. 145.

[12] *The Wealth of Nations* (Modern Library ed., 1937), pp. 4–5.

[13] Quoted in S. Giedion, *Mechanization Takes Command* (1948), pp. 217–18.

[14] Frederick Winslow Taylor, *Scientific Management* (1947), p. 106.

[15] *Segmented Work, Divided Workers* (1982).

[16] Allan Nevins and F. E. Hill, *Ford* (1954), 1:504–05.

[17] *Report of the United States Industrial Commission on Capital and Labor* (1901), 8:606ff.

[18] Quoted in Charles R. Walker and Robert H. Guest, *The Man on the Assembly Line* (1956), p. 46.

Henderson, Texas, c. 1920

Chapter 12
INDUSTRIALIZATION RUBS OFF ON LIFE

So far we have observed the impact of industrialization on the structure of business enterprise, on government, and on work. Yet if we could somehow manage to look simultaneously at the whole range of everyday life in 1865 and 1929, it would probably not be those economic aspects of industrialization that would first engage our attention. Rather, we would be struck by a series of other changes, also connected with the process of industrial growth, that would account for the wholly different "look" of the country at those two times.

URBANIZATION

The first of these changes would surely be the sharp contrast in the habitat of Americans. "The United States," writes Richard Hofstadter, "was born in the country and has moved to the city."[1] The growth of cities after the Civil War was both rapid and widespread. In 1860 Chicago had a population of 109,000 people; by 1900 it had 1.7 million. During the same period the population of Minneapolis grew from 2,500 to 200,000, that of Pittsburgh from 67,000 to 450,000. In 1865 no city had yet reached a million inhabitants; in 1929 there were five such cities. Even more striking, in 1865 only fourteen cities had populations over 100,000. By 1929, there were ninety-three such cities. Half the population was now classified as "urban"—that is, living in towns of 8,000 or more. Equally telling, between 1860 and 1920, for every urban dweller who moved to a farm, twenty farmers moved to a city.

From Farm to City

Who were these migrants? Small-town laborers in search of better jobs; farmers who were unable to secure a good piece of land or make their farms pay; rural dwellers who were tired of the narrow scope and isolation of rustic life; young Dick Whittingtons who believed that the streets of the cities were paved with gold.

Above all, however, it was the pressure of the economic transformation that served as the catalyst for urbanization. People came to cities to find work. The farm lands were booming in terms of output but not as places of employment. As we have seen, the new industrial machinery of agriculture steadily lessened the need for labor to bring in the crops. As the reapers and combines and tractors arrived in the fields, they displaced the farm hands who had previously done the reaping and binding and hoeing and plowing. It took twenty man-hours to bring in an acre of wheat in 1880; less than ten by 1930. As a result, the proportion of the total work force needed on the farm dropped from over half in the 1860s to less than a quarter in the 1920s.

Simultaneously, the expansion of industrial output steadily created new opportunities for employment in the urban areas. New York's sweatshops produced the blouses and skirts and shirts worn by Americans who never came within a thousand miles of the metropolis. Pittsburgh produced steel for the entire continent. Chicago slaughtered and packed the country's bacon and beef. And the cities were, par excellence, the locus of the burgeoning service tasks of trade, finance, government.

Urbanization changed not alone the distribution of our population but the quality of its life. America became a nation of city dwellers, enjoying the excitement of city life, suffering the evils of urban sprawl. For just as no one planned the overall economic expansion of the nation, so no one planned the expansion of the cities. As with industrialization, it was the lure of profit and the counterforce of competition that mainly directed the process of urbanization, with results that mixed gains and losses in often unexpected ways. Let us examine some of them.

The Tenement

One of the losses was the deterioration of the city, symbolized by the rise of the tenement. Because of steady population growth, urban real

Slum life, New York City, 1888

estate steadily rose in price. In Washington, D.C., for example, land that went for eight cents a square foot in 1882 was selling for forty-eight cents in 1887. In their quest for profits landlords subdivided and partitioned apartments, converted private residences into rooming houses, and built new tenement apartments to accommodate as many people as possible in the smallest amount of space.

In 1869 New York City had 14,872 tenements housing a population of 468,492; in 1890 there were 37,316 tenements with 1,250,000 dwellers; in 1900, 42,700 tenements contained 1,585,000 people. In some New York tenements as many as twelve families lived on one floor, in rooms that often had no direct ventilation. In 1867 the New York State Legislature passed "An Act for the Regulation of Tenement & Lodging Houses in the Cities of New York & Brooklyn," whose requirements tell us much about prevailing conditions. The law demanded that stairs have banisters, that roofs be kept in repair, that proper ventilation be provided, and that cellars could not be used as dwellings unless the ceiling was one foot above street level. In addition, the act stipulated that there must be one toilet for every twenty-one inhabitants, although it permitted the toilet to be located in the back yard.

In 1879, Henry C. Meyer, editor of the trade journal *Plumber and Sanitary Engineer,* sought to alleviate the tenement problem by announcing a prize for the design of an apartment building on a 25 × 100-foot lot that would best combine safety and convenience for the tenant and maximum profits for the investor. Of the 204 plans submitted, James E. Ware's design for the so-called dumbbell tenement was awarded first prize. This was a five- or six-story building, with front and rear rooms connected by a hall. Each floor had space for four families living in fourteen rooms—seven on either side, going back in a straight line—with two toilets (opposite the stairs) on each floor. The largest rooms in these tenements were $10^{1}/_{2}$ × 11 feet. Ventilation was provided by a narrow, enclosed, twenty-eight-inch indentation on the side of the building.

Yet even these reforms were inadequate. The air shafts formed by the indented flanks of the adjacent dumbbells failed to provide adequate ventilation. Moreover, they served as ducts to convey flames from one story to the next, and as garbage chutes that created a fetid odor.

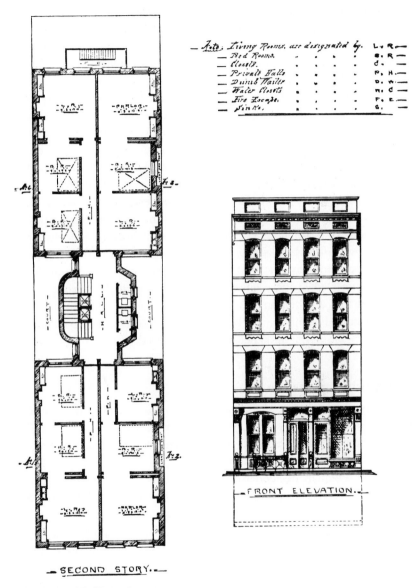

The "dumbbell" tenement

Playgrounds and open spaces were virtually nonexistent in most cities. Police and fire protection was inadequate. Garbage collection was haphazard, at best. City water was often impure. Sewers were smelly and often clogged. Disease could spread quickly under such conditions. In 1882, half the children in Chicago died before reaching the age of five. In one New York tenement area the annual death rate per 1,000 for the years 1883, 1884, 1885, and the first three-quarters of 1886 came to roughly 42 percent, as compared with roughly 26 percent for the city as a whole; nearly 62 percent of the deaths were children under five years of age, while in the city as a whole the percentage was just above 42. Like most cities, New York had become a city of extremes and contradictions, where the best and the worst, the highest and the lowest, existed side by side in sunshine and shadow, in splendor and squalor. The mansions of millionaire industrialists stood only a few blocks from ugly, unhealthy slum districts that housed the poor families who labored in their factories. Seeing the way people lived in these cities, southern visitors to New York once suggested that antebellum slaves on plantations lived more comfortably. Visiting Pittsburgh, Herbert Spencer, the English prophet of Social Darwinism, commented: "Six Months residence here would justify suicide."*

The Company Town

One person who believed that good housing and a healthy environment were essential to people's well-being was George M. Pullman of Chicago, the sleeping car king who had created the greatest railroad car–building organization in the world.

In 1880, Pullman decided to concentrate his operations outside of Chicago, where he would build a model city, named for himself, that

---

*We should note in passing that the conditions of tenement life were a stimulus to American reform movements. In Chicago Jane Addams founded the most famous settlement house in America, Hull House, providing services that ranged from day care for children to English classes for immigrants. Addams and her sister workers were also responsible for the passage of laws limiting female hours of work (an Oregon statute in 1908 set a limit of sixty hours per week), and for other kinds of factory legislation. In 1911 a fire broke out in the Triangle Shirtwaist Company in a New York tenement building. One hundred and forty-eight women perished in the blaze. Thereafter New York State passed thirty-five new factory inspection laws, and shortly other states began to require that manufacturers take out insurance against industrial accidents, so that injured workers could file claims for compensation.

would provide employee happiness, social progress, and employer profit. Accordingly, Pullman purchased over 4,000 acres of land in the Calumet region of Chicago (about eight miles south of the city) and engaged an architect and landscape designer to create a model work-home integration that would be both aesthetically pleasing and functional.

The typical cottage in Pullman was a two-story, five-room structure with a sink, water tap, gas fixtures for lighting and cooking, toilet facilities, and sufficient closet and pantry space. Although the rents for a comparably sized apartment were higher than in Chicago, the accommodations and surrounding environment were far superior.

But as mentioned, Pullman was also intended to serve as a profit-making enterprise. Pullman gave his workers expensive homes and libraries which he hoped would refine and uplift his workers' character and performance, but he expected a 6 percent profit on the capital he invested. As one student of his experiment points out, "Pullman was expected to show that man could be improved by proper surroundings and that American Industry could provide this without sacrificing profits."[2] But Pullman categorically refused to allow workers to own their own homes or to "sell an acre under any circumstances." Everything was rented, including the church. Moreover, Pullman permitted no saloons and insisted that his town manager visit workers' homes to enforce his forty-two page manual of tenants' regulations.

Virtually all Americans who were familiar with urban and industrial conditions were optimistic about Pullman, believing that it would usher in a new era in labor-management relations and urban planning. But although Pullman was a unique venture, it too contained a great deal of the residue of earlier company towns. "It was virtually impossible to come there without constant reminder that this was a company town," writes historian Stanley Buder, "and if the casual visitor was highly conscious of this fact, one can imagine the residents' awareness." Hence although the company's influence could not be measured, it could certainly be sensed.

Nor did Pullman pursue an enlightened attitude when dealing with its workers. In hard times, the company laid off workers and reduced wages while keeping rents constant; refused to accept any responsibility for industrial accidents; and employed such infamous tactics as blacklists and company spies. Surely such practices would one day reap the whirlwind, no matter how placid the town appeared. And in

1894, Pullman's workers struck to protest wage cuts he had ordered after the onset of the depression. The resulting strike spread to and included the American Railway Union, which supported the strikers by refusing to operate any trains that carried a Pullman car. In the end, President Grover Cleveland, arguing that the U.S. mails had to be delivered, ordered federal troops to Chicago to crush the strike.

Clearly many of Pullman's employees would have preferred the "free air" of the city to the iron-fisted authority of the company.

The Model Tenement

In sharp contrast to Pullman were the motives behind the worker-housing projects sponsored by a number of individual philanthropists and housing reformers. Their objective was to show that efforts to improve the living conditions of workers could be combined with "limited dividends," that is, profits of 5 percent annually. Among these model housing projects were Alfred T. White's Home Building development in Brooklyn, New York (1877) and Edward Waller's Francisco Terrace in Chicago (1895), which was designed by Frank Lloyd Wright.

Generally, these apartment buildings were constructed around a courtyard, thus providing playground space, and they usually offered communal facilities such as reading rooms and baths. The buildings were safe, clean, and well-ventilated, the apartments adequate for a working man and his family.

Reformers believed that the model dwellings would set a standard that other landlords would be forced to meet, partly because of public pressure, but mostly because of the workings of competition. Unfortunately, this solution to the housing problem did not take hold, even though most of the experiments succeeded in achieving their goal of philanthrophy plus a 5 percent profit. The great mass of urban workers, as well as newcomers in search of employment, were crowded into privately owned tenements that operated solely for profit.

The Ghetto

Among those who gravitated to the cities in search of jobs and housing were many blacks. With their arrival we witness the appearance of ghettos and the special problems that come in their wake.

Of all the nation's ghettos, probably the best known is Harlem, a thousand acres of concentrated misery that begins north of an ill-defined frontier across Manhattan Island and disappears in the dreary stretches of the Bronx. Few people realize that this was once one of the choicest neighborhoods in New York. Indeed, if we look at Harlem's housing we see that many of the decrepit brownstones and run-down apartment houses are the remains of what were once elegant town houses and expensive apartment dwellings built during the late 1800s.

What happened to Harlem? A building boom, fueled by extravagant and unrealistic expectations, played itself out in 1904. Vacancies began to appear, first scattered, then wholesale. As the neighborhood began to deteriorate, whites moved out and blacks were able to locate good housing at low prices. By 1914 some 50,000 blacks were in Harlem, many of them enjoying very good, low-priced housing. But this very good fortune served as a magnet to attract other, less well-housed, black families. Soon Harlem was overcrowded: by 1929 its population doubled, mainly by in-migration from out of state. Three-quarters of New York's blacks were now crowded into those 1,000 acres. Harlem was becoming a city within a city.

As population rose, so did rents, for landlords were quick to charge what the traffic would bear. Rents doubled between 1921 and 1927, and many black families—most of whom earned low wages—were forced to subdivide their apartments or to take in boarders. The ghetto syndrome began to appear: high rents, high density, low amenities. "The state would not allow cows to live in some of these apartments used by colored people," said the chairman of the city's Housing Reform Committee in 1927.[3] Overcrowding and unsanitary conditions soon took their toll. Between 1923 and 1927 the death rate in Harlem was 42 percent higher than anywhere else in New York.

Urbanization and Industrialization

The point, however, is not to lament the appearance of the ghetto, but to relate it to the larger development of industrial growth. The connection is not difficult to make. The rise of industrial employment and the decline of rural employment together served as a powerful stimulus to uproot blacks from their rural habitat. Bad as the city was, it was better than the rural slum; and as the nation's economy grew, it pulled the black population cityward. Between 1865 and 1929, millions of blacks left the South, most of them for city life in New York or elsewhere. During the 1920s alone, 600,000 blacks moved north, many of them to Harlem.

In the cities, the blacks provided an underlayer of cheap labor that served the economic needs of the growing industrial metropolis. Black males became the city's day laborers, its casual dockhands, its dishwashers, hallmen, bellboys. The black female workers became its servants, laundresses, cleaning women. The presence of the low-paid, easily abused black labor force provided a lubricant for the growing economy. The last to be hired and the first to be fired, the black worker served as a buffer for the white worker, absorbing much more than his or her share of unemployment when times were bad, yet not competing strongly enough to prevent the rise of white wages when times were good.

But there is a lesson to be learned from the rise of the great city, with its ghettos and slums. The big city also testified to the growing interdependence of economic life in an industrial society. In the 1860s many city dwellers still had their tiny truck gardens; in Homestead, a worker could still have one foot in the factory and one on the farm. By the 1920s the link between rural and urban life had been largely severed. The city dweller was now almost entirely dependent on the network of rails and roads that brought his food from a countryside hundreds of miles distant. The citizens of New York and Chicago ate wheat grown in Kansas and meat raised in Texas and lived in houses built of Vermont stone and Pittsburgh iron and steel. Without the intricate web of transportation that bound together a thousand trades and localities, the city could not have existed for a week.

Industrialization is inextricably bound up with this kind of interdependence. Yet the effects of urbanization extended far beyond even this deep-reaching change, touching life in innumerable ways: technical, cultural, political. Urban agglomerations that had grown up without plan or foresight had to find means of disposing of garbage and sewage on a mass scale. The city had to provide transportation from one area to another. It offered a new market for mass entertainment. It brought into being a class of office workers who sought to imitate their "betters" in stylish dress. It jostled races and cultures together: it was the city, not the country, that was the "melting pot." It was also the scene of loneliness and isolation for the newcomer: suicide rates rose from 3.18 per 100,000 in 1860 to 11.9 in 1922.

Residential street in a small town in Illinois, c. 1900

None of these problems was new, of course. Cities have always had their special attributes. But the extent and ubiquity of these urban traits were new. In 1860 cities were few in the United States and their excitement and despair were the exception in a land where rural placidity was the rule. By the first quarter of the twentieth century the city, with its strains and its vitality, had become the norm. It was a long while before the political structures and the prevailing beliefs and self-images of the nation caught up with the realities of its urbanized life: To some degree they have still not embraced the importance of the city. This lag is itself one reason why the city has remained a "problem." We continue to see our urban ills as intrusions upon, rather than as embodiments of, our economic evolution.

MACHINERY AND MATERIAL LIFE

A second change brought about by industrialization affected both city and country. It was the enormous acceleration of a trend whose beginnings we saw before the Civil War—the introduction of machinery into everyday material life. This change was so pervasive, so all-embracing, that it is impossible to itemize its particulars. Let us simply consider some of the differences that it brought.

Mobility

The first difference we notice is in mobility. In the 1860s the basic means of local transportation was the horse. But the horse was ill-suited to an urbanized nation: Where could a million New Yorkers or Chicagoans stable their steeds? Urban life became constricted, limited to journeys on foot or to occasional ventures on trains or steamboats.

But the constriction was not long-lasting. The first breakthrough was the development of the horse-pulled streetcar—the first urban mass transit. By 1895 the electrically powered trolley was running over 10,000 miles of track in the cities; indeed, by changing from one streetcar line to another you could even journey from New York to Boston.

Residential street in Chicago, c. 1906

Traffic jam, Chicago, c. 1910

Even more pervasive was the influence of the bicycle. It is hard to realize today how vast a change the bicycle ushered in. Small enough to be parked in a hallway, inexpensive enough to be bought by a working-class family, simple to maintain, the bicycle reopened the country to the city dweller. First introduced into the country in 1878, in less than two decades bicycle-manufacture had become a major industry. By 1900 the industry was turning out over a million vehicles, and an estimated four million people could be seen riding a strange assortment of high-wheelers, low-wheelers, bicycles built for two, bicycles with sidecars. The mass use of the bicycle also brought pressure on Congress to improve the road system of the country: the League of American Wheelmen was a kind of precursor of the American Automobile Association in the campaign for good public roads. As the census report for 1900 states, "It is safe to say that few articles ever used by man have created so great a revolution in social conditions as the bicycle."

Then, of course, there was the automobile. The first gas-powered auto appeared in the nation in 1892; in 1896 its inventors, the Duryea brothers, actually sold thirteen cars. That was the year in which a thirty-two-year-old mechanic named Henry Ford sold his first "quadricycle." In 1909, with the advent of the Model T, he sold 10,660 cars. By 1929 there were twenty-three million cars on the road—one for every five Americans.

The rise of the automobile industry affected economic growth in a number of ways. It was the prime center for the application of the mass-production techniques whose impact on labor we witnessed in our previous chapter. It was a stupendous source of employment— indeed, soon the largest employer in the country. It was the biggest customer for steel, rubber, sheet steel, lead, leather. It became the origin of one-sixth of all the patents issued in the country. With 2,471 plants in 1923, the automobile industry was the largest in the nation.

But we are interested in the automobile as a concrete manifestation of growth that changed material life. To the average American family it became the most prized (and most expensive) of all its possessions, save only its home. It was the means for cheap and easy travel that made Americans, always a restless people, into a nation of motorized vagabonds. It changed the location of industry and of workers' housing, for it was no longer necessary to live within walking distance of work or near a trolley route. It altered urban configurations: the move to the suburbs was made on rubber tires and would have been impossible without them. (Later, during the Great Depression, Will Rogers would claim that America went to the poorhouse in its automobiles.) It changed social habits. Vacationing became a national passion. Sex mores were radically affected by the car. The city stretched beyond its capacity by the vehicles that jammed its streets. Highways greatly increased in mileage: during the decade of the 1920s federal, state, and city authorities spent roughly $1 billion per year on highways and $400 million on city streets. The nation's police force had to be expanded to cope with a new major source of accidents, of theft, of exasperation. Not least, the car provided the greatest joy ride in the nation's history.

Power in the Home

Next to mobility, the most visible change in daily life was the increased use of energy. In 1860 the total amount of energy delivered by all "prime movers," such as steam engines, water wheels, windmills, and farm animals, totaled thirteen million horsepower. By 1930 the amount of energy used by the nation was 1.6 *billion* horsepower. Of this total, 1.4 billion was provided by that extraordinary power source, the automobile. But the power delivered by stationary motors of all kinds was also some twenty times as much as in 1860.

A great deal of this increased power was used by the factories of the nation, now mechanized to a degree unimaginable in 1860. But we are interested in the direct use of power by the average family as it ran the machines that were more and more part of the normal household's equipment. Here we have but to trace the growth of the use of electricity following Edison's installation of the first power-generating plant in New York in 1882. By 1907 only 8 percent of all homes had access to electricity, mainly because the problem of sending current over cables for long distances had not yet been solved. But by 1929, 85 percent of all nonfarm residences had wall receptacles that enabled them to "plug in" to this new source of energy. The residential use of electricity grew from next to nothing in the 1890s to nine billion kilowatt hours in 1929. In that latter year about 70 percent of the nation's industry was electrified. By 1930 the United States was using more electricity than the rest of the world combined.

Electricity brought power into the home. Perhaps the least revolutionary of its effects was the electric light, for candles or gas burners had provided reasonably good illumination before Edison perfected the carbon-filament lamp in 1887. The real change was the possibility of using machines in domestic life in a manner impossible before this extraordinary source of invisible, easily conducted energy became available. The washing machine and the refrigerator, the vacuum cleaner and the electric iron were the creations of electric power. Their effect on household life was dramatic. The availability of mechanical servants made it possible for the housewife to venture into the labor market and still to maintain her traditional role of "home-maker." Thus the advent of the working woman was intimately connected with the mechanization of household work.

Leisure habits were changed, too. As electric lights illuminated the night (and streetcars crisscrossed city streets), people were able to go to theatres, vaudeville houses, or just out for an evening stroll. Meanwhile, electricity also vastly increased the ability of households to communicate with one another. In 1887 there were 170,000 subscribers to the new telephone service; in 1917 nearly twelve million phones were in use. "What startles and frightens backward Europeans," said a visiting English author, "is the efficiency and fearful universality of the telephone."

Machines such as the electric washer had a dramatic effect on household life

The phone, and then the radio, served to open the ordinary household to events far beyond its previous ken. Together with the movies, those devices were probably more important than the schools as a force for social education and for the spread of sophistication. The jazzy, freewheeling spirit of the twenties would have been unthinkable without the electrical technology of communication. How few people had ever actually heard or seen Abraham Lincoln or Mark Twain! How few had not seen or heard Herbert Hoover or Al Jolson!

THE TRIUMPH OF INDUSTRIALIZATION

New household appliances were not the only changes in material life that the industrial era brought to the United States. There were also, for example, advances in medicine associated with the increased interest in and application of science. Life expectancy between 1865 and 1929 rose from just under forty years to just over sixty, mainly through the conquest of childhood diseases. The death rate from typhoid fell by 95 percent; from measles, by 75 percent.

Second, our overview has by-passed an important change in the tempo of life that also arose from the increased productivity of the age. This was the gradual decline in working hours from over sixty per week in 1865 to about forty-two in 1930. In 1923, after protesting for years that it could not be done, the U.S. Steel Works at Gary, Indiana, went from two grueling twelve-hour stints to three eight-hour shifts. In 1926 Henry Ford, who had already astonished the business world by instituting a five-dollar workday in 1914, announced that henceforth his plants would work on a five-day week. The International Harvester Company started another trend by granting its workers a two-week vacation with pay. Meanwhile, Ford reduced the price of his cars. When he introduced the Model T in 1908, it cost about $850. By 1925, a Model T cost $290, roughly the equivalent of three months' wages for factory workers.

Still another change was a greatly lengthened attendance at school. In 1929 30 percent of the seventeen-year-old population was in high school. This may not seem like a very high figure—today about 80 percent of this age group is in school—but in 1865 the percentage of seventeen-year-olds in school was two.

Not less significant, although less apparent on the surface, was the change in America's position in the world. Alone among the participants in the First World War, the United States emerged stronger than when it entered. Formerly a debtor to Europe—it entered the war with $3.5 billion in debts—it now became the great lender to Europe, with credits of $12.5 billion. By 1929 almost half of the world's industrial production was located in the United States. Meanwhile, the international thrust of business continued apace: Exports rose by a third between 1913 and 1929, and United States investment abroad in factories, mines and plantations rose from the $635 million we saw in 1897 to $7.5 billion.

In 1919, looking ahead to the postwar era, Woodrow Wilson had said: "The financial leadership will be ours. The industrial primacy will be ours. The commercial advantage will be ours."[4] He was right.

The National Feeling

All these new ways, and others that we have not included, constituted the reality of a vast economic transformation. Not all of it by any means was benign, as we have seen from our view of the ghetto, and its outcome would be anything but happy, as the impending—and wholly unsuspected—Depression would prove. Yet there can be no doubt that a general consciousness of prosperity was widely felt and much celebrated.

Americans were convinced they were on the threshold of a new era, a time of peace and prosperity. Given the economic statistics, it would have been difficult to cast cold water on this belief. National income rose from $63.1 billion to $87.8 billion between 1922 and 1929. Per capita income had jumped from $517 for the period 1909 to 1918 to $612 for the period of the 1920s. Despite generally shorter working hours, output per worker was up by 30 percent. Industrial production as a whole nearly doubled between 1921 and 1929. Two of today's most vexing problems, inflation and unemployment, were virtually nonexistent. The average annual rate of increase in prices between 1923 and 1929 was less than 1 percent and unemployment averaged only 3.7 percent of the labor force.

Another cause for the prevailing sense of well-being was the unusually friendly attitude of government toward big business. The tensions of the age of trust-busting were over. In their place was a strongly pro-business attitude, summed up in the words of President Calvin Coolidge that "the chief business of the American people is business." Secretary of Commerce Herbert Hoover virtually put his department at the disposal of big business, encouraging businesses in the same field to form trade associations to share information, and to act as a clearing-house for information on business opportunities abroad. Meanwhile, Secretary of the Treasury Andrew Mellon, one of the richest men in America, successfully urged that taxes on high incomes be lowered. Under Mellon's Revenue Act of 1926, a person with an annual income of $1 million had his or her taxes lowered from more than $600,000 to less than $200,000. This friendly attitude of government encouraged businesses to make new investments and this, in turn, stimulated eco-nomic growth.

"No Congress of the United States ever assembled," said President Calvin Coolidge in 1928 surveying the state of the Union, "has met with a more pleasing prospect." Coolidge was a very conservative man who believed that "The man who builds a factory builds a temple." His contemporary, Lincoln Steffens, was not. Once a famous muckrak-ing reporter for *McClure's* magazine, he had reported with enthusiasm on the early days of the Soviet Union: "I have been over into the future, and it works." Now Steffens was himself saying, "Big business in America is producing what the socialists held up as their goal: food, shelter, and clothing for all."[5]

Certainly Coolidge's successor, Herbert Hoover, regarded the prospect as bright:

> We in America [he said to a Stanford University audience in 1928] today are nearer to the final triumph over poverty than ever before in the his-tory of any land. The poorhouse is vanishing among us. We have not yet reached the goal, but, given a chance to go forward with the policies of the last eight years, we shall soon with the help of God be in sight of the day when poverty will be banished from this nation.

The Nation in 1929

It was assuredly a time of prosperity for the rich: the number of mil-lionaires, which reached 4,000 in 1914, had almost trebled by 1926, and the stock market was making new ones every year. But it was not only the rich who basked in the warmth of the late twenties. The Nia-gara of production testified to an unprecedented degree of national well-being, although—as we shall see in our next chapter—it was a well-being by no means enjoyed by everyone. In turn, the Niagara promoted that "democracy of things" we first noted in the mid-1850s. Fresh vegetables were now widely available, thanks to new techniques of storage and transport. The consumption of ice cream soared—up 45 percent just from 1919 to 1926. Automobiles, now colored in Versailles Violet and Florentine Cream rather than just funereal black, were owned by two households out of three. Rich and not-so-rich alike shaved with the Gillette Safety Razor, snapped pictures with their Kodaks, went to the movies (in December 1923 the movie attendance in Muncie, Indiana, was almost four-and-a-half times the population of the town), and shopped at Macy's, where "Goods suitable for millionaires" were available "at prices in reach of millions."[6]

Thus, if the technical achievement of the age of industrialization was hugely to augment the volume and to alter the composition of the nation's output, its social achievement was to bring about an era of self-conscious prosperity unlike any the country had known before. Especially among those who fared well, there was an acute sense of the American economy as a triumph of enterprise. There was only one problem: Although the national edifice of prosperity appeared to be built of granite, it turned out to be built on sand.

Notes

[1] *The Age of Reform* (1955), p. 23.

[2] Stanley Buder, *Pullman: An Experiment in Industrial Order and Community Planning, 1880–1930* (1967), pp. 52–3.

[3] Quoted in Gilbert Osofsky, *Harlem: The Making of a Ghetto* (1965), pp. 135–36.

[4] Ray S. Baker and William E. Dodd (eds.), *The Public Papers of Woodrow Wilson* (1925), 1:640.

[5] Quoted in William Leuchtenburg, *The Perils of Prosperity* (1958), p. 202.

[6] From an 1887 Macy's advertisement, as quoted in Daniel Boorstin, *The Americans: The Democratic Experience* (1973), p. 113.

Part IV
FROM LAISSEZ FAIRE TO MIXED ECONOMY

Construction of TVA's Fontana Dam
(1942–1945)

Migrant farm workers in the 1930s

Chapter 13
THE GREAT DEPRESSION

We turn now to a new aspect of the economic transformation of America. Up to now our narrative has mainly focused on two aspects of our principal theme. One has been the progressive development of material life—the life of work, of consumption, of command over the environment. Here the general thread has been the extraordinary alteration and enlargement that industrialization has brought about within daily life.

A second pattern of study has been concerned with the extension of what Fernand Braudel has called our economic life, the life that binds us into a working economic society. Here the main theme has been the widening and deepening of our connection with the market, the increasing complexity of our economic interdependency, and the growth of the business institutions that have shaped and channeled so many of our economic ties with society.

In all this overview, however, we have hardly mentioned Braudel's third great theme—the development of capitalism itself. That is, we have rarely stepped back to comment on the unfolding of that embracing web of institutions and relationships we call capitalism, with its central drive for the accumulation of capital, its division of society into a public and private realm, and its reliance on the guiding functions of the market mechanism.

Now, however, things change. With the advent of the Great Depression we encounter a phenomenon that cannot be grasped in terms of the routines and techniques of material life or through the pressures and pulls of the marketplace. To understand the Great Depression we must speak about capitalism as a *system* with tendencies and developmental characteristics of its own.

THE STOCK MARKET BOOM

This requires that we take a short lesson in economics—a lesson that will explain something about how capitalism works. It will also lead us to reflect on the momentum of growth that has played so central a role in our narrative. Thus our chapter will take us into realms of theory and speculation quite different from those that we have previously visited. We will, so to speak, mount to Olympian heights to look down on capitalism from the perspective of a historian of the future.

But we will begin far below these heights. The best way to learn about the advent of the Depression is to watch the spectacle that attracted the gaze of millions of Americans in the late 1920s—the stock market boom. In *Only Yesterday* social historian Frederick Lewis Allen has given us a vivid, if somewhat overdrawn, account of what we would have seen:

> The rich man's chauffeur drove with his ears laid back to catch the news of an impending move in Bethlehem Steel: he held fifty shares himself on a twenty point margin.* The window cleaner at the broker's office paused to watch the ticker, for he was thinking of converting his laboriously accumulated savings into a few shares of Simmonds. [One reporter] told of a broker's valet who made nearly a quarter of a million in the market, of a trained nurse who cleaned up thirty thousand following the tips given her by grateful patients; and of a Wyoming cattleman, thirty miles from the nearest railroad, who bought or sold a thousand shares a day.[1]

Behind the Boom

The market value of shares listed on the New York Stock Exchange soared from $4 billion in 1923 to $67 billion at the beginning of 1929. Stocks were going up for many reasons. One was that the profits of most corporations were rising. Between 1916 and 1925 the profits of large manufacturing companies totaled $730 million in an average year. From 1926 through 1929, their annual total profits jumped to an average of about $1,400 million. In 1929 profits were actually triple

---

*A "margin" means that stock has been bought by borrowing from the bank or from the brokerage firm to cover the difference between the value of the shares and the amount of the down payment.

those of 1920. Hence one reason for buying stocks was the expectation that dividends would rise. And they did. From 1920 to 1929, dividends almost tripled.

A second reason was that banks and brokerage firms were encouraging people to buy stocks by lending vast sums to potential buyers. Loans from brokers to enable individuals to buy stocks—loans that were often equal to half the value of the purchase—soared from just over $1 billion in 1920 to $6 billion in 1928. Who could resist the chance to become as rich as Croesus when you could buy $1,000 worth of stock by putting up only $500 of your own, borrowing the rest from a brokerage firm or a bank? Hundreds of thousands of people *didn't* resist. A million and a half people were stockholders, a far larger number than ever before and the number of shares traded on the New York Stock Exchange rose from 236 million in 1923 to 1.1 *billion* in 1928. In 1900 roughly 15 percent of all families owned some stock; in 1929, about 28 percent.

Finally, there was the allure of a seemingly foolproof method of getting rich. Many Americans were encouraged to join in the great stock market boom because they listened to the advice of trusted men. In 1928 John J. Raskob, a director of General Motors and chairman of the Democratic Party, projected the recent rise in stock prices into the future and predicted that riches could be within the reach of anyone who saved money. In an article for the *Ladies Home Journal* entitled "Everybody Ought to Be Rich," he said: "If a man saves fifteen dollars a week and invests in common stocks, at the end of twenty years he will have at least $80,000 and an income from investments of around $400 a month. He will be rich." In New York City a big electric sign over Columbus Circle blinked out the message: "You should have $10,000 at the age of thirty; $25,000 at the age of forty; $50,000 at fifty."

THE CRASH

Thus the growth in incomes that we traced in our earlier chapters was paralleled during the 1920s by a spectacular growth in wealth—alas, paper wealth. For on October 24, 1929, without any prior warning, the bottom suddenly dropped out of the market. The headlines in the *New York Times* for October 25 read:

Worst Stock Crash Stemmed by Banks;
12,894,650-Share Day Swamps Market;
Leaders Confer, Find Conditions Sound

What was meant by the "crash" was that investors all over the country decided that the market was "too high" and placed orders to sell. But no one can sell a security—or any other item—at whatever price he or she wishes. The seller has to find a buyer. And if the buyers are nervous and pessimistic, the price at which they will agree to buy the stock may be much lower than the sellers expected.

What happened on the morning of October 24 was that buyers were only willing to buy stocks at prices far below the prices of the preceding day. Montgomery Ward, a favorite, had "opened" at a price of eighty-three, that is, the first transaction was a sale at eighty-three dollars per share. By mid-morning, it was being traded at fifty. Goldman Sachs Trading Corporation, a speculative favorite, opened at eighty-one and dropped to sixty-five. General Electric slid from 315 to 283. Some stocks could not be sold at all—there were simply no buyers to take them at any price.

By noon the roar of voices on the stock exchange floor had reached panic proportions, and a group of bankers met to issue reassuring statements that "conditions were sound." On Saturday, October 26, President Herbert Hoover echoed this optimism by insisting that "the fundamental business of the country—that is, production and distribution of commodities—is on a sound and prosperous basis." For a week the market rallied as buyers lifted up their courage and sellers lost their terrified impulse to sell. Then on October 29 came an even more devastating day. As the *New York Times* wrote about it the next morning:

Stocks Collapse in 16,410,030-Share Day

Stock prices virtually collapsed today, swept downward with gigantic trading losses in the most disastrous trading day in the stock market's history. Millions of dollars in open market values were wiped out as prices crumbled under the pressure of liquidation of securities that had to be sold at any price. . . .

Efforts to estimate yesterday's market losses in dollars are futile because of the vast number of securities . . . on which no calculations are possible. However, it was estimated that 880 issues, on the New York Stock Exchange, lost between $8,000,000,000 and $9,000,000,000 yesterday.

And October 29 was not the end. In 1932 Frank Vanderlip, former president of the National City Bank of New York, a leading financial institution, surveyed the wreckage in an article in the *Saturday Evening Post:*

. . . The quoted value of all stocks listed on the New York Stock Exchange was, on September 1, 1929, $89,668,276,854. By July 1, 1932 the quoted value of all stocks had fallen to $15,633,479,577.

Stockholders had lost $74,000,000,000. The figure is so large that not many minds can grasp it. It is $616 for every one of us in America. It is, roughly, three times what we spent fighting the World War. . . . In the bursting of the New York Stock Exchange bubble, the value of all stocks fell to 17 percent of their September 1, 1929 price. . . . Never before, in this country or anywhere else, has there been such a general loss in "security" values.[2]

In 1932 the United States Senate held a hearing on the fate of some of those stocks:

SENATOR COUZENS: Did Goldman Sachs and Company organize the Goldman Sachs Trading Company?
MR. SACHS: Yes, sir.
SENATOR COUZENS: And it sold its stock to the public?
MR. SACHS: A portion of it. The firm invested originally in 10 percent of the entire issue for the sum of $10,000,000.
SENATOR COUZENS: And the other 90 percent was sold to the public?
MR. SACHS: Yes, sir.
SENATOR COUZENS: At what price?
MR. SACHS: At 104 . . .
SENATOR COUZENS: And what is the price of the stock now?
MR. SACHS: Approximately $1\frac{3}{4}$.[3]

Behind the Crash

What caused the crash? To this day we do not know what item of news, what rumor, what particular event may have started the collapse. Clearly there must have been an underlying nervousness among hundreds of

A run on a bank

thousands of stockholders, for the fall in prices soon fed upon itself. In addition, the collapse worsened because holders of stocks on margin—that is, on borrowed money—were forced to sell their securities to pay off their loans. Perhaps in the end we can only classify the Great Crash with other speculative busts that had happened elsewhere in history—land booms that came to nothing, crazes such as the tulip bulb speculative mania in seventeenth-century Holland, prior stock booms like the famous English South Sea "Bubble" of 1720.

What interests us is the impact of the crash on the economy. For as everyone knows, the Great Crash ushered in something worse—the Great Depression.

THE DEPRESSION OF THE 1930s

It was an oddly invisible phenomenon, this Great Depression [wrote Frederick Lewis Allen]. If one observed closely, one might note that there were fewer people on the streets than in former years, that there were many untenanted shops, that beggars and panhandlers were much in evidence; one might see breadlines here and there, and 'Hoovervilles' in vacant lots at the edge of town (groups of tarpaper shacks inhabited by homeless people); railroad trains were shorter, with fewer Pullmans; and there were many factory chimneys out of which no smoke was coming. But otherwise there was little to see. Great numbers of people were sitting at home, trying to keep warm.[4]

LABOR FORCE AND UNEMPLOYMENT, 1929–41
(NUMBERS IN MILLIONS)

Year	Labor Force	Unemployment Number	Unemployment % of Labor Force
1929	49.2	1.6	3.2
1930	49.8	4.3	8.7
1931	50.4	8.0	15.9
1932	51.0	12.1	23.6
1933	51.6	12.8	24.9
1934	52.2	11.3	21.7
1935	52.9	10.6	20.1
1936	53.4	9.0	16.9
1937	54.0	7.7	14.3
1938	54.6	10.4	19.0
1939	55.2	9.5	17.2
1940	55.6	8.1	14.6
1941	55.9	5.6	9.9

SOURCE: United States Department of Commerce, *Historical Statistics of the United States* (1960), p. 70.

However hard it was to see, the Great Depression was a vivid reality to virtually everyone. To begin with, unemployment soared beyond any previous experience. All through the long period of industrialization, recurrent periods of unemployment had plagued the economy, sometimes reaching as high as 10 percent of the work force. But those times of trial had always been brief and had always been followed by a resumption of growth, which brought with it job opportunities for almost everyone who wanted work.

The depression was different. The table on page 281 reveals its severity.

Nothing like this had ever happened before. For it was not only unemployment that the depression brought, but a total cessation of growth. In the nation as a whole, home-building came almost to a standstill—residential construction fell by 90 percent. Eighty-five thousand businesses failed, and production in those that survived was often reduced to half the volume of the 1920s. Wages reached levels that made sheer survival a problem: in Pennsylvania men were paid five cents an hour in sawmills; $7^1/_2$ cents in general contracting. In Ohio the earnings of office workers were cut by a third, those of store clerks by nearly half. Considering the nation as a whole, national income fell from over $80 billion in 1929 to under $50 billion in 1932. Thus, while the Great Crash had dashed American illusions about instant riches, the Great Depression threatened something much more fundamental. It brought into question the faith of Americans in the economic system itself. The system simply did not work.

Political Paralysis

At first no one believed that. "We have now passed the worst," said President Hoover in May 1930. One year later he declared the depression to be "over." Meanwhile business spokesmen continued to assert that things were "fundamentally sound":

> Charles Schwab, Chairman of Bethlehem Steel, December 10, 1929: "Never before has American business been as firmly entrenched for prosperity as it is today."
>
> John Edgerton, President, National Association of Manufacturers, December 1929: "I can observe little on the horizon today to give us undue or great concern."
>
> James Farrell, President, United States Steel, January 1931: "The peak of the depression passed thirty days ago."[5]

But as the situation stubbornly refused to mend itself, sentiment began to change. Among the unemployed an ugly mood of frustration and anger was surfacing. In 1932 a small "army" of unemployed veterans converged on Washington to demand payment of a bonus promised them for their service in the First World War. Hoover refused to meet with them. Instead, the veterans were attacked with bayonets and tear gas, to the shock and dismay of the nation. In the farm states, representatives of banks who arrived to take possession of farms that could not keep up their mortgage payments were met by groups of unsmiling men carrying clubs. Representatives of farm groups warned the Hoover administration that the countryside was ripe for revolution.

Worst of all, however, was the inability of the business leaders to provide a recipe for renewed prosperity, save for "prudence" on the part of government. A Senate committee in 1932 spent two weeks listening to businessmen give the following advice:

> Bernard Baruch, financier and advisor to many presidents: "Balance budgets. Sacrifice for frugality and revenue. Tax—tax everybody for everything."
>
> Jackson Reynolds, First National Bank: "I have [no remedy] and I do not believe anyone else has."
>
> Nicholas Murray Butler, President of Columbia University: "Government economy and balanced budgets."[6]

Heeding the counsel of business leaders and the philosophy of laissez faire, the government under President Hoover believed that the economy would restore itself if it were left alone. Although his administration did more than any previous administration to revive the economy, Hoover felt that no radical steps were called for. His administration bought some agricultural surpluses to help bring farm prices up, and it began a modest program of public works, including the building of Boulder Dam (later renamed Hoover Dam) on the Colorado. Mainly, however, it tried to persuade business to maintain wages, prices, and employment—that is, to conduct business as usual. In 1932 Hoover asked Congress to establish the Reconstruction Finance Corporation (RFC), which lent government money to banks, life insurance companies, railroads, and mortgage associations. The theory behind the RFC was that it would lend funds to large businesses at the top of the economic structure, and benefits would filter down to the people at the bottom through a sort of trickle-down effect. Later that year the Home Loan Bank Act further aided financial institutions in danger of bankruptcy. With more money available, these institutions could extend credit to mortgage holders and meet their depositors' needs for cash. This, it was hoped, would make it possible for more people to buy homes, which, in turn, would give a boost to the construction industry.

The Sins of Omission and Commission

All this did help somewhat. But what was striking was the administration's unwillingness to help the neediest—the unemployed. Before 1932 the federal government provided *no* funds for direct relief to the unemployed. Finally, in July of that year, the federal government began allocating relief money in the form of *loans* to the states. But by the end of 1932 the national government had released only $30 million for relief. Partly this was due to Hoover's belief that charity was the work of voluntary groups and institutions, not of the federal government. In 1930, for example, Hoover endorsed a $45 million appropriation to feed the livestock of Arkansas farmers during a drought, but he rejected a grant of $25 million for food for the farmers and their families. Partly it was due to the fact that the president could not bring himself to believe in the severity, or even the reality, of the plight of the unemployed. "No one is actually starving," he told reporters. "The hoboes, for example, are better fed than they have ever been. One hobo in New York got ten meals in one day."[7] Later, the president was actually to write about the many unemployed who eked out a living by selling apples on street corners: "Many persons left their jobs for the more profitable one of selling apples."

Inaction was the government's worst moral sin, but perhaps its greatest economic sin was in taking actions that unwittingly exacerbated the situation. Believing that the American business system was inherently sound and that the depression was a European import, Hoover signed the Smoot-Hawley Tariff Act of 1930, which raised tariff rates on imports to the highest levels in the country's history. This action had profound repercussions. By making it very difficult for foreign countries to sell their products to America, the tariff deprived European nations of a major source of revenue that would have

Louisville flood victims, 1937

enabled them to buy American goods (especially farm output) and to repay their war debts to the United States.

Nor did the government exercise its taxing and spending or monetary powers prudently. Arguing that a balanced budget was one of the major requirements for a nation's economic health, the government, in 1932, decreased its expenditures and actually enacted the largest tax *increase* up to that point in American history! Even more serious were the Federal Reserve Board's actions. During the speculative mania of the twenties, the monetary authorities could not bring themselves to check the unwise expansion of bank loans by raising the discount rate (the interest rate at which member banks can borrow from the Federal Reserve) or by taking other measures. But when the depression came and the crying need was for banks to encourage business by lending them money for expansion, the Federal Reserve Board suddenly tightened the monetary screws, *raising* interest rates and generally discouraging the financial community from helping its customers.

Yet, before we blame the Hoover administration out of hand for its undoubted mistakes, we must realize that most people did not understand how the depression could be cured—or why it did not cure itself. As time went on and the economy failed to recover, economists as well as businessmen felt baffled by events. The most frightening thing about the depression was that the nation was not only bankrupt in its affairs but bankrupt in its ideas.

BEHIND THE COLLAPSE

What *was* the cause of the Great Depression? The question leads us toward that lesson in economics mentioned at the outset of this chapter. But at least some of the reasons for the collapse do not require any special knowledge at all. Let us examine three of them before we turn to an analysis of the depression itself.

Apple seller, New York City, 1932

1. *The economy was extremely vulnerable to a crash.*

The get-rich-quick philosophy of the 1920s was not limited only to the public. It also infected the business community. An orgy of financial manipulation, wild speculative ventures, and reckless practices made the decade of the 1920s reminiscent of the period of the robber barons.

More to the point, these practices resulted in pyramids of corporations, each holding the stock of others. The pyramids were very profitable as long as the corporations on the bottom stood firm. But when one of them slipped—when one company in a pyramid failed— it often brought down the heap with it. For example, the structure of a giant utility company controlled by a Chicago financier named Samuel Insull was so complex that it was said, in all seriousness, that no one, including Insull himself, could understand it. (Insull held sixty-five chairmanships, eighty-five directorships, and seven presidencies of corporations.) One small part of the structure, Georgia Power & Light, was controlled by Seaboard Public Service Corporation, which was controlled by National Service Corporation, which was controlled by Middle West Utilities Corporation, which was controlled by Insull Utility Investments, which was controlled by Corporation Securities Company, which in turn was controlled by Insull Utility Investments. . . .

Thus despite endless assurances by businessmen that things were fundamentally sound, things were *not* fundamentally sound. Nowhere was this more true than in the banking industry. Banks were up to their ears in the very unsound business of lending money for security purchases; and when the market fell, the lending banks were grievously stricken. In addition, banks not only foisted all manner of unsound securities on the public but became convinced of the value of those very same investments and bought them themselves. Nor did the Federal Reserve Board use any direct controls,* such as raising the discount rate to check the speculative mania of the times. And not least, the acquisitive mania of the twenties tempted banks into practices that hardly squared with "soundness." For instance, the First National Bank (one of the leading New York banks) paid $450,000 to the son of the president of Peru for his services in connection with a

---

*It should be noted that the Federal Reserve Board did not have control over margin requirements until 1934.

$50 million Peruvian loan the bank was about to make at a considerable profit. The services of the president's son, it should be added, consisted entirely of his agreement not to block the deal.

Hence one terrible consequence of the crash was that it toppled many banks whose failure in turn toppled other businesses. In the first six months of 1929, 346 banks failed. By 1932, 4,835 banks had closed their doors. When they did so, it meant that depositors or businesses could not redeem their savings or checking accounts. In the years from 1929 to 1933 over nine million savings accounts were lost and countless businesses went bankrupt because they could not get their money out of the banks.

2. *There was trouble on the farms.*

The crash brought down the fragile banking structure, but even without the stock market there was trouble brewing during the 1920s. The trouble was not in the cities or the big corporations, or among the suburbanites who danced the Charleston, but in rural America. Here lived seven million of America's thirty million families. They did not dance the Charleston because they had no radios on which to hear the music—less than 10 percent of America's farms had electricity. This meant that over 90 percent of the farms were entirely excluded from the market for refrigerators and electric appliances and even electric light.

Moreover, the average farm household was not only poor but was growing relatively poorer. In 1910 an average farmer's income had been about 40 percent of an average urban worker's income. By 1930 it had fallen to less than 30 percent. More telling still, in 1919 farmers had received 16 percent of the national income; in 1929 the figure was 9 percent. Moreover, each year more and more farm families lost their ability to maintain their own farms. Unable to meet the mortgage payments on their properties, they went into sharecropping or tenantry: By 1929 four out of every ten farmers were tenant farmers.

Perhaps what was most ironic in this rural tragedy was that it was caused in substantial part by the very success of the industrial portion of the nation. One of the results of industrialization, as we have already seen, was that farm tasks were increasingly mechanized. This gave rise to a flood of output from the farms—a flood that

Other statistics show that between 1920 and 1929 per capita disposable income for all Americans rose by 9 percent, but the top 1 percent of income recipients enjoyed an explosive 75 percent increase in disposable income. The share of disposable income going to the top 1 percent rose by almost 60 percent in 1929.

One further statistical breakdown is necessary to round out the picture: In 1929 approximately 80 percent of the nation's families—roughly 21.5 million households—had no savings whatsoever. The 24,000 families at the top—0.1 percent—held 34 percent of all savings. The 2.3 percent of families with incomes of more than $10,000 controlled two-thirds of the nation's savings.

The consequence was not just a matter for tongue-clucking. Income was being diverted away from ordinary families, who would have spent it for the products of mass industry, into the hands of the rich, who spent it for luxuries or who did not spend it at all.

In other words, the prosperity of the 1920s was a good deal less substantial than it appeared on the surface. A rickety financial structure brought havoc when the stock market collapsed. A declining farm sector created an undertow of falling incomes in the agricultural areas where a fourth of the nation lived. The boom in profits and the swelling of topmost incomes came at the expense of a much-needed encouragement to mass buying power. Thus the economy operated very unevenly, bringing real riches to a few but a false sense of widely shared well-being to the nation at large. It was a prosperity based largely on speculation, easy credit, and foolish spending.

THE ANATOMY OF DEPRESSION

All these reasons help explain why the depression was so deep, so hard, so long. But they do not quite enlighten us as to the main question—namely, why an economy in full growth should suddenly go into a kind of paralysis. For that we need to take a brief lesson in economics.

Much of our understanding about the nature of depressions derives from a book published in the midst of the period, *The General Theory of Employment, Interest, and Money,* written by the English economist, John Maynard Keynes. Controversial at the time, Keynes's basic theories have by now become accepted by economists and governments all over the world. And like so many new theories that seem extraordinarily difficult at the time they are first pronounced, Keynes's essential ideas now appear very simple.

At the heart of Keynes's explanation of depression is a fundamental fact about a market economy: *the source of all its employment is spending.* Unless money is spent, money will not be received. Unless dollars are spent, neither businesses nor employees will get paid. Spending—*expenditure* is the more formal term—is the key to the generation of employment and income.

Who Does the Nation's Spending?

Keynes divides spenders into two groups: households and business firms. Households spend money for the goods and services they consume—consumer goods. These include food and clothing and automobiles and doctors' services and similar items. But consumers are not the only spenders in the economy. Business also spends money, not merely to keep its operations going, but to add to its plant and equipment, its capital wealth. We call this second kind of spending *investment.* A business invests when it is building a new factory, adding a wing to an existing establishment, piling up larger inventories to service its customers.

All that was familiar enough, even in the 1930s. But Keynes emphasizes a very important distinction between consumer spending and business spending. Consumer spending, he explains, is not usually marked by rapid changes (upward or downward), *unless consumers' incomes have previously changed upward or downward.* That is, households tend to spend a fairly steady proportion of their incomes. When their incomes fall—as in a depression—naturally they spend less. When their incomes rise, they spend more.

But it is different with business spending for investment. A business firm does not decide to build a new plant or to buy new equipment only because its *current* income is high. Indeed, we recall that Andrew Carnegie launched the great Thomson Steel Works even though there was a severe depression in 1873. Business spending for investment depends on businessmen's expectations of *future* sales. If a business firm expects to be able to sell more goods, it might spend money to enlarge its factory even though its current income is low. Vice versa, even if a business is highly prosperous, it might cut its investment spending if it feels that the future is not likely to continue as favorably as the past.

The Crucial Role of Investment

This gives us a first clue to the real meaning of the depression. *All depressions, or "recessions," or business slumps are brought about because the economy is not spending enough to create high levels of employment or income.*

That is exactly what caused the Great Depression. In 1929 the gross national product—the value of total final output—was $104 billion.* In 1932 the gross national product (GNP) had fallen to $56 billion. What caused the terrific collapse? The main reason is that the Great Crash, added to all the weaknesses that we have seen, sent a wave of pessimism through business. Businessmen simply cancelled their plans for business expansion in the face of deep and growing concern about the future.

---

*What is gross national product? *It is the market value of all the final goods and services produced by the economy in a year.* The word "final" means that the statisticians who compute GNP add up the value of all the "last" goods we produce but do not include the value of output that *goes into* those goods. Example: the statisticians count in GNP the market value of all the automobiles that are made, but not the value of the rubber, the steel, the paint, and the cotton cloth that various companies sell to the auto-makers. The reason is that the value of these goods is *included* in the value of the finished car. In the same way, GNP includes the value of the clothes that are made, but not the value of the cloth, the thread, and the buttons that are included in the selling price of the finished garment.

What are "final" goods? There are four kinds. First, there are all the domestically made *consumption goods* or services that households buy, such as autos and clothes. Second are the domestically produced *investment goods* that business buys, such as new buildings, machines, and additions to inventories. Third are the domestic goods or services that *government buys*—roads, public education, police, arms, and so forth. And fourth is the value of all *foreign goods* and services of all kinds bought by the nation, minus the value of all domestic production sold abroad. To recapitulate, then, *GNP is the total market value of the annual output of all domestic consumer output, all domestic investment output, all domestic public output, and all output sold abroad less foreign output imported into the country.*

Recently our national output has been calculated as GDP, not GNP—D standing for domestic instead of national. The change affects the way we treat the earnings of U.S. corporations abroad, and foreign corporations operating within the U.S. In dollars, the difference between GNP and GDP is small.

We can see the collapse in investment spending in the figures below:

INVESTMENT SPENDING (BILLIONS OF $)		
	Housing	**Other Construction**	**Plant & Equipment**
1929	4.0	5.0	5.6
1932	1.7	1.2	1.5

SOURCE: *Historical Statistics,* Bureau of the Census, 1975, Tables F57, F55, F56.

The Multiplier Effect

Between 1929 and 1933, investment spending of all kinds shrank by 88 percent! One-third of all unemployment was directly generated by the shrinkage in output of industries that supplied capital goods. Unemployment then spread throughout the economy as a consequence of the cutback in investment spending. As workers were fired and lower incomes were paid out by construction firms and steel plants and other businesses making capital goods, employees were forced to cut back their spending for consumer goods. In turn, because they bought fewer consumer goods, firms that sold clothing, food, housewares, and so forth began to fire some of their workers, or to lower their wages. Thus the sharp drop in investment spending spread throughout the economy, creating a "multiplier" effect as it went.

Indefinite Depression

Keynes's explanation of the mechanism of depression was very clear, and not too controversial. But buried in his analysis was a deeper implication. It was that there was no *automatic* cure for a depression. Only a resumption of spending—investment spending—could move an economy off dead center. But there was no mechanism that would bring this about from the normal workings of the system. An economy could remain in a stagnant condition indefinitely. A depression could go on forever.

It was this last part of Keynes's analysis that was most disturbing. For economists had always maintained that depressions would ultimately cure themselves, not merely because businessmen would recover their optimistic expectations and begin again to invest, but because the workings of the system would by themselves create the stimulus for reexpansion. As the economy contracted, economists argued, unused savings would pile up in the banks, forcing down the rate of interest to a point where businessmen would be irresistibly tempted to borrow and spend. After that, the upward march would resume.

Keynes's book dealt a disconcerting blow to that reassuring belief. For it pointed out that there would be no unused savings as a depression continued. Rather, savings would shrink along with investment as the economy ran downhill. Moreover, even if interest rates did fall, Keynes pointed out, businessmen would not invest if their expectations remained pessimistic. Hence the economy could go on in "equilibrium"—without any internally generated upward thrust—even though it was full of unemployed men and women and underutilized plants and equipment. That dead part of the economy might as well be on the moon, for all the positive effect it exerted on the business community.

Growth or Stagnation?

A full discussion of Keynesian economics is obviously far beyond the scope of this book. But we can see how Keynes's idea of a stagnant economy touches our own central theme. The economic transformation of America has been a narrative of capitalist growth. All through our historic journey, the theme of capitalist expansion—of a rising trajectory of output and income—has provided the setting in which occurred the changes in material and economic life to which we have paid heed. But now the Great Depression—the endless, endless depression—and the idea of an economy in stagnant equilibrium causes us to ask another question: Is growth the norm for capitalism? Is it a state of affairs to be taken for granted, with depressions viewed as temporary aberrations from the main path? Or is growth a prelude to something else, of which the Great Depression provided a frightening glimpse?

It may come as something of a surprise to learn that all the great economists have pictured capitalism as tending finally toward a kind of stagnant, stationary condition. Adam Smith, the first magisterial student of the system, believed that sooner or later a market society would accumulate all the capital it needed, after which it would begin to decline. David Ricardo and his disciple, John Stuart Mill, writing in the nineteenth century, also thought that capitalism would move toward a stationary condition—not because it had built all the capital it needed, but because profitable investment would become ever more difficult as wages and material costs rose as a consequence of expansion. Karl Marx also perceived the system as reaching a limit. Marx foresaw a series of "crises" generated by capitalism, each one resulting in a more concentrated structure of business and a more proletarianized lower class, until the tension within the system finally snapped, and capitalism came to an end.

Essentially then, almost all the great economists, Keynes among them, have expected that capitalism would eventually change so profoundly that it could no longer be called by its name. The main point of disagreement has been over the nature of the forces bringing about that change—Smith's exhaustion of investment opportunities, Ricardo's or Mill's squeeze on profits by rising costs, or Marx's complex dynamics of instability and concentration—and over the length of time the system could be expected to continue. In 1942, Joseph Schumpeter, perhaps the most distinguished conservative economist of the twentieth century, put the matter point blank. "Can capitalism survive?" he asked. "No," he answered. "I do not think it can."[9] However, Schumpeter hastened to add that it would take another fifty to 100 years before capitalism gave way before the advance of a kind of bureaucratic socialism.

The Social Structure of Accumulation

How does the Great Depression fit into these possible evolutionary tendencies of the system? An interesting answer has been proposed by economist David Gordon.[10] It focuses our attention on the milieu within which capitalism carries on its accumulative activity. This milieu begins in the workplace where capitalists must organize and oversee a work force to create a profitable flow of output, a relationship that sometimes works very well and sometimes very poorly. The milieu then extends into the interaction of business and government, where businessmen sometimes find their investment activities supported by public action, and sometimes find them blocked by it. It moves out still further into the realm of public opinion where businesses may encounter a favoring or hostile reception to their general aims. And it reaches out finally into the world economy within which each national economy must find its place.

Gordon calls this complex set of relationships and institutions *the social structure of accumulation.* It is in this social structure that he finds the crucial connection between growth and stagnation. For the network of relationships that supports capital accumulation in one period may become a hindrance in another. Thus we can distinguish between the normal business cycle, in which investment booms may be interrupted but quickly resume their course within a favoring milieu, from turning points, or crisis periods, in which investment comes to a halt because the milieu itself stands in the way of capital expansion. In these critical periods we need more than a recovery of business optimism. We need a social restructuring that will permit capital expansion once more to take place.

The Crisis of the 1870s

We have spent a good deal of time studying one such crisis period. This was the era of the Robber Barons, when capitalists struggled to cope with the disruptions of a new high speed, mass-volume technology. We watched as a framework of giant-business, created by vertical and horizontal integration, brought order into the chaos of cutthroat competition by replacing the unmanageable currents of the marketplace with the steadying guidance of management's visible hand.

The concept of a crisis period caused by an inadequate social structure of accumulation helps us put this period into a perspective of capitalist evolution. For we can see that the structure of the pre–Robber Baron period with its small-scale enterprises, its craft-organized labor force, and its nonregulative government, could not handle the economic pressures and strains caused by the technology of mass production. Indeed, in the milieu of the 1860s, the new technology did not produce growth but chaos and disorder. It required a wholly different social structure of giant organizations, "de-skilled" labor, and regulative government, before those technological forces could give rise to capital accumulation.

The 1930s as a Crisis Period

This brings us once again to the Great Depression. For now we can see that the era of the 1930s was also a time in which an older milieu was no longer able to provide the necessary support for the accumulation process. The difference was that the immediate problem of the 1930s was not technological. The big business system had more or less overcome that once formidable threat. But that selfsame system had brought into existence a new difficulty, previously absent. This was the tremendous downward momentum generated by the system when investment halted, for whatever reason. The economy of the 1930s was no longer an economic landscape of small enterprise with a few great enterprises towering over the whole. It was the great enterprises themselves that constituted the main elements of the system. In place of an economy that resembled a pile of sand, there had arisen an economy that resembled a great steel scaffolding. A pile of sand can withstand a heavy blow without losing its stability. A scaffolding whose main members are weakened comes toppling down with a crash.

Essentially the crisis of the 1930s was caused by the vulnerability of a structure of business that had become interlocked on a previously unknown scale. It was the collapse of the scaffolding that caused the extraordinary damage, the sense of an economy in ruins. Perhaps, as some business leaders affirmed, the system would in time recover its optimism and begin once again to grow. But it was time that was running out. The country was exhausted. There was no patience left.

But what was to be done? With the gift of hindsight we know the answer, as did Keynes and a few others at the time. In part it was to use government powers to restore order to shattered elements of the system, such as the banking structure. In part it was to use government to emplace a floor of security beneath the nation's households. And most important of all, it was to use government spending itself as a means of imparting momentum to the economy—a task that had formerly been solely entrusted to business investment spending. In a word, the overriding task was to rescue the capitalist economy by altering its social structure of accumulation in ways that would make the government vastly more responsible for the functioning of the economic mechanism.

None of that was very clearly seen by most of the nation's business leaders or its politicians. Indeed, the idea of creating such a new "socialistic" milieu was as foreign and as unwelcome to most leaders in the 1930s as was the idea of fostering an economy of "trusts" in the 1860s. Yet in one period of crisis as in the other, changes of vast extent were carried out, despite the absence of any clear blueprint for the future, and over the protests of those who felt that the changes were against their interests. And in one period as in the other, after the changes had been made, the new social structure of accumulation did generate a new era of growth, and the long upward trajectory of the system was renewed.

How did this far-reaching change come about? To find out we must pick up our narrative as a discredited and discouraged Republican administration leaves office in 1932 and a new Democratic president takes over, with very few convictions except that *something* had to be done.

Notes

[1] *Only Yesterday* (Bantam ed., 1946), p. 349.

[2] Nov. 5, 1932, pp. 3–4.

[3] Quoted in John Kenneth Galbraith, *The Great Crash* (1955), pp. 69–70.

[4] F. L. Allen, *The Big Change* (1952), p. 148.

[5] Arthur Schlesinger, Jr., *The Crisis of the Old Order* (1957), pp. 162–63, 177.

[6] Quoted in Schlesinger, *The Crisis of the Old Order*, pp. 457–58.

[7] Quoted in William Manchester, *The Glory and the Dream* (1974), p. 41.

[8] David Shannon (ed.), *The Great Depression* (1960), p. 27.

[9] *Capitalism, Socialism, and Democracy* (1942), p. 61.

[10] David Gordon, Michael Reich, and Richard C. Edwards, *Segmented Work, Divided Workers* (1982), pp.9–10, 22–26.

National Industrial Recovery Act banners, 1933

Chapter 14
THE NEW DEAL

On election day, 1932, Franklin D. Roosevelt won an overwhelming victory over Herbert Hoover. The popular vote, 22,800,000 to 15,750,000, and the Electoral College vote, 472 to fifty-nine, tell only part of the story. In addition to carrying every state south and west of Pennsylvania, and capturing more counties than any previous candidate, the new president had taken from Hoover all but six of the forty states the ex-president had won in 1928. With the exception of the election of 1912, when the Republican Party was split between Taft and Theodore Roosevelt, no Republican presidential candidate had ever been defeated so soundly.

THE HUNDRED DAYS

The nation had unequivocally declared its need for a new policy to deal with the depression. In the four months before Roosevelt took office the depression deepened and worsened. When inauguration day finally came, on March 4, 1933, the country was glued to its radio receivers to hear what the new president would say. What they heard was this:

> First of all, let me assert my belief that the only thing we have to fear is fear itself—nameless, unreasoning, unjustified terror. . . . I shall not evade the clear course of duty that [confronts] me. I shall ask the Congress . . . for broad Executive power to wage war against the emergency, as great as the power that would be given to me if we were in fact invaded by a foreign foe. . . . I pledge you, I pledge myself to a new deal for the American people.[1]

Roosevelt's clarion call was magnetic. "America hasn't been as happy in three years as they are today," wrote Will Rogers the next day. "No money, no banks, no work, no nothing, but they know they got a man in there who is wise to Congress, wise to our so-called big men. The whole country is with him."[2] That weekend the new president received 450,000 messages confirming Rogers' opinion.

Financial Crisis

About few subjects have so many volumes been written as about the "New Deal"—those two words Roosevelt first uttered casually in his acceptance speech before the Democratic convention in Chicago in 1932. Not since Lincoln or Theodore Roosevelt had a personality so engaged the public. Millions of Americans hung pictures of Roosevelt in their living rooms and felt him to be a member of their families.

What the country desperately wanted from FDR was action—almost any action—rather than a continuation of Hoover's policy of waiting for the economy to cure itself. The public was not disappointed. The New Deal began with what historian Arthur Schlesinger, Jr., has called "a barrage of ideas and programs unlike anything known to American history." In the first dazzling "Hundred Days," March 9 to June 16, 1933, over fifteen major pieces of legislation were passed.

The most pressing problem that the president had to address himself to was the financial crisis, which had now reached a point of near panic, with more banks closing every day. Even before he convened Congress into emergency session, Roosevelt issued an executive order declaring a nationwide bank "holiday." Thereafter he instructed his first Secretary of the Treasury, William Woodin, to prepare an emergency banking bill within five days. When the special session of Congress convened on March 9, it gave its approval to actions Roosevelt had in fact already taken. The Emergency Banking Act gave the President unequivocal control over gold and currency movements, outlawed the hoarding of gold, sanctioned the issue of new Federal Reserve Bank notes, and established a procedure for reopening those banks that possessed liquid assets and for reorganizing those that did not.

The Emergency Banking Act represented a bold extension and assertion of government power. Curiously, the bill was written at lightning speed by conservative bankers and by Hoover's own Treasury officials and was then passed unanimously, *sight unseen,* by the

President Franklin D. Roosevelt

House of Representatives! A few days later, some sixty million Americans turned on their radios to hear the first of Roosevelt's "fireside chats." In informal, fatherly tones, the president's voice conveyed a spirit of national purpose and demonstrated one of his many charismatic qualities—the power to persuade. After describing the complex banking structure in simple terms, he told the country that the banks would be safely opening in the twelve Federal Reserve Bank cities the next morning. They opened safely, because people believed Roosevelt and did not rush to withdraw their deposits. Indeed, by the end of the month net inflows of currency into banks amounted to $1.25 billion. "Capitalism," a member of Roosevelt's advisory team (the so-called brain trust) later wrote, "was saved in eight days."[3]

Other Financial Legislation

Subsequent banking legislation established the Federal Deposit Insurance Corporation to guarantee bank deposits up to $5,000 ($100,000 today), divorced investment and commercial banking, and broadened the power of the Federal Reserve Board. These measures also had an immediate impact. People began to deposit rather than withdraw money, and bank failures were sharply reduced.

In retrospect, the "obscure, unpretentious, unwanted Federal Deposit Insurance Corporation" (as John Kenneth Galbraith has described the measure, which was opposed by the American Bankers Association* and endorsed only halfheartedly by the administration) may well have been the most important single piece of financial legislation passed by the Roosevelt administration. As Galbraith points out, for the first time an utterly reliable lender of last resort—the federal government itself—was squarely committed to the safety of bank accounts. No more powerful measure of financial or psychological endorsement was ever taken by the government.

Closely related to the reorganization of the banking structure was Roosevelt's determination to curb financial abuses, particularly in the securities market. Writing to Congress on March 29, 1933, he stated: "What we seek is a return to a clearer understanding of the ancient truth that those who manage banks, corporations, and other agencies handling or using other people's money are trustees acting for others."[4]

Within a year the country saw the birth of the Securities and Exchange Commission (the SEC) charged with broad powers to oversee the issuance of new securities, to insist on the divulgence of full information regarding new issues, and to establish an agency to maintain a watchful eye over the operation of that great gambling casino, the stock exchange. It would be too much to say that the Banking Act, the Federal Deposit Insurance Corporation, and the SEC cured American finance of all its problems or prevented financial misdeeds in the future. But with these acts, and the Public Utility Holding Company Act that prohibited the old pyramiding of utility companies, the New Deal effectively removed the worst elements of the financial crisis that was threatening to undermine the system itself.

---

*Big bankers opposed the act because they believed it would give unsound banks "a license for reckless behavior that the supervision authorized by the legislation could not hope to restrain." Hence the sound establishments would "have to accept responsibility for the recklessness of the worst." See Galbraith, *Money* (1975), p. 197.

Unemployment

The New Deal was not so successful in combating unemployment. For one thing, Roosevelt was himself a strong believer in balanced budgets for government,* and therefore he shrank from the full application of a Keynesian remedy of government spending, whatever the effect on the deficit. We will go into this in more detail later in this chapter. But despite the inhibitions imposed by a genuine desire to achieve budget economies, the New Deal did attack the problem of unemployment and human suffering far more vigorously than its predecessor.

On April 5, 1933, Roosevelt created the Civilian Conservation Corps to provide jobs in reforestation and conservation projects for young men between the ages of eighteen and twenty-five. Wearing their forest-green CCC uniforms, over $2^{1}/_{2}$ million youths planted 200 million trees, not only beautifying the land but establishing windbreaks to prevent the erosion that had devastated many farm lands.

Then, in May, Roosevelt signed into being the Federal Emergency Relief Administration, headed by Harry Hopkins, a confidant and trusted adviser. The FERA had $500 million to allocate to state and local relief agencies, but Hopkins was convinced that jobs, not money, were the prime requisite to restore confidence. Hopkins persuaded the president to sponsor the Civil Works Administration, a federally sponsored program to employ people in building roads, schools, playgrounds, airports, or to teach. Before Roosevelt finally disbanded the CWA because of its mounting costs, it had given work to over four million people and had channeled some $950 million into the economy. Then, in 1935, Hopkins was put in charge of another alphabet agency—the WPA (Works Progress Administration). By 1943 this agency had employed $8^{1}/_{2}$ million people and had spent a total of $11 billion.

In a nation that had not yet heard of Keynes and that was still wedded to the ideas of laissez faire, all this was a radical departure indeed.

---

*During his campaign for the presidency, Roosevelt had attacked the Hoover administration for "being the greatest spending Administration in peace times in all our history. . . . "Indeed, Roosevelt's second piece of Hundred Days legislation, the Economy Act, was an effort to honor his pledge to cut government spending. The purpose of the measure was to help balance the budget by slashing veterans' benefits and allowances by $400 million and by reducing by $100 million the pay of federal employees.

Yet few voices were raised in protest. For the country knew, as did Roosevelt, that the alternative to these experiments in government employment was the risk of an interminable depression with massive unemployment. No one dared run that risk.

Industry and Labor

One of Roosevelt's pet proposals for ending the demoralization of the economy was the National Industrial Recovery Act. The NIRA was a curious mixture of things, designed to please many constituencies. It contained the authorization, for example, for the Public Works Administration (with a budget of $3.3 billion), a works project that supplemented the WPA. It contained a clause specifically guaranteeing workers the right to unionize and to bargain collectively with their employers. It outlawed much child labor. It established a precedent for the government regulation of minimum wages and hours. Not least, it allowed business to do legally what it had sought in vain to do through pools, trusts, and collusion—namely, to establish industrywide prices and codes of fair practice. The hope was that the act would turn the sluggish industrial economy around and, at the same time, usher in a new era in labor-management relations. Internecine warfare among firms in the same field would be avoided and the threat of strikes would be minimized.

The National Recovery Administration (NRA) did not achieve all its objectives by any means, and its use of government powers to protect labor on the one hand and to legalize "trusts" on the other offended many people. Though it was greeted with much initial enthusiasm, there was a general sigh of relief among several government offices when the act was finally declared unconstitutional by the Supreme Court in 1935.* But by then the NRA had served its purpose of restoring orderly markets in many areas, and its specific reforms were soon continued under new legislation (the Fair Labor Standards Act) aimed at establishing minimum wages and maximum hours in certain

---

*In the case of *Schechter v. United States*, the high court ruled unanimously that Congress had delegated too much of its law-making power to the boards that administrered the industrial codes established under the measure. Roosevelt, however, continued to believe in the NRA approach of government-business-labor cooperation and never abandoned the idea of trying to restore it.

Works Progress Administration workers

industries, at abolishing child labor, and most important, at protecting the rights of labor. According to James MacGregor Burns, the passage of the Wagner Act in 1935, which once again assured the right of unions to organize and to bargain collectively, was "the most radical legislation passed during the New Deal" because it helped to create "powerful unions that . . . would furnish votes, money, and organization to future liberal coalitions." Under the auspices of the Wagner Act, and the National Labor Relations Board which it created to run union elections and settle disputes, union membership jumped from 3.2 million in 1932 to 8.3 million in 1938.[5]

Agriculture

The NRA had something for business and something for labor. But the Roosevelt program for farm relief was incorporated in another major piece of legislation. This was the AAA—the Agricultural Adjustment Act of 1933. The AAA went much further than Hoover's efforts to help the farmer through the government purchase of some surplus crops. It aimed to break the vicious circle of farm poverty by making it possible for farmers to do collectively what they could not do individually—to limit their production so that the price of their products would rise.

The program was intended to work through compulsory restrictions on the production of designated crops, together with government subsidies for staple commodities such as wheat, cotton, and pork. However, since crops were already growing when the law was enacted, Secretary of Agriculture Henry A. Wallace felt it necessary to tell farmers to destroy their produce in the field. Thus, while millions of Americans were still hungry, cotton planters received $100 million for plowing under ten million acres of growing crops, and farmers were paid to kill six million baby pigs and 200,000 pregnant sows! Yet, if the program revealed an appalling insensitivity, it did succeed in its overall objectives. More than 30 million acres were taken out of cultivation, and farm prices rose from depression lows to more normal levels. By 1936 the farm sector had doubled its income, and there was no more talk of revolution brewing in Ohio.

Soon thereafter a much more imaginative program made up for the government's failure to deal more sensibly with the problem of farm surpluses. This was its effort to bring economic growth to a backwater region through the establishment of a federal power-generating system, the Tennessee Valley Authority. During the First World War the government had built a hydroelectric plant at Muscle Shoals, Alabama, to provide power for the manufacture of synthetic nitrate explosives. Although farmers and other interest groups succeeded after the war in warding off plans to hand these facilities over to private enterprise, they failed in their efforts to have the site come under federal control. Now Roosevelt hoped to turn one of the country's most underdeveloped areas into an experimental laboratory for extensive social planning. The TVA constructed dams and powerhouses, established programs for flood control, soil conservation, and reforestation, and produced electricity and fertilizer. Moreover the TVA became a "yardstick" that enabled the government to measure the fairness of the rates charged by private power companies.

Together with the power generated by the TVA, one other New Deal action dramatically altered the course of the farmer's life—the Rural Electrification Administration of 1935. One statistic sums up its accomplishment. Before 1935, nine out of every ten farms had no electricity; by 1950, nine out of ten had electric light.

Social Security

We have not yet discussed what is perhaps the most important single measure that the New Deal passed: Social Security. After signing the measure on August 15, 1935, Roosevelt remarked: "If the Senate and the House of Representatives in this long and arduous session had done nothing more than pass this bill, the session would be regarded as historic for all time."[6]

Essentially, the Social Security Act established a national system of old-age insurance. Once workers reached the age of sixty-five they would receive retirement benefits paid for by taxes on their wages and their employers' payrolls. Payment would, up to a point, vary with the amount each individual earned. The act also created a federal-state system of unemployment insurance and provided for federal-state joint assistance to the destitute, to the handicapped, and to dependent mothers and children.

Not all Americans approved of this unparalleled legislation. "Never in the history of the world," said conservative Congressman John Taber, "has any measure been brought in here so insidiously designed as to prevent business recovery, to enslave workers, and to prevent any possibility of the employers providing work for the people." Congressman Daniel Reed agreed: "The lash of the dictator will be felt and twenty-five million free American citizens will for the first time submit themselves to the fingerprint test."[7]

These were not isolated criticisms, nor did they match the more strident invective that was hurled at Roosevelt. Many businessmen regarded the president, who came from a wealthy New York family, as a "traitor to his class," and the reforms of the New Deal, far from being welcomed by them, were bitterly resisted and interpreted as the entering wedge of socialism. In 1934 some of these arch-conservative businessmen formed the American Liberty League, around which anti–New Dealers from both parties coalesced.

The innovations of the New Deal were also regarded suspiciously by another conservative element in society—the nation's courts. One after another of the major New Deal efforts, such as the Agricultural Adjustment Act* and the National Industrial Recovery Act, were declared unconstitutional by a Supreme Court that viewed with alarm the efforts of the federal government to use the powers of the Constitution to regulate and restrain economic life. Even some of the most liberal justices felt that Roosevelt exceeded the proper bounds of executive power. Not until the Eisenhower years in the 1950s was the new role of the government finally accepted as a necessary element in a highly organized industrial system, rather than as a threat to that system.

THE NEW DEAL IN PERSPECTIVE

Can we sum up the economic accomplishments of the New Deal as a whole? Looking back on its array of accomplishments from the perspective of our last chapter, we can see that the New Deal can be regarded as an attempt—a quite unconscious attempt—to alter the social structure of accumulation in three ways.

First, *the New Deal was an effort to make the system work in certain areas in which it had failed.* The stock market crash, the farm disaster, the bank failures, massive unemployment—these were not merely localized or transient failures that could be safely left to the dynamic forces of the economy to cure. The public had waited too long to believe that things would straighten out by themselves. What was needed was a new assurance that serious problems affecting the livelihood and lives of millions of wage-earners would not be allowed to fester unheeded. If the economy did not function reliably by itself, the public wanted the government to make it work.

That is what the New Deal tried to do, though not always with success. For all the accusations of "socialism" that were hurled against it, the New Deal was essentially conservative in its intent. As evidenced

---

*The AAA was declared unconstitutional in the case of *United States v. Butler* (1936). In a six to three decision the Court held the AAA's processing tax—the means by which farm subsidies were financed—to be unconstitutional. According to Justice Owen Roberts, the tax expropriated "money from one group for the benefit of another."

by the authorship of the emergency banking legislation, it sought not to replace the business system with another totally different system but to amend the business system to make it succeed.

Second, *the New Deal was an effort to create a new relation between government and citizenry in economic life.* The belief that prevailed throughout the years of American economic growth had been that the best guardian for each able-bodied citizen was himself. This was indeed an integral part of the philosophy of laissez faire. When Herbert Hoover spoke of "the American system of rugged individualism" and deplored agencies for relief and for the provision of a retirement income, he was speaking not just as an individual whose view of the economy inclined him in a conservative direction, but as a true spokesman of a philosophy endorsed by large numbers of the business community.

What Hoover and the business community failed to realize was that the basis for a system of rugged individualism had been eroded by the very success of the industrial growth of the economy. In 1890, for example, twice as many Americans lived in rural areas as in urban ones. When growth slackened in the industrial centers and unemployment grew, at least some affected families could move in with their relatives on the farm. In the 1930s, as we have seen, the proportion of rural and urban dwellers had swung the other way. Almost 60 percent of the nation lived in urban areas; so it was no longer possible for a recession affecting large numbers of workers to be cushioned by a reliance on country cousins. The workable basis for rugged individualism had gone with the industrialization and urbanization of the country. The New Deal was not an effort to make people dependent on government for security in case of economic trouble. It was a response to a situation in which no other solution was possible.

Third, *the New Deal was an effort to renew growth, not merely by repairing the weaknesses of the nation's financial and farm sectors, but by using the government as a means of spending to supplement the laggard expenditure of private investment.* Certainly the idea was very far from Roosevelt's mind when he took office at the very bottom of the depression. Campaigning for the presidency, he urged "balanced budgets," just like everyone else, and the idea of a large and aggressive program of public spending as a way of swelling the nation's output was as foreign to him as it was to the most conservative of the nation's businessmen. What was different about Roosevelt and the New Deal, in its early days, was a sense of the human urgency of the situation. Herbert Hoover was able to speak of the unemployed shivering at wintry street corners with their little piles of apples for sale as having *chosen* their economic condition. In contrast, Roosevelt and his advisers saw the unemployed as the victims of an economic disaster for which they were not responsible and over which they had no control. Hence they responded to the immediate situation by hastily throwing together the collection of emergency programs that we have seen.

Of course this necessitated the spending of money by the government. Federal Emergency Relief increased from $6 million in 1933 to $115 million in 1935. Expenditures by the Civilian Conservation Corps began in 1933 at $141 million and grew to $332 million in two years. The Civil Works Administration spent $215 million in the first year of Roosevelt's term and more than double that the next year. These are all very small numbers to us, who are used to billions and tens of billions rather than mere millions, but they were very large numbers in a day when the total military expenditures of the government were less than $700 million in a normal year. Do not forget, either, that in the 1930s gross national product was less than $100 billion, whereas today it is over $6 trillion.

As a result of these emergency measures, total government spending rose. In 1932, the last year of the Hoover administration, the federal government spent $4.6 billion for all purposes—education, highways, national defense, postal services, relief, and so forth. By 1935 the total was up to $6.5 billion; by 1936, $8.4 billion—an unprecedented sum. Helped along by this "pump-priming," business began to spend more too—spending for business investment rose from $0.9 billion in 1932 to $11 billion in 1937. Consumer spending rose as well, supported by the new dollars flowing into households: consumers spent $46 billion in 1933 and $67 billion in 1937.

Disappointing Results

On the face of it, then, it would seem that the effort to restore growth was a success. Real gross national product had fallen to a low of $74 billion in 1933—off by one-fourth from the high of 1929. By 1937 it was back to $109 billion. Unemployment, which had reached the dreadful total of almost thirteen million men and women in 1933, was down to 7.7 million by 1937.

Yet it is clear, at second look, that the program was at best only a partial success. For despite the recovery under the impetus of federal spending, gross national product in 1937 was still only 5 percent above its peak in 1929—instead of really growing, the economy was only catching up (and was far below the trend of the past). And although 7.7 million unemployed was a good deal less serious than thirteen million, it still meant that 14 percent of the labor force was unable to find work, compared with only 3 percent in 1929.

Chart 1 shows us what was happening with government spending and GNP. Notice how government spending rose, helping to push up GNP but hardly bringing it above the level of 1929 prosperity.

Chart 2 shows the problem even more clearly, for now we place the New Deal period in a longer-range historical context. The second chart shows the long, irregular upward slope of growth prior to the Great Depression, the subsequent collapse, and then the recovery following on the New Deal. Note that by 1937 the economy had not yet reached the "trend line" established by the pre–New Deal period.

The Doldrums

Why was the economy in 1937 barely above the level of 1929? Why had not the bold new program of the New Deal quickly brought the country back onto the long "growth path" of the past?

If we had been able to visit Washington or the main industrial centers of the country in 1937, the answer we would have heard was that the government was doing "too much." James Farley, chairman of the Democratic Party, warned Roosevelt: "The one criticism which is being constantly hammered home and which seems to be having the most effect is the charge that the President and his Administration are carrying on an orgy of public spending. . . ."[8]

Farley's opinion was widely held. After resigning as Roosevelt's director of the budget because he believed that the president was spending too much, Lewis Douglas wrote the president: "I hope, and hope most fervently, that you will evidence a real determination to bring the budget into actual balance, for upon this, I think, hangs not only your place in history but conceivably the immediate fate of western civilization."[9] Ironically, Roosevelt himself worried that he was spending too much money. In 1937, when the economy seemed on the way toward a modest recovery (as we can see from Chart 2), he

CHART 1
Pre-New Deal and New Deal Periods

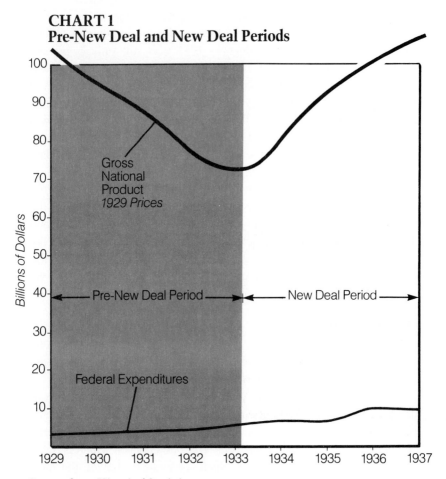

Source: from *Historical Statistics.*

slashed spending, sharply cut the rolls of the WPA, and turned off the "pump-priming" expenditures of the PWA.

The result was disconcerting. Government expenditures fell by a billion dollars—but gross national product fell by $5 billion! Out of the blue, another selling wave hit the stock market, which dropped a staggering 40 percent. Worst of all, unemployment jumped from 7.7 million to over ten million.

The severity of the collapse of October 1937 actually exceeded that which followed the Crash of '29. During the next nine months,

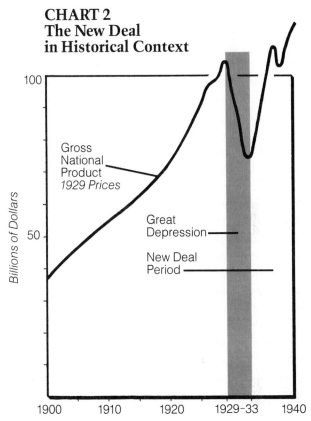

**CHART 2
The New Deal
in Historical Context**

Gross
National
Product
1929 Prices

Great
Depression

New Deal
Period

Billions of Dollars

100

50

1900   1910   1920   1929-33   1940

Source: from *Historical Statistics.*

national income fell 13 percent, industrial production by 33 percent, employment in manufacturing industries by almost 25 percent, and payrolls in general by 35 percent.

There was very little choice as to what to do next. The PWA was hurriedly given additional funds; government spending increased by over $1 billion; unemployment slowly fell to 9.4 million in 1939, then to eight million in 1940. The country resumed its sluggish recovery. In 1939, gross national product went up to $111 billion—just above the 1937 level—and finally, in 1940, it climbed to $121 billion, surpassing by a mere 16 percent the level of 1929.

The Dilemma of Government

What *was* the trouble? Looking back, we can see that much of the stagnation was in fact caused by the *belief* that the New Deal was doing "too much." Frightened by the policies of an activist, anti–laissez-faire administration, the business community never gained enough confidence to bring its own spending for investment purposes up to the levels of the 1920s. In 1929, businesses had poured $16 billion into new equipment, new plants, and home and office building. In 1937, the best year of the early New Deal, private investment was only $11.7 billion (and it fell to half that the following year).

Thus the critics were not entirely wrong when they blamed the doldrums on the policies of the New Deal, with its "dangerous" spending proclivities. But the critics were right only because the business community was so alarmed by New Deal spending that business spending for investment never regained its pre–1929 momentum.

Indeed, from our present-day perspective, we can see a quite different reason for the failure of the New Deal spending program. *The New Deal did not spend nearly enough!* Precisely because business did not spend predepression amounts for investment, the full-scale applications of Keynesian policies would have meant that the government should have spent twice or even three times as much as it did, financing its spending by borrowing money from the public in exchange for government bonds.

But that truly bold policy was quite impossible in a period when even the modest measures of the New Deal were enough to inspire fears of "socialism" and when government borrowing was not seen as an alternative to private investment borrowing but as a reckless and dangerous policy. Thus the New Dealers were caught in a trap. They were unable to spend enough to restore the full momentum of growth, but they were also unable to cut back their spending programs without sending the economy into a tailspin.

The War

No one knows how this dilemma of policy might have eventually been resolved, for suddenly events took a dramatic change that provided a decisive demonstration of the power of government spending. In 1939 war broke out in Europe; in December 1941 the Japanese bombed Pearl Harbor. Suddenly the nation found itself in a position of peril before which all quarrels about economic policy seemed trivial. The clear necessity, to which all agreed, was to mount a gigantic war effort—to build an armada for the sea, and another for the air, and simultaneously to equip a vast army for the land. All this required the expenditure of stupendous sums, and no one worried about the fact that only government could raise those sums by taxing and borrowing. Again Keynes was correct, for in 1940 he wrote: "It seems politically impossible for a capitalistic democracy to organize expenditure on the scale necessary to make the grand experiment that would prove my case—except in war conditions."[10]

Thus government spending skyrocketed—in the first six months of 1942 the government placed over $100 billion in contracts. GNP boomed. And unemployment quickly fell almost to zero:

THE EFFECTS OF WAR SPENDING (CURRENT PRICES)		
Federal Purchases ($ billions)	GNF ($ billions)	Unemployment (millions)
1940	6.0	99.7	8.1
1941	16.9	124.5	5.6
1942	51.9	157.9	2.7
1943	81.1	191.6	1.1
1944	89.0	210.1	.7
1945	74.8	211.9	1.0

SOURCE: *Historical Statistics,* Series F67, F47, D85.

To be sure, with the outpouring of military spending there was some inflation—consumer prices were about 28 percent higher in 1945 than they had been in 1940. Price ceilings imposed by the government helped prevent much greater wartime inflation. But even if we adjust the GNP figures for this inflationary influence, there is no doubt that growth was fully resumed. Chart 3 shows us the dip caused by the cutback in spending in 1937, and then the great surge that followed with the onset of spending during the war.

Many volumes have been written about the Second World War. Most of us study the war as a heroic chapter in the defense of democracy, or as a great contest between rival political systems. Yet history can be "read" from many angles, bringing into focus themes that give it special meaning for different purposes.

**CHART 3
The 1938
Slump**

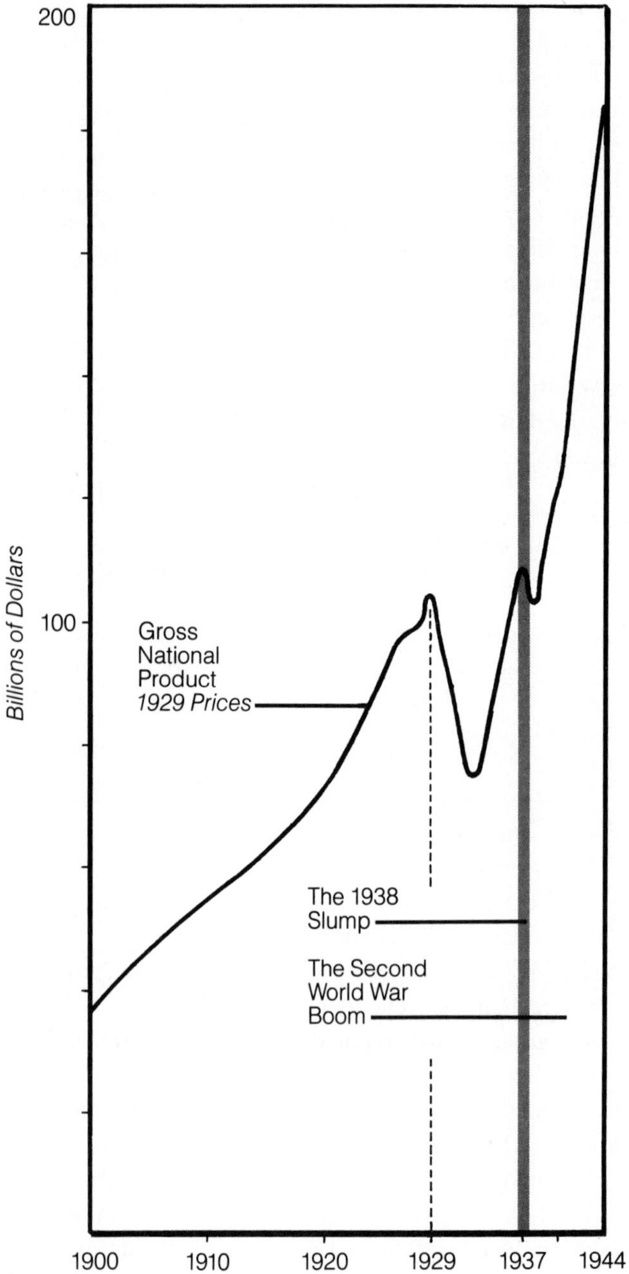

200

Billions of Dollars

100

Gross
National
Product
1929 Prices

The 1938
Slump

The Second
World War
Boom

1900   1910   1920   1929   1937   1944

Source: from *Historical Statistics*.

As students of economic history, we "read" the chapter of the Second World War in an unusual light, just as we read the history of the Civil War in an unaccustomed way. From our perspective, it is the burst of economic growth brought about by war spending that provides the main lesson. It shows that government spending can indeed play a decisive role in creating economic expansion, just as private investment spending did in the past. To put it differently, we can see that a new social structure of accumulation in which government spending could play a decisive role in providing the forward thrust of the system was indeed possible.

The new structure of accumulation was, however, put into place under special circumstances. The imperatives of war provided a rationale that overrode all kinds of objections that would otherwise have impeded government spending at anything approaching wartime magnitudes. Thus the great question to be answered was whether growth could continue after the war, when government spending would necessarily be pulled back to a much more modest place. As we shall see, that question continues to be asked—and answered in different ways—down to our present day.

Notes

[1] *The Public Papers and Addresses of Franklin D. Roosevelt* (1938), 2: 11ff.
[2] *How We Elect Our Presidents* (1952), p. 141.
[3] Raymond Moley, *After Seven Years* (1939), p. 155.
[4] *Public Papers and Addresses,* 2: 93–94.
[5] *Roosevelt: The Lion and the Fox* (1956), pp. 218–19.
[6] *Public Papers and Addresses,* (1938), 4: 325.
[7] Quoted in Arthur Schlesinger, Jr., *The Coming of the New Deal* (1958), p. 311
[8] Quoted in Arthur Schlesinger, Jr., *The Politics of Upheaval* (1960), p. 621.
[9] Quoted in William Leuchtenburg, *Franklin D. Roosevelt and the New Deal* (1963), p. 91.
[10] Quoted in Richard Hofstadter, *The Age of Reform* (1955), p. 309.

Satisfied shoppers

Chapter 15
FROM POSTWAR BOOM TO POSTWAR INFLATION

The war was over in 1945, but the euphoria of victory was tempered by an undercurrent of anxiety. The Great Depression had left an invisible scar on the American character, and the end of the war signalled to many the reappearance of a time of economic troubles. Predictions of gloom and doom filled the air: it was darkly said that twelve million veterans, trained to fight, would not meekly submit to the mass unemployment that seemed an all too likely consequence of the decline in war spending.

The Fair Deal

The person charged with the responsibility of leading the nation through this time of worries was Harry S Truman, catapulted into the presidency after the death of Franklin Roosevelt on April 12, 1945. Truman found himself immediately on the horns of a dilemma. On the one hand, he wanted to remove as many wartime controls as possible to encourage a resumption of private spending. On the other hand, he feared that dismantling controls too rapidly would unleash a flood of pent-up spending that would bring inflation and inequity. Complicating his problem was the mood of the public, tired of a long period of belt-tightening and eager to spend its war-swollen savings. And most difficult of all was the disappearance of a national purpose. With peace at hand, every group thought first and foremost of its own interest. Thus labor demanded higher wages but insisted that price controls be retained; industrialists demanded higher prices, but asked that the government continue to control wages; farmers pressed for a retention of price supports for their crops but opposed any price controls on their output.

Truman tried valiantly to reconcile these diverse and contradictory interests, setting forth a program of domestic reforms that came to be called the Fair Deal. In many ways it was a continuation of the main lines of the New Deal–strengthening New Deal legislation on Social Security and minimum wages, extending New Deal price supports and public housing programs, and pioneering with legislation aimed at creating health insurance and a government commitment to full employment. Many of these objectives were gained. But in one critical area Truman failed. He could not convince Congress—or the public—of the need to continue wartime controls over prices.* Cautiously Truman responded to the general demand for a free economy. First he ended the wartime rationing of scarce goods like gasoline. Then he signed a bill cutting taxes by some $6 billion. Finally in June 1946 he lifted all price controls except those on rent.

The result was all too foreseeable. Prices skyrocketed as consumers scrambled for goods. Food prices rose by more than 25 percent between 1945 and 1947. The inflation rate for 1946 was a staggering 18.2 percent. Worse, the rise in prices predictably sparked a demand for higher wages. When management refused to meet these demands, a wave of strike activity coursed through the nation—in 1946 alone nearly 5,000 strikes affected 4.5 million workers. Recognizing that unions were well organized, management decided to negotiate settlements and to pass along the costs of the new contracts to their customers.** Thus began an upward spiral of wages and prices that has continued as a central inflationary mechanism to our own day.

---

*During the war the Office of Price Administration worked assiduously to control eight million commodities and services through both rationing and price controls. Its efforts were rewarded: Consumer prices rose only 30 percent over 1939 levels, whereas in World War I, with no rationing and price controls in place, prices had more than doubled.

**In 1947 a Republican-led Congress tried to undo what it regarded as a privileged position for labor under the Wagner Act. Led by Senator Robert A. Taft of Ohio, it passed the Taft-Hartley Act, outlawing the closed shop (an arrangement under which job applicants had to join a union before they could be hired). In addition, the Taft-Hartley Act gave the president the authority to obtain court injunctions forcing striking unions to call off their strike for an eighty-day "cooling off" period. Truman vetoed the bill, but Congress passed it over his veto.

POSTWAR GROWTH

For all these shaky beginnings, the American economy showed remarkable strength and resilience in weathering the reconversion period. Government spending did fall precipitously between 1945 and 1946, from $83 billion to $31 billion, but the rush of pent-up consumer and business spending was large enough to hold the fall in GNP to scarcely more than 1 percent. In addition, as the production process picked up speed and as industrialists switched back from war to peacetime outputs, supply soon caught up with demand, and the initial inflationary burst petered out. In fact, the increase in supply was so great that prices were effectively stabilized after 1948, until the Korean War broke out in 1950. Not least, to the nation's immense relief, the transfer from the military to the civilian work force was managed without the expected difficulties. The Office of Mobilization and Reconversion had predicted that eight million people were likely to be out of work by the spring of 1946, but in fact postwar unemployment never rose above 2.7 million.

The Great Boom

Thus contrary to all expectations, the economy found itself launched on a great boom, rather than headed toward a repetition of the Great Depression. And it *was* a great boom—the longest and most successful period of expansion in American history. Between 1945 and 1970, the nation's real output of goods and services—that is, its gross national product, corrected for inflation—doubled. The median real income of families rose almost as fast: There were a third more households in 1970 than there had been after the war, but the average household's consumption of goods and services was nevertheless almost twice as high as it had been in 1947. In current dollar figures, gross national product in 1970 was almost at the trillion-dollar mark, a hitherto unimaginable number that was becoming a TV newscast cliché, and the median family was enjoying an income of $10,000 a year, a number that seemed very large to most Americans. Meanwhile, real per capita income growth rose 5.9 percent between 1946 and 1950, another 15.2 percent in the 1950s, and an even more impressive 31.7 percent in the 1960s.

Affluent teenagers, c. 1965

It is not surprising, then, that the short-lived euphoria of the imme-diate postwar victory slowly became a long-lived euphoria of national prosperity. The words "economic growth," previously unknown to most economists much less to ordinary Americans, entered the national consciousness, as commentators and presidents alike pro-jected the current trend into the future and painted a vision of an America that was now middle class in its income as well as in its aspi-rations.

Looking Back on the Boom

Two forces were responsible for the wonderful two and a half decades that followed the Second World War. One was the outpouring of dammed-up private expenditures, part household, part business, that had been held back for four years during the war. Thus the boom was in part simply the product of normal economic expansion, accelerated by the long-denied needs of a starved household and business com-munity.

But the other stimulus was new, and very important. It was the boost given to production, both directly and indirectly, by government. As we have mentioned, federal expenditures fell sharply for two years when the war stopped. Here is where the rush of private spending headed off a major economic contraction. But very shortly thereafter, government spending began to rise again. In some degree it was buoyed by the needs of states and localities for schools, roads, hospitals, fire-fighting equipment—all deferred, like household or business spending, during the war. More important was the renewal of federal spending for arms. With the onset of the Cold War in general and the Korean War in particular, arms spending became a major economic stimulus. In 1947 the military budget was roughly $9 billion. By 1949, when the Defense Department was formed, outlays had climbed to $13 billion. Four years later they topped $50 billion. By 1970 they were $74 billion.

Arms expenditures were thus an indisputable source of the initial growth surge, but they were by no means the sole source of the long boom. Indeed, from the mid-1950s on, military expenditures were a steadily *declining* portion of gross national product. Now, however, came the last and perhaps most significant contribution of the government: the rise of welfare expenditures. In 1950 these expenditures amounted to about $23 billion, just short of 9 percent of GNP. By 1970 the total was $146 billion, 15 percent of GNP. Here was the propulsive stimulus that took over after the boost of war spending stopped.

The growth of welfare spending was by no means a return to New Deal "relief." Rather, it embraced a broad series of programs that aided many sectors and groups within the economy. An early instance was the GI Bill of Rights, which provided demobilized veterans with loans to start new businesses and subsidies to continue their educations. About one million veterans entered college under the Bill, and another million used the Bill to open their own business. By the time the Bill ended in 1956, it cost the government $14.5 billion. Another was the rapid increase in federal aid to education at every level from elementary through college. Still another was the slow growth of payments for health programs, culminating in the Medicare and Medicaid programs of the late 1960s. But most important by far was the widening and strengthening of the Social Security program. Under Truman, Social Security outlays had reached a level of $2 billion a year, but the number of individuals covered was not much larger than in the late 1930s. The leap occurred under Dwight D. Eisenhower, the conservatively inclined but pragmatic general who became the Republican successor to Truman. Eisenhower was responsible for a dramatic increase in the number of families covered by Social Security. Ten million households, previously uncovered, were brought under the Social Security umbrella, and expenditures rose from $2 billion to $11 billion.

A New Economic Structure

Taken together, the federal, state, and local expenditures within GNP—partly for arms, partly for welfare, partly for domestic improvements—provided an indispensable underpinning for the long boom.* In 1929 the contribution to GNP of all these streams of government spending had been less than 10 percent. The spending of the federal government alone, for both goods and services and welfare, had been less than 2.5 percent of GNP. By 1970 federal spending for "warfare and welfare" had risen to over 20 percent of GNP, and the spending of all levels of government, including states and localities, to almost a third of GNP. To put it differently, whereas private investment spending was (in round numbers) 50 percent more than all government spending in 1929, by the 1970s it was 50 percent less.

The direct economic stimulus of government was therefore a major element in the long boom. But it was not the only reason for the two and a half decades of almost uninterrupted growth. Along with the increase in expenditures had also come a change in the relationship of government and business—that is, a change in the social structure of accumulation. The change had two main aspects. *First, there was a general acknowledgment of the necessity for government to provide floors under the economy.* The floors ranged from agricultural subsidies of various kinds to minimum wages, which were raised under Eisenhower; from widened Social Security to lengthened and strengthened unemployment benefits; from federally assisted state welfare programs to federally run job-training programs. By making the government an active force for personal income security, the threat of a demoralized and disgruntled work force was avoided, and the groundwork laid for a stable political climate, a necessity for business investment.

---

*An important contribution was the Interstate Highway Act of 1956, which committed the federal government to pay 90 percent of the construction costs of interstate highways.

Second, the business community was gradually brought around to an acceptance of government as a guarantor of economic stability. As the prestigious Rockefeller Panel Reports stated in 1958, "Public expenditures in support of growth are an essential part of our economy. Far from being a hindrance to progress, they provide the environment within which our economy moves forward."[1]

THE CHANGING ROLE OF GOVERNMENT

To be sure, the idea of a mixed economy did not emerge overnight or without resistance. In retrospect we can see that it began with the passage of the Employment Act of 1946 under President Truman, committing the government to the promotion of "maximum" employment through fiscal (tax and budget) and monetary policies. The law also required the president to submit an annual economic report to Congress, and created the three-member Council of Economic Advisers to assist him.

The Employment Act marked a new stage in the evolution of government's role in the economy. In the first part of the nineteenth century, the government was a *promoter* of business, underwriting "internal improvements," granting land to railroads, and helping infant industries to take root. A second stage was the emergence of the government in the latter half of the century as a *regulator of the economy,* using its powers to assure the orderly workings of individual markets or industries—witness the emergence of the ICC and antitrust policies. With the Employment Act came a third stage. The government now took on the function of *guarantor,* taking as its prime objective the maintenance of socially acceptable rates of growth and levels of employment.

The transition of the national government from promoter, to regulator, to guarantor of economic growth gained further support under Eisenhower and a conservative Republican Congress. Eisenhower tried to steer a middle course between the conservative policies of the Republicans of the 1920s and the New Deal liberalism of the 1930s, but veered in the direction of the Old Guard. His plan was to turn over as many federal programs as possible to the states. Among the federal programs that Eisenhower wanted dismantled and restructured on the basis of private enterprise was the TVA, which the president saw as a symbol of "creeping socialism." "If I do anything,"

Eisenhower said after his first inaugural, "it's going to be less govern-ment and not more government."[2] Yet the exigencies of the time forced him to abandon many of his orthodox ideas and to extend many of the "welfare" provisions of the New Deal. In 1954, for exam-ple, Eisenhower signed bills extending Social Security benefits to more than seven million Americans, raising the minimum wage to one dollar an hour, and adding four million workers to those eligible for unem-ployment benefits. Another important piece of legislation, the Soil Bank Act of 1956, authorized payments to farmers who let portions of their land lie fallow in order to reduce production. As a result, one dollar of every six dollars that farmers and agricultural corporations earned at harvest time came not from sales but from government sub-sidies—for crops that were never planted.

After the start of the first of three recessions during his administra-tion (1953–54, 1957–58, and 1960–61), Eisenhower told his cabinet that the Republican Party must be prepared to use the full power of gov-ernment to prevent "another 1929." As a result, despite Eisenhower's deep desire to cut government spending, federal disbursements rose from $68 billion when he took office in 1952 to $92 billion when he left in 1960, and the federal government incurred the largest deficit in its peacetime history.

More Intervention

The idea of a mixed economy became still more explicit under John F. Kennedy, to whom it was a foregone conclusion that government intervention was a necessity. Under his presidency, the government entered into economic affairs much more freely than it had under Eisenhower. Wage "guidelines" were initiated to help dampen the wage–price spiral of inflation. Minimum wages were further increased and Social Security extended. Assistance was provided for regional development of the backwater areas of the country.

But Kennedy's greatest departure from traditional economic policy took place in January 1963. The economy was hesitating on the verge of what seemed to be a potentially serious recession, with rising unemployment levels. Urged on by his advisers, Kennedy proposed a bold step. He asked Congress to reduce taxes by $13.5 billion *without reducing government spending.* That is, he asked Congress deliber-ately to incur a government deficit, using the government's borrowing powers to finance its spending. The result, he explained, would be a stimulus to the economy, because consumers would have more money to spend. As GNP rose, government tax revenues would also rise, and in the end the budget would be balanced at a higher level of GNP than if there had been no tax cut to stimulate total output.*

Kennedy's proposal to incur a deliberate government deficit produced a furor, and the tax cut was not actually passed until Lyndon Johnson assumed the presidency after Kennedy's death. By that time the idea had begun to win the approval of much of the business community.** Meanwhile, Johnson extended the idea of the mixed economy in other directions. His program for a Great Society brought new departures for government, including direct aid to the nation's elementary and secondary public schools and a far-reaching program of Medicare for people over sixty-five. But Johnson's most ambitious program was the Economic Opportunity Act of 1964, which launched a frontal assault on poverty. The purpose of the law was to help poor people improve their ability to earn money. Thus it established a Head Start program to give extra help to disadvantaged children even before they entered school, a Job Corps to train school dropouts, and an adult education program. Between 1965 and 1970 nearly $10 billion was committed to Economic Opportunity Act programs.

Income Distribution

As a consequence of efforts made by the Eisenhower, Kennedy, and Johnson administrations, the distribution of income in the United States showed a considerable change compared with the distribution

---

*The question of government deficits is a complicated one, better covered in an economics course than in a survey of economic growth. A key aspect of the problem lies in the "internal" character of government debts. By internal, we mean that a government debt is usually held by its own citizens. Because government has the power to tax, it can always raise the necessary funds to pay off its bonds when they come due, or to pay interest on them. By way of contrast, a corporation, no matter how large, has no way of forcing people to buy its products so that it can pay back its debts. The power to tax is what makes government debts entirely different from private debts. That is why it is said, quite correctly, that a government debt, held by its own citizens, is a debt that a nation owes to itself.

**In *The Fiscal Revolution in America* (1969; p. 372), economist Herbert Stein referred to this tax cut as "the act, which more than any other came to symbolize the fiscal revolution."

before the war. The table below shows the shift in overall shares among the lower, middle, and top groups in the nation:

DISTRIBUTION OF FAMILY INCOME (BEFORE TAX)		
	Percent of all incomes	
	1929	**1971**
Lowest 40 percent of families	12.5	17.4
Next 40 percent	33.1	41.1
Top 20 percent	54.4	41.6
Top 5 percent	30.0	14.4

SOURCE: *from Historical Statistics;* 1929, series G319–324.

Much of this change was the direct consequence of the welfare programs undertaken during the long boom. Between 1959 and 1969, the number of persons whose incomes fell into the brackets officially classified as "poverty" or "near poverty" declined from thirty-nine million to twenty-four million, and the percentage of the population in these low income brackets fell from 22.4 to 12.1.* Poverty thereafter continued to decline slowly until the 1980s, when it took a sharp turn upward as a result of cutbacks in welfare programs under the Reagan administration.

FROM GROWTH TO INFLATION

Measured in terms of growth or distribution, then, the long boom was an unparalleled success. Why, then, did it come to an end?

The first answer is that it produced inflation. Already noticeable in the 1960s, inflation became a matter of growing national concern as

---

*Mention should here be made of a highly influential book, *The Other America,* published in 1962 by Michael Harrington. Harrington's study graphically brought to the attention of the American people the existence of poverty in the midst of prevailing affluence. In particular, he cast light on the culture of what he termed "the invisible poor," the roughly fifty million Americans who lived a hand-to-mouth existence, wrestling daily with physical disease, mental illness, and a pervasive feeling of hopelessness. Harrington's book was a call to arms to eradicate poverty, and struck a responsive chord with many Americans, including Presidents Kennedy and Johnson.

Inflation protest, Brooklyn, New York

the boom went on. From 1950 to 1960 the average rate of inflation in the United States was about 2 percent a year. During the last five years of the 1960s, the average inflation rate climbed to 4 percent. In the first five years of the 1970s it reached 6 percent. In the next five years it rose to 9 percent. After 1980 it moved into the double digit range, over 10 percent.

Why the rise in inflation? An enormous amount has been written on the subject, but no single explanation of inflation has been generally accepted comparable to Keynes's explanation of stagnation. Nevertheless, we understand a good deal about the process. In 1973 the Organization of Petroleum Exporting Countries (OPEC) took advantage of a tight market for oil, following the Arab–Israeli War, to boost the price of oil fourfold within a matter of a few months. The resulting "oil shock" hit all capitalist nations like a tidal wave, and was regarded by everyone as a tremendous impetus to inflation.

But why was the rise in oil prices *inflationary*? Suppose that the Pennsylvania coal mines had managed to form a cartel in 1873 and had quadrupled coal prices. Would that have produced inflation? Far more likely, it would have resulted in a sharp depression. Coal mines would have shut down, steel mines curtailed their operations, householders gone without coal. This imaginary but very persuasive "counterfactual" scenario causes us to ask an illuminating question: What happened between 1873 and 1973 so that the identical shock—a rise in energy prices—could give rise to such opposite results?

The question is not hard to answer. If coal prices had been boosted in 1873, there would have been no additional purchasing power to enable coal buyers to maintain their levels of coal consumption. Either coal miners or producers of some other goods would have been put out of work for sheer lack of demand. But in the 1970s no such constraints held back the system. On the contrary, when the price of oil rose, additional amounts of purchasing power were quickly created by government to assure that the needed dollars would be there. Householders, faced with higher costs of living, found that their pay checks were larger or their Social Security checks increased because wages and salaries were informally adjusted to changes in the cost of living, and Social Security checks were "indexed" by law to compensate for them. Industries, faced with higher costs of production, turned to banks for more credit, and the banks provided them with that credit with the blessings of government. Thus the increase in oil prices, far from constituting a drain on purchasing power, became a stimulus for the creation of additional purchasing power through the mechanisms of the mixed economy and the welfare state.

These mechanisms were certainly not the only reason for the onset or the persistence of inflation. Inflation received its disastrous first push from the Vietnam War. It was "exported" to Europe by the high-handed manner in which the United States conducted its international economic affairs. It was aggravated by the increasing concentration of business and labor power, and because industries in the vital manufacturing core of the system reached a tacit agreement with unions under which wages were steadily raised and the resulting higher costs passed along to consumers in higher prices.

Not least was a dangerous change in expectations shared by business and the public alike. In the unsupported economy of the 1920s the prevailing wisdom was that "What goes up must come down." Hence a certain wariness tempered the behavior of all but the most speculative-minded. But as prices began to move inexorably upward, a new conventional wisdom displaced the old: "What goes up today is likely to go up more tomorrow." Such inflationary expectations become powerful mechanisms for creating the very kind of behavior that itself accelerates inflation.

Thus there were many specific causes for inflation. Yet the imaginary comparison of OPEC and a coal cartel brings home a central point. It is that the structure of capitalism itself had become inflation-prone by virtue of the very institutional changes that had laid the basis for its postwar growth. Had the mixed economy and the welfare state been taken away from mid–twentieth century capitalism, its inflationary tendencies would almost certainly have disappeared as well. But so, too, would its remarkable prosperity.

The Effects of Inflation

It took some time before inflation became a central political issue. Eisenhower's administration was more concerned about preventing or cushioning the minor recessions that occurred during his term of office than with holding back the rise in prices. Kennedy and then Johnson were first absorbed in efforts to stimulate the economy—the Kennedy tax cut to which we have referred—and thereafter in trying to finance the unpopular Vietnam War without raising taxes. As a consequence, the inflation problem itself did not become a main focus of political concern until Richard Nixon's administration. From January 1969 to August 1971 the cost of living increased by 14.5 percent. In mid-August, 1971, Nixon announced a ninety-day price-wage freeze, to be followed in November by a system of wage and price controls.

The system of controls worked—for a while. But pressures were clearly building up behind it, like a river rising behind the frail bulwarks of a sandbag levee. When he was reelected in 1972 Nixon removed the controls, and with a rush the flood spread out across the countryside. From an inflation rate of 3.4 percent while the controls still held, the cost of living rose by 9 percent in 1973 and by nearly 12 percent in 1974.

Nixon's successor, Gerald Ford, was ideologically opposed to a reimposition of controls. Instead he sought to bring inflation under control by reducing federal spending and encouraging the Federal Reserve Board to tighten credit. Ford's hope was that a moderate rise

Urban unemployment office, 1983

in unemployment would hold back both labor and management from pursuing their wage–price spiral.* The result was the worst slump since the Roosevelt recession of 1937–38. Unemployment rose to nearly 9 percent of the work force by mid-1975. By the next year the inflation rate had been cut to less than 5 percent, but the rise in unemployment was more than Congress or the public were willing to tolerate. Ford was reluctantly persuaded to stimulate the system by cutting taxes. By early 1976 the economy had responded sufficiently well so that he could announce that the recession was over. Alas, so was the lull in inflation, which soon began its upward course again.

From Stop-Go to Full Stop

The dilemma of choosing between inflation and unemployment was not just an American problem. All through the Western world, the drift toward accelerating inflation was being met with similar policies—and similar failures. Efforts to arrest inflation by slowing the economy

---

*Ford suggested that patriotic citizens should wear WIN buttons (Whip Inflation Now) to evidence their support for his policies.

down through tight money policies that restricted the abilities of banks to make loans and through stringent fiscal measures soon resulted in unacceptable increases in unemployment. Thereafter the red light of restrictive policies was rapidly changed to a green light of expansive policies. As a result, all over the world capitalist economies displayed stop-go symptoms—first enjoying some respite from inflation only to encounter rising unemployment; then easing the unemployment situation only to come up against a renewed burst of inflation.

The dilemma came to a head in the United States under the administration of Jimmy Carter, a Democrat. Elected in 1976, Carter determined that inflation required a much more vigorous and tough-minded policy of monetary austerity, and he appointed Paul Volcker to be Chairman of the Federal Reserve System to bring the growth of the money supply under much tighter control. Volcker stepped harder on the monetary brakes than anyone had dared to up to that time. By refusing to allow bank reserves to expand as rapidly as in the past, he brought about a credit squeeze that pushed interest rates steadily higher. The prime rate—the interest rate charged by banks to their best commercial customers—rose from below 7 percent to over 12.5 percent. By 1980, the last year of the Carter presidency, the prime rate was an unprecedented 15 percent, and the Consumer Price Index was soaring at an annual rate of 18.2 percent, the highest in U.S. history.

Predictably, the consequences of tight money were painful. Businesses—especially small and medium sized firms—were unable to finance their inventories or their normal borrowings, and began to contract their activities. Unemployment grew from 5.8 percent of the work force in 1979 to 7.1 percent in 1980. Economic growth came to a total halt; corrected for inflation, the economy actually contracted in 1980, the first post–World War decade in which American purchasing power actually declined. In 1980 Americans earned 5 percent less in real income than in 1970. But even the growing disarray in the system could not stop the momentum of inflation, now mainly kept going by "indexing" Social Security payments and wage contracts—that is, adjusting them annually to stay abreast of inflation. In 1980 the inflation rate rose to 12.4 percent, despite the tightest money and the largest unemployment in the nation's postwar history.

Thus the great boom ended in the great inflation. This was not just an American dilemma. To a lesser degree, the same disappointing end to the great boom was experienced in other capitalist nations, especially in Europe. By the early 1980s, no way had been found to bring about sustained economic growth without suffering inflationary consequences. The stage was set for one of those pendulum swings that seems to affect American political history—and as a consequence, its economic history as well.*

Notes

[1] *Prospect for America*, p. 279

[2] Quoted in Herbert Parmet, *Eisenhower* [1972], p. 174.

*For a stimulating discussion of political cycles in American history, see Arthur Schlesinger, Jr., *The Cycles of American History* (1986).

President Reagan relaxing in California

Chapter 16
THE CONSERVATIVE ERA

The pendulum swing was ratified in the 1980 presidential election, when—in a mood of frustration—the public turned to Ronald Reagan, a conservative Republican. Reagan carried forty-four of the fifty states, and his party gained control of the Senate for the first time since 1954 and added thirty-three seats in the House. The Reagan juggernaut ushered in an era of conservative hegemony that would persist until President George Bush was defeated by Governor Bill Clinton of Arkansas in the election of 1992.

Those twelve years of conservative authority are the basis for the title of this chapter and the theme of its content. It is too early to attempt anything like a historian's perspective on the complex political and social currents and consequences of the Reagan–Bush years. But it is not too soon to attempt an appraisal of the problems that dominated them and the adequacy of the response that was forthcoming.

THE CONSERVATIVE BANNER

The regnant economic philosophy of those dozen years was clearly "conservative," a label worn by Presidents Reagan and Bush as proudly as Kennedy and Johnson had worn the badge of liberalism. Moreover, there was no mistaking conservatism's first and most important objective. It was to reduce the role of government in economic affairs. In his inaugural address Ronald Reagan said, "In this present crisis, government is not the solution to our problems; government is the problem. . . . "* According to historian Robert Dallek, "no president in American history entered the White House more determined to reduce the role and size of government than Ronald Reagan."[1] In one of his first acts as president, Reagan ordered the portrait of Thomas Jefferson removed from the East Wing of the White House, replacing it with that of Calvin Coolidge, whose pro-business philosophy of government is already familiar to us. Reagan hailed Coolidge for having cut taxes four times. "During the Coolidge years," he said, "we had probably the greatest growth in prosperity that we've ever known."[2]

Cutting Government

Reagan was determined to unleash energies that he believed had been dammed up by administrative regulation and anti-business legislation. Blaming this on Democratic "excesses," and sensing general dissatisfaction with—even a loss of confidence in—government policies of "tax and spend," Reagan undertook a large-scale trimming of welfare programs, a dismantling of government regulations, and a diminution of government in all areas except the military.

No sooner did Reagan enter office than he called on Congress to reduce by billions of dollars such well-established federal programs as Medicare, welfare subsidies for the working poor, urban aid, food stamps, and school lunch programs. In July 1981 Congress agreed to most of the president's demands, and Reagan followed up with a second round of domestic spending cuts in September of that year.

Another purpose of the spending cuts was to push forward Reagan's program to establish a "New Federalism" which would transfer over to the states many of the social services then under federal funding and supervision. According to Reagan, local governments were far better equipped to measure and to meet the needs of the citizenry than the far removed, bureaucracy-laden government in Washington.

Having lightened expenditure, the administration next advocated, and Congress passed, the largest tax cut in American history. The

---

*It is worthy of note that conservatism was gaining vitality as a rallying-ground throughout the world. In May 1979 Margaret Thatcher's Conservative Party came to power in England. After Reagan's election, conservative governments were placed in office in Canada, West Germany, and Italy. Voters were expressing their dissatisfaction with government-dominated solutions to economic problems, and increasingly calling on their governments to follow conservative policies to expand their economies.

Economic Recovery Act of 1981, as the law was called, reduced individual income tax rates by 25 percent over a period of three years, and lowered the top rate on unearned income from 70 to 50 percent. Other sections of the new measure provided an investment tax credit, and a system of depreciation allowances making it possible to recover capital costs more rapidly.

The conservative philosophy behind the act can be seen in its deliberate tilting of tax relief in favor of the rich. The 31.7 million tax-paying families earning $15,000 or less were to receive only 8.5 percent of the reduction, whereas the 12.6 million families earning $50,000 or more were to get 35 percent of the savings. The greatest gains by far were enjoyed by the topmost 1 percent. In 1977 this group paid 36 percent of its average income of $350,000 in income taxes. By 1983 the average income of the top 1 percent had risen to $400,000 but the average tax levy had dropped to 22 percent.[3]

Supply-Side Disappointments

Reagan's economists predicted that this measure would stimulate saving, investment and growth precisely *because* it was aimed at upper-income groups whose initiative was believed to be crucial in determining the pace of economic life. This philosophy was called "supply-side" economics, in contrast to the "demand side" that typically depended on government spending to increase output. According to supply-side thinking, well-to-do families would spend their tax savings on consumption, lifting the economy out of the doldrums, or would invest their tax savings in new ventures, providing an even more important stimulus for jobs and production. Thus additional income at the top would trickle down to those below, bringing new economic vitality as its dividend.

Fatal Contradictions

Would trickle-down economics have worked? We cannot really say, because the program was marked from the start by two glaring inconsistencies. The first was a failure to realize the spending cuts that had been so boldly announced. Spending for Medicare, for example, increased from $32 billion when Reagan was inaugurated, to $132 billion when his successor left office. Social Security expenditures rose from $118 billion to over $300 billion. And the largest peacetime build-up of military strength swelled the military budget from $130 billion to double that. In addition, although the tax burden of the rich was greatly reduced, that of the middle and working classes was greatly increased by higher payroll taxes. Between 1978 and 1990, for example, the Social Security payroll tax increased 30 percent.* In all, when Reagan entered office in 1981, total federal tax revenues were $599 billion. Twelve yars later, they were $1,091 billion. Thus the years saw neither a massive scaling back in total federal spending or in federal tax receipts. Supply-side was more of a slogan than a reality.

Second, Reagan's plan also banked heavily on squeezing inflation out of the system by continuing a policy of very tight money. This directly contradicted the desired effects of supply-side incentives. Supply-side policies were supposed to spur the economy on; tight money was supposed to hold it back. In this conflict of objectives, tight money won. Inflation fell from 12.4 percent in 1980 to less than 7 percent in 1982, and the discount rate—the rate at which the Federal Reserve loans money to member banks—fell from a record 21.5 percent in early 1981 to 10.5 percent in the summer of 1982.

But tight money also meant that loans were hard to get. As businesses desperately cut costs and unions agreed to cut wages, production and consumer spending came down along with prices. During the last three months of 1981 GNP fell by 5.3 percent and unemployment rose to a six-year high of 8 percent. At year's end one-third of the country's industrial capacity was idle; real take-home pay was below that of ten years earlier; agricultural income dropped precipitously, resulting in an increase in farm foreclosures, auctions, and bankruptcies; and the number of Americans living in poverty was 60 percent higher than in 1979. Supply-side hopes had become depression realities.

---

*Why does the Social Security payroll tax claim a higher portion of the earnings of the middle and working class than of the rich? In part it is because this tax has a ceiling above which no more payments need be made. As of January 1993 that ceiling was 7.65 percent of the first $57,600 in earnings and 1.45 percent of the next $77,400. In addition, the tax exempts investment income, such as interest and capital gains. Thus the payroll tax is like an income tax in reverse, exempting high rather than low incomes. As a result of this and other increases in state and local taxes, by the middle years of the 1980s, the middle-bracket taxpayer bore a heavier tax burden than the more well-to-do citizen.

A homeless person in Washington D.C.

A Rebound—and New Problems

Fortunately for Reagan, the economy rebounded dramatically just before the 1984 election. Gross national product rose 6.8 percent in 1984, the highest increase since 1951, and mid-year employment statistics seemed to indicate a complete turnaround: Unemployment fell to 7.1 percent, a four-year low, and inflation dropped to 4 percent, the lowest since 1967. Against these successes, the ever-popular president* soundly defeated his Democratic opponent, Walter Mondale, winning forty-nine of the fifty states.

Merger Mania

Meanwhile, however, a different problem was beginning to emerge in the corporate sector. We have seen how a great merger movement

---

*One of Reagan's much-noted skills was an ability to distance himself from bad news. Representative Patricia Schroeder of Colorado said that Reagan was "perfecting a Teflon-coated presidency. . . . He sees to it that nothing sticks to him."

brought about a concentration of industry in the late nineteenth century. Another such movement, not quite so dramatic, brought further concentration in the 1950s and 1960s. Thereafter the statistics of concentration seemed to stabilize, as we see in the table below.

Suddenly, beginning in the mid-1980s, this condition changed dramatically. A new merger wave broke out that dwarfed all earlier periods of corporate agglomeration. During the relatively stable years before this wave, the annual number of mergers among the largest corporations came to less than 100, and the total value of assets involved in all mergers amounted to only about $5 billion a year. When the merger mania began, those numbers changed out of all recognition. In 1984, 2,999 "big" mergers took place, involving $124 billion in total assets. The next year the number was even higher, and in that year at least five mergers involved sums larger than the total value of all mergers during the premerger decade.

Behind the Merger Wave

What was the cause of this frenzied acquisitiveness? Two factors seem of paramount importance. The first was the financial impetus that resulted from a combination of high interest rates and inflation. Together these depressed the price of corporate shares on the stock market to the point at which the cash value of the assets of many companies, such as the oil reserves of the petroleum group, were worth a good deal more than the market's valuation of the companies that owned them. This presented financiers and aggressive competitors with the chance to buy out undervalued corporations, and then to realize bonanza profits by selling off their assets for much more than the entire company had cost.

The second cause of the merger frenzy was a change in the attitude

LARGEST MANUFACTURERS' SHARE OF ASSETS						
	1948	**1960**	**1970**	**1981**	**1982**	**1983**
100 largest corporations	40.2	46.4	48.5	46.8	47.7	48.3
200 largest corporations	48.2	56.3	60.4	60.0	60.8	60.8

SOURCE: *Statistical Abstract of the United States,* Table #866.

Heavy trading on the New York Stock Exchange

of government. The much more benign attitude of the Justice Department toward mergers removed an obstacle that had formerly dampened the enthusiasm for merger. As a result, the drive to deregulate as many industries as possible set the stage for a general competitive consolidation within those industries. As the airlines, for example, were progressively released from the supervision of the Federal Aviation Authority, airlines began to gobble one another up, radically reducing the number of carriers, and changing the route and the rate structures of the industry.

Hostile Mergers

The merger wave also differed from earlier waves in another respect. Previous merger waves were largely the consequence of a widely shared desire to minimize competition. Hence all parties to the merger cooperated eagerly to bring it about. During the wave of the 1980s, "hostile" takeovers dominated the scene—purchases of one company by another, or by financial raiders interested only in making a killing for themselves, not in creating a more stable industrial pattern.

Two new developments accounted for this change. One was the anonymity of most corporate managements, whose names were unknown to their stockholders, unlike the days of owner-managers like Ford or Carnegie. As a result, when shareholders received offers for their stock from the raiders at a price far above the current market value, they paid little heed to the appeals of existing management to remain loyal to them. Similarly, large institutional investors, such as pension funds and life insurance companies, also looked kindly on hostile takeovers, since bidding wars for control of a company tended to boost share prices.

A second element was that hostile takeovers were often made possible because banks were willing to lend the raiders large amounts of money, often on frail security. The merger deals were then financed by using the bank's money to buy out stockholders, after which the raider typically unloaded his bank debt onto the company he had acquired, causing the company to issue high-interest, high-risk "junk bonds." These bonds, with their tempting coupons, were then sold to the public, thereby raising the money to reimburse the bank for its original loan. Later these free-and-easy financing methods were stopped by the Federal Reserve Board, but for a time they were a source of immense financial purchasing power that fueled the merger process.

Consequences of the Wave

The effects of the merger wave are not as clear-cut as its causes. For the wave has had supporters as well as opponents. Those who have looked favorably on it believed that the wave of takeovers was a bitter but necessary medicine for a slack and lazy business community. As a result of the merger wave, say its defenders, corporations are today lean and mean, as they must be if they are to hold their own in the increasingly rough competition of the global market. On the other side of the argument, opponents of the merger process point to the damage that has been done to many corporations by forcing them to exchange equity for debt—that is, to exchange shares of stock that carried no legal obligation to pay dividends, with bonds whose interest payments had to be met. In all, something like $200 billion of new debt has been added to U.S. corporations as a result of the merger wave. The obligation to "service" this debt—that is, to pay interest on it—saddles the corporate world with a huge expense that must be met before any profit can be had.

By and large, the conservative administrations saw the positive side of the merger movement. It will be some time, however, before we know which side of the argument has won the day. It is quite likely that surviving corporations will be leaner and meaner, and therefore better able to hold their own in the world's market. But there is no doubt that many companies will have dropped by the wayside because of their inability to handle their massive new debt load. In the end, the validity of the conservative view may perhaps be determined not by the winners, but by the ability of the losers to reenter the business scene. On the success of that largely overlooked aspect of the merger movement will depend the economic fate of hundreds of thousands, perhaps even millions, of workers and middle managers, displaced by no fault of their own.

The Reagan Finale

Although somewhat diminished by alleged scandals within his administration and by questionable uses of power in foreign affairs, Reagan's popularity was still powerful enough for him to turn over the presidency in 1988 to the Republican candidate, Vice-President George Bush. Bush easily defeated his Democratic rival, Governor Michael Dukakis of Massachusetts. Paradoxically, it was during Bush's administration that American capitalism won its greatest ideological victory abroad, but suffered a most telling defeat at home.

THE BUSH YEARS

The ideological triumph was the downfall of Communism, an event of momentous importance in world history. The fall occurred with lightning speed, as mass movements ousted Marxist–Leninist regimes throughout Eastern Europe. On November 9, 1989, the Berlin Wall, a symbol of Communist repression and the Cold War since 1961, was torn down. But the fatal blow was struck in August 1991, when the people of Moscow, led by the popularly elected president of Russia, Boris Yeltsin, heroically resisted a coup that tried to depose President Mikhail Gorbachev and to restore power to the old guard. The bloodless victory sealed the fate of the hardliners and opened the way for the democratic reorganization of the Soviet Union. That transformation is still far from complete, and may yet founder, but the very possibility would have been impossible to imagine in the opening days of the Bush presidency.

Americans greeted these events with great pride and high expectations, hoping not only for the dawn of an era of peace and order abroad, but for the possibility of a "peace dividend" at home, as military expenditures were diverted to much needed peacetime projects. They were soon disappointed on both counts. Events in Eastern Europe, Germany, Yugoslavia, and in the former Soviet territory made it plain that a peaceful and stable era was not yet at hand; and the rapid emergence of serious domestic economic problems made it equally evident that the end of the Cold War would not, in itself, bring about a resumption of strong economic growth for the United States. On the contrary, from the date of Bush's administration to that of his leaving office, there was essentially no real growth in average personal income. The last years of his administration were marked by another recession, almost as painful as that which tight money had brought on in the early 1980s.

The Neglect of Infrastructure

What was the cause of these economic difficulties? Many of them had their roots in earlier neglect. One of these, without question, was a crippling decline in the quantity and quality of the "infrastructure" of the economy. Infrastructure refers to the publicly owned productive capital of a nation—its roads and dams, harbors and airfields, public research facilities, educational institutions, and the like. This public capital does not normally *make* goods, which are usually produced in the private sector, but it determines to an important degree the efficiency with which private goods can be produced. Business clearly depends on good road, rail, and air transport, on water, power, and postal facilities, as well as on purely private physical capital. In this light, infrastructure can be likened to the roadbed that determines how fast a train can run.

During the years of the conservative era, the national infrastructure was allowed to deteriorate to an unprecedented degree. According to the figures of the Office of Management and Budget, federal investment in public capital was cut by a third from 1976 to 1990; education and training by almost 40 percent;* physical capital by almost 30 percent; research and development by the same. Economist David Alan Aschauer, to whose research we owe the first full-scale airing of the problem, has estimated that total nonmilitary public investment in the 1980s was only half that of the previous decade and only one-fourth the level of the 1950s and 1960s. In fact, public investment had been neglected to such an extent that, according to Aschauer's estimates, a dollar spent in the public sector raised GNP by considerably more than a dollar spent for private investment.[4]

The Role of the Public Sector

By the end of Bush's term the extent and consequences of the neglect of public capital had become obvious. But behind that neglect lay a view of the economy that placed private activity as the source of economic progress and well-being. That was not the view of Adam Smith, whose *Wealth of Nations* was often taken to be the blueprint for a capitalist system. There Smith wrote that government had three duties to its citizens. The first two were the provision of national defense, and the establishment of a framework of law and order—activities that coincided very well with the aims of conservative presidencies.

But the third duty spelled out by Smith was quite different: it was

the duty of erecting and maintaining certain public works and certain public institutions, which it can never be for the interest of any individual, or group of individuals, to erect and maintain, because the profit could never repay the expense. . . , although it may frequently do much more than repay it to a great society.

---

*It has long been a fundamental American belief that education is the surest means of bettering society. Moreover, all through the nineteenth century that belief was manifested in public expenditures that made Americans the best-educated people in the world. During the conservative era, that trend came to an end. By the late 1980s, per-pupil expenditures were higher in Switzerland, Sweden, Norway, Japan, Denmark, Austria, West Germany, and Canada than in the U.S. At the same time, public funding for retraining workers dropped by more than 50 percent in the 1980s. The result was a shortage of skilled workers in America, quite unlike the case in Europe or Japan. In France, for example, companies are required either to allocate a percentage of their gross earnings to worker training or to pay a tax into a nationwide training fund.

Smith is making clear that government has a positive economic function to perform—namely, the provision of adequate public works, including, by Smith's explicit mention, public education. That is a view of the economy that the conservative era forgot. During the Reagan and Bush administrations several aides used to sport neckties with Smith's profile on them, but the policies of those years give no reason to believe that the aides had read his great work.

The S&L Disaster

The infrastructure problem festered silently until it was suddenly "discovered" in the late 1980s, several years after motorists had discovered the problem for themselves along the nation's decaying highways. A second issue burst into prominence in a much more dramatic fashion. It was a financial crisis of a kind that the country had not experienced since the 1930s, when there was a nationwide failure of the banking system.

This time the disaster was limited to savings and loan institutions (S&Ls), principally based in the Southwest. By the late 1980s, S&Ls were collapsing with alarming regularity and mounting consequence. As with the infrastructure problem, however, the seeds of the disaster were sown during the Reagan years.

Traditionally, S&Ls were engaged in the narrow business of taking small deposits and providing mortgage loans. They were non-profit mutual associations owned by their depositors, and had limits on the interest they could pay those depositors. During the deregulation-minded Reagan administration, the S&Ls successfully lobbied Congress to expand their operations. Soon they were converted to for-profit, stockholder institutions that could compete for depositors by bidding up interest rates, and for borrowers by making loans on virtually everything. Because Reagan was opposed to any regulation that might affect business profits adversely (he actually appointed opponents of regulation to enforce its rules!), his administration trusted that banks, as well as other businesses, would police themselves. Congress was also at fault. It happened that S&Ls were significant contributors to election campaigns, and Congress failed to make adequate provision for the monitoring of their business practices. As a result, billions of dollars disappeared in the form of unsound bank loans—usually for highly speculative projects utterly unsuited for banking investment, and sometimes in shady dealings that echoed the manipulations and reckless practices of the 1920s.

So widespread was the S&L debacle that it soon affected major banks of hitherto substantial standing. Fortunately, the government repaid depositors for their federally insured accounts. But that "bailout" was very expensive. It appears that the total cost of the S&L failure will eventually exceed $500 billion over a thirty-year period.

Behind the S&L Crisis

Once more, we stop to ask whether there was greater significance in this debacle than sheer mismanagement or skullduggery. Here the issue seems to be the criteria that are applied to the question of regulation itself. On the one side is efficiency. This is the side from which a

Depositors in Randallstown, Maryland wait to withdraw their money

conservative philosophy principally draws its strength. The wastefulness of many government procedures make them a natural target. The cost overruns of public undertakings, the endless delays in approving new processes and products, the avalanche of paperwork, the layers of bureaucratic self-protection of government-in-general are its anathema. And there is reason for this anti-government orientation. Left to themselves, the costs of government can be fatal to the vitality of any society, as exemplified in the progressive decline of the Soviet economy, leading to its collapse.

There is, however, another criterion. It is self-protection. The conservative view, which seeks its justification in a desire to maximize the energies latent in a capitalist system, tends to overlook the damage that can be inflicted by those selfsame energies. The excesses of the S&L disaster testify to the harm that can ensue when private energy is allowed to overstep the boundaries dictated by social prudence. The precept to be borne in mind is that all private economic activity has public consequences, just as all public economic activity has private consequences. The conservative era tended to emphasize the second injunction and to ignore the first.

Fiscal Difficulties

A third major issue can likewise be traced to President Reagan's term in office, although it did not become acute until his successor took charge. It was the problem of a federal deficit that had apparently become uncontrollable.

The federal deficit refers to the amount that the national government borrows from the public by issuing Treasury bills and notes and bonds.* When Reagan came into office in 1981, the deficit was $74 billion, or less than three percent of GNP. By 1992, as Bush left office, the deficit had grown to $340 billion, or 5.7 percent of GNP. Over the same years the gross national debt, which is the sum of all outstanding government borrowings, had grown from $629 billion to over $4 trillion, or from a sum equal to 23 percent of GNP to one equal to 68 percent of GNP.

---

*A Treasury bill has a short maturity, usually thirty, sixty, or ninety days; a note comes due in a year; and a bond over a longer period, up to thirty years.

Expenditure Profligacy

What accounted for this alarming increase? Two elements can be clearly identified. One was the failure of the two administrations to put a cap on expenditures. We have already noted that Reagan's enthusiasm for cutting government back did not extend to the military budget, or to the two rapidly growing areas of social expenditure, Medicare and Social Security. President Bush, likewise, could not effectively deal with the military build-up or the tremendous growth in medical costs. Nor was Congress willing or able to check the rising tide of spending.

In turn, expenditure profligacy can be attributed to two factors. Military spending was supported partly because of the severe employment costs that cutbacks would impose on many states and localities, and partly because both Congress and the president were unwilling to relinquish America's place as a super power—a role dramatically realized in January 1991 when the Gulf War prevented Iraq's conquest of Kuwait and blocked its threat to Saudi Arabia.

The rise in social expenditure must be explained differently, in the presence of very large needs for which there existed no alternative to federal programs of support. By way of example, roughly thirty-five million Americans had no health care benefits, another fifteen million were underinsured, and another ten million were covered only by an inadequate Medicaid system. The paradox was that U.S. medical costs were at an all-time high. In 1992, the nation's total expenditures on health care was $838.5 billion, or approximately 14 percent of GNP. This was the highest percentage of any nation in the world. Certainly there were no easy solutions to America's health care crisis, but equally clearly, the stage was set for government to take the lead in developing a comprehensive program to provide all Americans with an affordable health care umbrella. But that brings us beyond the reach of this chapter.

Tax Phobia

But the problem of growing deficits must be attributed as well to a quite different source. Americans consider themselves to be a very heavily taxed people, and punish representatives who dare to vote for tax increases. In fact, Americans are almost the lowest taxed of any industrial nation. The Organization of Economic Cooperation and Development (OECD), representing the chief industrial nations in the world, has pointed out that American tax revenues, as a percentage of GNP, are the second lowest among their twenty-four member states, exceeded only by Turkey. German tax revenues, for instance, equal some 38 percent of its GNP, France's revenues are equal to not quite 44 percent, those of the Netherlands or Belgium are close to 50 percent. Our ratio of tax revenues to GNP is 28 percent.

Thus, if we were willing to tax ourselves in the same proportion as do our OECD counterparts, there would be a much smaller deficit. Raising our tax collection ratio to that of Germany would have increased our intake in 1992 by about $130 billion, or more than a quarter of that year's deficit. Raising it to the level of France would have brought in an additional $150 billion, enough to cut the deficit by over 40 percent.

Why are we such inefficient tax collectors? One part of the answer is probably that we rely on much more strongly disliked tax measures than do our fellow industrial nations. We raise about 36 percent of our tax revenues through the income tax, compared with less than 30 percent for Germany and just under 12 percent for France. To many economists, the income tax is the fairest of all taxes, insofar as it is usually proportional to one's income, but that is not the way it is regarded by those who pay it. Rightly or wrongly, households feel that the government is trespassing when it levies a tax on the incomes they have earned, whereas taxes on gasoline or goods in general may be resented but are not regarded in such a politically charged fashion.

If we were to adopt a gasoline tax or a value-added tax—a kind of national sales tax—our tax revenues would certainly rise, our deficit fall, and our tax tempers cool.*

A Question of National Character?

In such a fiscal program there is nothing inherently incompatible with a conservative economic philosophy, as witness its application by many conservative governments overseas. Perhaps the difficulty lies at

---

*An interesting analysis of the American tax phobia will be found in *No Pain, No Gain,* by Louis A. Ferleger and Jay R. Mandle (1992).

a deeper level. The sociologist Seymour Martin Lipset has called to our attention two countries that shared a very similar experience but reacted very differently to it. The countries are the United States and Canada, and the shared experience was the taming of a wilderness to their west. From this common experience, however, the two nations spontaneously chose two strikingly different culture heroes. The Canadians chose the scarlet-coated Northwest Mounted Police, the symbol of law and order. The Americans chose the cowboy.[5] A nation that admires the values of cowboy life—and they are not inconsiderable—is not likely to welcome a larger government role, no matter what the means of financing may be.

The Concentration of Wealth

This view reflects not merely a conservative view, but a peculiarly American brand of conservatism, one that celebrates and rewards business success more lavishly than other capitalist nations. The table below lists executive compensation in the biggest firms in the United States compared with other nations:

AVERAGE CORPORATE EXECUTIVE COMPENSATION*		
	Top 30 firms	**All firms**
United States	3,200,000	747,000
Britain	1,100,000	399,600
France	800,000	448,500
Germany	800,000	364,500
Japan	500,000	371,800

*Includes bonuses and stock options.
SOURCE: *New York Times,* Jan. 10, 1992.

More specifically, in 1990, chief executive officers (CEOs) of American companies earned 119 times as much as their average workers, whereas CEOs of Japanese companies earned only eighteen times as much. Moral questions aside, a nation whose economy is built on mass production runs an economic risk from a highly unequal income distribution.

Although conservatives may argue that this structure may generate more savings from its prosperous upper class, the economy as a whole is likely to suffer from the diminished purchasing power of its middle and lower classes. This is precisely what occurred during the conservative years. Despite economic expansion, income became concentrated in fewer and fewer hands. Looking at the nation as a whole, during the 1980s the income of the top 20 percent of U.S. families went up 19 percent, while the poorest 20 percent lost 9 percent of their income. Over the same period, the share of national income received by the wealthiest 20 percent climbed from 41.6 percent to 44 percent, while the 60 percent in the middle ranks experienced a slight decrease in income. Put simply, the rich got richer and the poor poorer. This concentration of wealth reversed three decades of growing equality, and marked the 1980s as the first decade since the 1930s in which large numbers of Americans actually suffered a serious decline in living standards. According to economist Paul Krugman, "The growing gap between rich and poor was arguably the central fact about economic life in America in the 1980s."[6] This bears not only on the question of the American tax phobia, but on the forces that may have been responsible for turning an era of high economic hopes into one of disappointing attainments.

Deficit Fears

One last aspect of the fiscal problem deserves mention. It is the extraordinary degree of alarm that has been generated by the term "deficit." Let us remember that deficits mean borrowing, and that with government, as with corporations and households, there is borrowing for good purposes as well as bad. A government that borrows to pay interest on its own debt or to pay the salaries of its regular employees is misusing its borrowing powers as badly as a corporation or a household that borrows for the same purposes. But a government that borrows to finance infrastructure is pursuing a course that is in no wise less prudent than a company that borrowed to finance a new productive venture or a household that borrows to send its children to college.

The difference is that it is very easy to tell from the public or the private records of companies and households what they borrow for, and thereby to judge whether their debts will become a burden or a source of growth. That is not the case with the way the United States keeps its national accounts. We count as revenues only our tax income, but measure our expenditures by adding both normal expenses and our public capital expenditures. Every company and household, and every industrial country other than our own, separates the two accounts so that one can tell at a glance whether the borrowing is for a good purpose or a bad one. Proper accounting may well reveal that our deficit is too large. But we cannot ascertain *how* large until we have sorted out those expenditures that should certainly be paid for by taxes (such as interest on the national debt) from expenditures such as infrastructure that have a prima-facie claim to be financed by borrowing.

Adopting a "capital budget" would not ensure that our government will use intelligence and responsibility to determine how much to borrow and for what purposes to use it. But it would at least give us an indication whether the government is in fact profligate or stingy, thoughtful about tomorrow's needs or neglectful of them.

America and the World Economy: The Making of a Debtor Nation

One further problem deserves our notice: This was a dramatic reversal of America's position in the world of international economic affairs. With few exceptions, the United States had enjoyed a substantial advantage as a world producer, starting well before World War I and mounting to a seemingly impregnable superiority after World War II. The superiority was not only the consequence of our safe distance from the world's battlefields, but also the result of our vaunted technological and organizational edge in industrial production. Thus, a quarter of a century after the end of World War II, the United States was exporting, on average, something like $10 billion a year more than it imported. Our position as an international producer seemed assured.

It was not. Beginning in the 1980s, our long-standing favorable balance began to turn negative. In 1982 our balance on goods and services was a *negative* $20.6 billion—that is, we bought that much more goods and services from the world than we sold in return. The next year that negative balance more than doubled. In 1984 it doubled again, to reach the total of $102.7 billion. Three years later the adverse balance had become an astounding $143.1 billion. We had moved from a trade creditor—that is, a trader who regularly sold more than we bought—to a world debtor on current account.

By 1988 the tide in trade again turned, and our balance on current account began to decline. By 1991 our adverse balance was down to $21.8 billion, and the worst of the crisis seemed over, although we continued to run uncomfortably large adverse balances.

Behind the Trade Problem

What lay behind this disconcerting change? Two explanations can be put forward. One is historical. Scarcely had World War II ended than the United States realized that the devastation wrought by the conflict seriously threatened its own domestic economy and international well-being. Europe had lost some thirty million people in the war; Japan, about two million. Entire cities were levelled or damaged; factories were destroyed; infrastructure was demolished; farm lands charred and ravaged. This was not a world in which capitalism and democracy could thrive. On the contrary, it was a world open to political turmoil, poverty, revolution, and, worse still, to Communist takeover. To promote international stability, and to maintain an "open door" world for American commerce, the United States took the lead in rehabilitating war-torn Europe and Japan. The cornerstone of this program was the Marshall Plan (1947), which ultimately channeled $13 billion into European restoration.

As the currents of international trade and finance were re-established, Europe and Japan quickly recovered from World War II, and America—the world's leading exporter and producer of manufactured products—prospered accordingly. By the 1980s the international economy was in the midst of its fourth postwar decade of growth. In the 1970s alone, world trade increased sevenfold, growing much faster than world GNP.

Although the United States remained the largest and richest economy in the world, it was inevitable that sooner or later its overwhelming pre-eminence would ebb. Products that foreigners could once purchase only in America became available elsewhere. Improvements in agriculture abroad reduced the world's dependency on American farm exports. Meanwhile, Americans "discovered" a wide variety of new, well-made, well-priced products manufactured abroad. As a result, from 1960 to 1983 U.S. merchandise exports expanded tenfold, but U.S. merchandise imports expanded twenty-five-fold. Hence, part of the changing balance of trade can be traced quite simply to the reemergence of Europe and Japan, as the disasters of World War II were gradually repaired.*

The Dollar Soars

The other explanation is more complex, and we shall only sketch it briefly here. It involves not merely the changing strength of the U.S. economy versus its competitors, but the entrance of new, special forces that affected our place in the world economy. These forces originated with the decision of the Reagan administration (and before that, of the Carter administration) to look to the Europeans—and later to the Japanese—as a promising source of dollars to help finance the deficit. This policy had two effects. First, it raised the value of the dollar on the foreign exchange market because Europeans rushed to invest the proceeds earned from their flourishing trade with the U.S. in the high-interest bonds of the Treasury. As a consequence, foreign goods became dirt cheap as the rising dollar bought more and more yen or francs or marks. One of these basement bargains was the cost of living abroad, which led, in turn, to a boom in foreign travel—tourism actually became the largest single industry in the world!

. . . and Then Plummets

At the time, of course, as the high dollar made foreign goods cheap to Americans, it made American goods expensive for foreigners. American exports suffered as a consequence, and pressure rose within the United States to "devalue" the dollar—that is, to take measures to lower its price in terms of other currencies. This became official policy in 1985, and within two years the dollar had fallen almost 50 percent against the Japanese yen and the German mark. Now America became the bargain basement of the world.

Thus foreign exchange fluctuations help explain the downs and ups of American fortunes in the world trade market. But they also had another, quite unexpected result. As the dollar took a precipitous fall, it brought a demand not just for U.S. exports but for American capital

---

*There is also a second reason. Europe and Japan not only regained their strength but began to forge ahead of the United States in the management of their national economies. This is a question to which we will turn in our next chapter.

assets—stocks and bonds, real estate, entire corporations. In 1980 only 3 percent of America's manufacturing assets were foreign-owned; by 1988, 12 percent were owned by overseas investors—German, Swiss, Japanese, French, and others.

This was a new and unsettling experience. We had ourselves long been major holders of foreign corporations, and never thought about it when General Motors or IBM or General Electric picked up a company here and there; but we did not like it when "American" firms such as the record division of RCA or Purina Mills or Firestone were bought, respectively, by a German conglomerate (Bertelsmann), a British oil company (British Petroleum), and a Japanese corporation (Bridgestone).

Thus the vicissitudes of the American trade balance and the American dollar are important not merely for the immediate problems they brought, and will continue to bring, but because they announce that the 1970s, 1980s, and 1990s have ushered in a sea change for America. The sea change is the immersion of American economic life into world economic life; or to depict the same phenomenon from a different perspective, the advent of a truly global economy in which America plays only one part.

U.S. arrival of foreign-made cars

The End of an Era

That is a change of huge significance for the future, and it will play its part in the chapter to come that looks toward that future. But first we must conclude this chapter. We left our survey of the period with the advent of the Bush presidency, and an account of some of the major problems it faced. Other problems also began to assume national importance, not least of them social pathologies of a kind that the country had not witnessed since the depression years. As many as a million Americans were homeless—begging on city streets and huddled on sidewalks at night. A nationwide drug epidemic became a matter of universal concern. Crime assumed greater importance than ever before. By the end of the president's term, these problems had brought the country to a standstill. A serious recession began in 1990—unemployment resumed its upward march, real output in the nation declined, and a growing sense of unease was almost palpable, with one important exception: The White House continued to declare that the economy was fundamentally sound and would soon recover.

Although Bush had replaced Calvin Coolidge's portrait with that of Theodore Roosevelt's, he did not use the presidency as a "bully pulpit" to initiate economic reforms or inspire the citizenry. The fundamental policies of the Reagan years continued. This provided the Democrats with a central issue on which to fight the election campaign of 1992. In Governor Bill Clinton of Arkansas they found a candidate who understood the political appeal and the economic importance of promising to break the stalemate in Washington, and to replace an apparently indifferent and passive administration with an engaged and concerned one.

Clinton's election was more than just a sign that the president had badly misjudged the economic situation. It was evidence of the end of an era in which government was automatically regarded as the problem, and the inauguration of an era in which government would be regarded as a means to deal with many problems. Whether or not the Clinton presidency will succeed to grappling with the vast issues of the times cannot be foretold; but there it may be that the pendulum of American political and economic sentiment had again swung, as has been the case so often in the past.

Notes

[1] *Ronald Reagan: The Politics of Symbolism* (1984), p. 63.
[2] Robert McElvaine, *The Great Depression* (1984), p. 14.
[3] Robert S. McIntyre, *Challenge* (Nov./Dec. 1991), p. 28, fig. 5.
[4] David Alan Aschauer, *Public Investment and Private Sector Growth* (1990).
[5] Seymour Martin Lipset, *The First New Nation: The United States in Historical and Comparative Perspective* (1963), p. 251.
[6] *The Age of Diminished Expectations* (1992 pb. ed.), p. 25.

Bill Clinton on the campaign trail

Chapter 17
AMERICAN CAPITALISM: RETROSPECT AND PROSPECT

Our discussion has taken us to the very edge of the present, with its uncertain and unwritten future. This now seems a good place to halt our journey and to look back over the terrain we have traversed, before venturing a glance—of necessity speculative and hazardous—into the possible shapes of things to come.

We have traced the main lines of the economic transformation of the United States. Can we find large-scale patterns in that transformation? Are there lessons to be drawn from the past? Clarifications that can be applied to the present? The questions suggest that we must find a frame of reference other than the chronology of events that have provided our thread for the last several chapters. Let us therefore return to the organizing principle of our initial chapter—an organizing principle that we have always kept in sight, but that can now once again be placed at the center of our inquiry. Let us look back over the past and reflect on what has happened to material life, to economic life, and to capitalism itself in America.

MATERIAL LIFE

Material life, Fernand Braudel tells us, is the foundation on which all else is raised. It comprises the work we do, the products we create, the forces of nature that we capture within our tools and machines, the techniques and learning we invent and retain. Nothing has changed so astonishingly in America—indeed, in all capitalist nations—as material life. To imagine the work, the products, the tools, and techniques of the Pilgrims requires an effort of the imagination sufficient to bring wax figures in museums to life. It is difficult to reconstruct the material life of the Lowell mill, the Homestead steel plant, even the Ford River Rouge plant. All that seems hopelessly distanced from modern material life.

In what ways distanced? First it is clear that we do different kinds of work than in the past. In 1620 everyone in America was in immediate touch with nature. In 1820 70 percent of all working persons were still farmers or farm employees. By 1900 fewer than 40 percent were engaged in agriculture. Today less than 3 percent of the labor force works in farming—and even that group does not till the soil so much as steer tractors and combines, work complicated farm machinery, fly crop duster planes, tend automatic milking machines, and worry about the cost of chemical fertilizers. Contact with the soil, in the close and intimate relationship of the Pilgrims and the sturdy homesteaders of the past, is now almost vanished.*

What, instead, do Americans do? The great exodus from agriculture has resulted in the swelling of two other major branches of endeavor—services, which employ about three-quarters of our employed labor force,** and manufacturing, which gives work to about 16 percent.

Only thirty years ago we employed 30 percent of the labor force in manufacturing. Does that mean that we are therefore in danger of losing our industrial strength? Here it is useful to reflect that the fall in manufacturing employment is dwarfed by the drop in agricultural employment which, half a century ago, was ten times as large a work force as it is today. Yet we never hear that we have too few agricultural workers to enable us to feed ourselves. This is because it is not

---

*With the exception, all too easily passed over in a bird's-eye view such as this, of the migrant (and immigrant) labor that plays a vital part in harvesting many crops. This ragged work force, often grossly abused and exploited, is still only a small percentage of the total American labor force, but it is growing rapidly and should not be lost from sight.

**The breakdown of the service sector warrants a footnote because it always surprises people. About eighty-five million men and women work in "services." The largest group, twenty-eight million, are in miscellaneous personal occupations that range from health care to restaurants, from ministers to scientists. The next group consists of nineteen million in retail trade. Then come the fifteen million in government—state and local, not federal. They are followed by almost seven million in finance, insurance, and real estate, and just over six million in wholesale trade. Next are not quite six million in transportation. Last we find about three million in the federal government.

the volume of employment that establishes our capacity to produce, but the productivity of that labor force; that productivity in turn is established by the quantity and quality of the machinery that labor uses.

Thus a small manufacturing labor force may be perfectly capable of making a vast volume of output, provided—and this is a very important proviso—it is well educated and trained, and surrounded with "intelligent" and fast-working mechanical aids. In fact, a considerable portion of our labor force in "services" adds productivity to manufacturing labor by supplying it with information, communication, research, and other such output-generating inputs.

High Technology

Two new capabilities have altered modern technology beyond its traditional limits. One of these is the ability to pry apart matter to release the volcanic forces within the atomic nucleus—an ability whose consequences for humanity are of overwhelming, perhaps suicidal, and possibly of life-giving importance. The djinn of nuclear capability has been let out of the bottle and it is very doubtful that it will ever again be induced to retreat within a safe container. Breaching the nuclear threshold is in itself enough to mark off the modern age from all that has gone before, even though, to date, nuclear power has not made a significant difference to the actual texture of material life.

Less awesome, but more freighted with significance, is a second technical advance—the development of the power to harness microcircuits in vast numbers, capable of processing and storing information in a manner that greatly narrows the gulf between brain and machine. The computer is a technical advance every bit as revolutionary as access to nuclear power, and much more immediately apparent in the fabric of daily existence.

Here is where the productivity-generating capacity of the manufacturing sector may collide with the job-creating capacity of the service sector. For the possibility inherent in the human like "skills" possessed by computers raises the possibility that work in the service and the manufacturing sectors may be increasingly performed by computerized machinery, just as work in the agricultural sector has been virtually taken over by machines. If the "robotization" of work becomes in fact a profitable avenue for development, the needs for unskilled or

Computer semiconductors

semi-skilled labor in both manufacturing and service occupations may be severely reduced.* Correspondingly, the need for highly trained, "knowledge-intensive" labor is likely to rise, although not necessarily by enough to make up for the reduced need for relatively less educated workers.

This raises important and disquieting possibilities. Can we equip most men and women for the kinds of work that will be in demand? Will there be enough positions for all who will seek them? If not, will "work" take on the form of a two-tier spectrum—an upper tier with something of the standing and expertise that we now associate with professionals, and a lower tier doing little more than oiling the great self-directing machinery of society? Such a picture has overtones of the anti-utopian fiction of Aldous Huxley's *Brave New World*. Huxley's scenario is certainly not a destination toward which we are inexorably pushed, but it is one that the changing character of material life may force us to confront unless we act to prevent it. Probably the most effective way to do so is to increase our expenditures on education in general, and on producing a highly trained labor force in particular.

ECONOMIC LIFE

The prospective possibility of a far-reaching transformation in the material life of America raises the question of what has happened to its economic life.

Economic life, we recall, is the manner in which we are integrated as individuals into a working social whole. Mainly this takes place through our engagement with the marketplace which we enter to sell our skills and work energies and to buy the products made by the skills and energies of others. Today our entanglement in the market is so complete that it is useful to recall that it was not always so. Only a hundred years ago, our farmer and artisan forebears were by no means as inextricably tied into market relationships as we. As recently as 1900, at least a third of the nation—its agricultural population—was still self-supporting to some degree, capable of sustaining its existence with only minimal recourse to the outside world through exchange. To be sure, even in 1900 everyone bought and sold in stores, and no one

---

*At this writing there are estimated to be some 37,500 mechanical robots "working" in U.S. industry. Japan, the world leader in robotics, claims to use seven or eight times as many.

lived in hermit-like isolation. But the agricultural fraction still represented a substantial group that could have produced its own subsistence, like the Pilgrims, even if all market relations had vanished.

No such stratum of near independence exists today. The market has become the ubiquitous and universal solvent of daily life, the mechanism on which the overwhelming majority depends for the provision of the most essential as well as the most trivial of its daily needs, and to which it turns for access to that essential means of gratifying those needs—money income.

The Supranational Economy

The economic transformation of America has thus constantly widened the screen on which was projected the drama of market activity. But the widening has not merely been in terms of the numbers of Americans who have come to depend on the market as buyers and sellers. The screen has also widened beyond the boundaries of the national economy until the forces of supply and demand that affect our well-being now come from all quarters of the globe, not merely from activities within our national borders. We have already caught a glimpse of this supranational economy in our last chapter. Now it is time for a more careful look.

Modern-day global enterprise is not merely an enlargement of the far-reaching trading enterprises of the past. It is a wholly new internationalization of production itself. Thus the "American" Chrysler Corporation builds its most successful car in Canada; the "Japanese" Honda is produced in the United States; and the Pepsi-Cola company makes its products in 500 plants located in 100 countries. The Phillips, Asea-Boveri, and Electrolux companies, all members of the so-called "Club of the 350" largest multinational companies, are in many ways too large to be contained in their "home" economies of the Netherlands, Switzerland, and Sweden.

Modern-day transnational business operates on a scale, and at a level that lifts it above the nation-states in which it locates its operating units. The magnitude of this flow has become enormous. According to a recent study of the United Nations Center on Transnational Corporations, the combined sales of the "Club of the 350" in 1985 amounted to one-third of the combined gross national products of all industrial countries, and exceeded the aggregate GNPs of all the developing nations, including China.[1]

The internationalization of the market is also compounded by the extraordinary transnational reach of banking and finance. By the 1990s, most of the world's big banks had opened branches in other nations—branches that were not subject to the credit controls that applied to their home offices, because no central bank (such as the Federal Reserve) had the authority to impose regulations or restrictions on an enterprise that lay within the sovereign territory of another nation.

As a result, the very meaning of a nation's "own" money began to blur. In 1990, for instance, the value of all commercial bank deposits within the United States—the bulk of what is called our "money supply"—came to about $826 billion. But the value of the dollars deposited in foreign branches of U.S. banks, or in banks of other nations, came to over $3,000 billion. There had thus grown up a vast pool of dollars, called Eurodollars, located abroad. This makes it very difficult for the Federal Reserve to control effectively the volume of bank credit, insofar as big corporations can easily borrow dollars abroad. Yet another indicator of the vast expansion of the reach of international finance is that the estimated global value of *daily* trading in foreign exchange is $1 trillion.

THE IMPACT OF TRADE

These astonishing figures testify to the degree to which economic linkages and relationships have leaped over national boundaries. No less sobering is the extent to which ordinary trade—the imports and exports of goods that are conveyed by boat or plane rather than being produced abroad—have also broken down the compartmentalization of the world. In 1950 the total values of exports from and imports into the United States, compared with the total value of goods—not services—produced in the U.S., was about 12 percent. This is a good measure of our exposure to the forces of the international market in the production of manufactures or raw materials. For all intents and purposes it meant that the U.S. economy was a "closed system," reliant to a modest extent on exports, more or less indifferent to the volume of imports.

Within forty years this had changed out of all recognition. By 1990, the ratio of exports and imports to GNP was 40 percent. Nowhere was the power and penetration of the international market more evident

Worker protests plant closing in Flint, Michigan

than in the collapse of America's place in steel and autos, traditionally the twin pillars of its industrial might. In 1950, U.S. steelmakers were the undisputed leaders of the world, accounting for 50 percent of all world steel output. By the 1990s, U.S. steelmakers had been reduced to one of the least efficient world producers and accounted for only 12 percent of world output. Despite the high cost of transporting steel, 19 percent of the U.S. market had been won by foreign makers, and American steel mills had been forced to ask for protective trade barriers to save themselves from still further losses.

Even more shocking was the debacle in automobiles. After the war the United States imported a mere $50 million worth of automotive vehicles and parts. America was virtually the only efficient auto maker in the world. By 1960, however, imports had grown ten times; by 1970 the value of 1960s' imports had again increased tenfold; and by 1990, imports had once more increased their value tenfold. This was a thousandfold increase over the 1950 level—enough to raise imports of Japanese, German, English, Swedish, and other cars to some $44 billion a year. Shortly thereafter, Japan became the world's largest auto producer and GM's no. 2 competitor in the United States became Toyota.

It was not in steel and automobiles alone that the international market breached the formerly impregnable dikes of American industrial strength. The computer industry, an American invention, was for all intents and purposes a Japanese-dominated field. In machine tools and electrical equipment, cameras and color TVs, tires and motorcycles, all erstwhile American-led fields, the United States market was being increasingly served by foreign makers.

Economic life in America had thus not only exposed its work force to the flux of the market, but had subjected the greatest of its corporations, like the weakest of its citizens, to the power of the market's forces. By 1982, Chrysler Corporation, a mighty U.S. giant, had escaped bankruptcy only by congressional bailout. U.S. Steel, J.P. Morgan's giant, had essentially quit the steel business and renamed itself USX Corporation, to indicate its new, rather vague, "field." IBM, long a world-renowned company, posted a loss of $5.46 billion for the last quarter of 1992, the biggest single loss in corporate history. Perhaps most significant of all, a considerable portion of American business and financial opinion, long wedded to the ideas of free trade, was beginning to think along protectionist lines, asking whether America's place in the international economy could be made secure without some form of legislative protection against the onslaughts of the world market.

A Two-Level System?

The trend toward worldwide economic activity makes it patently clear that the United States, like all advanced countries, must prepare itself to meet the challenge of global competition. What gives this question a new degree of urgency is the fear that competition will take place not merely by exporting goods but by exporting capital and that the export of capital will take the form of high-tech machinery worked by low-skilled (and very low-paid) workers.

This is by no means a merely alarmist possibility. The average factory wage in the boom city of Shenzhen in China is one-thirtieth or one-fortieth of the average Japanese wage, and the average Japanese wage is not yet as high as our own.[2] It is little wonder, then, that some foresee a day when high-productivity machinery will be uncrated in Shenzhen to create a factory capable of matching the quality, and of vastly beating the price, of anything that America has to offer. On a less dramatic scale, something like this has already been the bitter experience of American workers who have lost millions of jobs—500,000 in automobile production alone—as American firms found themselves unable to meet competition from low-wage areas such as Mexico, and have moved part of their manufacturing operations across the border in order to forestall low-wage competition.

This prospect adds yet another dimension to the world of the supranational corporation. The new dimension is that international competition will now endanger the economies of all high-wage countries—not merely of laggard ones—because the prospect of a two-level economy with Shenzhens around the world would seriously lessen the purchasing power of labor in all high-wage capitalisms. In this prospective world, we are not so much at loggerheads with Europe and Japan as in the same boat with them.

Three Strategies for the Future

What could be the outcome of such a two-level world economy? Three possibilities seem open. The first is to continue the commitment to free and unhindered trade, a central tenet of American (although not so much of European) international economic policy since the end of the Second World War. The theory behind this policy recalls the views of the English economist David Ricardo, first set forth in his *Principles of Political Economy and Taxation,* published in 1817. Ricardo explained how two countries could profitably trade, even if one of them were more efficient in the production of "everything" than its counterpart. Differences in climate, resources, and the like would always make it profitable for each country to concentrate its efforts on the commodities in which its *comparative* advantage was greater, thereafter selling those products to the other.

The idea of specialization in international production remains a valid and important one. Imaginably, America might be better off if its industrial machinery were produced in, say, Mexico, while we concentrated in the output of something like highly skilled services. The difficulties arise when we face the problem of retraining the millions of workers who would be affected. Many years would lapse before the work force of our industrial sector had become the technicians, educators, scientists and high-skilled professionals in which our national comparative advantage lay. In the meanwhile, we could easily face serious problems of economic dislocation and social and political unrest. Hence, a policy of complete laissez faire, allowing the market to determine the employment levels and directions of the work forces of the advanced countries, seems unlikely.

Protectionism

A second response is even older than free trade. It is to exclude certain goods, or classes of goods, from domestic markets because of the economic disruption they might cause. The most common means of carrying out such a protectionist policy is the tariff, whose place in our history we have already observed.

Tariffs are by no means the only, or the most effective means of protecting domestic markets today. Quotas on allowable imports, or direct negotiations with foreign nations that result in their "voluntary" curtailment of exports, play a large part in the foreign economic policies of all industrial nations. For instance, the tonnages of steel or Japanese cars allowed into the United States are established by agreement, not by competitive price. At present, roughly 25 percent of all U.S. imports, double the amount of two decades ago, are subject to nontariff restrictions.

GATT, EC, OPEC

Efforts to regulate international trade, in one form or another, have been a well-nigh ubiquitous feature of the postwar world economy. As early as 1947, the United States and twenty-two other nations attempted to ensure an open trading system by entering into a General Agreement on Tariffs and Trade (GATT). Among other things, the agreement sought to implement a so-called most-favored-nation principle—that is, each nation had to treat all other nations in exactly the same way: the lowest tariff, the fewest restrictions, the easiest access awarded to anyone had to be given to everyone. In subsequent years GATT served as a forum for U.S.–sponsored "rounds" of trade talks among its members, now numbering 108. During the Kennedy Round (1963–67), for example, tariffs were reduced an average of 36–39 percent. The outcome of the most recent round of negotiations, the Uruguay Round, is still unclear.

GATT, it must be noted, was established in the same year as the Marshall Plan, and like that program it had a political aspect to it. GATT was an effort not only to revitalize the European economy but effectively to prohibit the establishment of trading blocks which could, in turn, develop into political or military alliances. As a result, GATT prohibited bilateral agreements among its members. But these are precisely the types of negotiations that appear now to be taking place among nations. As a result, the future role of GATT is, at this point, very uncertain.

More promising have been the efforts of nations with common geographical boundaries to open their borders to their neighbors and integrate their economies. The outstanding example of this development was the economic unification, on January 1, 1993, of the twelve nations comprising the European Community (EC), thereby creating the world's largest economic market, 337 million people. Yet at the same time that many nations have worked to establish closer economic ties, others have entered into cartels to protect their comparative advantages. Cartels are international pooling agreements that allocate world markets, establish minimum prices, and restrict output. Since the 1970s, the word cartel has become synonomous with OPEC, the Organization of Petroleum Exporting Countries. From its founding in 1960 until the Arab–Israeli War of 1973, OPEC was little more than a paper organization. Thereafter, it became the first commodity cartel to use its raw material assets as an effective economic and political weapon. What power OPEC will be able to wield in the future brings us not only into the subject of energy but also into the area of foreign policy, each a topic beyond the scope of this discussion.

No economist likes protectionism, because it has a tendency to spread like a virus. Steel is protected today, machine tools tomorrow, television sets the day after. In the end, jobs are protected, but the nation's overall productivity suffers, and with it, its real purchasing power. Nonetheless, if the two-level global economy acquires the importance that is imaginable during the coming decades, a resurgence of protectionist sentiment is very likely.

Managed Trade

A third policy is a kind of compromise between the two. Called "managed" trade, it seeks to combine the productivity gains of at least a limited free exchange with the safeguards of protectionism. It does so by tempering the bargaining process so that the Shenzhens can only enjoy a share of a developed country's market to the degree that they abide by standards of environmental protection, workers' safety, and similar policies. Observance of these standards adds considerably to the cost of production in the underdeveloped nations, and thereby narrows their cost advantages.

The Challenge to Sovereignty?

One last aspect of managed trade merits a word. The real challenge of a two-level world is that the multinational corporations are often the supplier of the high-tech equipment that combines with low-wage labor. What we then find is that transnational production presents problems that escape the regulatory reach of the nation-state. Too large to reach into the wage settlements of Shenzhen, too small to serve as a regulator of transnational flows of production or human migration, the nation-state is losing its effectiveness in regulating and guiding international exchange and supranational production. What new forms of regulation and guidance the twenty-first century may bring we do not know, but this issue is likely to become a key challenge in the years ahead.

AMERICA IN THE TWENTY-FIRST CENTURY

This now brings us back for a last look into the half-visible, half-invisible American future. For it is clear that to a greater extent than ever before, this future will be inextricably entangled in the changing structure of world economic affairs.

Why America Was a World Leader

It is useful to begin to look forward by looking back. Economic historians Richard Nelson and Gavin Wright have argued persuasively that the American technological leadership of the Western world from the middle to the late nineteenth century was based on several factors.[3] One was the sheer extent and riches of the continental market of the United States. In a day in which modern-day possibilities of transportation were unknown, these conveyed tremendous competitive advantages to American industrial leadership.

A second advantage lay in the characteristics of American leadership itself. We have seen the gradual replacement of the swashbuckling robber barons of American industry by organized management. The American variant of this movement, with its emphasis on "scientific management," became a symbol of organizational skills and techniques that were another source of American leadership.*

A third reason was a growing recognition of the role of education in promoting productivity and technology. Before World War II, Americans enjoyed roughly twice as much secondary education as did their European competitors. In addition, as late as 1969, total U.S. expenditure on R&D (research and development) was still double that of England, Germany, France, and Japan *combined*.

These general sources of America's uncontested economic superiority had disappeared by the 1960s. To begin with, extraordinary developments in the technology of international transportation greatly diminished the importance of the American market. Belgian lettuce flew overnight on jumbo jets to markets in New York and San Francisco; gigantic tankers made possible a world oil market; automatic machinery opened the manufacture of components to unskilled work forces in Mexico City, Bangkok, or Turkey. Thus, the world's work

---

*U.S. managerial technique was even admired by Lenin!

became globalized in a manner that militated against the advantages that American labor had once personified.

Second, the American advantage in managerial skills and technical know-how also became ever less visible. Because of its continuing emphasis on military-connected R&D, American preeminence in peace-related innovations began to fall behind. This was not a sign of diminishing creativity, but of a diminishingly effective application of that creativity. By 1980, a number of countries were outspending the U.S on peacetime R&D as a percentage of GNP.* Although American scientists continued to lead the world in the capture of Nobel Prizes, American industry lost its lead in capturing the markets for automotive and jet plane and bullet-train transportation. Not least, the education needed to match the new levels of advanced technology was clearly better supplied abroad than at home, judging by international comparisons of mathematical grade scores, in which Americans regularly finished last.

As a result, each year America has been producing too few scientifically and technically trained people. By way of example, only 6 percent of U.S. college degrees are taken in engineering, as compared with 20 percent in Japan and 37 percent in Germany.

Falling Behind or Convergence?

Thus, from many perspectives it seems that America has been losing the unquestioned primacy in economic strength that it has enjoyed for a century. There is, however, another way of assessing the present and prospective state of affairs. What we are witnessing is not so much an American decline as a foreign catch-up; this catch-up is the consequence of an increasingly shared culture of technology and management throughout the industrial world.

"We believe," write Nelson and Wright, who propose this "convergence" thesis, "that the internationalization of trade, business, and technology is here to stay. This means that national borders mean much less than they used to regarding the flow of technology, at least among nations that have made the now needed social investments in

---

*All through the 1980s, we have lagged behind our competitors, spending 1.8 percent of GNP on nondefense R&D, compared with 2.6 percent for Germany and 2.8 percent for Japan.

education and research facilities. . . . It is increasingly difficult to create new technologies that will stay contained within national boundaries for very long in a world where technological sophistication is widespread and firms of many nationalities are ready to make the investments needed to exploit new generic technologies."[4]

This does not mean that individual countries may not forge ahead or fall behind. Indeed, as Nelson and Wright hasten to add, there is another interpretation of convergence—namely, that America is indeed slipping backwards, precisely because it is failing to provide the educational and infrastructural investments needed to stay abreast of its European and Japanese competition. "While we argue," say Nelson and Wright, "that the principal factor driving convergence over the last quarter century has been internationalization, we do not dismiss the possibility that the United States may be in the process of slipping into second, third, or fifth rank in productivity and per capita income. . . ."[5]

Labor–Management Relations

What could be the cause of such a relative decline in American economic capability? One possibility that has attracted the attention of many commentators is the American failure to establish a satisfactory framework for labor–management relations, a framework within which the full cooperation and participation of labor could be achieved. In part this helps explain the decline in productivity in the United States. Between 1982 and 1989, the average annual increase in productivity per worker hour in the U.S. was 1 percent, as compared with 2.7 percent in West Germany and 3.1 percent in Japan. These figures, coupled with earlier statistics, have led Paul Krugman to conclude that "the two decades since 1970 have seen the worst U.S. productivity performance of the century."[6]

Certainly there is no lack of evidence that American labor fell far short of the performance offered abroad. Here the testimony is offered by the litany of complaints, growing all through the 1960s, 1970s, and 1980s, about the poor quality of American workmanship. Indeed, in its World Competitiveness Report for 1990, the Swiss-based World Economic Forum, which evaluates business policies and standards, ranked the U.S. twelfth in product quality. Japan was ranked first. It was this poor quality, not cheaper prices, that drove American buyers to Japanese Sonys and Hondas, German Volkswagens, Swedish machinery, and similar foreign wares. Americans were willing to pay more for Sony TVs because their image was noticeably sharper and their color reproduction more lifelike and vivid. Similarly, they were willing to pay more for Hondas than for Chevrolets because their performance was better, their fuel efficiency superior, and their frequency of repair lower. Already by 1979, imports claimed 94 percent of television domestic sales. By 1980, 50 percent of all consumer electronics products, 90 percent of the cutlery, and one of every four autos bought in the U.S. was foreign made.

What was the cause of this widely noticed difference in labor attitudes? Many observers singled out as the central difficulty the antagonisms and suspicions held by labor, resulting in a tight control over factory floor operations, and the counterpart attitudes of management that reinforced these stiff and generally obstructive union postures. American managers tended to treat their workers as an expensive nuisance to be decently paid, hard worked, and otherwise ignored. German managers, in contrast, had become accustomed to union representatives on their boards of directors; Swedish managers experimented with work flows that allowed workers to determine their own pace of production; Japanese companies went to great length to secure lifetime employment for their workers and to make all employees feel that their company was part of their community. As a result of this last-mentioned policy, Japan's worker turnover rate is just 3.5 percent per annum, as compared with America's turnover rate of 4 percent per month. In other words, Japan has fewer job switches or firings in a year than the U.S. has in one month.

These managerial attitudes were not simply the expression of kindlier attitudes abroad. Most of them were concessions that had been won from management by strongly unionized and politically unified labor movements. In America, a weaker labor movement was unable to win such concessions. Paradoxically, then, the inefficiency that has characterized American labor–management practices may be the consequence of the failure of American management to accord labor its due respect.

A Social Contract

A second attempt to discover a broad explanation for the American slippage turns our attention away from the relation between management and labor to that between management and government. It is the nature of capitalism that this relationship is inherently tense and difficult. Yet in many foreign capitalisms a degree of mutual understanding, cooperation, and support has been attained between the public and the private spheres that far exceeds anything that we have achieved in the United States.

American business attitudes toward government are typically as narrow and antagonistic as American labor attitudes toward management: Many businessmen speak of "the government" as if it were an enemy that occupied the capitol. And government attitudes toward business are also unsatisfactory—chaotic and constrained, insecure and unfocused. As a result, government in America has lagged far behind governments in other capitalisms in formulating a coherent *social contract*—a policy in which government, with business and labor cooperation, determines targets for economic encouragement or retrenchment, and then uses its broad powers to realize these specific objectives.[7]

Such a social contract can serve two purposes. First, it can lessen the inflationary pressure that builds up in all modern capitalisms as soon as a boom gets under way. This pressure makes it exceedingly difficult for an economy to pick itself up by its own bootstraps through a program of sustained public investment, because inflation starts to rear its ugly head as soon as employment picks up. But the very same inflationary pressure prevents a sustained boom, even if it is propelled entirely by private investment. In both cases, the onset of rising employment is quickly followed by rising prices; these in turn call for anti-inflationary policies of tight money or fiscal retrenchment that lessen the inflationary threat—and also the prospects of economic progress.

A Three-Way Bargain

We do not know by what means this inflationary threat can ultimately be tamed, but at this writing Germany and Japan have made promising gains in establishing a kind of anti-inflationary arrangement among labor, management, and government.

Under this arrangement each side gives, and each side gets something it needs. Labor gives up the drive for wage settlements in excess of those compatible with productivity increases, and labor gets both political legitimacy and economic security. Legitimacy comes with a seat on corporate boards for participation in matters of corporate labor policy; security is gained through apprenticeship training and unemployment insurance. These government programs facilitate job changeovers as management modernizes or alters production processes.

Management also gains and gives. It gains the right to deploy labor as it wishes on the factory floor, without encountering the usual suspicions or resistance from labor unions. In turn, management gains assurances of government financial assistance for modernization programs that exceed the normal bounds of corporate finance, as well as cooperation from both labor and government in any inter-firm arrangements required to maintain global market shares.

Finally, government is able to plan a long-term program of public investment with a much higher degree of protection from inflationary pressures. In turn it must provide a new kind of economic leadership—so-called *industrial policy*—that saddles it with a high degree of economic responsibility and a corresponding risk of political failure.

Thus, a social contract can set the stage for a greater control over inflation and a more coherent direction of national economic energies in a new setting where inflation and globalism pose new and difficult challenges. This is not a blueprint for "planning" that in any way resembles the disastrous centralized system of the former USSR and its satellites, but it is certainly different from the relatively unguided capitalism of the twentieth century. The world of twenty-first century capitalism seems likely to require a more organized and socially responsive form of capitalism than in the past, and some form of social contract appears to be the most promising response it may make.

A Spectrum of Capitalisms

One realization emerges clearly from this overview. Capitalism is capable of many institutional and organizational forms—not only from one country to the next, but from one period to the next. As material life changes, so does economic life. As ideas and ideologies change, so does the relation between politics and business. As capitalism changes in its complex structure, new dynamics emerge, giving another impetus to the process of economic evolution.

This very property of changefulness leads to the first general pronouncement for the coming century. It is that capitalism is likely to present a spectrum of social variants, all of them clearly members of the same basic social formation, but not all of them equally successful. By members of the same "formation" we mean that all will be motivated by the quest for capital; all of them marked by the presence of two realms, one economic, one political; and all of them essentially coordinated by a market mechanism. When we say that not all will be equally successful, we mean that among the many permutations of these three identifying elements, not all will function with equal success in securing the social morale, the political peace, and the economic vitality needed to carry on.

This is not a prognosis peculiar to our time in history. At any time in the past 200 years one might have said that so dynamic a system as ours was likely to evolve into a spectrum of forms, some of which would prosper as societies, polities, and economies more than others. That is not to say that one could have foreseen the specific characteristics of the Dickensian capitalism of England, the Balzacian capitalism of France, the Bismarckian capitalism of Germany, or even the exuberant capitalism of America. But certainly the future would have pointed to a fan-shaped trajectory of evolution, with some of these national variants carrying on tasks of accumulation, managing the delicate interplay of polity and economy, and mastering the use of and the control over the market with a greater degree of concord, unity, and vigor than others.

The Crucial Variable

That seems a plausible way to describe those attributes that will most likely determine the success of capitalisms in the coming century. But we shall add a more specific prognosis. The crucial variable for businesses in the twenty-first century is not their relative success in finding technologies and techniques to generate capital. The internationalization of the system seems certain to bring about a greater degree of conformity than in the past. Neither is it the form of the market mechanism. Once again, the spread of common technologies and modes of management seems likely to lead in the direction of more uniformity of national market mechanisms than in the past. The crucial variable, to our eyes, seems to lie in the relationship between the worlds of business and politics, the realms of economics and government.

Put differently, the decisive element appears to reside in the appropriate combination of laissez faire and planning—on the one hand, allowing capitalism to express its self-generated energies; on the other, guiding and supplementing those energies with various means of public encouragement and discouragement. Having said that, we do not presume to know what combination will prove the most fruitful. All we say—and that is already risk enough for any historian—is that we believe *this* is where the decisive determinations will lie.

Limits of Adaptability

One further prognostication seems necessary. We appear to be moving toward one challenge for which there is no visible remedy. It is the ecological dangers to which the modern industrial processes give rise, of which by far the most awesome is the possibility of climatic change. Global warming, as it is called, is a large-scale ecological process whose causes and consequences lie outside the scope of this book.[8] While still uncertain with respect to its speed of advent, there

Heavy smog over Denver, December 1983

seems to be a growing scientific consensus that industrialization itself is a major source of carbon emissions which, once in the atmosphere, form a kind of greenhouse whose invisible panes entrap solar energy, causing a rise in the ambient temperature of the earth.

The arresting feature of this process is not just its glacier-like encroachment. It is that the control over global warming lies outside any form of social control. This is because carbon emissions do not recognize national boundaries. They also do not arise from any single form of socioeconomic organization. Capitalism produces ecological dangers and so do all known kinds of socialism. Once carbon is released into the atmosphere it can no longer be charged to any geographic source or national origin, and its effects will be distributed with complete indifference as to the origins of the problem.

How is this challenge to be curtailed and controlled? How can global warming rights be granted—or denied—to poorer nations, or more ecologically concerned nations, or more deserving nations? The problem calls for remedies that surpass the political and economic limits and capabilities of our time. It is a problem that is likely to loom ever larger in the twenty-first century and to have moved to the foreground by the advent of the twenty-second.

Beyond Capitalism?

Ecology is the most fearsome challenge, but not the only one that dwarfs capitalism, as such. Anyone who looks out over the disarray of the post–Cold War world, with its seething racial and ethnic hatreds, its horrendous extremes of poverty and wealth, its population explosions and risks of local population extinctions, must recognize that humanity in its perhaps ten thousandth year of what we call civilization is still a very insecurely anchored achievement of the human species.

Against that perspective, capitalism diminishes in importance but also takes on a special significance. Capitalism is the name for the social arrangements with which we will have to come to grips with vast problems of unprecedented consequences. We do not know how adequately these arrangements can cope with these challenges, nor do we know what other social arrangements might prove to be necessary.

What we *do* know is that in this period great decisions will be made that will powerfully affect our capability to deal with the problems ahead. We can certainly vanquish the remediable evils of poverty and ignorance. We can marshal our scientific resources to minimize and perhaps hold at bay the destruction of the ecosphere. We can begin to construct the first transnational agreements that will be needed to coordinate a unified global economy and a patchwork global sovereignty. We can become aware of our responsibilities to the future, and of the contribution we can make to it by becoming the most adaptive, the most forward-looking capitalism—not of the twentieth century, but of the twenty-first.

Notes

[1] *Report on Transnational Corporations,* cited in *The Nation,* May 18, 1992, p. 652.

[2] Paul Kennedy, *Preparing for the Twenty-first Century* (1993), p. 178.

[3] Richard R. Nelson and Gavin Wright, "The Rise and Fall of American Technological Leadership," *Journal of Economic Literature* (December 1992), 1931–64.

[4] *Ibid.,* 1961.

[5] *Ibid.*

[6] *The Age of Diminished Expectations* (1992 pb. ed.), p. 12.

[7] See Ira Magaziner and Robert Reich, *Minding America's Business* (1982).

[8] For an up-to-date review see Kennedy, *Preparing for the Twenty-First Century.*

SUGGESTIONS FOR FURTHER READING

Chapter 1 ———————————————————————————

ECONOMIC TRANSFORMATION AS A THEME OF HISTORY

The organizing principle for this work as a whole is based on Fernand Braudel's magisterial *Civilization & Capitalism, 15th–18th Century* (3 vols., 1979–1984). For the rise, development, and meaning of capitalism, see Max Weber, *The Protestant Ethic and the Spirit of Capitalism* (1930); R.H. Tawney, *Religion and the Rise of Capitalism* (1937); Henri Sée, *Modern Capitalism: Its Origin and Evolution* (1928); Maurice Dobb, *Studies in the Development of Capitalism* (1947); R. Hilton (ed.), *The Transformation from Feudalism to Capitalism* (1976); Karl Polanyi, *The Great Transformation* (1973); and Robert Heilbroner, *The Making of Economic Society* (9th ed., 1993).

Chapter 2 ———————————————————————————

OUT OF THE EUROPEAN CRADLE

For historical background, see Henri Pirenne, *Economic and Social History of Medieval Europe* (1956); Carlo M. Cippola, *Before the Industrial Revolution: European Society and Economy, 1000–1700* (1980); and Douglass C. North and Robert Paul Thomas, *The Rise of the Western World* (1973).

The spice trade is covered in Donald F. Lach, *Asia in the Making of Europe* (1965), and E.P. Cheyney, *European Background of American History, 1300–1600* (1961). The fullest account of mercantilism can be found in Eli Heckscher, *Mercantilism* (1935). See also Joyce Appleby, *Economic Thought and Ideology in Seventeenth Century England* (1978), and T.K. Rabb, *Enterprise and Empire* (1967).

The Age of Discovery is the subject of *The Rise of the Atlantic Economies* (1973), by Ralph Davis; *The Age of Reconnaissance* (1981), by J.H. Parry; and *The European Discovery of America* (1971–74), by Samuel Eliot Morison.

On the unintended results of the interaction between the Old World and the New, see Alfred Crosby, *Columbian Exchange: Biological and*

Cultural Consequences of 1492 (1972). The impact of New World treasure on the economy of the Old World is analyzed in Earl J. Hamilton, *American Treasure and the Price Revolution in Spain, 1501–1650* (1934).

For the rise of capitalism and the Commercial Revolution, see John U. Nef, *Industry and Government in France and England, 1540–1640* (1940), and E.E. Rich and C.H. Wilson (eds.), *The Economy of Expanding Europe in the Sixteenth and Seventeenth Centuries,* volume IV of the *Cambridge Economic History of Europe* (1967).

Chapter 3
THE COLONIZATION OF AMERICA

Important background studies of England include Peter Laslett, *The World We Have Lost* (1965); Keith Wrightson, *English Society, 1580–1680* (1968); D.C. Coleman, *The Economy of England, 1450–1750* (1977); Carl Bridenbaugh, *Vexed and Troubled Englishmen, 1590–1642* (1968); Wallace Notestein, *The English People on the Eve of Colonization, 1603–1630* (1954); and D.B. Quinn, *England and the Discovery of America, 1481–1620* (1974).

For the colonization of America, see Charles M. Andrews, *The Colonial Period of American History* (1934–38), John E. Pomfret, *Founding the American Colonies* (1970), and Wesley Frank Craven, *The Colonies in Transition, 1660–1713* (1968).

On the colonial economy in general, see John J. McCusker and Russell R. Menard, *The Economy of British America, 1607–1789* (1985); Edwin J. Perkins, *The Economy of Colonial America* (1980); Gary M. Walton and James F. Shepherd, *The Economic Rise of Early America* (1979); and the relevant chapters in two studies by Stuart Bruchey, *The Roots of American Economic Growth, 1607–1861* (1961), and *Enterprise: The Dynamic Economy of a Free People* (1990).

Colonial agriculture is covered in L.C. Gray, *History of Agriculture in the Southern United States to 1860* (1933); P.W. Bidwell and J.I. Falconer, *History of Agriculture in the Northern United States, 1620–1860* (1925); Howard S. Russett, *A Long Deep Furrow: Three Centuries of Farming in New England* (1976); James Lemon, *The Best Poor Man's Country: A Geographical Study of Early Southeastern Pennsylvania* (1972); and James A. Henretta and Gregory H. Nobles, *Evolution and Revolution: American Society, 1600–1820* (1987).

Important studies on the Chesapeake region include T.H. Breen, *Tobacco Culture* (1985); Edmund S. Morgan, *American Slavery,*

American Freedom: The Ordeal of Colonial Virginia (1975); Allan Kulikoff, *Tobacco and Slaves: The Development of Southern Cultures in the Chesapeake, 1600–1800* (1986); Aubrey C. Land, *Colonial Maryland* (1981); and Gloria L. Main, *Tobacco Colony: Life in Early Maryland, 1650–1720* (1982). On the international market for tobacco, see Jacob M. Price, *Capital and Credit in British Overseas Trade* (1980).

The economy of the British West Indies is covered in two excellent works: Richard S. Dunn, *Sugar and Slaves* (1972) and Richard B. Sheridan, *Sugar and Slavery: An Economic History of the British West Indies, 1623–1775* (1974).

On indentured servitude, see A.E. Smith, *Colonists in Bondage: White Servitude and Convict Labor in America, 1607–1776* (1971); David W. Galenson, *White Servitude in Colonial America* (1981); and Robert Heavner, *Economic Aspects of Indentured Servitude in Colonial Pennsylvania, 1771–1773* (1977).

The African slave trade is covered in Philip D. Curtin, *The Atlantic Slave Trade: A Census* (1969); James A. Rawley, *The Transatlantic Slave Trade* (1981); and Herbert S. Klein, *The Middle Passage: Comparative Studies in the Atlantic Slave Trade* (1978).

On colonial commerce, see James F. Shepherd and Gary M. Walton, *Shipping, Maritime Trade, and the Economic Development of Colonial America* (1972).

Chapter 4
SETTING THE ECONOMIC STAGE

The subject of the colonial population is treated in J. Potter, "The Growth of Population in America, 1780–1860," in D.V. Glass and D.E.C. Eversley (eds.), *Population in History* (1965), and Robert Wells, *The Population of the British Colonies in America Before 1776: A Survey of Census Data* (1975). See also Bernard Bailyn's *Voyagers to the West* (1986).

On colonial merchants, see Bernard Bailyn, *The New England Merchants in the Seventeenth Century* (1955); Stuart Bruchey (ed.), *The Colonial Merchant* (1966); James Hedges, *The Browns of Providence Plantation: The Colonial Years* (1952); and C.L. Heyrman, *Commerce and Culture: The Maritime Communities of Colonial Massachusetts, 1690–1750* (1984).

Colonial currency is given extensive treatment in Leslie V. Brock, *The Currency of the American Colonies, 1700–1764* (1975); Curtis Nettels, *Money Supply of the American Colonies before 1720* (1934); and Joseph Ernst, *Money and Politics in America, 1755–1775* (1973).

The working classes are discussed in Gary B. Nash's *The Urban Crucible* (1976).

On the distribution of wealth, see Alice Hanson Jones, *Wealth of a Nation to Be* (1980); Jackson Turner Main, *The Social Structure of Revolutionary America* (1965); and P.H. Lindert and Jeffrey Williamson, *Long-Term Trends in American Wealth Inequality* (1977).

Chapter 5
THE DECLARATION OF ECONOMIC INDEPENDENCE

Economic frictions between the colonies and the mother country are discussed in Thomas Barrow, *Trade and Empire* (1967); Edmund and Helen Morgan, *The Stamp Act Crisis* (1953); Benjamin Labaree, *The Boston Tea Party* (1964); and O.M. Dickerson, *The Navigation Acts and the American Revolution* (1974).

Merrill Jensen's *The Articles of Confederation* (1940) and *The New Nation* (1950) are standard on the 1781–89 period. See also Curtis Nettels, *The Emergence of a National Economy, 1775–1815* (1962), and E. James Ferguson, *The Power of the Purse: A History of American Public Finance, 1776–1790* (1961).

For the Constitutional Convention, consult Charles A. Beard, *An Economic Interpretation of the Constitution of the United States* (1965); R.E. Brown, *Charles Beard and the Constitution* (1956); and Forrest McDonald, *We The People: The Economic Origins of the Constitution* (1956).

Early industrialization is covered in Barbara M. Tucker's *Samuel Slater and the Origins of the American Textile Industry, 1790–1860* (1984).

Jefferson's views on agriculture are discussed in Drew R. McCoy, *The Elusive Republic: Political Economy in Jeffersonian America* (1980), and Joyce Appleby, *Capitalism and a New Social Order* (1984).

The Hamiltonian program is set forth in great detail in Forrest McDonald, *Alexander Hamilton* (1974), and Jacob E. Cooke, *Alexander Hamilton* (1982).

Chapter 6
PREPARATIONS FOR THE AGE OF MANUFACTURE

For a general overview of the period, see Charles Sellers, *The Market Revolution: Jacksonian America, 1815–1846* (1991). The best general account of developments in transportation is George Rogers Taylor,

The Transportation Revolution, 1815–1860 (1951). Other useful studies include L.C. Hunter, *Steamboats on the Western Rivers* (1949); R.E. Shaw, *Erie Water West: A History of the Erie Canal* (1966); Erik Haites et al., *Western River Transportation: The Era of Early Internal Development* (1975); Harry Scheiber, *The Ohio Canal Era* (1965); and Carter Goodrich (ed.), *Canals and American Economic Development* (1972).

Two complex quantitative studies that try to measure the impact of the railroad on American economic development are Robert W. Fogel, *Railroads and American Economic Growth* (1964), and Albert Fishlow, *American Railroads and the Transformation of the Antebellum Economy* (1965).

On the life of the early New England textile operatives, see N.J. Ware, *The Industrial Worker, 1840–60* (1924); Caroline Ware, *The Early New England Cotton Manufacture* (1931); Hannah Josephson, *The Golden Threads* (1949); Thomas Dublin, *Women at Work: The Transformation of Work and Community in Lowell, Massachusetts, 1826–1860* (1979); and Alice Kessler-Harris, *Out to Work: A History of Wage-Earning Women in the United States* (1982).

Other important studies on the antebellum working class include Paul G. Faler, *Mechanics and Manufacturers in the Early Industrial Revolution: Lynn, Massachusetts, 1780–1860* (1981); Alan Dawley, *Class and Community: The Industrial Revolution in Lynn* (1976); Sean Wilentz, *Chants Democratic: New York City and the Rise of the American Working Class, 1788–1850* (1984); Jonathan Prude, *The Coming of Industrial Order: Town and Factory Life in Rural Massachusetts, 1810–1860* (1983); Anthony F.C. Wallace, *Rockdale: The Growth of an American Village in the Early Industrial Revolution (1978);* Mary H. Blewett, *Men, Women, and Work: Class, Gender, and Protest in the New England Shoe Industry, 1789–1910* (1988); and two studies by Bruce Laurie, *Working People of Philadelphia, 1800–1850* (1980), and *Artisans Into Workers* (1989).

For the transformation of American law and its impact on the development of American enterprise, see Morton Horwitz, *The Transformation of American Law, 1780–1860* (1976), and R. Kent Newmeyer, *The Supreme Court Under Marshall and Taney* (1969).

Corporations and banking are covered in Ronald E. Seavoy, *The Origins of the American Business Corporation, 1784–1855* (1982), and Bary Hammond, *Banks and Politics in America from the Revolution to the Civil War* (1957).

Technological developments are covered in Nathan Rosenberg, *Technology and American Economic Growth* (1972); Donald Hoke, *Ingenious Yankees* (1989); David A. Hounshell, *From American System* to *Mass Production, 1800–1932* (1984); H.J. Habakkuk, *American and British Technology in the Nineteenth Century* (1962); David J. Jeremy, *Transatlantic Industrial Revolution* (1981); and D.H. Stapleton, *The Transfer of Early Industrial Technologies to America* (1987).

Chapter 7 —————————————————————————————
THE STRUCTURAL TRANSFORMATION

Economic growth and change is covered in Paul A. David, "The Growth of Real Product in the United States Before 1840," in *Journal of Economic History,* 27 (June 1967), and Lance E. Davis et al., *American Economic Growth* (1972). For the distribution of wealth, see Lee Soltow, *Men and Wealth in the United States, 1850–1870* (1975).

On the importance of cotton to the United States economy in general and the southern economy in particular, see Douglass C. North, *The Economic Growth of the United States, 1790–1860* (1961); William N. Parker (ed.), *The Structure of the Cotton Economy of the Antebellum South* (1970); and Gavin Wright, *The Political Economy of the Cotton South* (1978).

On slavery in general, see Kenneth M. Stampp, *The Peculiar Institution* (1956); Eugene D. Genovese, *Roll, Jordan, Roll* (1975); and John W. Blassingame, *The Slave Community* (1972). For slavery and its effects on the economic development of the south, see A.H. Conrad and J.R. Meyer, *The Economics of Slavery* (1964); Eugene D. Genovese, *The Political Economy of Slavery* (1965); and Harold Woodman (ed.), *Slavery and the Southern Economy* (1966).

Slave culture and community are discussed in Albert J. Raboteau, *Slave Religion* (1978); L.W. Levine, *Black Culture and Consciousness* (1977); and Herbert G. Gutman, *The Black Family in Slavery and Freedom, 1750–1925* (1976). On planters, see James Oakes, *The Ruling Race* (1982).

Economic developments during the Civil War era are discussed in Ralph Andreano (ed.), *The Economic Impact of the American Civil War* (1967); Allan Nevins, *The Ordeal of the Union* (1947); L.M. Hacker, *The Triumph of American Capitalism* (1940); and E.D. Fite, *Social and Industrial Conditions in the North During the Civil War* (1910).

For a full account of the 1863–77 period, see Eric Foner, *Reconstruction* (1988). On the economic and social effects of emancipation on freed blacks, see R.L. Ransom and Richard Sutch, *One Kind of Freedom* (1978); Robert Higgs, *Competition and Coercion: Blacks in the American Economy, 1865–1914* (1977); and Leon Litwack, *Been in the Storm So Long* (1979).

The "New South" is the subject of *Origins of the New South, 1877–1913* (1951), by C. Vann Woodward, and *The Promise of the New South* (1992), by Edward L. Ayers. See also Gavin Wright, *Old South, New South* (1986).

Chapter 8
THE AGE OF THE BUSINESSMAN

Two well-written introductions to the period are John A. Garraty, *The New Commonwealth, 1877–1890* (1968), and Robert H. Weibe, *The Search for Order* (1967).

Important general studies of industrialization include Samuel P. Hays, *The Response to Industrialism* (1957); H.G. Vatter, *The Drive to Industrial Maturity: The U.S. Economy, 1860–1914* (1975); E.C. Kirkland, *Industry Comes of Age* (1961); Allan Nevins, *The Emergence of Modern America: 1865–1878* (1927); T.C. Cochran and William Miller, *The Age of Enterprise* (1968); Robert Higgs, *The Transformation of the American Economy* (1971); and Glenn Porter, *The Rise of Big Business* (1973). *American Business Cycles, 1865–1897* (1959), by Rendigs Fels, is an important specialized study.

There are several excellent studies on the growth of particular industries. See, for example, R.W. and M.E. Hidy, *Pioneering in Big Business, 1882–1911: History of the Standard Oil Company* (1955); H.F. Williamson and A.R. Daum, *The American Petroleum Industry* (1981); and H.C. Passer, *The Electrical Manufacturers* (1972).

On businessmen, see Matthew Josephson, *The Robber Barons* (1934); Edward C. Kirkland, *Dream and Thought in the Business Community, 1860–1900* (1956); Irwin G. Wyllie, *The Self-Made Man in America* (1954); and Louis Galambos and Barbara Barron Spence, *The Public Image of Big Business in America* (1975).

Social Darwinism is covered in Richard Hofstadter, *Social Darwinism in American Thought* (1955), and Cynthia Eagle Russett, *Darwin in America* (1976).

There are two excellent biographies of Andrew Carnegie: J.E. Wall, *Andrew Carnegie* (1970), and Harold Livesay, *Andrew Carnegie and the Rise of Big Business* (1975). On Jay Gould, see Maury Klein, *The Life and Legend of Jay Gould* (1986).

Chapter 9
THE TECHNOLOGY OF INDUSTRIALIZATION

For the technology of steel production, see Peter Temin, *Iron and Steel in the Nineteenth Century* (1964). See also W.P. Strassman, *Risk and*

Technological Innovation (1981), and two works by E.E. Morison, *From Know How to Nowhere* (1974), and *Men, Machines, and Modern Times* (1966).

The best introduction to business organization in these years are the studies by Alfred Chandler, Jr.: *Strategy and Structure* (1962); *The Visible Hand: The Managerial Revolution in American Business* (1977); and *Scale and Scope: The Dynamics of Industrial Capitalism* (1990).

On the corporation, see G.H. Evans, *Business Incorporations in the United States.*

Chapter 10
FROM TRUST TO ANTITRUST

In addition to many of the works cited in the previous two chapters, see Ralph Nelson, *Merger Movements in American Industry* (1959), and Naomi Lamoreaux, *The Great Merger Movement in American Business, 1895–1904* (1985).

On Rockefeller, see the outstanding biography by Allan Nevins, *Study in Power* (1953). For Morgan, see Ron Chernow, *The House of Morgan* (1990).

Two important studies on antitrust are Hans P. Thorelli, *The Federal Antitrust Policy* (1955), and William Letwin, *Law and Economic Policy in America: The Evolution of the Sherman Antitrust Act* (1981). The Interstate Commerce Commission is discussed in Ari and Olive Hoogenboom, *A History of the ICC* (1976).

The careers of three important critics of monopoly are discussed in John L. Thomas, *Alternative America: Henry George, Edward Bellamy, Henry Demarest Lloyd and the Adversary Tradition* (1983). For an overview of Roosevelt's and Wilson's response to big business, see John W. Chambers, *The Tyranny of Change: America in the Progressive Era* (1980); George E. Mowry, *The Era of Theodore Roosevelt, 1900–1912* (1958); and Arthur S. Link, *Woodrow Wilson and the Progressive Era, 1900–1917* (1954).

Chapter 11
WORKERS AND WORK

For a general statement on the role of labor, see Stanley Lebergott, *Manpower in Economic Growth* (1964). Nell I. Painter, *Standing at Armageddon: The United States, 1877–1919* (1987), is excellent on the struggles of working people in these years.

The Knights of Labor are discussed in N.J. Ware, *The Labor Movement in the United States, 1860–1895* (1929), and Leon Fink,

Workingmen's Democracy (1982). The AFL is the subject of Philip Taft's *The AFL in the Time of Gompers* (1957). See also S.B. Kaufman, *Samuel Gompers and the Origins of the American Federation of Labor* (1973), and Harold Livesay, *Samuel Gompers and Organized Labor in America* (1978).

For a sampling of the important testimony taken by the Senate Committee on Education and Labor in 1883, see John A. Garraty (ed.), *Labor and Capital in the Gilded Age* (1968).

For women at work, consult Alice Kessler-Harris, *Out to Work* (1982), and B.M. Wertheimer, *We Were There: The Story of Working Women in America* (1977). Other valuable works for this chapter include David Montgomery, *Beyond Equality* (1967); Montgomery, *The Fall of the House of Labor* (1987); Herbert Gutman, *Work, Culture, and Society in Industrializing America* (1976); D.T. Rodgers, *The Work Ethic in Industrial America* (1980); Charlotte Erickson, *American Industry and European Immigration, 1860–1885* (1957); G.N. Grob, *Workers and Utopia* (1972); Irwin Yellowitz, *Industrialization and the American Labor Movement* (1977); David Brody, *Steelworkers in America* (1960); Melvyn Dubovsky, *Industrialism and the American Worker, 1865–1920* (1975); Daniel Nelson, *Managers and Workers: Origins of the New Factory System in the United States, 1800–1920* (1975); Nelson, *Frederick W. Taylor and the Rise of Scientific Management* (1980); and David Gordon et al., *Segmented Work, Divided Workers: The Historical Transformation of Labor in the United States* (1982).

On the Homestead Strike, see Leon Wolff, *Lockout* (1965), and Paul Krause, *The Battle for Homestead, 1880–1892* (1992).

A brilliant, although disputed, analysis of labor from a Marxist point of view is presented in Harry Braverman's *Labor and Monopoly Capital: The Degradation of Work in the Twentieth Century* (1975).

Chapter 12 ─────────────────────────────
INDUSTRIALIZATION RUBS OFF ON LIFE

There are several excellent introductions to the topic of urbanization. See Howard P. Chudacoff and Judith E. Smith, *The Evolution of America Urban Society* (1988); Blake McKelvey, *The Urbanization of America* (1963); Sam Bass Warner, *The Urban Wilderness* (1972); and Raymond A. Mohl, *The New City: Urban America in the Industrial Age, 1860–1920* (1985).

For slums and tenements, see Robert Bremner, *From the Depths: The*

Discovery of Poverty in the United States (1956); Roy Lubove, *The Progressives and the Slums* (1974); and Allen Davis, *Spearheads for Reform: The Social Settlements and the Progressive Movement, 1890–1914* (1967).

On Harlem, see Gilbert Osofsky, *Harlem: The Making of a Ghetto, 1890–1930* (1965). See also Allan H. Spear, *Black Chicago: The Making of a Negro Ghetto, 1890–1920* (1967), and Kenneth L. Kusmer, *A Ghetto Takes Shape: Black Cleveland, 1870–1930* (1976).

On Pullman, see Stanley Buder, *Pullman* (1967), and Almont Lindsey, *Pullman* (1942). Alfred T. White's approach to model tenements is discussed in his *Better Homes for Working People* (1885).

On machinery and material life, see Siegfried Giedion, *Mechanization Takes Command* (1948).

Chapter 13 ───────────────────
THE GREAT DEPRESSION

Useful introductions to the period include F.L. Allen, *Only Yesterday* (1931); J.W. Prothro, *The Dollar Decade: Business Ideas in the 1920s* (1954); William Leuchtenburg, *The Perils of Prosperity* (1958); Geoffrey Perrett, *America in the Twenties* (1982); J. Potter, *The American Economy Between the World Wars* (1974); and Michael E. Parrish, *Anxious Decades: America in Prosperity and Depression* (1992).

On economic thinking during these years, see William J. Barber, *From New Era to New Deal: Herbert Hoover, The Economists, and American Economic Policy, 1921–1933* (1985).

For the stock market collapse, see John Kenneth Galbraith, *The Great Crash* (1955), and Robert Sobel, *The Great Bull Market: Wall Street in the 1920s* (1968).

On the Great Depression, consult John A. Garraty, *The Great Depression* (1986); Robert McElvaine, *The Great Depression* (1984); Michael A. Bernstein, *The Great Depression: Delayed Recovery and Economic Change in America, 1929–1939* (1988); Charles P. Kindleberger, *The World in Depression* (1970); Broadus Mitchell, *Depression Decade* (1947); Albert U. Romasco, *The Poverty of Abundance* (1968); and Caroline Bird, *The Invisible Scar* (1966).

The plight of the unemployed is covered in John A. Garraty, *Unemployment in History: Economic Thought and Public Policy* (1978), and Irving Bernstein, *The Lean Years: A History of the American Worker, 1920–1933* (1960). The activities of the Federal Reserve Board are the subject of Milton Friedman and A.J. Schwartz, *The Great Contraction,*

1929–1933 (1965), and Peter Temin, *Did Monetary Forces Cause the Great Depression?* (1975).

Two useful guides to Keynesian economics are Alvin Hansen, *A Guide to Keynes* (1953), and Robert Lekachman, *The Age of Keynes* (1975).

Chapter 14
THE NEW DEAL

William Leuchtenburg's *Franklin D. Roosevelt and the New Deal* (1963) is still the best single-volume study. Other important works include Arthur Schlesinger, Jr., *The Age of Roosevelt* (1957–60); J.M. Burns, *Roosevelt: The Lion and the Fox* (1956); Paul K. Conkin, *The New Deal* (1975); Albert U. Romasco, *The Politics of Recovery: Roosevelt's New Deal* (1983); Daniel Fusfeld, *The Economic Thought of Franklin D. Roosevelt and the Origins of the New Deal* (1956); and Harvard Sitkoff (ed.), *Fifty Years Later: The New Deal Evaluated* (1985).

Chapter 15
FROM POSTWAR BOOM TO POSTWAR INFLATION

Important general overviews include H.G. Vatter, *The U.S. Economy in the 1950s* (1963); John Diggins, *The Proud Decades, 1941–1960* (1989); Geoffrey Perrett, *A Dream of Greatness: The American People, 1945–1963* (1979); William Leuchtenburg, *A Troubled Feast: American Society Since 1945* (1979); Otis L. Graham, Jr., *Toward a Planned Society: From Roosevelt to Nixon* (1976); and James L. Sundquist, *Politics and Policy: the Eisenhower, Kennedy, and Johnson Years* (1968).

On the Truman Administration, see David McCullough, *Harry Truman* (1992), and Alonzo L. Hamby, *Beyond the New Deal* (1973). The Employment Act of 1946 is discussed in S.K. Bailey's *Congress Makes a Law* (1980). On the Eisenhower Presidency, see Stephen E. Ambrose, *Eisenhower: The President* (1984), and C. Alexander, *Holding the Line* (1975). See also Mark H. Rose, *Interstate: Express Highway Politics, 1941–1956* (1979). The Kennedy years are covered in Arthur M. Schlesinger, Jr., *A Thousand Days* (1965); Irving Bernstein, *Promises Kept: John F. Kennedy's New Frontier* (1991); J.F. Heath, *Decade of Disillusionment: The Kennedy–Johnson Years* (1975); and A.D. Donald (ed.), *John F. Kennedy and the New Frontier* (1966). Johnson's Great Society is discussed in V.D. Bornet, *The Presidency of Lyndon B. Johnson* (1983); Charles Murray, *Losing Ground: American Social Policy, 1950–1980* (1983); James T. Patterson, *America's Struggle Against*

Poverty, 1900–1985 (1986); and M.E. Gettleman and D. Mermelstein, *The Great Society Reader* (1967). Nixon's years in office are covered in James A. Reichley, *Conservatives in an Era of Change: The Nixon and Ford Administrations* (1981), and Stephen E. Ambrose, *Nixon: The Triumph of a Politician, 1962–1972* (1989). On Ford, see John Osborne, *White House Watch: The Ford Years* (1977). Carter's administration is studied in Clark Mollenhoff, *The President Who Failed* (1980), and Ervin C. Hargrove, *Jimmy Carter as President* (1989).

Important specialized studies for these years include John Kenneth Galbraith, *American Capitalism* (1952); Galbraith, *The Affluent Society* (1978); Michael Harrington, *The Other America* (1962); John W. Kendrick, *Postwar Productivity Trends in the United States, 1948–1969* (1973); Herbert Stein, *The Fiscal Revolution in America* (1969); Stein, *Presidential Economics: The Making of Economic Policy from Roosevelt to Reagan and Beyond* (1984).

Chapter 16
THE CONSERVATIVE ERA

Useful introductions to the Reagan adminstration include Lou Cannon, *President Reagan: The Role of a Lifetime* (1991); Robert Dallek, *Ronald Reagan: The Politics of Symbolism* (1984); Gary Wills, *Reagan's America* (1987); and Haynes Johnson, *Sleepwalking Through History: America in the Reagan Years* (1992).

For subjects covered in the text, see Paul Craig Roberts, *The Supply-Side Revolution* (1984); Benjamin Freidman, *Day of Reckoning: The Consequences of American Economic Policy Under Reagan and After* (1988); Joseph A. Pechman, *Federal Tax Policy* (1987); Pechman, *Who Paid the Taxes, 1966–85?* (1985); Roy C. Smith, *The Money Wars: The Rise and Fall of the Great Buyout Boom of the 1980s* (1990); David Alan Aschauer, *Public Investment and Private Sector Growth* (1990); Kevin Phillips, *The Politics of Rich and Poor: Wealth and the American Electorate in the Reagan Aftermath* (1990); Paul Krugman, *The Age of Diminished Expectations: U.S. Economic Policy in the 1990s* (1992); Lawrence J. White, *The S&L Debacle* (1991); Robert Eisner, *How Real is the Federal Deficit?* (1986); Robert Heilbroner and Peter Bernstein, *The Debt and the Deficit* (1989); David Calleo, *The Bankrupting of America: How the Federal Budget Is Impoverishing the Nation* (1992); Robert Reich, *The Work of Nations* (1991); Robert Kuttner, *The End of Laissez Faire: National Purpose and the Global Economy After the Cold War* (1991); Lester Thurow, *Head to Head: The Coming Economic Battle*

Among Japan, Europe, and America (1992); Edward M. Graham and Paul R. Krugman, *Foreign Direct Investment in the United States* (1989); I.M. Destler and C. Randell Henning, *Dollar Politics: Exchange Rate Policymaking in the United States* (1989); and Allen J. Lenz, *Narrowing the U.S. Current Account Deficit* (1992).

Chapter 17 —————————————————————————————
AMERICAN CAPITALISM: RETROSPECT AND PROSPECT

In addition to many of the works cited in the previous chapter, see, for general overviews, Robert Heilbroner, *Twenty-First Century Capitalism* (1993), and Paul Kennedy, *Preparing for the Twenty-First Century* (1993).

On multinationals, see Richard Barnet and Ronald Müller, *Global Reach* (1974), and two works by Mira Wilkins: *The Emergence of Multinational Enterprise* (1970), and *The Maturing of Multinational Enterprise* (1975).

International commerce is discussed in Gary C. Hufbauer and Jeffrey J. Schott, *North American Free Trade* (1992); Walter Russell Mead, *The Low Wage Challenge to Global Growth* (1990); John H. Jackson, *Restructuring the GATT System* (1990); and Thomas R. Howell (ed.), *Conflict Among Nations: Trade Policies in the 1990s* (1992).

On Labor-management relations, see Barry Bluestone and Irving Bluestone, *Negotiating the Future: A Labor Perspective on American Business* (1992). See also Michael L. Dertouzas et al., *Made in America: Regaining the Productive Edge* (1989); and William J. Baumol et al., *Productivity and American Leadership* (1989).

Industrial policy is discussed in Otis L. Graham, Jr., *Losing Time: The Industrial Policy Debate* (1992). For the environment, consult Al Gore, *Earth in the Balance: Ecology and the Human Spirit* (1992), and William R. Cline, *Global Warming: The Economic Stakes* (1992).

PICTURE CREDITS

Index